Human Resource Management in the Hospitality Industry

An Introductory Guide

EIGHTH EDITION

Michael J. Boella, MA, FHCIMA, MCIPD
Faculty Fellow, School of Service Management,
University of Brighton
Visiting Professor, University of Perpignan

Steven Goss-Turner, MSc, BA, FHCIMA, MCIPD
Head of Teaching
Deputy Head of School
Faculty of Management and Information Sciences
School of Service Management
University of Brighton

ELSEVIER
BUTTERWORTH
HEINEMANN

AMSTERDAM • BOSTON • HEIDELBERG • LONDON • NEW YORK • OXFORD
PARIS • SAN DIEGO • SAN FRANCISCO • SINGAPORE • SYDNEY • TOKYO

Elsevier Butterworth-Heinemann
Linacre House, Jordan Hill, Oxford OX2 8DP
30 Corporate Drive, Burlington, MA 01803

First published 2005
Reprinted 2006

British Library Cataloguing in Publication Data
A catalogue record for this book is available from the British Library

Library of Congress Cataloguing in Publication Data
A catalogue record for this book is available from the Library of Congress

ISBN 0 7506 6636 6

For information on all Elsevier Butterworth-Heinemann
publications visit our website at www.bh.com

Working together to grow
libraries in developing countries

www.elsevier.com | www.bookaid.org | www.sabre.org

ELSEVIER   BOOK AID
             International   Sabre Foundation

Typeset by Integra Services Pvt. Ltd., Pondicherry, India
www.integra-india.com
Printed and bound by MPG Books Ltd., Bodmin, Cornwall

Mike Boella

For Juliet, Jo, Elena and Luci and all who provided the motivation, information and support that made this book possible.

Steven Goss-Turner

To My Girls, Janice and Molly

Contents

List of figures

A note to the eighth edition

It is over 30 years since the first edition of this book appeared and it is a source of great satisfaction that it is still read around the world as a key text for existing and future managers. However, the time had come for new views and perspectives to be included; so it gave me great pleasure when Steven Goss-Turner, a colleague with whom I have worked for many years, agreed to join me in the eighth edition of this book. Steven brings both invaluable senior management experience and an academic approach to this, the eighth, edition. His contribution has been invaluable.

Michael J. Boella, MA, FHCIMA, MCIPD

Foreword

Bob Cotton, OBE, FHCIMA
Chief Executive
British Hospitality Association
February 2005

For as long as any of us in hospitality can remember, the industry has had a staff and skills shortage. This was as true of the 1960s as it is today but, with the expansion of the industry since then, the only change is that the shortage has got worse. Unfortunately, it is likely to get even worse in the future. If the industry expands as the government is forecasting, it will create a further 500 000 jobs by 2010. Added to the present staff shortages (there are an estimated 200 000 vacancies at any one time), it is clear that recruitment and retention is an overwhelming pre-occupation of managers and employers in the industry and will remain so unless we do something about it.

What can be done? To begin with, we should not assume that, in an industry of over two million workers, there is not some overmanning. Even if it is only 1 per cent, that is 20 000 people who are not meaningfully employed; if it is as much as 5 per cent, then the figure becomes even more concerning. So ensuring that the people we have already recruited are fully occupied is the oft-forgotten first step. Raising levels of productivity by better work scheduling, better training, better employment practices, better communications and better reward systems will undoubtedly reduce the industry's recurring need to recruit more and more staff. In this way, encouraging existing staff to work smarter – not harder – must be the immediate priority of every business in the industry.

How best to do this? It takes no genius to recognise that a hospitality business stands or falls on the staff it employs – on the welcome they provide, on the efficiency with which they perform their tasks and on their ability to interact with their colleagues and with the customer. Staff are the primary asset to the business, yet the hospitality industry's training effort in the last 40 years has been patchy, to say the least. Clearly, there is some very good training but, with over 300 000 separate hospitality businesses, the majority of them small and independent, it is not surprising that too many have resorted to poaching rather than training in the past.

What have not helped the industry are the constant changes in the country's training and education structure and in the qualifications provided at all levels – to such an extent that the old certainties of the past have been completely eroded. Many employers, who understood the standards reached by students who had attained City and Guilds 706, or an OND or HND, are now floundering in a sea of misunderstanding as they struggle to come to terms with NVQs – which are, themselves, now destined to be abandoned – and other qualifications.

With the advent of People 1st, the Sector Skills Council for the industry, there is now a debate about what qualifications are needed and how they may be offered. This has been exacerbated by the alarming reduction in the number of craft catering courses, often in favour of more popular tourism courses. This represents a huge challenge to the hospitality industry. At the other end of the scale, the growth in the number of universities offering degree-level courses in hospitality has been equally alarming. Does the government's dictum that 50 per cent of all school-leavers should obtain university-level qualifications really reflect the hospitality industry's needs? Hardly – but individual employers have little or no influence on what is a national policy that is encouraging every school-leaver to believe that vocational qualifications are somehow second-rate. And is it any surprise that employers, themselves, are understandably confused that apprenticeships – despised some ten years ago as old fashioned and out-of-step with modern requirements – are now (rightly) being re-introduced in the guise of Modern Apprenticeships?

Every human resource manager is facing a scenario of constant change so Michael Boella's eighth edition of his standard work, *Human Resource Management in the Hospitality Industry*, is as timely now as ever it was when it was first published in 1974.

The book is not only a model textbook for students, which has been tested by time. With new legislation appearing every year, which impacts on the people that a business employs and on how it employs them, the book has become required reading for both human resource managers and employers who have to work in an environment of flux and change.

The book's emphasis on the need for a professional approach to human resource management is also timely. If staff are to be motivated to work smarter in such a tumultuous work environment, they must have leadership. But systems also have to be put in place so that there is the right kind of support for every eventuality. The book emphasises the need for leadership and outlines the systems that must back it up.

Michael Boella, now with his co-author, Steven Goss-Turner, has over 40 years of experience in human resource management and teaching in hospitality. His deep understanding of the needs of managers and of students aspiring to management positions is legendary. Eight editions have proved the book's rightful place as a classic in hospitality literature. We will never overcome the staff and skills shortages without taking careful note of what it so sensibly tells us.

Foreword

Philippe Rossiter, MBA, FHCIMA, FCMI, FTS, FRGS, AIL
Chief Executive
Hotel & Catering International Management Association
April 2005

At the conclusion of his foreword to the 7th edition of this seminal work, my predecessor at the HCIMA said, quite simply, 'Roll on the eighth edition.' Well, here it is; as fresh, vibrant and pertinent a contribution to the subject of hospitality management as it was when first published over 30 years ago.

This longevity illustrates two key aspects of this essential text. Firstly, the subject of human resource management is perennial, even if we have changed our vocabulary somewhat. In this respect, *Human Resource Management* is now more widely employed than the term *Personnel Management*, used in the title of the book's first edition. Indeed, we no longer refer to the *Hotel & Catering Industry*, now preferring the all-encompassing *Hospitality Industry*. Yet the fundamentals which provide the foundation for the sound management of people remain timeless, whether one is talking about recruitment, training, task organisation or appraisal. At the same time, the environment in which we all work constantly changes and evolves, responding to both technological advances and shifts in society's perceptions of human relationships in every context. Often, such changes are reflected in employment legislation, and there is little doubt that, in this area alone, we have witnessed a substantial growth over the last thirty years. This underscores the second reason for the timeless contribution of Michael Boella and Steven Goss-Turner to the subject, as each successive edition has brought the book right up to date, with relevant case studies being used in an imaginative and informative fashion.

This dual approach of promoting sound management practice within a contemporary setting lies at the heart of the HCIMA's philosophy as the hospitality industry's professional body. As if to illustrate this message, I am pleased to see that the book contains sections covering the HCIMA's *Risk Management Guide* and its *Hospitality Assured* business excellence standard, alongside its more traditional *Code of Conduct* for members. Enduring relevance is as important for a professional association as it is for an essential text such as *Human Resource Management in the Hospitality Industry*; Michael Boella and Steven Goss-Turner must be congratulated on their skill in retaining the book's immediacy and relevance to a wide audience of managers at all levels and students alike.

This book is written by authors who not only know their subject, but also recognise the needs of hospitality managers in all sectors. More importantly, Michael Boella and Steven Goss-Turner are able to set those management challenges in the context of readily understood environments, thereby making the subject 'come alive'. This approach has created a book which is easy to use and understand; a copy should be found in every hospitality manager's office!

Preface

When the first edition of this book was written in the 1970s, personnel management in the hospitality industry was practised by a handful of employers and even in these cases it was confined to a few functions of personnel management such as recruitment and training. Today, thirty years later we can say that human resource management (HRM) in the hospitality industry has grown in its impact and status, with an increasing number of HR Directors being appointed at executive Board member level. However, it is clear that in such a fragmented industry, with many thousands of businesses of all sizes, there is still much to do, developing further a positive image of the sector as a first choice for the best talent.

Each new edition has been prompted by a variety of changes that have affected the hospitality industry, including political, legal, economic, social and technological changes and this edition is no different. Many of these changes have had considerable influence on the management of the industry's human resources; the introduction of the minimum wage being just one example, another being the development of internet-based recruitment. Another issue that has recently begun to emerge is a growing awareness of the 'stakeholder' society and a concern among more enterprises for the environment, for communities in which the business takes place and ethical behaviour.

One key economic element has been the growth of many hospitality companies into global actors – one company, InterContinental Hotels Group, added 42 hotels in the Americas alone to its portfolio in a four-month period in 2004! Such a rapid growth has an almost insatiable appetite for human resources at all levels and this can only be achieved through a professional HR function. The issues of HRM across multi-site companies and in an international context have been developed to a greater extent in this edition.

Together with this globalization trend, the need to meet shareholder expectations creates other pressures which often result in changes to the managment of an enterprise's human resources. Such changes may include more flexible but often polarized and distanced workforces, outsourcing of large sections of a business activity, reliance on agency staff and short-term contracts. All of which can create a purely economic relationship with little room for loyalty. Another consequence of such economic pressures is flatter organization structures with more empowered or enabled workers, but often with fewer internal promotion and personal development prospects.

At the same time, many employers, some conscious of these trends, are improving their human resource management practices through participating in a range of schemes such as Investors in People, the British Hospitality Association's Excellence through People, and the Hotel and Catering International Management Association's Hospitality Assured schemes.

Such trends and developments create tremendous paradoxes for contemporary hospitality managers. Whilst many companies wish to recognize the needs of all their stakeholders, they also have to remain competitive in a global market.

We are grateful to all those who have made this latest edition and earlier editions possible, including the many companies and associations that have allowed us to use their material. These include: the British Hospitality Association, Choice Hotels, the Chartered Institute of Personnel and Development, Croner Publications, De Vere Hotels, Flamingo Lodge, Forte Hotels, Hilton Hotels, the Hospitality Training Foundation, the Hotel & Catering International Management Association, Marriott Hotels, Pan Pacific Hotels, and Sheraton Hotels.

Finally, we both are very grateful to the committee of the Hotel and Catering Personnel and Training Association (Fiona Rassell in particular) for the privilege of judging the annual awards for excellence in human resource management. This has certainly given us insights into what is being done at the leading edge of human resource practice by some of the most influential operators in the industry.

Michael J. Boella, MA, FHCIMA, MCIPD
Steven Goss-Turner, MSc, FHCIMA, MCIPD
January 2005

PART 1

The Hospitality Industry HRM Context

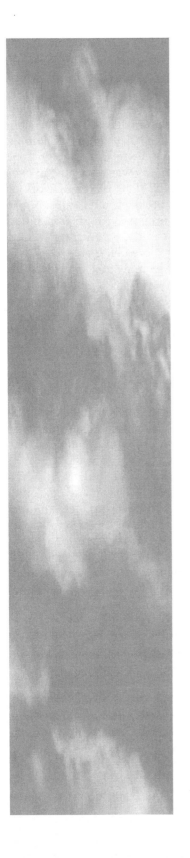

Background to the industry's workforce

Since the middle of the twentieth century, in spite of many economic ups and downs, the leading developed nations of the world have seen many fundamental and far-reaching changes within society. The major one, with little doubt, must be a vast improvement in economic wealth, which, in turn, has led to considerable improvements in standards of living for the majority of the people living and working in these countries. These changes have involved improved productivity and a redistribution of the workforce away from the primary and secondary sectors into service industries and, increasingly symbolic of the twenty-first century, into knowledge (information) industries and occupations.

From the hospitality industry's perspective, there are many accompanying societal changes with great significance for the industry's operators. These include increased disposable incomes, more time for leisure (although it is reported that this trend is reversing in some countries), easier and cheaper travel and, as a consequence of improved lifestyles and medical services, increased longevity, resulting in increasing populations and demographic restructuring. Alongside this, the media in their many different forms are informing and shaping people's behaviour as never before.

The contributions made by the hospitality industry to this general rise in standard of living are considerable and varied, providing essential products and services, leisure services, large-scale employment and wealth creation. Tourism, of which the hotel and catering industry is a principal element, is now claimed to be the world's fastest growing industry and also one of the leading earners of foreign currency. The total value of tourism to the UK in 2003 was estimated to be £76 billion, with overseas visitors spending close to £12 billion of that figure in foreign currency (British Hospitality Association, 2004). The value to the nation's 2002 Gross Domestic Product of specific hospitality sector services was estimated at over 4%. The fact that millions of people eat meals at or near their places of work or study, rather than at home, would not be possible without restaurants, cafés, public houses, fast food and takeaway establishments and in-house catering facilities. Furthermore the improved standard of living and increased discretionary income enjoyed by the majority of people has resulted in many more being able to enjoy a vast range of hospitality products which in earlier times were restricted to the affluent in society.

Nevertheless, for many people these improvements have been accompanied by a degree of economic polarization, with the differentials in wealth, earnings and standards of living getting wider. In the past, efforts to protect the weakest or less well-off have taken many forms, which included various approaches to minimum-wage regulation. Until the late 1980s this was achieved through statutory wages councils. These councils set minimum conditions in industries where union power and collective bargaining was particularly weak – a number of different sectors of the hotel and catering industry being covered by wages councils. However, in the 1980s the Conservative government took the view that this mechanism interfered with the free market economy, and disbanded wages councils. It was only in 1999, following the return of a Labour government in 1997, that we saw the return to statutory minimum wage (the National Minimum Wage) and maximum hours regulation (the Working Time Directive).

The UK hospitality industry, with its ever-developing range of products and services, has seen vast growth in recent years. The high streets of towns are now as much a forum of branded restaurants and coffee houses as they are for general retailers. Whilst there have been substantial technical improvements, and conditions in the industry may have improved over what they were in the past, the relative status of the industry as an employer, compared with other employers, has not improved significantly. Admittedly at the top of the scale, some highly skilled workers such as chefs, who are in short supply, can command very high incomes, but at the other end of the scale, kitchen porters and cleaners, for example, would earn considerably higher wages for broadly similar work in other employment sectors. This is in spite of efforts being made by some of the larger companies in the industry to improve conditions. Among the reasons must be the fact that most employees only generate around £40,000 per year (based on data taken from *Trends and Statistics 2004*, British Hospitality Association, 2004) for their employer and of this between 10 and 40% will be taken up by labour costs, the remainder going towards material costs, property costs, fixed costs and profit. With few exceptions, catering services do not lend themselves easily to mechanization, although there are now signs that significant changes in productivity may be forthcoming in the future. As a result, the industry is heavily labour-intensive and labour costs dominate many profit-and-loss accounts.

The reasons for the relatively slow rate of improvement in the industry's conditions of employment are considerable, including an understandable reluctance on the part of many proprietors and managers to be among the first to charge higher prices for their services, particularly when Britain is reported to be already among the most expensive of tourist destinations. Another reason, however, is probably that the trade union movement exerts little influence in most sectors of the industry; the wages councils never were a real substitute and it is questionable whether the minimum wage will have a significant effect. A third reason is that the industry's workforce consists largely of people drawn from the secondary labour market, i.e. those people who use the industry on a short-term basis (such as students, housewives, school leavers) and who are prepared to accept low pay since they may not be the primary breadwinner. Because of low pay, low union presence and the high proportion of staff drawn from the secondary labour market, the industry has its own less obvious but costly labour problems, including such phenomena as a high labour turnover rate, institutionalized pilfering, and low service standards in many establishments.

It is, of course, to be expected that some aspects of working in the hospitality industry may be unattractive when considered alongside other sectors. There are intrinsic and largely unavoidable challenges such as having to work evenings, weekends and bank holidays. Other problems, however, can certainly be reduced or eliminated by determined management action. These problems include unnecessary split-shift working, staff reliance on tips, ignorance of methods of calculating pay and distributing service charges, and management's reluctance to involve staff in matters that affect their working lives. A number of reports have highlighted these difficulties which, together with some management attitudes and practices, undoubtedly cause much of the industry's labour problems. Even today, for example, many employers and managers expect all employees, whatever their position and wage rate, to be dedicated to their jobs, to have a vocational fervour towards their work and to sacrifice leisure time for pay that is not high by general economic standards. This attitude is not confined to the commercial and more entrepreneurial sectors of the industry but is found as a discordant element in many organizations. These same employers and managers fail to recognize that their own motivation to work is usually completely different from that of their staff, and that many work people throughout the community are becoming less work orientated for various reasons. Employers in industry must reconcile themselves rapidly to the fact that the majority of potential staff are less likely to be singularly and vocationally committed unless ways and means are found to harness what some researchers claim is a natural motivation to work. And employers in the hospitality industry must recognize this position. Staff, if they are to stay and develop, expect competitive conditions of employment and motivational management approaches, and unless these are offered the industry's staffing problems will persist.

At the 1999 International Hotel and Restaurants Association Human Resource Think Tank in The Netherlands this issue was discussed and it was concluded that a distinction now has to be made between 'loyalty' and 'commitment', loyalty being a two-way long-term attitude of trust and reliance between employer and employee, whereas commitment is perceived as a shorter-term professional/economic relationship which endures so long as each is dependent upon the other.

The British hospitality industry, its workforce and the British economy

The value of the hospitality and tourism sectors to the UK economy have been emphasized earlier, and has encouraged the government to take increasing heed to the issues faced by the industry such as during the recent foot-and-mouth disease outbreak which had a devastating impact on many tourism and hospitality businesses. The increasing value of tourism and hospitality to the UK economy can be seen in Figure 1.1.

	2000	2001	2002	2003
Overnight stays by UK residents	26.1	26.1	26.7	26.5^p
Spending by overseas visitors	12.8	11.3	11.7	11.9^p
Day trips by UK residents	32.7	33.4	34.2	34.2^p
Fares to UK carriers	3.2	3.2	3.2	3.3^p
Total	74.8	74.0	75.8	75.9

^{p} Provisional.
Day visits figures have been adjusted in line with RPI.

Figure 1.1 Value of tourism to UK (£bn), 2000–2003
Sources: UK Tourism Survey/UK Day Visits Survey.

The 2003 Labour Market Review (Hospitality), commissioned by the Hospitality Training Foundation, reports that the hospitality industry workforce increased year on year by 189,058 to a total of 1.67 million, around 8% of the UK workforce as a whole. This statistic is endorsed by the British Hospitality Association's *Trends and Statistics 2004*, noting that dependant on the definition of ancillary hospitality workers such as cleaners, the total hospitality labour force can be considered to top the two-million mark. Figure 1.2, from the British Hospitality Association (BHA)'s report, illustrates workforce differences and changes within the various sectors of the hospitality industry.

To achieve this level of societal and economic significance, hospitality sector proprietors, local authorities, management and employees within the industry provided for the needs of millions, including working people, holidaymakers, business travellers, school children, students and hospital patients. The industry is now a vital part of the British economy and over the last ten years has slowly but increasingly been recognized as such through a wide range of government initiatives involving direct collaboration with the industry, such as working with the government's New Deal, the BHA's involvement with the Tourism Strategy Working Group and the appointment of permanent secondees from the industry to the government's sponsoring department.

	England		Wales		Scotland		Northern Ireland		UK	
	2002	2003	2002	2003	2002	2003	2002	2003	2002	2003
Hotels	225,952	235,651	12,938	14,354	36,810	38,904	4045	4045	279,745	292,954
Restaurants	424,771	447,674	24,810	24,810	49,803	52,636	9090	11,327	508,483	536,447
Pubs, clubs and bars	227,089	279,154	11,926	14,556	16,878	20,489	5237	6063	261,130	320,262
Food and service management	167,721	175,459	8047	8047	13,636	14,367	2894	3430	192,298	201,303
Hospitality Services	252,815	261,430	16,770	18,461	23,157	24,357	11,445	11,778	304,187	261,430
Total	1,298,348	1,399,368	74,491	80,228	140,284	150,753	32,720	36,643	1,545,883	1,612,396

Figure 1.2 Employees in hospitality businesses, 2002 and 2003
Source: ONS Labour Force Survey.

Tourism and travel

The increased demand for tourism and international travel services is a worldwide development and one consequence is the internationalization of many of the leading hotel companies. One consequence of this for the British hospitality industry's employers is that many potential employees now look overseas for employment. At the same time many foreigners come to the UK, in many cases, to learn English.

The growth in demand for business travel, conferences, exhibitions and short courses

An important feature of technologically advanced societies is the need for business people, professionals, administrators and others to travel and to meet. According to the BHA, business was the purpose in 2003 for 22.3 million trips in the UK by UK residents and 7 million trips by overseas visitors. These trips equate to a spend of about £6 billion by UK residents and £3.4 billion by overseas visitors. The impacts of terrorism and the '11 September 2001' attacks in New York have caused a temporary reduction in growth in this aspect of tourism and hospitality but the long-term prospects are still very positive. This overall growth in tourism creates demands for additional jobs.

Social and demographic changes

The industry is, of course, responding to major changes in the demand side of the industry, i.e. the consumer side. Demographic changes alone, such as the increased proportion and number of older people, have created demands for more products catering for their needs, and the reduced number of young people (Figure 1.3) is creating both demand and labour market problems. Among the younger population, changes in eating habits – a shift to 'grazing', for example – have created opportunities for many different types of fast food outlets. The move to healthy eating too is responsible for a range of new products and a related growth in vegetarianism.

Year	Under 16	16–34	35–54	55–64	65–74	Over 74	Total
1991	20	29	25	10	9	7	57.8
1995	21	27	26	10	9	7	58.6
2001	20	25	29	10	8	7	59.5
2011	18	24	29	12	9	7	60.5

Figure 1.3 Population by age (million), UK
Source: Central Statistical Office.

A breakdown in the traditional socioeconomic usage of different catering products is probably of significance. No longer are most different products used exclusively by particular socioeconomic groups. Instead, the use of catering products, to a greater extent than previously, is determined by the occasion (behaviourally determined) rather than by the socioeconomic group.

The changing hospitality industry

Within the hospitality industry itself there are important developments that have long-term implications for the industry. First, as hospitality businesses became larger (i.e. owning more establishments) and as individual establishments have become larger and more complex, there was in the 1980s an expansion of numbers in junior and middle management, particularly in the non-line functions. In the late 1980s and the 1990s, however, economic pressures have led to a reduction, a 'delayering', of such roles. This is discussed later in this book.

Also during recent years hotel and catering organizations have become more market orientated. This has led to increased market segmentation and to many of the larger companies establishing specialist subsidiary companies which are concerned with a range of highly specialized products. This has involved, in some cases, considerable changes in products and management, or the negotiation of franchise-type agreements with international branded names such as McDonald's, Burger King and Pizza Hut.

This last development is associated with the rapid growth of fast food outlets in Britain and elsewhere in Europe. The nature of such operations, dependent as they are on the maintenance of rigorous operational and quality standards, has altered the face of British popular catering and is putting many of the traditional operators in jeopardy.

Fast food, high-street catering is still a relatively easy and inexpensive field to enter, but nowadays success demands considerable expertise and promotional effort, which are increasingly becoming beyond the resources of the independent. The franchise side of the industry is growing therefore along with franchising generally.

In the hotel sector, similar developments are evident in the growth of the consortium movement, by which individual hotel businesses can collaborate with other similar establishments in order to compete effectively against the large national and multinational companies, especially in the areas of marketing and global distribution and reservation systems.

While the industry has established its importance from an economic point of view, it could be hoped that those employed in the industry would be reaping rewards that echo this increased importance. In many cases this may well be so, with key people such as chefs and waiters at leading restaurants and good managers earning high rewards.

However, as reported above, the industry does still have a reputation for low pay, which is also discussed later in the book, because it is not as simple a matter as outside observers appear to think. The value of tips, food, accommodation, laundry and savings on fuel and fares all have to be taken into account: anyone 'living in' avoids some of the heavy daily transport and accommodation costs. Also it must be borne in mind that a very large proportion of the industry's workforce is drawn from a secondary labour market. Because of this, many work people may not have high value skills to offer, or alternatively their motives to work may put a premium on the convenience of their work (location, hours, family), for which they will sacrifice higher incomes. In fact, recent research from Bath

University, published in 1999, found that 'catering workers are in the half of the population most happy with their jobs despite poor pay and image':

Job	Satisfaction rating (%)
Restaurant and catering managers	55
Bar staff	50
Chefs and cooks	47
Catering assistants and counterhands	44
Waiters and waitresses	40
Kitchen porters and hands	40
Publicans, innkeepers, licensees	40

The most satisfied workers were child carers, with a satisfaction rating of 60%. The lowest were metal workers, with a rating of 20%. Professor Michael Rose of Bath University concluded 'that part-time women were more satisfied than full-timers and men in similar positions . . . and staff satisfaction tended to drop with improved skills and greater access to alternative jobs' (*Caterer and Hotelkeeper*, 16 September 1999). Lucas (2004) supports the general tone of the Bath findings, utilizing evidence from the 1998 Workplace Employment Relations Survey, declaring that many hospitality employees are more positive about their jobs than many in better-paid sectors.

Undoubtedly, low pay in the industry exists, but it is not something that can be put right overnight. Britain's hotels and restaurants are already reported to be among the most expensive in the world, so increases to tariffs are not the answer. Instead, a thorough reappraisal of the services offered and the consequent manning levels and staff training may lead to greater productivity. In this field, strides have been made; capital investment is made to replace the most menial tasks, and efforts are made to improve the standard of training. However, increased productivity in service industries is not as easy to achieve as in many other industries without making radical changes to the nature of the service itself. To some extent this is happening, particularly through increasing the amount of customer participation, whether this be by buffet-style breakfasts or by automated check-in and check-out procedures such as those developed by Formule 1, the budget division of the French Accor group. The subject of productivity is discussed more fully in Chapter 18.

Most improvements and efforts seem to be made at the tip of the iceberg, mainly among the larger companies. Much the greater numerical proportion of the industry is made up of smaller employers who each employ a few staff only and who for a variety of reasons are not able or prepared to evaluate their own business methods as rigorously as is required in today's aggressive business climate. One consequence is the growth of the larger companies at the expense of smaller companies, which is a phenomenon not confined to the hospitality industries, but is a general phenomenon of consolidating, industrialized societies.

Changing working patterns

In 1986 the National Economic Development Office (NEDO) published its report *Changing Working Patterns*, which identified major changes in working patterns which have taken place in recent years. The reported trends continued into the late 1990s.

The report came to a number of conclusions. First, it was found that firms were aware of the need to alter working practices. The awareness varied according to the impact of recession on sectors, such that manufacturing firms were much more aware of the need for change than were service sector firms. One concomitant of these changes was an increased level of communication within the workforce and a decline in union opposition to change.

The second major finding was that the main constraints to more flexibility were inadequate skill levels and training resources and also status differences due to staff/manual differentiation and union membership. These constraints were less important in the service sector.

The third finding was that 'distancing', the process by which employers use contractors, agents, etc. to replace employees, had been confined mainly to ancillary or support services such as catering, cleaning, security and transport.

Fourthly it was found that peripheral forms of employment had grown since 1980. Such employment tended to lack continuity and security and such workers enjoyed substantially worse non-pay benefits. The work tended to require low level skills; peripheral status tended to inhibit investment in training; and consequently advancement opportunities were limited. Any claimed benefits flowing from peripheral employment were limited to a small number of freelance professionals in shortage occupations.

Finally it was concluded that there had been a growth in segmentation of the labour market and 'this seemed likely to increase the volatility of employment patterns, giving rise to more short-term, interrupted employment while at the same time reducing access to core status'. In addition, NEDO expected firms to shift their recruitment orientation to workers not aspiring to core status, particularly if service sector employment continued to grow. This finding was reinforced by the statement made by the Institute of Directors which proposed that the government take measures to break traditional work patterns and encourage self-employment, part-time jobs and working from home (Institute of Directors, 24 June 1987). Between 1987 and 1996 the government took a wide range of measures to 'free up' the labour market, such as the abolition of wages councils. With the return of a Labour government we witness the return of increased government intervention such as the introduction of minimum wages and maximum hours.

Such changes in the structure of the labour market and the workforce have not finished by any means yet. They appear to be following Engel's law, which states that there 'is an increasing demand for the more sophisticated final service functions' (quoted from Gershuny and Miles, 1983). It is predicted by many that the proportion employed in manufacturing will continue to decline, even to numbers similar to those employed in agriculture, because of the ease with which manufacturing can be mechanized, robotized, computerized and outsourced to other countries. In 2004, the Department for Trade and Industry published statistics which suggested that manufacturing accounted for only 15% of the UK's GDP.

In essence, therefore, major structural changes are taking place in the workforce, and in methods and organization of work. These can be summarized as follows:

1 Employment in manufacturing is declining as productivity is improved through automation and outsourced to other (lower wage) countries, such as China and Taiwan.
2 Employment in personal services is increasing.

3 There will be fewer full-time jobs for men.

4 There will be more part-time jobs for women.

5 There will be growth in the secondary labour market and a decline in the primary labour market.

6 There will be an increase in white-collar employment.

7 There will be a decline in manual employment.

8 There will be a decline in full-time work, with more people doing more than one job, including professionals pursuing a so-called 'portfolio' career.

9 There will be a reduction in job security.

10 Technological change causes redistribution and reorganization of work as evidenced by the outsourcing to other countries such as India of much routine information processing and call-centre work.

These trends were anticipated some 20 years ago by Charles Handy (1984), who wrote that the full-employment society was becoming the part-employment society, that the one-organization career was becoming rarer and that sexual stereotyping at work was no longer so rigid.

It is worth adding that such changes in working patterns are not all imposed by employers. In many cases it is the supply side of the labour market, the employees, who demand conditions such as more flexible working practices and family-friendly policies on the employer. This is evidenced today by employers asking when potential employees would be available for work, rather than insisting on traditional shift patterns. The trend towards few full-time jobs is supported by the *Labour Market Review 2003* (Hospitality Training Foundation 2004), which reported that only 48.1% of the hospitality workforce is full-time, a 2.7% fall since 2001. Figures 1.4–1.8 express important workforce data and demographic characteristics (gender, weekly earnings, age, sectoral and by occupation) of the hospitality industry in 2002/2003, as reported in the British Hospitality Association's 2004 *Trends and Statistics Report*, and the *Labour Market Review 2003* produced by the Hospitality Training Foundation and VT Plus Training.

	Males		Females	
	2001	2003	2001	2003
Hotels	42.6	44.5	57.4	55.5
Restaurants	46.8	48.6	54.0	51.4
Pubs, clubs and bars	35.5	37.0	64.5	63.0
Food and service management	29.8	29.9	70.2	70.1
Hospitality services	4.5	20.4	95.5	79.6
Hospitality industry	38.4	38.3	61.6	61.7

Figure 1.4 Numbers employed in the hospitality industry by gender (%), 2001 and 2003, UK
Source: ONS Labour Force Survey.

	2000	2001	2002	2003
Hotel and accommodation managers	402.90	380.50	396.00	416.10
Restaurant and catering managers	350.30	368.30	410.30	421.30
Publicans and club stewards	333.50	340.30	363.80	345.90
Chefs/cooks	266.30	273.60	286.00	296.40
Waiting staff	194.60	208.20	211.40	218.20
Bar staff	184.80	198.60	217.00	217.90
Hotel porters	215.50	222.00	233.80	229.90
Kitchen porters and catering assistants	186.70	196.70	209.80	228.40

Figure 1.5 Average gross weekly earnings for full-time staff on adult rates in core occupations (£), 2000–2003, UK
Source: New Earnings Survey.

	16–19		20–29		30–49		50–64		Over 65	
	2002	2003	2002	2003	2002	2003	2002	2003	2002	2003
Hotels	19.8	19.5	23.7	24.1	36.1	36.2	18.6	18.5	1.8	1.7
Restaurants	27.3	26.9	30.1	30.2	32.1	32.6	10.0	9.7	0.5	0.5
Pubs	25.3	23.6	35.8	36.8	24.4	26.7	13.2	12.0	1.3	1.0
Contract catering	4.6	4.6	14.4	13.9	58.9	58.9	19.2	19.6	3.0	3.1
Hospitality services	9.9	9.9	13.0	13.9	50.0	49.4	25.2	24.9	1.8	1.8

Figure 1.6 Employment by age category (%) in hospitality businesses, 2002 and 2003, UK
Source: ONS Labour Force Survey.

Labour turnover and employment

The industry has, for many years, had a reputation for a very high level of labour turnover. Twenty years ago the Hotel and Catering Industry Training Board (HCITB) published its report Manpower Flows in the Hotel and Catering Industry, which predicted that there would be in the region of 1.4 million vacancies per annum, 3% arising from growth, 2% from retirements and the remaining 95% from staff turnover. It found the following gross turnover rates: managers 19%; supervisors 94%; craftspeople 55%; and operatives 65%. Cafés and public houses had the highest rates of losses, caused largely by young people using the industry as an interlude between school or college and a full-time career.

Ten years later the Hotel and Catering Training Company (HCTC), the HCITB successor, predicted a modest growth in jobs, about 140 000 between 1995 and 2000. Labour turnover for all sectors was 26.8% per annum with the commercial sector rate almost double that of the catering services sector (where catering for a profit is

	Full-time				Part-time			
	2001	%	2002	%	2001	%	2002	%
Hotels	177,339	74.6	164,108	58.7	60,381	25.4	115,677	41.3
Restaurants	241,710	62.3	250,208	49.2	146,268	37.7	258,275	50.8
Pubs	104,234	41.9	98,291	37.6	144,534	58.1	162,839	62.4
Contract catering	35,430	32.0	102,195	53.1	75,290	68.0	90,103	46.9
Total hospitality businesses	558,713	56.7	614,802	49.5	426,473	43.3	626,894	50.5
Hospitality Services	164,858	42.9	128,876	42.4	219,427	57.1	175,311	57.6
Total UK hospitality industry	723,571	52.8	743,678	48.1	645,900	47.2	802,205	51.9

Figure 1.7 Employment status of workforce by sector: 2001/2002, UK
Source: Labour Force Survey.

	Full-time				Part-time			
	2001	%	2002	%	2001	%	2002	%
Hotel and accommodation m'gers	16,240	88.0	35,129	73.3	2215	12.0	12,827	26.7
Restaurant and catering m'gers	69,465	89.0	134,411	87.6	8586	11.0	19,058	12.4
Publicans and club stewards	29,398	89.0	47,043	92.2	3634	11.0	4005	7.8
Chefs/cooks	149,535	69.0	186,188	70.1	67,182	31.0	79,298	29.9
Waiting staff	45,482	25.0	52,719	23.9	136,445	75.0	168,149	76.1
Bar staff	49,984	26.0	54,390	27.4	142,261	74.0	143,774	72.6
Hotel porters	7479	86.0	10,546	74.9	1218	14.0	3532	25.1
Kitchen porters and catering asst's	100,990	29.2	125,566	29.9	244,864	70.8	294,813	70.1
Total	468,573	43.6	645,992	47.1	606,405	56.4	725,456	52.9

Figure 1.8 Employment status of workforce by core occupation: 2001/2002, UK
Source: Labour Force Survey.

not normally the main objective, e.g. in hospitals). Labour turnover is still a challenge in the year 2005 and is dealt with in detail in Chapter 14.

Although labour turnover can appear to be relatively high among some sectors and some employers, it is vital that proper comparisons are made and also to recognize that not all labour turnover is the consequence of poor employment practices. Many smaller employers cannot offer careers or career progression, so employees will naturally move from one employer to the other, but remaining in the industry. Some refer to this as 'circulation' as opposed to 'turnover', because the employees concerned are not lost to the industry.

In other cases many employers recruit directly from the secondary labour market, i.e. workers who are not committed to a particular industry. Many workers such as school leavers, students and 'long-term tourists' are seeking short-term employment, sometimes just to earn holiday money or to learn the language, before starting their studies or returning home. Among some employers, particularly in the fast food sector, there is a very high level of labour turnover, often attracting candidates experiencing their first entry into the job market, but it is anticipated and can be properly managed.

Although some reports categorize the industry's problems very much in statistical terms, it is possible to illustrate some of the problems in more human terms. These range right through the employment process from initial selection to the termination of employment. All of these aspects will be discussed at more length later, but it is important to see some of the industry's practices in terms that are related to the employee – the individual – who is subject to an employer's employment practices.

Initial selection

At one end of the scale there are employers who use only expert techniques, including group selection procedures and psychological tests. In addition, many companies and the Hospitality Training Foundation are now training managers and supervisors in most of the skills of management, such as interviewing techniques. At the other end of the scale, however, are many employers who do not even acknowledge receipt of application forms. One unemployed manager applied to over 50 employers and received less than 20 acknowledgements. Another employer used box numbers for the express purpose of avoiding the need to acknowledge applications. On the other hand many employers are frustrated by the casual approach to employment of employees – with many simply not turning up for a prearranged interview. Recruiters in the sector are also restricted in their selection criteria by the number of qualified applicants across the industry, the *Labour Market Review* for 2003 calculating that 21% of the near two million workforce have no qualification at all.

Induction and training

This is an area that has shown some improvements in the last few years. However, there are still serious problems which are completely ignored by many managers; for example, some managers or supervisors do not have the empathy to recognize that skills such as laying a table formally, making a bed correctly, using computers or even telephones, which are second nature to themselves, may be worrying to some, such as a middle-aged returner who has come out to work for the first time after many years.

A related problem is the large number of small- and medium-sized employers, and managers in large companies, who continue to insist upon 'experience' rather than being prepared to recruit and train new staff, in spite of the fact that about 80% of the industry's workforce do not need other than ordinary life and social skills.

In a more general sense, there is still the argument that because of tight staff budgets there is no time to train, so to acquire training skills is not worthwhile.

Some managers are persuaded, however, that even with understaffing or reduced staffing, training does take place somehow and that training skills become more, not less, necessary as staff levels are reduced.

Pay

The New Earnings Survey 1998 and the Low Pay Commission Report 1998 both confirm that pay in the industry is among the lowest in the UK. Such a reputation was not enhanced when some employers, following the introduction of the minimum wage in 1999, cut back on some staff benefits such as late-night taxis, or used tips and service charges to compensate for the consequent increase in labour costs.

In 2004 median earnings in the industry were around £260 per week, with managers averaging around £416 per week and kitchen porters and catering assistants averaging around £228 per week (*Trends and Statistics 2004*, British Hospitality Association, 2004). These rates do not compare favourably with many other industries (see Figure 1.5). The *Labour Market Review 2003* reported that salary levels increased at only 0.8% in hospitality from 2002, as against a 4.5% average increase across all industries.

While there are many instances of high rates of pay in the industry, top executives are in the six-figure bracket, the image overall is not good in this respect. Reliance, in some sectors, on tipping still exists to a greater extent than some consider desirable. The practice of paying employees the basic or near basic wage and also putting notices on tariffs that service charges are included has had the effect of diverting guests' tips into company revenue. In many cases this practice has had an adverse effect on net earnings. First, all of the service charge may not be distributed to the staff, and second, income from such a source is taxed (VAT and income tax), which was not done previously. In spite of this it is to be hoped, from the tourist industry point of view, that the practice of 'all inclusive pricing' (including service charge and VAT) will become common practice in Britain, as it is in some other European countries. However, this practice will have to be linked to a fair system of distribution and the establishment of realistic minimum rates.

In these circumstances, where low pay and distrust of the employer's wage practices exist, it is to be expected that pilfering on a significant scale takes place. A report based upon an Open University case study, 'Room for Reform', claimed that pilfering appears to be an institutionalized part of wage bargaining in hotels. Management often recognized it as a way to boost inadequate pay (see Mars and Mitchell, 1979).

Today, 'fiddles' range from straightforward short-measuring and short-changing of customers to supplying one's own household with cleaning materials, toilet paper, light bulbs, crockery, cutlery and even towels and other linen. Some fiddles are quite sophisticated and operate at quite high levels. It has been known for managers to redecorate their own homes at their employer's expense, or for a manager to deduct 'the cost of grass cutting' from the hotel's petty cash and to arrange for a farmer to pay the manager for some acres of hay taken from the same land. In regular spot surveys, not one industrial release student questioned had not witnessed pilfering.

Such practices, however, must be seen in proper perspective, bearing in mind that some other industries, trades and professions provide vastly more lucrative opportunities than those provided in the hospitality industry.

Women

Women, according to the 2004 Office of National Statistics Labour Force Survey (reported in *Trends and Statistics 2004*, British Hospitality Association, 2004), make up 62% of the industry's workforce (see Figure 1.4). This figure equates to around one in five of all female employment in Britain. Most women employed in catering are employed in operative or subcraft level jobs, although women's proportion of supervisory or management jobs is substantial, about 50%. This is probably the highest proportion of women managers in all of Britain's industries, and may be one explanation of the relatively low rate of pay of the industry's managers (see Section 'Pay').

About 75% of women's jobs in the commercial sector are part-time. Around 800 000 are employed in the main commercial sectors and 900 000 are employed in the subsidiary sectors of the industry, i.e. those where catering is an ancillary rather than the main service, such as schools and hospitals. One explanation of this concentration is part-time work in that this enables women to combine work with their family responsibilities.

Personnel management in the hospitality industry

Until the early 1960s, personnel management as a specialist function in the hotel and catering industry was almost non-existent. Where it did exist, it was devoted to small elements of personnel management, such as recruitment and training. It was not until the introduction of employment legislation, such as the Contracts of Employment Act 1964 and the establishment of the Industrial Training Board, that personnel managers began to appear in the industry in many numbers. Today all of the larger companies now employ personnel or human resource (HR) specialists and personnel management is seen as an essential part of the organization. There is still, however, too little regard paid to it by many employers. Personnel managers are frequently junior managers learning the ropes at the staff's expense. The fact that 76% of the establishments in the sector employ fewer than 10 staff (*Labour Market Review*, 2003) is also a naturally critical factor in determining the extent to which Human Resource Management (HRM) can be professionalized across the industry.

Within larger hotels and at senior level in the larger companies, personnel work appears to be taken more seriously. Even so the determining factor appears to be one more of attitude to human resource issues rather than the size of business in itself. Where human resource or personnel professionals are employed, HR management has become more sophisticated.

Some evidence of the increasing sophistication of the human resource function within the industry is to be found in the Hotel and Catering Personnel and Training Association's (HCPTA) annual awards for excellence in human resource management. Each year hospitality companies submit human resource activities for consideration for these awards. Many of the ideas submitted show considerable concern for the employers' human resources. These range from the distinctive branding of the HR function as a separate activity (or 'product') within the company (Choice Hotels) through a range of training initiatives to schemes concerned with the care of company pensioners (Forte Granada). Other such schemes submitted have included the 'decasualization' of casual workers (Mayday). Further encouraging evidence about the increasing professionalism in hospitality sector HRM comes in the recent research and writings of Kelliher and Johnson (1997), Hoque (2000) and Lucas (2004).

Also, two of the industry's most influential bodies have set in motion a number of significant initiatives that should have long-term effects on the industry's labour force and how it is perceived by government and the larger community. This is at the same time as employers generally are implementing similar initiatives, such as the Confederation of British Industries (CBI) benchmarking of human resource practices. This is part of a wider CBI initiative known as Probe which is benchmarking a range of other management areas too, such as service provision.

Excellence through People – British Hospitality Association

The British Hospitality Association in 1998 started their Excellence through People scheme, which was partly a response to the Department of National Heritage's report (1996) which listed a familiar range of complaints about the industry's employment practices, including poor wages, long hours and high labour turnover. The report went on to state that 'the tourism and hospitality industry faces the threat of a self-perpetuating vicious circle that is harmful to profitability and competitiveness ... The negative image of many jobs in the industry – low pay, low skill, low status – discourages many people from joining the industry, thus taking us back to the beginning of the vicious circle.' Figure 1.9 shows the BHA's Excellence through People 'Ten Point Code'. In 2004 the BHA reported that about one thousand organizations were accredited.

Excellence through People is based on a ten point code of good employment practice. It commits employers to:

Recruit and select with Care
(so that you can promote a positive image and attract quality staff)

1 Equal opportunities
2 Recruitment

A good employer attracts, selects and employs quality staff, whether full-time or part-time or casual, who are legally entitled to work in the UK.

Offer a competitive employment package
(so that the staff you take on know what to expect and are well cared for)

3 Contract of employment
4 Health and safety

A good employer ensures that staff are fully aware, in writing, of their terms and conditions of employment and provides a healthy and safe work environment for them.

Develop skills and performance
(so that standards of customer service and productivity can be enhanced)

5 Job design
6 Training and development

A good employer constantly seeks to increase productivity, business efficiency and customer service by improving staff competence, motivation, effectiveness and job satisfaction.

Communicate effectively
(so that you and your staff are working towards the same goals)

7 Communications
8 Grievances and discipline

A good employer ensures that staff know what is expected of them, keep them informed of performance and has arrangements for dealing with discipline and grievances.

Recognise and reward
(so that you can retain highly motivated staff)

9 Performance review
10 Rewards and recognition

A good employer takes steps to keep and motivate quality staff by rewarding them equitably by means of a well-understood remuneration package.

Figure 1.9 Ten point code
Source: British Hospitality Association.

Hospitality Assured – HCIMA

The Hotel and Catering International Management Association (HCIMA) has also set up its Hospitality Assured scheme, supported by the BHA, which sets out to recognize and reward high standards of customer service in the hospitality industry. The process for achieving Hospitality Assured consists of customer research and feedback and assesses a business' performance in standards of service and business excellence, with prominence given to aspects such as the customer promise, business planning, standards of performance, service delivery, training and development. It was reported in December 2004 (Croner Technical Brief No. 46), that 130 corporate organizations have now been accredited, representing 3500 outlets and over 50,000 employees. Further information may be gained from the HCIMA (e-mail: hospitalityassured@hcima.co.uk), or from the website (www.hospitalityassured.com).

Investors in People

Investors in People (IiP) was launched to 'improve business performance and secure competitive advantage'. The scheme has four main principles:

- Commitment – to invest in people to achieve business goals.
- Planning – how individuals and teams are to be developed to achieve these goals.
- Action – to develop and use the necessary skills in a programme directly tied to business objectives.
- Evaluation – measuring progress towards goals.

By 1997 around 1400 hospitality establishments, employing over 280 000 people, were involved in the standard, and 451 had achieved IiP status (British Hospitality Association, 1998). In 2002 this number had grown to 1067 which had achieved IiP status.

Further Reading and References

British Hospitality Association (1998) *British Hospitality: Trends and Statistics 1998*, London: BHA.

British Hospitality Association (2004) *British Hospitality: Trends and Statistics 2004*, London: BHA.

Croner Technical Brief (2004) *Hospitality Assured*, Kingston-upon-Thames, UK: Wolters Kluwer.

Department of National Heritage (1996) *Competing with the Best: People Working in Tourism and Hospitality*, London: Department of National Heritage.

Gershuny, J. and Miles, I. (1983) *The New Service Economy*, London: Frances Pinter.

Handy, C. (1984) *The Future of Work*, London: Blackwell.

HCITB (1978) *Manpower in the Hotel and Catering Industry*, London: HCITB.

HCITB (1984) *Manpower Flows in the Hotel and Catering Industry*, London: HCITB.

Hoque, K. (2000) *Human Resource Management in the Hotel Industry*, London: Routledge.

Hospitality Industry Congress (1996) *Hospitality into the 21st Century*, Henley: Henley Centre.

Hospitality Training Foundation (2004) *Labour Market Review (Hospitality) 2003*, London: HTF and VT Plus Training.

Hotel and Catering Training Company (1994) *Catering and Hospitality Industry 1994*, London: HCTC.

Kelliher, C. and Johnson, K. (1997) Personnel management in hotels: An update: A move to human resource management?, in *Progress in Tourism and Hospitality Research*, Vol. 3, No. 4, 321–331.

Low Pay Commission Report 1998, London.

Lucas, R. (2004) *Employment Relations in the Hospitality and Tourism Industries*, London: Routledge.

Mars, G. and Mitchell, P. (1979) *Manpower Problems in the Hotel and Catering Industry*, London: Heinemann.

Medlik, S. (1999) *The Business of Hotels*, 3rd edn, Oxford: Butterworth-Heinemann.

National Economic Development Office (1986) *Changing Working Patterns*, NEDO.

The New Earnings Survey (1998), London: Office of National Statistics.

Questions

These questions have been designed so that the first question in every case can be answered from material in the preceding chapter or chapters. Subsequent questions may need reference to the books contained in the reading list and maybe to other sources as well, such as the Labour Market Trends published by the Department for Education and Employment. The last question, in most cases, requires knowledge and experience of the industry, acquired, for example, through normal employment, holiday work or industrial placement.

1 Describe the size and nature of the hospitality industry's workforce. What are the outstanding features?

2 Describe the size and nature of the hospitality industry's workforce relative to the UK's total workforce.

3 What factors are likely to influence the hospitality industry's workforce in the future?

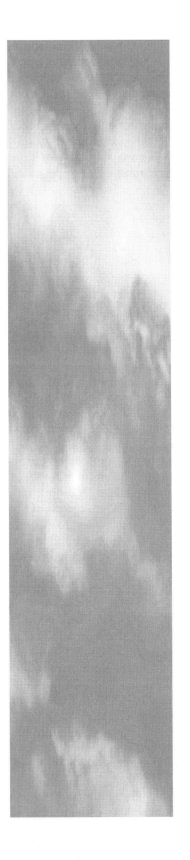

Human resource management

An enterprise's human assets or, put more conventionally, its human resources tend to be one of the most significant costs for most hospitality enterprises. In most hotels the payroll is the single biggest cost item, whilst in restaurants and bars it is usually second only to material costs. Furthermore, human resources are usually the first point of contact between an enterprise and its customers. The effective management of these human resources is therefore vital to the success of the enterprise. In smaller enterprises, management of the staff is by line managers who are often also the owners of the business. In larger enterprises the line managers will be assisted in staff management issues by human resource or personnel managers.

In talking with many personnel and human resource managers and in looking at many of the writings and research on human resource management, it is apparent that the role played by these human resource specialists varies considerably from employer to employer. These roles can be likened to the skills and functions involved in the building industry. At the basic level are the technicians such as electricians and plumbers. The human resource or personnel equivalent would be the recruiter or trainer. Above the technicians comes the builder, who carries out the wishes of the client by coordinating the activities of the various technicians. The human resource equivalent is the personnel manager, responsible for executing senior line managers' directions by carrying out a range of tasks himself or herself and/or by coordinating the personnel technicians. Above the builder comes the architect, who is responsible for interpreting the client's wishes and advising the client about the best solutions. In the human resource context the equivalent is a human resource manager who is directly involved in business policy making and implementation.

Human resource policies are normally a part of an organization's overall policy, which will consist of a number of components (Figure 2.1). The extent to which they are a subpolicy or an essential component of the overall policy may be a key indicator of how an organization values its human assets and its human resource or personnel function.

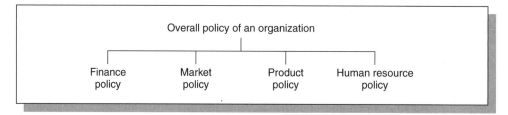

Figure 2.1 The components of an organization's policy

Virtually every management decision affects, to a greater or lesser extent, the people working in the organization. Most decisions are made within an organization's policy framework, explicit or implicit. Policies represent the aims, purposes, principles or intentions of an organization and provide the framework or guidelines for management decisions. Policies, sometimes expressed as 'mission statements', may be written down, as is the case with many larger organizations. Alternatively they may be merely inferred by decisions taken. Some companies in the hotel and catering industry, such as McDonald's, have a policy to operate within a narrow product sector. Other companies, such as Whitbread and Accor, have a policy to operate within many market sectors. These policies provide the management with the framework within which they make their decisions; e.g. where to expand, what to divest, how to expand, such as through organic growth, franchise, or merger and acquisition.

A debate has long raged concerning the differences between human resource management and personnel management. Some hold the view that human resource management is merely a new name for personnel management, whereas others consider it to be a new and different view of the way human resources are managed by the enterprise.

David Guest has written (*Personnel Management*, January 1989) that there are probably three popular approaches to defining 'human resource management'. The first is merely a retitling of personnel management, the second approach emphasizes the strategic aspects of managing human resources, and the third approach suggests that human resource management is 'distinctively different' from personnel management.

Ian Beardwell and Len Holden (1997) state that 'the term Human Resource Management has come to be used ... as a description of the management of employees'. These authors then go on to discuss a range of different perspectives suggesting that human resource management may be:

- the renaming of the traditional personnel function
- a managerial fusion of personnel management and industrial relations
- an enabling and development role for the individual employee
- a strategic managerial function aimed at determining and achieving organizational goals.

Storey (2001: p. 6) defines HR management as 'a distinctive approach to employment management which seeks to achieve competitive advantage through the strategic deployment of a highly committed and capable workforce, using an integrated array of cultural, structural and personnel techniques'. Storey points to the strategic qualities of contemporary human resource management, that HR policies are increasingly integrated with business strategies. Storey also refers (2001: p. 9) to the frequent description of HRM as being either 'hard' or 'soft' in characteristic. The hard approach to HRM (also known as the 'Michigan' dimension) stresses the need for a business-oriented style, with an emphasis on productivity, efficiency in utilization of human resources and the achievement of business goals. The soft approach (known as the 'Harvard' dimension), considers much more the achievement of goals of mutual benefit to both employee and organization, with greater emphasis on motivation and commitment of the human resource, shared values and worker involvement. In relation to the hospitality industry it is clear that due to its reliance on a capable and service-oriented workforce, there is a need to ensure true alignment between business strategies and plans and the HRM strategies and plans (see Holbeche, 2001). This concept of 'fit' between business and HR policy is much discussed in recent literature, based on the assumption that if HRM is more in line or contingent with the external environment and the organization's business strategy, then higher performance will result and the competitive edge is assured (Legge, cited in Storey, 2001). Another strand of thinking on HRM stresses the value of organizational culture, of individual commitment and mutuality of objectives and beliefs of both organization and employee (Beardwell, Holden and Claydon, 2004; Lucas, 2004). An emphasis on the elements that form the organization's culture is also a strong boost for the significance of HRM policies and practice, as most of such elements, from behaviours and rituals to communications and reward systems, may be influenced by the people management of the business, especially in the service sector.

From this brief description of human resource management it is apparent that good human resource management should be the responsibility of all managers – not just personnel managers. And if the Institute of Personnel Management's (IPM, now the Chartered Institute of Personnel and Development (CIPD)) original definition of personnel management is examined, it is apparent that there are strong similarities:

Personnel management is a responsibility of all those who manage people, as well as being a description of the work of those who are employed as specialists. It is that part of management which is concerned with people at work and with their relationships within an enterprise. It applies not only to industry and commerce but to all fields of employment.

> Personnel management aims to achieve both efficiency and justice, neither of which can be pursued successfully without the other. It seeks to bring together and develop into an effective organization the men and women who make up an enterprise, enabling each to make his or her own best contribution to its success both as an individual and as a member of a working group. It seeks to provide fair terms and conditions of employment, and satisfying work for those employed.

The main distinction is that the CIPD's definition is rather general and pluralist (i.e. it indicates a balancing of the employer's and employees' interests) whereas the definitions put forward by Guest and Storey are more concerned with resourcing so that the organization's desired outcomes are achieved (a unitarist approach).

For the purpose of this book, human resource management is to be discussed as the concern of all managers, whereas personnel management is to be discussed as the activities of specialist personnel managers.

Human resource and personnel policies should embrace a number of different but interrelated issues. The first may be to do with deciding to be a 'leader' or 'follower' on the terms and conditions offered. A second may be concerned with human resource policies such as career prospects and to what extent an employer sets out to offer long-term secure careers to a significant proportion of the workforce. A third may deal with employee involvement and management style. To what extent do senior management really want to involve staff in decisions? One general feature of the top US companies identified by Peters and Waterman (1982) in the book *In Search of Excellence* has been a statement of company credo, and, in particular, the emphasis this has put on policy towards employees. Maybe it is this third type of concern which distinguishes human resource management from personnel management.

Personnel management as a specialist function

Personnel management, as a distinct specialization of management, is relatively new and consequently its specialist role and definition vary much more than is the case for older established specializations such as management accounting. In addition, because it leans heavily on the social sciences, its definitions and duties are more fluid.

To some, personnel management is seen as no more than the welfare branch of the company – concerned with looking after individual employees when in need. In 1986 two writers suggested that the personnel function could be described in one of three ways: clerk of works, contracts manager or architect (Tyson and Fell, 1989). In 1989 Nick Georgiades, at the European Association for Personnel Management Conference, suggested other roles: administrative handmaiden, policeman, toilet flusher, sanitary engineer. To others, it is the 'in-house staff agency', and in yet other cases the personnel management function is integrated completely into company activity. It is concerned with assisting in the harnessing of the employees' energies so that the enterprise operates efficiently, and it is also concerned with ensuring that the enterprise meets fully its social responsibilities to every employee. This is evident in the HCIMA's Hospitality Assured scheme and the Investors in People and the BHA's Excellence through People schemes (see Chapter 1).

This is no easy role, and frequently the personnel manager is seen, particularly in the private sector, as no more than a cost centre, or as the company's social conscience, by those managers who have to 'make the profits'. This should not be the case, because it must be recognized that for most organizations, there are two major functions: one is to achieve the 'group goals' such as increased sales or profits or, in the public sector, to provide services; the other is 'group maintenance', i.e. the role of creating and maintaining the group so that it can achieve its goals. Personnel managers assist management to achieve their objectives in the most effective manner by ensuring conditions of employment that attract, retain, motivate and obtain the commitment of the appropriate labour force.

Effective personnel management requires imagination in obtaining a fair share of the available labour. Consequently, good personnel policies can make considerable contributions to the success of an undertaking, and although their efforts frequently cannot be measured accurately in monetary terms, management should not be able to visualize doing its job effectively without the support of such policies. As Professor Ghoshal of INSEAD said, 'the role of HR is to support, not supplant' (*People Management*, May 1995). Figure 2.2 shows some of the issues of concern to HR managers whilst Figure 2.3 shows the main functions and responsibilities normally covered under the specialist personnel management function.

absenteeism	harassment
alcohol abuse	health and safety
annual hours contracts	
assertiveness	information technology
	internationalism
benchmarking	
bullying	law of employment
change management	organization structures – business process
communications	re-engineering
competencies	
continuous professional development	outplacement
culture and cultural change	outsourcing
delayering	part-time working
discipline	performance-related pay
distancing	psychological tests
drug abuse	
	quality and human resource management
empowerment	
equal opportunities – discrimination	racial discrimination
on grounds of gender, race,	re-engineering
age, disability	
ethics	sexual discrimination
	smoking at work
'family friendly' policies	
flexible working – flexible contracts	trade unions
flexible pay systems	
	violence

Figure 2.2 Some issues in human resource management

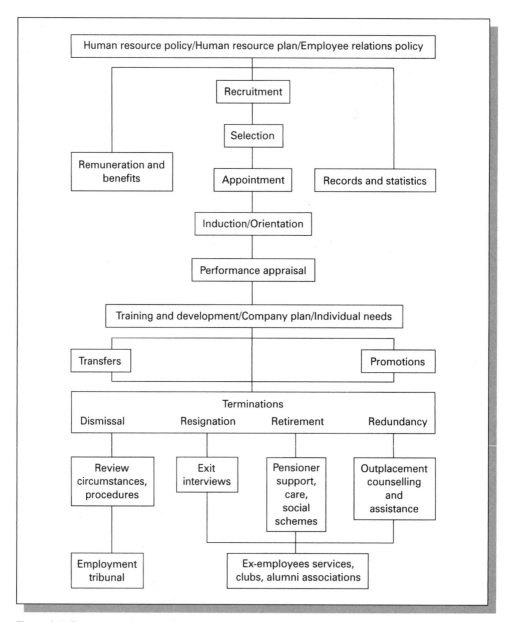

Figure 2.3 Elements of the specialist personnel management function

Human resource policies

Human resource policies do not develop in a vacuum, however. They are, as stated earlier, an expression of the style of management of an organization, an expression of its values. Human resource policies should be dynamic, both changing with and bringing about changes in the behaviour of the workforce and the organization. The part a personnel department can play in helping to formulate human resource policies will depend crucially on its current standing in the organization. However, its importance can often be estimated by looking at the levels of risk with which the function is involved. Figure 2.4 illustrates the different levels of risk with which an organization's personnel department can be associated.

Level of activity				
	High risk strategy			Leadership strategy culture
	Medium risk		Work group climate	
			Management practice	
	Low-risk tactical casework	Individual needs and motivation		
		Individual	Work Group	Organization
		Focus of Activity		

Figure 2.4 The level of personnel work
Source: Personnel Management, February 1990.

In order to arrive at a clearer understanding of the relationship between human resource policies and the style of management of an organization, it is necessary for managers and students of management to look at the findings of those who have studied the behaviour of people at work.

One of the problems in attempting such a task is the amount of published work available and the wide variety of opinions it expresses. Therefore only what this author considers the most important points have been selected. (Anyone wishing to study the subject should refer, as a starting point, to the reading list at the end of this chapter.)

People at work

The study of people at work falls within the province of the social sciences which are concerned with studying the relationships between individuals, groups of individuals and their environment. The knowledge obtained can be used in two principal ways, namely to understand and predict changes, i.e. to focus on 'content', and to bring about change, i.e. to focus on 'process' (see Mullins, 2005). The fundamental conclusion to be drawn from the work of behavioural scientists (Figure 2.5), and Abraham Maslow in particular, is that humans are satisfaction-seeking animals motivated primarily by their biological needs. Hotel and catering managers should be more conscious of the truth of this than most others. In addition, and unlike most other animals, once humans' biological needs are satisfied,

1841–1925	Henri Fayol (France)	Claimed to be the earliest known proponent of a theoretical analysis of managerial activities. He defined management as five functions: • to forecast • to organize • to command • to coordinate • to control.
1864–1920	Max Weber (Germany)	Responsible for defining three types of legitimate elements or criteria, including a clearly defined hierarchy, objective selection.
1856–1915	Frederick W. Taylor (USA)	The founder of the movement known as 'scientific management'. He proposed four 'great underlying principles': • the development of a true science of work • the scientific selection and progressive development of the workman • the bringing together of the science of work and the scientifically selected and trained man • the constant and intimate cooperation of management and men.
1880–1949	Elton Mayo (USA)	Often referred to as the founder of the Human Relations movement. His work demonstrated the importance of groups in affecting the behaviour of individuals at work. He is most famous for the Hawthorne investigations which led to a fuller understanding of the 'human factor' at work.
1903–1981	Rensis Likert (USA)	Showed that effective supervisors and managers tended to be 'employee centred' rather than 'job centred'. Likert distinguished four systems of management: • exploitive/authoritative • benevolent/authoritative • consultative • participative. He favoured the participative system, although other systems could also produce high productivity.
1906–1964	Douglas McGregor (USA)	Famous for theories X and Y. In theory X, people are assumed to dislike work and need direction and control. In theory Y, people are assumed to enjoy work and external control is not necessary. Managers' assumptions about their subordinates shape their behaviour.
Born 1923	Frederick Herzberg (USA)	Famous for demonstrating that factors that lead to dissatisfaction (hygiene factors) are quite different from those that lead to satisfaction (motivators). Determinants of job satisfaction are: • achievement • recognition • work itself • responsibility • advancement

Figure 2.5 Eleven theorists who have contributed to management thinking

		• company policy and administration • supervision • salary • interpersonal relations • working conditions.
1908–1970	Abraham Maslow (USA)	Maslow saw human needs in a form of hierarchy, for which he is famous; as one set of needs is satisfied, another emerges. Their order is: • physiological needs • security and safety needs • affiliation or acceptance needs • esteem needs • self-actualization.
Born 1909	Peter Drucker (USA)	Famous for developing the concept of 'management by objectives' (MbO). He believes that there are five basic principles of management: • set objectives • organize • motivate and communicate • measure performance • develop people.
	Edgar Schein (USA)	Known for his work on motivation – introducing the concepts of the 'psychological contract' and the 'career anchor' into the language of management. His work also included the study of corporate culture – an organization's set of artifacts, values and assumptions.
	Amitai Etzioni (USA)	Developed the classification of managers' power and workers' involvement

Managers' power	**Workers' involvement**
Coercive	Alienative
Utilitarian	Calculative
Normative	Moral

Figure 2.5 *continued*

further needs emerge – mainly of a social nature. This manifests itself in the pursuit of status, security, power and other outward signs of success. Most people may not be conscious of these needs that drive or motivate them. If, however, management can recognize them, they can take appropriate steps to ensure that these driving forces can be used to the advantage of both the organization and the individual.

The first need, the need for bodily comfort, is satisfied relatively simply by adequate meals and housing. Most advanced nations, recognizing that the satisfaction of this need is essential to the survival of individuals and of society, ensure by and large that no one needs to go without food and shelter. Individuals in our society, therefore, no longer accept that working merely for food and shelter is an end in itself. There are many cases where people are financially better off being unemployed rather than employed, and consequently they choose to remain unemployed. One report indicated that although pay is the single most important aspiration of unemployed people, satisfying and stimulating work and good relations with colleagues and managers are also regarded as being important (Hall, 1989). Most people expect much more from their employment than being able merely to purchase food and shelter.

Physical security is also these days very largely assured by the state. Regulations designed to protect the community and the individual from injury or disease penetrate every aspect of our daily lives, ranging from traffic to hygiene regulations. When people fall ill or suffer injury, the state cares for them so that they do not fear the consequences to the same extent as they may have done in the past or that they might in many other countries today. Therefore, seeking employment with low physical risk or with benevolent employers is no longer as important as it may have been a century or even fifty years ago. Consequently, because some basic needs are now largely guaranteed by the state, they no longer provide the motivation that they once did; some say that this provision has created a 'dependency culture' in some sections of the population. Instead, other and much more complex needs – the social needs – have emerged.

Satisfactory relationships with other people are among the highest of our needs. To work with, and for people we get on with, is something most of us like to do, and it is no doubt a major force attracting many people into the hospitality industry. In looking at staff turnover it should be noted that the greatest numbers leave in the earliest days of employment – the period when relationships have not developed. On the other hand, one of the main reasons why people stay in their jobs when all other conditions should encourage them to leave is their relationship with those at work, including colleagues, bosses, subordinates and customers.

In modern society another aspect of our relationship with others which plays a significant part is our need for social acceptance. Frequently this depends on our job and our way of living. By certain indications society locates us on the social ladder, but many people not content with their position attempt to move up. Social mobility has increased considerably even in the last 30 years and the main evidence is change of occupational status, type of housing, earning more money, obtaining a variety of other status symbols such as motor cars, longer holidays, thicker carpet in the office, etc., or even by changing from one occupation or employer to another with a higher social standing. This fact unfortunately deters many people from working in the hotel and catering industry because many of its jobs, in spite of being highly skilled, are not awarded the status awarded to other jobs demanding the same or maybe less skill. It is in this area that the industry's trade and professional bodies need to do a great deal of work. This problem is not unique to Britain. At the International Hotel and Restaurants Association Conferences in Tel Aviv in 1995 and in The Netherlands in 1999 the delegates resolved that national bodies worldwide needed to put greater effort into improving the perceived standing of hotel and catering work. The contribution of HRM (or lack of it) in hospitality firms towards image improvement has been a frequent criticism of the sophistication of HRM practices in the sector. However, recent research within UK hotels has revealed a general improvement in the quality of HRM, in the perceived value of jobs in the sector relative to other economic activities, and indeed of a favourable comparison with HRM approaches in those other activities (Hoque, 2000).

Next on the list of human needs comes the need to satisfy one's own ambitions and aspirations. This usually means making the maximum use of one's intellectual, social and manual skills. It may include the desire to be a company chairman or, more modestly, the wish to produce a satisfactory piece of workmanship. Today, with the undoubted economic need for mass production and consequent simplification, whether it be the production of in-flight meals or motor cars, a person's need for this satisfaction is constantly overridden. It is one of the strongest needs of working people and one for which they often make considerable sacrifices. Much research shows that people will put in long hours in difficult conditions even for low pay when intrinsic job satisfaction is high.

Finally – having satisfied all these needs – security of their continuing satisfaction is itself another and, these days, a growing need. Mergers and acquisitions along with automation now threaten many more people than ever before, and even those who a few years ago could feel secure no longer do so. The current trend to distancing and outsourcing, i.e. employing people on short contracts, through agencies, etc., whilst increasing an employer's flexibility, reduces job security. Seeking this security now plays an important part in employment relations and many people leave insecure employment for what they believe to be a secure alternative position. It is usually found that where job security is higher, such as in the public sector, labour turnover is lower – completely unlike the rate of labour turnover in some sectors of the hotel and catering industry, where job tenure is often short and notoriously precarious. Job security normally leads to a stable and skilled labour force with many of the consequent efficiencies. On the other hand, job security can be such that it can work against the best interests of the organization, with abuse abounding, such as excessive absenteeism and the protection of the grossly inefficient, as is the case in many public sector organizations.

When all these needs are satisfied, it is argued that an employee is more likely to offer stable and competent service, but, if any one of these needs remains unsatisfied, they will almost certainly behave in one of a variety of ways, some of which are contrary to the business interest.

First, they may seek employment elsewhere which offers more likelihood of a satisfying job. Second, they may seek other compensations, such as extra money or more time-off. If they have leadership qualities, they may become the focus for group, rather than individual, aspirations or dissatisfaction, and this may lead them to play an active part in trade union affairs or other similar activities. Third, they may just opt out and seek their satisfaction outside work, for example, at home or in club activities. In between these three distinct patterns of behaviour there are many degrees that most managers will recognize, including absenteeism, lateness, waste, pilferage and, of course, lack of cooperation or even sheer obstructionism, not all of which is blamed on management.

The behavioural scientist F. Herzberg developed a theory that suggests two largely independent sets of factors influence work behaviour. One set of factors, the 'hygiene' factors (such as work conditions), influence mainly the level of dissatisfaction. Improving the hygiene factors removes causes of dissatisfaction but without motivating the worker. Room temperature illustrates the point: ideal temperature goes unnoticed and does not motivate a person; a temperature that is too hot or too cold creates discomfort and demotivates.

The other set of factors are known as 'motivators' (achievement, praise, work itself). These actually make people feel positive about their work and have to be built into work in order to motivate the workforce. Ideally the hygiene factors should be put right at the same time.

Some alternative models of excellence in human resource management

Research conducted by the London School of Economics (see Guest, 1989) identified a number of different approaches to personnel management. These are as follows.

A paternalist welfare model

This approach emphasizes the need to look after employees as a means to the employees, in turn, looking after customers. An oft-quoted example from the past is Marks and Spencer or the former Trusthouse Forte.

A production model

The principal role of the personnel department is to support continuity of production by ensuring a proper supply of human resources, properly regulated through clear and consistent industrial relations guidelines. The Ford Motor Company is cited as an example.

A professional model

This model is based upon demonstrated and acknowledged competence of the personnel department in such technical areas as selection, training, pay and industrial relations. Examples include Shell and ICI.

A human resource model

This reflects a people-orientated focus throughout the organization, including respect for the individual, full utilization of individual abilities and sophisticated policies for employee involvement. An example of such a company is IBM.

Modern-day Taylorism

A variant of the production model, this is found in parts of the service sector. An example is McDonald's.

Which approach for which organization?

Most organizations will have to pay much closer attention to their human resource policies as labour markets become tighter, and expectations and aspirations of working people become heightened. Which of the above models or variants on these models will be the most suitable depends upon a whole range of different influences. The five different models above suggest that there are different solutions for different product markets and different technologies.

Human resource management and styles of leadership

A finding of considerable importance, highlighted by Douglas McGregor in his book *The Human Side of Enterprise* (1960), is that most people behave in the way expected of them and consequently live up or down to their superiors' expectations. Therefore the relationship between employee and boss can be described as a dynamic one: the higher the expectations made (within reason) of an employee, the higher the performance, and consequently even higher expectations can and will be made of and met by him or her in the future.

The style of management is therefore of vital importance in an organization because this determines to a large extent whether employees obtain satisfaction from their jobs and whether managers will achieve their business objectives.

The 'authoritarian' manager generally manages by issuing orders and instructions leaving little or no opportunity for discussion or even explanation. Very similar to this style is the 'unitarist' style, which is based on a reliance on traditional market forces and hierarchical systems with a clear split between the responsibilities of management and those of the workforce.

There are also the 'democratic' managers, who recognize that they are not only leading but are also part of a team and that this requires the others in the team – the staff – to be involved in decisions through discussion and explanation. The expression 'pluralist' is often used nowadays to describe such a style of management which recognizes that the aspirations of all sections of the workforce are to be taken into account in the decision-making process. A recent manifestation of democratic management is 'empowerment', discussed in the next chapter.

The third manager, the laissez-faire type, abdicates responsibility – leaving his or her staff to face the problems that are rightly more the manager's. The staff are left to face complaints from customers without the authority to rectify or overcome causes of disruption.

These three very simplified descriptions of styles of management have been included to illustrate that there are several different ways of managing and there are complex interactions between the individuals, the tasks and the environment, which usually determine a particular style of management.

There also exist different attitudes towards the workforce. Amitai Etzioni (1980) has produced a useful classification of the power used by managers to ensure compliance, and as with McGregor's theory, it can be shown that particular styles have particular effects. Etzioni states that there are three principal management orientations to workers. First, there is the use of coercive power, in which fear of the consequences is the main motivator. Those managers who bewail the passing of the 'divine right of dismissal' most probably fall into this category. The second category is the utilitarian use of power. This depends upon the manipulation of material rewards such as wages, and is commonly seen in large manufacturing industries where the predominant reward for work done is money. It is also seen in the hotel and catering industry, particularly in the way seasonal and casual workers are employed. Etzioni's third category is normative power. This rests largely upon the use of prestige, esteem and social acceptance. The managers of many organizations are motivated very much in this way, seeking power, responsibility, recognition, acceptance, titles, bigger cars, admission to prestige-carrying committees, etc.

Etzioni goes on to argue that each management type has a corresponding form of worker involvement. First, there is an alienative involvement which signifies that the employee has strong negative attitudes towards the employer. Normally this would persist only where no reasonable employment alternatives exist, but such an attitude might be manifested in various forms of sabotage, theft or, worst of all, arson (which does occur in hotels and restaurants). Second, Etzioni identifies a calculative involvement which is based on money or material exchange. Casual workers in catering are very likely to have this attitude towards their employers. Third, there is a moral involvement which signifies that the employee identifies closely with the employer's and colleagues' values and objectives. Employees will carry out their work because they value the objectives of the work.

In addition, Storey (2001) writes that an examination of many personnel texts will show that for much of its history, personnel management has been a management process or function concerned with achieving compliance from employees. More recently, however, there has been concern with achieving full employee commitment. Figure 2.6 illustrates an example of how this commitment can be expressed strategically.

Having given these brief outlines of some important contributions to our understanding of work people's behaviour, it must be emphasized that there are many other important contributions which, perforce, have had to be omitted. Our purpose, however, is to show that there are different, often mutually supporting, explanations of behaviour which state that different styles of management engender different worker attitudes.

Related research also demonstrates that there is no such thing as a universal leadership or management quality. Instead, successful management and leadership is contingent upon the interaction of a whole variety of factors, among which the nature of the goods and services being offered and the market itself are critical.

OUR VISION

> **Providing A Preferred Hospitality Experience by Exceeding Expectations and Caring Without Compromise**

OUR VALUES

(A) **Commitment to people and team**
- *Caring*: We recognise the well-being of guests, staff and their families as the core to our success.
- *Diversity*: We value the diversity of personal interests, cultures, races, creeds, colours and sexes and will always provide equality of opportunity.
- *Fairness*: We reward people based upon merit and expect everyone to accept personal responsibility for their actions. We are willing to forgive honest mistakes.
- *Growth*: Our commitment to manage growth creates opportunities for our people to develop.
- *Investment in people*: We will hire the best people who share our values. We are committed to helping people achieve their full potential through education, training and skills development in a work environment which encourages feedback advancement, reward and recognition.

Figure 2.6 Mission, vision and value of Pan Pacific Hotels and Resorts
Source: Reproduced by courtesy of Pan Pacific.

- *Integrity*: We generate mutual respect for each other through honesty, truthfulness, maintaining our honour and keeping our work.
- *Empowerment*: Our people will be empowered with the skills, tools and authority to ensure that guest expectations are exceeded.
- *Openness in communication*: We will listen intently to understand, clearly state our expectations, provide appropriate and timely feedback, and share information and ideas. It is OK to say 'I don't know', or 'I don't agree'.
- *Openness of mind*: We will be receptive to new ideas and value the freedom of one's mind and thoughts.
- *Respect*: We have mutual respect for each other's talents and value dearly the contribution of all our associates.
- *Teamwork*: We believe in the strength and value of working together and cooperating for a common purpose.

(B) **Commitment to business excellence**
- *Creativity*: We value originality and being in the forefront of new ideas.
- *Excellence/Quality*: We will constantly strive to achieve the highest level of quality given the existing environment.
- *Flexibility*: Flexibility in management style allows us to diversify beyond the confines of the hospitality industry and to adapt to changes.
- *Fun at work*: We encourage the belief that work should be enjoyable and seek to provide a happy, fulfilling and stimulating work environment.
- *Guest and customer driven*: Consistently understanding our customers' needs and meeting, even exceeding their expectations.
- *Global mindset*: Knowing no boundaries or borders, operating on a global scale, setting a world standard of quality and understanding that each hotel's success affects Pan Pacific Hotels and Resorts worldwide.
- *Pride*: We take pride in becoming a leader and making a significant difference by providing the best hospitality while relentlessly pursuing perfection.
- *Profit oriented*: We seek to ensure a healthy profit, which enables growth and furthers the well-being of the staff, the company, shareholders and owners.

(C) **Commitment to community**
- *Community involvement*: We value our relationships, our involvement and our respected standing within the community.
- *Environmental sensitivity*: We will work towards being environmentally responsible in all aspects of our business.
- *Heritage*: We value the local culture, traditions and customs.
- *Safe Environment*: We strive to provide a safe environment for our guests and our employees.

Figure 2.6 *continued*

A steady, non-seasonal trade, as encountered in much industrial catering, will call for a style of management very different from that required by a busy seasonal hotel. Circumstances and time, therefore, can make a manager who would have been a failure in one situation, a success in another. See also Chapter 20.

Further Reading and References

Armstrong, M. (1997) *A Handbook of Human Resource Management*, 7th edn, London: Kogan Page.
Beardwell, I. and Holden, L. (1997) *Human Resource Management*, 2nd edn, London: Pitman.
Beardwell, I., Holden, L. and Claydon, T. (2004) *Human Resources Management—A Contemporary Approach*, 4th edn, Harlow: Prentice Hall.

Etzioni, A. (1980) *Modern Organization*, Englewood Cliffs, NJ: Prentice Hall.

Guest, D. (1989) *Personnel Management*, January.

Hall, M. (1989) *Great Expectations*, Brighton: Brighton Polytechnic.

Handy, C. (1985) *Understanding Organizations*, London: Penguin.

Holbeche, L. (2001) *Aligning Human Resources and Business Strategy*, Oxford: Butterworth-Heinemann.

Koontz, H. and Weirich, H. (1994) *Management*, 10th edn, London: McGraw-Hill.

Hoque, K. (2000) *Human Resource Management in the Hotel Industry*, London: Routledge.

Lucas, R. (2004) *Employment Relations in the Hospitality and Tourism Industries*, London: Routledge.

McGregor, D. (1960) *The Human Side of Enterprise*, New York: McGraw-Hill.

Mullins, L. (2005) *Management and Organisational Behaviour*, 7th edn, Harlow: Prentice Hall.

Peters, T. and Waterman, R. H. (1982) *In Search of Excellence*, New York and London: Harper and Row.

Pugh, D. S. and Hickson, D. J. (1997) *Writers on Organizations*, 5th edn, London: Penguin.

Rothwell, S. (1984) In search of excellence, *Personnel Management*, London: CIPD.

Storey, J. (ed.) (2001) *Human Resource Management – A Critical Text*, 2nd edn, London: Thomson Learning.

Torrington, D., Hall, L. and Taylor, S. (2002) *Human Resource Management*, 5th edn, Harlow: Pearson Education.

Tyson, S. and Fell, A. (1989) *Evaluating the Personnel Function*, London: Hutchinson.

Questions

1 Describe the alternative types of human resource policies that can be adopted by employers.

2 Using an employer from the private (commercial) sector and another from the public sector, compare and contrast their approaches to human resource management.

3 Discuss the nature of human resource policies that are likely to be necessary in the future to attract, retain and motivate staff. (Divide staff into a number of different categories, e.g. full-time, part-time, casual, management, supervisory, operative, craft, unskilled, male, female.)

4 Evaluate the human resource policies of an employer you know well.

PART 2

Effectively Resourcing the Hospitality Organization

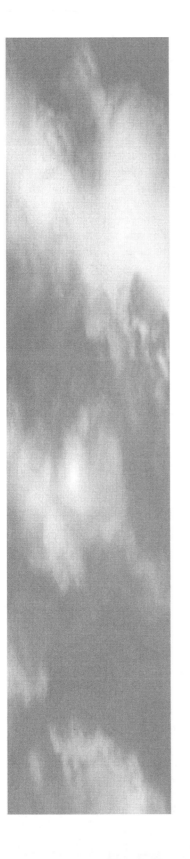

Job design

Although the term 'management' (in its abstract sense) has almost as many definitions as there are managers, it is generally understood to refer to the art or practice of achieving required results through the efforts of others. Drucker says that management is a practice rather than a science (*Professional Manager*, 1993). There is today, however, considerable debate about what precisely it is that motivates people to achieve the results required of them. At one extreme there are those of the scientific school of management (see Chapter 2) who believe that all that is necessary is to select the right people, give clear directions and enough money, and the required results will be achieved. On the other hand there are those from the human relations school (see Chapter 2) who believe that organizational objectives will only be achieved by recognizing to the full the needs and expectations of working people. Whichever view prevails, however, it is generally held that people produce their best performances when they know clearly what is expected of them. W. Edwards Deming, one of America's great management gurus stated, 'People need to know what their jobs are' (*Personnel Management*, June 1992). Consequently if an undertaking's objectives are to be achieved, it follows that all its managers and work people must know clearly the results they are expected to produce. Such a statement of an organization's expectations of its employees can be made either orally or in writing. There are many who believe that the written word is less likely to be misunderstood and that the need to think carefully before putting words to paper generally produces more logical and effective results than oral statements.

It is for such reasons that clear, precise job descriptions are given to people at work, because once a job is clearly described on paper there should be little room for subsequent misunderstandings. As a result the job should be performed more efficiently. Having said this, in the hospitality industry, with its large number of small establishments, there are many work people who do not have or need job descriptions. Furthermore there is a view that job descriptions and the related hierarchies merely serve to slow down effective communication. Tom Peters says that the only way to compete in an ever-faster world is for 'a revolution in structure to create a world with no barriers between functions' (*Financial Times*, 23 February 1990).

However, before producing job descriptions it is essential to realize that the job description should be the result of a process referred to as job design (Figure 3.1). First, job design can be seen as the process by which the employer sets out to maximize the output of the workforce – a scientific-school-of-management approach. For many employers this remains the sole objective. Second, there is increasing recognition that if job design is to be effective, the resulting jobs must satisfy a variety of stakeholder interests.

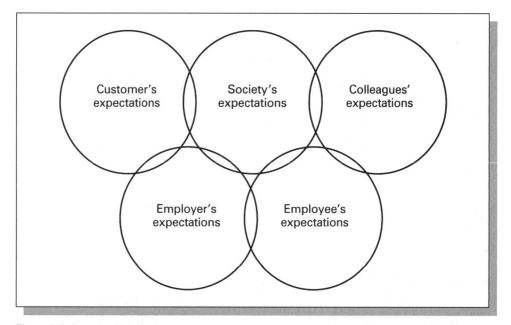

Figure 3.1 Aspects of job design

This second approach recognizes Drucker's view that it is important to distinguish between efficiency and effectiveness: 'Managers must in the end be measured by their economic performance, though this is not necessarily synonymous with maximum profits . . .' (Kennedy, 1991). Designing jobs for short-term efficiency may result, for example, in high labour turnover with a drop in customer satisfaction and hence in long-term effectiveness.

Third, of course, job design must result in customer satisfaction. Fourth, most people work in teams or groups, so colleagues' expectations have to be considered. And, finally, the job must be designed in such a way that society's expectations (e.g. health and safety, pollution) are satisfied (see Figure 3.1).

Approaches to job design

In setting out to design any job, therefore, it is essential to recognize the expectations of all stakeholders involved. The actual approach adopted will depend on an amalgam of these sets of expectations; for example, where customers and employers want fast service with minimum personalized contact, such as in many fast food operations, the resultant job may emphasize speed at the cost of job satisfaction. The consequence may be high labour turnover, which may well be acceptable, even desirable, to the employer where there is a steady supply of replacement labour.

Job specialization

This approach to organizing work has been around for thousands of years and has led to civilization as we know it today. However, as an approach to organizing modern industrial production it was developed by a number of practitioners and theorists, including F. W. Taylor the founder of scientific management. Major principles resulting from the scientific management approach are as follows.

Science of work

The need for scientific methods of observing, measuring and analysing work activities to replace existing unsystematic approaches.

Standardization

Using the resulting knowledge, efficient working methods and performance levels can be set for work.

Selection

Systematic and scientific approaches to selecting workers with relevant qualities and abilities, together with planned training for the work involved.

Specialization

Both management and workers should concentrate upon specific functional activities involving a limited range of tasks for which the individual's abilities and training enable expert performance. (From Torrington and Chapman, 1983.)

There have been two main consequences of the application of these ideas. First, areas of expertise and responsibility have become much more specialized, particularly in the technical and management areas. There are now many more specialists in management than there were fifty years ago, even ten years ago. Second, and in contrast, particularly at an operative level, job content is simplified through reduction of the number of tasks each operative performs to a very limited number so that the need for skill and training is minimized.

The apparent economic benefits of job simplification, however, were accompanied by many problems, such as industrial strife and alienation, the causes being put down to that same job simplification. In contrast, the findings of behavioural scientists were showing that work people could not be treated as mere components of machines: instead they had a range of needs to be met by the work they performed. As a consequence other approaches to job design became necessary.

Job rotation

One reaction to job simplification was job rotation. This provides individuals with some variety in either the working conditions (i.e. where or when the basic job is done) or the actual tasks performed. The jobs, however, remain simple; they may provide little stimulation and may not satisfy self-esteem needs.

Job enlargement

Job enlargement, in contrast, extends the range of tasks performed and is aimed at reducing boredom, increasing interest in work and increasing self-esteem. Job enlargement, however, brings about the very problems that work simplification sets out to eliminate, such as the need for greater knowledge, skill and training.

Job enrichment

Job enlargement, as described above, extends horizontally the range of tasks to be performed by an individual by adding tasks of a similar nature. It does not, however, meet the more complex expectations such as the need for autonomy. Job enrichment instead extends vertically the range of tasks by increasing an individual's responsibility and autonomy through adding elements of the job which may have been the responsibility of supervisors or management, such as planning, organization and control. Such an approach has been adopted by a number of leading companies in the hospitality industry. For example, room attendants have been given additional responsibilities, resulting in reduction in the number of supervisors.

Sociotechnical systems

This approach to job design sets out to bring together an employer's technical system (e.g. buildings and equipment) and the social system comprising the work people. This is because the scientific school aimed to maximize the technical system, seeing the work people as components. In contrast, the human relations theorists concentrated on maximizing the satisfaction of human needs. These two approaches can be seen to be incompatible. It is necessary to look at an organization as a sociotechnical system which compromises between technical efficiency and group needs.

In the sociotechnical system of job design three major factors are considered. These are: first, the need to recognize the needs that are met by formal and informal groups; second, work is allocated to groups that are able to identify clearly with the work; third, the group is given a high degree of autonomy over its work. Such an approach can be seen in the increased autonomy of many work groups (see the discussion of empowerment).

Quality circles

Quality circles (QCs) trace their origin to post-war Japan and the Japanese desire to change the image of Japanese products as cheap imitations of Western products. Quality circles evolved as a result of an increasingly literate workforce being able to participate in problem solving. The quality circles movement spread from Japan to the USA in the 1970s and to the UK in the late 1970s.

The principles of QCs are:

- QCs should be introduced in a totally voluntary way and should only grow as and when volunteers wish to join.
- QCs are based on a McGregor theory Y (see Chapter 2) concept of working people; i.e. they are willing and able to participate in solving problems that affect them.
- QCs should be unbureaucratic and need only brief action notes following each meeting.
- QCs, as with any other crucial approach to management, need middle and senior management commitment.
- QCs focus problem solving at the point at which problems occur, and therefore release middle and senior management time.

Quality circles are based upon the working group. Groups of about four to ten volunteers who work for the same supervisor meet about once a week, for about an hour, to identify, analyse and solve their own work-related problems. Discussions should be free from hierarchical restraints. Members take ownership of departmental issues and no longer see problems as other people's problems. Quality circle members will need some training in appropriate techniques, such as brainstorming, used to identify and suggest solutions. In addition they will need to be trained in problem-solving techniques. In some cases smaller numbers of employees may be involved, in which case such groups are sometimes referred to as 'quality bubbles'.

The benefits of QCs may be at least threefold: first, problems are solved; secondly, attitudes that identify with the organization's goals are developed; and thirdly, the quality of supervision and communications is improved.

Obviously it can be seen that if QCs are developed and operated effectively their influence on job design can be very significant. In particular, job design becomes a dynamic process with the possibility that jobs could be constantly changing in detail.

Job design, therefore, is the process that sets out to harness the energies of human resources in order to achieve an organization's objectives. In turn, job descriptions are the written results of the process of job design.

In some cases, particularly in the industry's smallest establishments, written job descriptions are not used and may be too formal and rigid. In other situations brief descriptions only may be sufficient, whereas in yet others quite detailed and complex documents are called for. The degree of detail needed in describing the various elements of a job varies from job to job and from organization to organization. There are, however, two main documents: job descriptions and job specifications. They are described below. In addition a brief description of management by objectives is included in this chapter because it describes a methodical and systematic approach to the design and description of jobs and setting of objectives.

Empowerment

In the last few years the word 'empowerment' has entered the management vocabulary. Other words are sometimes used, such as 'enabling'. The French use the word *responsabiliser*: 'to make responsible'. The concept has had a mixed reception, partly because empowerment has been associated with reduction in the layers of management of many organizations.

This reduction in the number of layers of management is partly the result of recession, new technologies and also competitive pressures. An associated reason has been the development known as 'business process re-engineering' (BPR) by which many organizations have analysed closely the way they carry out their organizational functions. Consequences of BPR have included delayering, i.e. reducing the number of levels of management; empowerment, i.e. giving more responsibility lower down the hierarchy; and outsourcing, i.e. subcontracting non-core activities.

In its simplest form, empowerment is a management philosophy that allows work people to take on responsibilities that were once the prerogative of management. This might include making operative staff responsible for the quality of their own work or whole teams of staff responsible for organizing how they work as a team. Examples include major hotel chains eliminating assistant housekeepers and making the room attendants totally responsible for the quality of the work they do. In another company the restaurant teams were given the responsibility of organizing the whole of the restaurant service operations. Management roles change in such a situation, managers becoming coaches, counsellors and facilitators rather than supervisors (see Ashness and Lashley, 1995). As Lashley and McGoldrick (1994) write, 'an increasing number of firms are considering employee empowerment as part of their human resource strategy for competitive advantage'. They go on to point out, however, that it is not the only strategy open to employers, suggesting that some have taken a too simplistic view of empowerment as a business solution.

Job descriptions

Job descriptions are a broad statement of the scope, purpose, duties and responsibilities involved in a job. Their main purposes are to

1 give employees an understanding of their jobs and standards of performance
2 clarify duties, responsibilities and authority in order to design the organization structure
3 assist in assessing employees' performance
4 assist in the recruitment and placement of employees
5 assist in the induction of new employees
6 evaluate jobs for grading and salary administration
7 provide information for training and management development. (Figure 3.2)

There are two distinct but equally important parts to the full description of jobs. The first is the statement of conditions for which employees contract to do work; some time ago in the UK it was recognized that the definition of conditions was not generally adequate, with the result that the Contracts of Employment Act became law in 1963. Now the Employment Rights Act 1996 requires that certain information about conditions of employment such as hours of work, job title and length of notice be

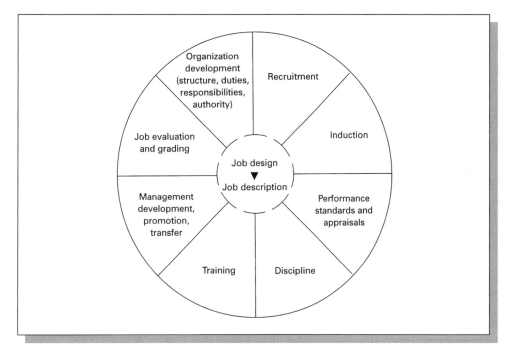

Figure 3.2 Job descriptions: the hub of personnel management

given to employees. This subject, together with other legal reasons for producing and issuing comprehensive job descriptions, will be dealt with in subsequent chapters.

The second part of describing jobs requires the provision of information to employees, which specifies clearly what results are expected of them and indicates how their performance will be measured.

Job descriptions should contain the following main elements:

Job identification

This section identifies the job by title, department and level in the hierarchy.

Scope of job

This section provides a brief description of the scope of a job.

Content

This section is a detailed statement and normally includes a list of duties and how these are performed, and what standard of performance is required.

Conditions

This section describes any particular conditions that make the job more, or less, difficult; for example, if a public house is situated in a rough area, this will need to be highlighted.

Authority

This section describes any limits to the employee's authority such as cash limits, authority to make contracts on behalf of the employer, and authority to engage or dismiss subordinates.

Figure 3.3 shows a typical job description for a chef and Figure 3.4 shows one for a waiter/waitress. A major criticism of many job descriptions is that, by prescribing tasks and responsibilities, they can work against the overall objectives of the organization. This is particularly so in service organizations where staff need to understand that their role is to provide a service, even when it is not in their job description. Martin Kaye (1995) writes, 'rigid job descriptions . . . are becoming redundant. People increasingly do not have a "job" they have a "role" and to keep up with this new industrial revolution it is necessary to turn away from job analysis towards role analysis.' An example of role analysis might specify that members of staff have customer satisfaction as one of their roles. In this way staff might take on (or own) a customer's problems rather than decide that the problem is not in their job description and try to pass the problem and the customer on to someone else.

Title	Chef
Department	Food and Beverage
Scope	All hotel food preparation operations
Responsible to	Food and Beverage Manager
Responsible for	1 *Personnel*: all kitchen staff including kitchen manual staff 2 *Equipment*: all kitchen fixed and removable equipment and kitchen utensils
Lateral communication	Restaurant Manager, Front Office Manager, Head Housekeeper
Main responsibilities	The planning, organization and supervision of food preparation in the hotel including: 1 Menu compilation according to agreed costed recipes 2 Purchasing of foodstuffs, kitchen materials and equipment from nominated suppliers within agreed budget levels 3 Portion and waste control 4 Control of labour and other variable costs within budget levels 5 Arrangement of staff rosters 6 Training of new staff 7 Hygiene and cleanliness 8 Fire precautions 9 Security of all kitchen supplies, equipment, utensils and silverware
Limits of authority	Engagement and suspension of all subordinates until circumstances can be reported to the Food and Beverage Manager
Hours of work	As agreed with Food and Beverage Manager

Figure 3.3 Job description for a chef

JOB DESCRIPTION

CHOICE HOTELS
EUROPE

Name:
Hotel:
Job Title: Waiter/Waitress
Department:
Responsible for: Stock/Equipment/Staff
Responsible to:
Internal Contacts: Kitchen/Laundry/Porters/Maintenance/Reception/Bar
External Contacts: Clients/Laundry/Suppliers
Overall Objectives: Prepare and clear down the Restaurant for service. Warmly welcome clients.
Order, serve and clear both food and liquor, selling up at all times.

KEY TASKS	HOW MEASURED
1. Preparation of the Restaurant for Service	All requirements to be clean and available
2. Welcoming and seating of the guests	Correct greeting and acknowledgement
3. Taking food/drink orders and selling up	Clear explanation of dishes. Increasing sales
4. Service of food and drink	Speed and courtesy. No accidents
5. Providing the correct accompaniments	Avoiding guests' having to ask for them
6. Offering a high standard of help and service	No complaints
7. Receiving payment for goods provided	All items charged and paid for
8. Farewell to guests	Seeing them return
9. Observing Hygiene, Health, Fire and Safety Regulations	EHO: Hazard and Accident Reports - cleanliness and safe working practices

Areas personally responsible for but not delegated

Constraints
No smoking/drinking whilst on duty
Access to other public areas is forbidden without prior permission

Other duties may be added from time to time according to business needs and at the discretion of management.

Name of Job Holder _____   Name of Supervisor/Manager _____

Signature (Job Holder) _____   Signature (Supervisor/GM) _____

Date: _____   Date _____

JDwaii2a/DTP/8/96

Figure 3.4 Job description for a waiter/waitress
Source: Reproduced by courtesy of Choice Hotels.

Job specifications

In many cases more detail than is normally contained in a brief job description may be necessary for a job to be performed satisfactorily. A detailed statement of the job may be required, specifying the precise skills and knowledge needed to carry out the various component tasks of the job. This information may be contained in a document, often referred to as a job specification. Alternatively, the information may be contained in such documents as manuals of operation, operating instructions and the like. Extracts from a job specification for a waiter/waitress are shown in Figure 3.5.

Duties	Knowledge	Skill	Social skills
1 Preparation			
1.3 Preparation of butter, cruets and accompaniments	1 Correct accompaniments for the dishes on the day's menu	Operation of butter pat maker. Preparation of sauces, e.g. vinaigrette	
3 Service of customers			
3.3 Taking orders	1 Procedures for taking wine and food orders 2 Menu and dish composition 3 Procedure for taking requisitions to kitchen, bar dispense and cashier		1 Assisting customers with selection in order to maximize sales 2 Informing customers of composition of dishes
8 Wine dispense	Product knowledge 1 Suitable wines for dishes on the menu 2 Suitable glasses for different wines 3 Correct temperatures for red, white and rosé Licensing law 1 Young persons 2 Drinking up time	1 Presenting bottle 2 Opening bottle 3 Pouring wine	1 Assisting customers with selection 2 Dealing with complaints 1 Refusing service 2 Asking people to 'drink up'
11 Preparation for cleaners after last customers have left			
11.3 Stripping tables	1 Safe disposal of ash tray contents 2 Disposal of cutlery, crockery, linen, cruets		

Figure 3.5 Extracts from a job specification for a waiter/waitress

Within the last few years job descriptions and specifications have become much more highly developed in the hospitality industry. Many companies use training booklets which serve several important purposes, including the provision of

- job descriptions
- trainers' programme
- trainees' *aides-mémoire*
- list of duties
- list of tasks
- standards of performance
- interviewer's checklist
- training checklist.

Not only are these booklets very useful for selection, induction and training purposes, they may also be useful for discipline purposes and even for 'due diligence' in cases of prosecution or litigation. If someone has been trained to do something, and the fact is recorded, then certain standards can be expected.

Job analysis

This is sometimes considered to be a document describing a job in detail, but the term is more commonly used when referring to the technique of examining jobs in depth.

Preparation of job (or role) descriptions and job specifications

Some managers like to prepare job descriptions and other such documents with the employees concerned, and, generally speaking, this is by far the best approach. Frequently, however, this principle can apply only to supervisory and management grades, because the jobs of operative grades are often so clearly defined that discussion, apart from explanation, would only raise hopes that would be disappointed when it became apparent that no changes were forthcoming. Furthermore, it is not always possible to involve the employee concerned, because the need for job descriptions often does not make itself apparent until a person has to be recruited. Even so, with the increasing development of participative approaches such as QCs and empowerment, it is very likely that the involvement of operative staff in the design of their own jobs will increase in the hospitality industry as in other sectors.

The preparation of job specifications normally requires a more skilled approach than that needed for the preparation of job descriptions. The uses to which such documents are to be put should determine who prepares them; for example, if job specifications are to be used for training purposes, they should be prepared by training specialists and the line management concerned. On the other hand, if they are to be used as a basis for work measurement, work study specialists should work with line management.

Whatever form the description of jobs takes, however, vague terms such as 'satisfactory levels of gross profit' should be avoided and, instead, actual quantities or levels should be specified, such as 'a gross profit of 65% is to be obtained'. It is good practice also to incorporate budgets and forecasts into job descriptions, since these set specific and quantified targets. Additionally, documents such as manuals of operation or training booklets may be directly related to job descriptions.

Because of the vital part played by job descriptions and specifications, particularly in such things as induction, training, job evaluation and performance appraisal, their preparation should be monitored by one person or department to ensure consistency. They should be regularly updated and a copy should be held by the jobholder, by his or her superior, sometimes by the superior's boss as well and, of course, by the personnel department (where one exists).

Some job-design tools

Job design, as indicated above, can involve a number of different skills and techniques. These can include the following.

Work study

This divides into method study and work measurement.

Method study

A part of work study concerned with recording and analysing methods and proposed methods of work, the purpose being to develop more effective ways of doing things.

Work measurement

A technique used to measure the time an experienced worker will take to perform a task or job to a predetermined standard. Measurement may be carried out by direct observation, by sampling or by using 'synthetic' values, i.e. times determined for particular movements.

Ergonomics

The study of the relationship between a worker and his or her work equipment and environment. In particular it is concerned with the application of anatomical, physiological and psychological knowledge to working situations. The aim of ergonomics is to produce safe and effective equipment for working people, using physical and psychological knowledge.

Management by objectives

Management by objectives (and various similar approaches) is an approach to management which, if operated effectively, influences all levels and activities of an organization. By concept it is typical of a democratic style of management, although, in practice, it is often introduced by other types of manager. It usually relies heavily on specially designed job descriptions and similar documents. It seeks to integrate all of an organization's principal targets with the individual managers' own aspirations.

Management by objectives requires the establishment of an undertaking's objectives and the development of plans to achieve these objectives and of methods for monitoring progress. At the same time each manager must be personally involved in the preparation of his or her own department's targets and in the means of achieving these targets. Objectives should not be handed down by superior to subordinate, but should be agreed between the two after all factors have been considered.

Only the critical areas (key result areas) of each manager's job are defined, the objectives where possible are quantified and means of checking results, or identifying obstacles, and of achieving objectives are developed. Planning and improvement go on continuously through review meetings between superiors and subordinates held at regular intervals. The procedure is illustrated in Figure 3.6 and an extract from an MbO job description is shown in Figure 3.7.

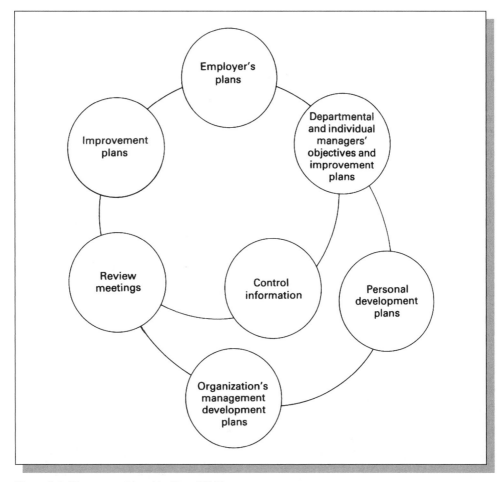

Figure 3.6 Management by objectives (MbO)

Manager, White Hart Restaurant: Objectives for six months ending 30 June

Key result area	Performance standard	Current level of achievement	Control information	Improvement target	Improvement plan
1 Gross profit (a) catering	63%	58%	Monthly stocktake	Achieve budget	Review selling and purchase prices, introduce more high-yield dishes, by 30 April.
(b) liquor	60%	58%	Monthly stocktake	Achieve budget	Alter sales mix, introduce premiumpriced beer, discontinue sale of cheaper draught beer.
2 Sales volume	£60,000 per month	£66,000	Takings sheets	Increase to £84,000	Promote new private function room, spend £2000 on promotion during first quarter.
3 Labour	23%	26%	Weekly wages sheet	Reduce to budget, 23%	Increase staff only for booked functions, no more staff to be recruited except to replace those who leave.

Figure 3.7 Management by objectives: example of performance standards and improvement plans

Where MbO concepts have been used in hotels and catering to set standards, it is generally found that the performance standards of operative staff are 'guest centred', i.e. they are concerned with identifying the standards of service to be provided to the guest. The performance standards of heads of departments, on the other hand, are 'profit centred', i.e. they identify the cost criteria for producing the services for the guest. Heads of departments are, however, directly responsible for ensuring that the operational performance standards are met by department staff, so their performance standards may incorporate quality management standards as well as profit-centred standards.

Current issues to be faced in job design

With the rapidly changing nature of the workforce and labour market, including skills shortages and the raised expectations of working people, job design now has to consider a wider range of factors than merely designing the task and work content of jobs. Job designers, i.e. most managers, will need to focus more than before on the conditions of work rather than just the job content. Such issues will include more flexible working hours, providing support for women returners, more autonomy, etc. in addition to eliminating menial tasks and tasks requiring scarce skills. Other dimensions include the need to ensure that forms of discrimination are not created or perpetuated, intentionally or unintentionally, through job design.

Job design in hospitality operations

At one extreme, job design can simplify work so that little skill and training are needed. Trends in this direction are very apparent in the hospitality industry in several sectors including fast food operations and the use of cook-chill and cook-freeze in many different operations, including schools, hospitals, banqueting and flight catering. A major reason why the process is sometimes referred to as 'decoupling' is that the production and service elements are totally separated – pre-prepared meals being produced away from the service point. Such systems are concerned mainly with the 'production elements' of many products. However, because of the significant 'customer contact' element, it is difficult to 'simplify out' many of the tasks that customers expect as part of the service and which employees themselves find rewarding, such as tasks involving social interaction.

Further Reading and References

Armstrong, M. (1999) *A Handbook of Human Resource Management*, 7th edn, London: Kogan Page.

Ashness, D. and Lashley, C. (1995) *Employee Empowerment in Harvester Restaurants*, Brighton: Human Resource Management in the Hospitality Industry Conference Document, University of Brighton.

Beardwell, I., Holden, L. and Claydon, T. (2004) *Human Resource Management—A Contemporary Approach*, 4th edn, Harlow: Pearson Education Ltd.

D'Annunzio-Green, N., Maxwell, G. and Watson, S. (2002) *Human Resource Management—International Perspectives in Hospitality and Tourism*, London: Continuum.

Handy, C. (1985) *Understanding Organisations*, London: Penguin.

Humble, J. (1979) *Management by Objectives in Action*, London: McGraw-Hill.

Kaye, M. (1995) *Employee Motivation and Effective Rewards*, Croners Pay and Benefits Briefing No. 77, Kingston-upon-Thames: Croner Publications.

Kennedy, C. (ed.) (1991) *Guide to Management Gurus*, London: Century Business.

Lashley, C. and McGoldrick, J. (1995) *The Limits of Empowerment*, Brighton: Human Resource Management in the Hospitality Industry Conference Document, University of Brighton.

Mullins, L. (2005) *Management and Organisational Behaviour*, 7th edn, Harlow: Prentice Hall.

Robertson, I. T. (1985) *Motivation and Job Design: Theory and Practice*, London: Institute of Personnel Management.

Torrington, D. and Chapman, J. (1983) *Personnel Management*, 2nd edn, London: Prentice Hall.

Torrington, D., Hall, L. and Taylor, S. (2002) *Human Resource Management*, 5th edn, Harlow: Pearson Education.

Questions

1 Describe the different approaches to job design.

2 Discuss the various influences that need to be taken into account when designing jobs.

3 Discuss what future influences are likely to influence job design.

4 Discuss how job design may differ when applied to management and non-management jobs.

5 Evaluate the approach to job design used by an employer you know well.

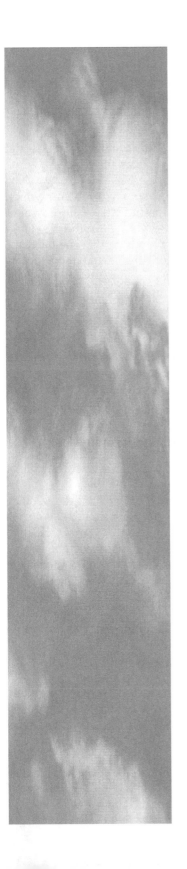

• • • • 4

Recruitment

The hospitality industry not only in the UK, but throughout much of the world appears to have recruitment problems associated with a poor image as an employer. At the international level this has been highlighted by the International Hotel and Restaurants Association resolutions in Israel in 1995 and The Netherlands in 1999 that national associations should take initiatives to improve the image of the industry as an employer.

In the UK many reports over the years, some summarized in earlier editions of this book, have highlighted the persistent nature of many of the issues confronting employers and employees. Two such reports are summarized below, but, in essence, they repeat the findings of earlier reports, emphasizing the persistent nature of poor employment practices in some sectors of the hospitality industry.

One such report, concerned with recruitment and retention problems in hotels, restaurants and public houses in London, identified ten clear messages for the industry's employers. These were (reported in *Tourism Training Initiative Newsletter*, April 1989) as follows:

- Tackle the industry's image: not that it has a bad one, but that it does not have one.
- Emphasize the importance of personal qualities.

- Distinguish between jobs and careers.
- Publicize the full rewards package, e.g. meals, travel costs, bonuses.
- Foster job satisfaction.
- Explore the way jobs are structured and consider other labour markets.
- Target recruitment well.
- Explain to unemployed people that work does not always remove rights to benefits.
- Look for ways to attract young people into the permitted areas of the licensed sector.
- Use the unusual working hours as an attraction rather than as a barrier.

Great Expectations (Hall, 1989) identified a number of similar problems which essentially reinforce the persistent nature of some of the industry's employment practices. The main findings of *Great Expectations* were that Brighton's hotel industry did not meet the aspirations of those seeking work and that the industry needed to improve its methods of management in a number of separate but interdependent areas including recruitment, induction, training and welfare, career structures, conditions of employment, industrial relations and management styles, pay and recruitment of women.

The hospitality industry in the UK, led largely by some major employers and by the BHA and HCIMA initiatives, appears to be attempting to tackle both the image and the recruitment problems. The industry was one of the earliest groups of employers to join the government's New Deal scheme. In addition Springboard, a specialist branch of the Employment Agency, is encouraging a range of recruitment initiatives throughout the country.

Recruitment advertising in the hospitality industry

The quality of recruitment advertising in the hospitality industry varies considerably. At one end of the scale, the large companies such as Hilton and Whitbread are able to employ the best of expertise in designing recruitment advertisements. At the other extreme are the small operators who, with no expertise and very limited resources, have to design advertisements which, not surprisingly in many cases, are ineffective. For example, media research has demonstrated that inclusion of earnings in a recruitment advertisement increases the effectiveness of the advertisement and yet the majority of advertisements in the *Caterer and Hotelkeeper* do not include earnings levels.

By itself, good recruitment cannot overcome the problem of high labour turnover. This has to be tackled by keeping all conditions of employment under constant review and by making appropriate improvements to conditions as circumstances dictate. The nature of the hospitality industry, however, is such that most people holding management or supervisory positions are going to be faced frequently with the need to recruit people to fill vacancies.

Employers need to recognize that they recruit not just from their primary markets, but also from secondary labour markets. In addition recruitment needs to appeal to 'passive' job seekers, i.e. those not actively seeking a job change (and those who influence them, such as parents and teachers) and not just the active job seekers.

Furthermore, employers now operate in a 'buyers' market (i.e. many potential employees have a range of opportunities). One only has to look at the application forms from some leading high-street employers to see that they ask their applicants for the times that they are available for work – a big contrast to a few years ago when employers dictated the hours of work, on a take it or leave it basis!

Labour markets

In order to recruit successfully, however, it is important to have an understanding of labour markets, in the same way as in promoting products and services it is essential to know the nature of the target markets.

Labour markets have a number of characteristics, including their size, technological complexity, elasticity, pay levels, geographical distribution and status (e.g. primary or secondary). For the purpose of this book the primary and secondary markets will be discussed in a little more detail.

Primary labour market

The primary labour market consists of those people who through education, training and experience are committed to an industry, sometimes even a sector of an industry. In the hospitality industry these include hotel managers, chefs, hotel receptionists, hall porters and cocktail bar staff. Such people intend to develop their careers in the industry and in many cases view their opportunities nationally, even internationally. As a consequence many of these people are mobile, both geographically and organizationally.

Secondary labour market

The secondary labour market consists of people, on the other hand, who have skills of use to an employer, but who may not be committed to a career in a particular industry. They probably attach more importance to a geographical area than to a career. Typically the secondary labour market contains housewives, students and unskilled working people who choose to work in a particular industry in order to earn a living rather than because of a strong commitment to that industry. The secondary labour market also includes people with skills that may be common to many industries, such as secretaries, maintenance people, book-keepers and accountants.

International labour market

With the enlargement of the European union in 2004 and the addition of the new member states' labour markets the opportunities for employers to find employees from an enlarged labour market have widened considerably.

However, the competition for the best staff will be severe as many industries in the UK continue to suffer from significant skills and numbers shortages. The hospitality industry will be no exception and because of its concentration in city centres with high rental costs (for the staff) hospitality businesses can anticipate challenging times in the labour market.

Discrimination

Whatever the reason for recruitment, plans have to be prepared in the context of employment legislation, which covers issues such as the employment of children and women, sex, age and race discrimination and the employment of disabled people.

Working in Hotels (1991), a Commission for Racial Equality report, found that the hotel industry had done little to achieve equal opportunities for ethnic minorities – ethnic minorities being found mostly in unskilled jobs. (Figure 4.1 is an example of an equal opportunities statement.)

This booklet gives an overview of our commitment to equal opportunities in employment.

A comprehensive policy document providing definitions, policy details and checklists for action is available in each business unit. Both manager and members of staff intend it for reference. Please ask your Personnel and Training Manager if you would like to see it.

WHAT is our policy?
Out mission is EQUAL EMPLOYMENT OPPORTUNITIES FOR ALL.

Our aim is to ensure that no employee or job applicant receives less favourable treatment on the grounds of gender, marital status, disability, age, colour, race, nationality, ethnic or national origin; or is placed at a disadvantage by a condition or requirement which cannot be shown to be justifiable irrespective of those grounds.

MAKING IT HAPPEN
The following is a brief summary of the points covered by our policy to translate it into practical actions.

Recruitment and Selection
• Job profiles and specifications should set out clearly the skills, experience and qualifications required for the post and should stipulate only justifiable requirements for the job.
• Job advertisements and instructions to agencies should not unlawfully preclude or discourage applications from under-represented groups.
• Questions on application forms should not suggest that the employer might take into account factors, which would, or might, discriminate unlawfully. Application forms should be available in an alternative format, e.g. on computer disk.
• Selection criteria used should only reflect the standards required.
• Consideration should be given to flexible working arrangements such as flexible working hours, part-time and term-time working, job sharing, career breaks.
• Disabled people should be given full and fair consideration for employment, having regard to their particular aptitudes and abilities and any reasonable adjustments which can be made. If an existing employee becomes disabled, the objective should be the continued provision of suitable employment, either in the same or an alternative position, appropriate training being given if necessary. Disabled employees should share in opportunities for training, career development and promotion.
• Full utilisation should be made of the support and facilities available to assist the employment of disabled people.

Training and Development
• Policies and procedures regarding selection for training and development should be examined and monitored to correct any bias or imbalance.
• Appraisals should also be carried out in a non-discriminatory way and without making stereotypical assumptions.
• All staff should receive appropriate training in the implementation of our equal opportunities policy.
• All staff with relevant experience and ability should be considered for promotions and transfers.

Terms and Conditions of Employment
Terms and conditions of employment and all benefits, facilities and services should be reviewed regularly to ensure that there is no unlawful or indirect discrimination.

Figure 4.1 Hilton UK equal opportunities statement
Source: Reproduced by courtesy of Hilton UK.

WHY do we have a policy?
Because it makes good business sense to do so.

Firstly, our customers come from a wide variety of grounds and it makes good sense to employ a workforce which reflects that diversity and can identify with those customers' needs.

Secondly, in an employment market where good, well-motivated employees are increasingly in demand, it is important to ensure that we recruit from as wide a base as possible to obtain and retain the best people for the jobs we have.

Thirdly, the variety of skills and attributes, which a diverse workforce possess, can contribute to more dynamic and effective teams. A diverse group of individuals 'can all bring something to the party'.

Fourthly, all employees thrive better in an environment where everyone is treated as an individual and given the opportunity to do their best.

WHO is responsible for the policy?
Everyone in the Company has a responsibility for the policy.

THE BOARD OF DIRECTORS are responsible for monitoring and reviewing the policy in the light of present and future legislation and changing social circumstances.

PERSONNEL SPECIALISTS are responsible for advising managers on the application of the policy and for ensuring that all training and documentation in connection with monitoring, recruitment, selection, training, promotion and relevant employment procedures are administered in accordance with the policy.

MANAGERS are responsible for setting standards, for promoting an equal opportunity culture within the workforce for whom they are responsible, and for ensuring the effectiveness of the policy.

EMPLOYEES are responsible for abiding and ensuring the consistent application of the policy.

WHEN does the policy apply?
The policy applies to all employees and prospective employees, regardless of hours or length of service and covers every stage of the employee journey from pre-recruitment advertising through to termination of employment and appeals against dismissal.

WHERE is the policy applicable?
At all sites operated by the Hilton in the UK and to all acts done in the course of employment. This includes a wide variety of locations including training courses, social events for staff and agencies instructed by us. Also included are any terms and conditions imposed by Hilton in relation to casual employees or employees of sub-contractors or concessionaires. Also included is any unlawful discrimination (see definition below) perpetrated by the third parties (e.g. guests) which is within the control of the Company.

WHAT is unlawful discrimination?
The Sex Discrimination Act and Race Relations Act identify two types of unlawful discrimination – direct and indirect.

Direct discrimination consists of treating a person less favourably on the grounds of gender, marital status, colour, race, nationality, ethnic or national origin than others are, or would be treated in the same – or similar – circumstances.

Indirect discrimination consists of applying a requirement or condition, which has a discriminatory effect on a certain group – even though there may have been no effect on a certain group – even though there may have been no intention to discriminate. For example, a requirement for five GCSEs may discriminate indirectly against someone who was educated in another country.

Figure 4.1 *continued*

The Disability Discrimination Act defines unlawful discrimination somewhat differently. Unlawful discrimination occur when, for a reason which relates to the disabled person's disability, the employer treats the disabled person less favourably than they treat, or would treat, others to whom the disability does not apply AND:

- The employer cannot show that the treatment is justified.
- The employer has failed to consider making an adjustment and whether it is reasonable.
- The employer is unable to justify failing to make the adjustment.

It is also unfavourable to victimise someone who, in good faith, has made an allegation of discrimination.

In Northern Ireland it is also unlawful to discriminate on religious grounds, specifically between Protestants and Catholics.

WHAT TO DO if there is a problem?
Although we are striving for equality of opportunity in employment, there will be times when individuals have a problem related to equal opportunities. In such cases, the Company will take its responsibilities seriously and will wish to investigate properly – and deal with – any complaint that our equal opportunities policy is not being adhered to. Any breach of the policy may be regarded as a disciplinary offence.

If you have a complaint, it should be raised initially through the grievance procedure, details of which are contained in your contract of employment. If you request that the matter be dealt with informally in the first instance, your wishes will be respected. If your complaint is of a personal or sexual nature, which makes it difficult to talk about the matter to your line manager, you may contact the Vice President, Human Resources at Maple Court directly.

Problems could include harassment. Harassment includes any behaviour of a sexual or racial nature, or related to a person's disability, which causes embarrassment or offence. Such behaviour can be intimidating and unpleasant and we will not allow our employees to be subjected to it. It should never be thought of as a joke. Any employee found to be harassing another will be subject to disciplinary action, up to and including dismissal.

Figure 4.1 *continued*

In addition to the statutory obligations of not discriminating on the grounds of gender, race or disability, there are employers who decide not to discriminate in other ways also, for example, on the grounds of a person's age. In any event, with the demographic increase of average age of people in the UK, employers may find that discrimination on grounds of age is no longer a practical proposition, since the older age groups will provide an increasingly important source of labour in the future, although the employers' forum on age reported in 1999 that little real progress was being made in changing attitudes to the employment of older people. (See the HCIMA Managing Diversity and Equal Opportunities Briefs in the appendices.)

The recruitment process

Recruitment is the process used to attract suitable applicants from whom the most suitable person may be selected for a particular job. It depends upon having the proper information available, including a job or role description (see Chapter 3), a personnel specification and a knowledge of the labour market. The process starts with the production of a personnel specification, based on a job description or job specification and ends with the appointment of a successful candidate.

Personnel specification

From the job description a 'personnel specification' – a description of the type of person most likely to be able to carry out the job described by the job description – can be prepared. The precise nature of a personnel specification will depend upon the degree of sophistication or otherwise of an organization. Figure 4.2 is an example of one used by Marriott. 'Personal qualities' are discussed in Chapter 5.

From the job description in Figure 3.3, therefore, a personnel specification could be drawn up and might look something like Figure 4.3. If considered necessary or useful, distinctions could be made between 'essential' or 'desirable' attributes.

From the information in the job description and personnel specification subsequent recruitment steps can be decided upon.

Internal recruitment

The first step always in filling a position is to consider promoting or transferring existing employees. Considerable dissatisfaction can be caused by bringing new-comers in over the heads of present staff, which is often done with the intention of causing as little disturbance as possible to the organization. Unfortunately, because the hopes of some individuals in the organization may be frustrated, they may leave or behave in other unsatisfactory ways and the long-term effect is therefore far more damaging.

It is good management practice, therefore, for all vacancies in a company, and particularly those that may be seen by existing employees to be promotions, to be advertised internally on the staff noticeboard or by circulars. Circulating details to supervisors only is generally not satisfactory, since some employees may, for various reasons, fear that their supervisors will not put them forward. Many employers encourage existing employees to recruit new employees. See the Choice Hotels scheme in Figure 4.4.

External recruitment

The next step, if no existing staff are suitable, is to go on to the labour market. This is where most problems arise and where most money and effort can be wasted. The numerous and varied means of recruitment include

1. newspapers: national, local and trade
2. agencies, including the Department for Education and Employment and the Youth Employment Offices
3. executive selection and management consultants
4. posters, e.g. on London Underground, in one's own premises, postcards in local post-office windows
5. colleges
6. the armed forces
7. The internet/online recruitment agencies.

Marriott.
HOTELS · RESORTS · SUITES

COURTYARD.
Marriott

PERSON SPECIFICATION

(To be completed with Job Description prior to recruitment)

JOB TITLE .... LOCATION ....

	Minimum Requirements	Desired Requirements	Undesirable Factors
Appearance & Health General Health Physical Capabilities Apperance/Image Speech Others			
Attainments Education Job Training Job Experience Others			
Special Aptitudes Manual Dexterity Numerical Dexterity Communication Skills Languages Others			
Disposition Self Reliance Maturity Confidence Assertive/Leadership Temperament Pleasant/Friendly Others			
Circumstances Family Commitments Accommodation Travel Mobility (Transfers) Others			

COMPLETED BY .... DATE ....

AUTHORISED BY .... DATE ....

Figure 4.2 Example of person specification form
Source: Reproduced by courtesy of Marriott Hotels.

Job title	Chef de cuisine
Sex	Male/Female
ESSENTIAL Qualifications	
(a) educational	No formal requirements
(b) technical	City and Guilds of London 706/1/2 or formal apprenticeship, NVQ Level 3
Experience to include	(a) experience in all kitchen departments
	(b) experience of controlling a brigade of not less than five
	(c) recent experience of good quality à la carte service (up to 200 covers a day)
Personal qualities	(a) able to control mixed staff of English, Continental and Asian nationalities
	(b) stable employment record (e.g. no more than three jobs over the last ten years)
Personal circumstances	(a) able to work late (11 p.m.) about three nights a week
	(b) will have to live out
DESIRABLE Qualifications	Qualified skills trainer
Experience	Large-scale banqueting

Figure 4.3 Personnel specification for a chef

The choice of media is critical to success and always depends on the type and level of vacancy and whether prospective employees are part of a local, national or an industry labour market, i.e. a primary or secondary labour market. Generally, the higher level appointments will be advertised nationally; for example, if a company is seeking to appoint an area manager for a group of hotels, the national press such as the *Daily Telegraph* or the *Sunday Times* could be used in conjunction with the trade press. On the other hand, if a waiter or waitress is required, local employment agencies and the local press will probably be adequate.

The likely mobility of applicants is of course vital and in this industry, where accommodation is often provided, even less qualified categories of employees are often part of a national or even international labour market and hence are prepared to move large distances. Because of this the trade press can be used effectively. If, for example, a living-in bar cellarperson is required, this could be advertised in a trade paper such as the *Caterer and Hotelkeeper* as well as in the local press and through agencies. Figure 4.5 illustrates some suitable sources.

Advertising

The ability to use the right media is absolutely vital today particularly as major operators are now extremely sophisticated in their use of media. But it is no longer enough to choose one medium as opposed to another. Many employers are increasingly adopting 'multi-channel' recruitment also using their websites as the early steps in their selection process.

One of the recruitment needs, particularly for larger companies, is to develop a comprehensive interaction between the various media so that, for example, a press

Comfort Quality Clarion

CHOICE HOTELS
EUROPE

NEW EMPLOYEE INTRODUCTION
BONUS SCHEME
£50.00

Invite a friend – colleague – relation or just an acquaintance to join the Company and you will earn yourself

£50.00

It's as simple as that.

The first £20.00 will be added to your wages when the person you have introduced has completed the first ***full month's employment*** with the ***remaining £30.00*** being paid ***after 4 months with the Company.***

Simply complete Section 'A' below and hand this form to your Manager.

SECTION 'A'

Introducing: *Mr/Mrs/Miss* ....

Address: ....

.... *Tel No:* ....

For the permanent position of ....

at ....
(Hotel/Unit Name) *(Location)*

I confirm the above named person has been introduced to the Company solely on my recommendation and has no offer of employment with the Company at the present time.

Name: .... *Signature:* ....

Date: .... *Position:* ....

Hotel/Unit Name: .... *Location:* ....

Section 'B' ***(Office use only)***

Confirmation of new employee engaged:

Name: .... *Hotel/Unit Name:* .... *Location:* ....

Position: .... *D.O.C.* ....

Date of First Payment: .... *Date Paid:* .... *GM. Signature:* ....

Date of Second Payment: .... *Date Paid:* .... *GM. Signature:* ....

WHY NOT ENTER OUR 'SUGGESTION SCHEME' £5–£250 – 'NEW BUSINESS BONUS SCHEME' £25–£1,000 OR TAKE A "WEEKEND BREAK" AT DISCOUNTED PRICES

'Applicable only to properties owned or managed by Friendly Hotels PLC'

SERVICING EUROPE
HUMAN RESOURCES
CHOICE HOTELS EUROPE

C\GENERAL\REF034D\HR\05\99

Figure 4.4 New employee introduction bonus scheme

advertisement will lead a potential applicant to an interactive website. Many large companies are now outsourcing such processes to specialist commercial 'job board' firms.

Whilst the internet has grown significantly, newspapers, particularly local newspapers, still remain the most used media for recruitment. Whilst around

Staff to be recruited	Sources and/or type of media	Examples
Senior executives, e.g. area managers, regional managers, hotel managers	National press Trade press Consultants Agencies Internet Job boards, company websites	*Daily Telegraph* *Caterer and Hotelkeeper* Executive selection consultants, head hunters Ecco, Job Centres
Departmental heads, managers of small units, public house managers, etc.	Trade press Specialized sections of national press Agencies Armed services Local radio Internet Job boards, company websites	*Caterer and Hotelkeeper*, HCIMA Journal – Hospitality *Daily Telegraph*, *Lady* (for housekeepers, etc.), *Daily Mail* Ecco, Job Centres, Resettlement officers of armed services Capital Radio
Skilled employees, e.g. cooks, waiters	Local press, including London evening papers and European Union local press Local colleges Agencies Government Training Centres BHA (foreign employees) Local radio and TV Areas of high unemployment Internet Job boards, company websites	*Evening Argus*, *Evening Standard* Ecco, Job Centres
Semi-skilled/unskilled employees, e.g. cleaners, porter, kitchen hands, part-timers, bar staff, fast-food operatives	Local press Agencies Local colleges Internet Job boards, company websites Notices and posters Social Services, e.g. probation officers Regional Development Authorities Local radio and TV Salvation Army YMCA YWCA	*Daily Echo* Ecco, Job Centres, Universities, Colleges of Technology (students) Displayed in local post office and shop windows or in own premises

Figure 4.5 Recruitment sources and media (external)

70% of employers now use their own websites to advertise vacancies, 40% are now using commercial job boards (2004). On the job-seekers side around one in four adults now favour the internet. But a survey also 'found that the use of agencies and headhunters was widespread' (British Market Research Bureau for Recruitment website reed.co.uk).

The web, whilst adding considerably to the recruiters' armoury, must not be seen as a replacement of older methods – instead it should be seen as just another weapon in the armoury. More direct methods, often a contemporary reworking of traditional methods, are also often utilized, such as specially printed table-top recruitment flyers in fast food outlets and pub-restaurants. Older, well-tried methods ranging from staff recruitment notices in pub windows through to open days will continue to play a crucial role.

It is evident that a large part of any recruitment can be expected to rely on various forms of advertising and, therefore, apart from the choice of media, the drafting of advertisements is important. To recruit successfully these days, in the face of expert competition from other employers, it is no longer enough just to place an advertisement. It has to be a good advertisement. Some suggested rules for creating an effective advertisement are given below:

1 Be honest.
2 Catch likely candidates' attention with a suitable headline.
3 Hold their attention by giving clear, factual information including
   (a) locality
   (b) job content
   (c) prospects
   (d) qualifications
   (e) experience
   (f) conditions of employment.
4 Keep the language simple if it is directed at unskilled applicants.
5 Stimulate interest in the employer and promote their image, but remember that the priority is to fill a vacancy, not to advertise the establishment.
6 Avoid box numbers.
7 Avoid meaningless statements such as 'attractive wage' or 'salary according to qualifications'.
8 Test the advertisement on others before finalizing it.
9 Describe what action has to be taken in order to apply.
10 Stimulate the reader to act by telling them to call in, write or telephone.

Advertising a vacancy should be the method by which an employer communicates to potential employees that they are seeking to fill a vacancy. If the advertisement is vaguely worded, it may encourage too many unsuitable applicants or, worse still, it may not attract the most suitable people.

A well-designed advertisement will do more than just communicate basic information in words; it can, by its graphic design, say a lot about the employer and their style.

There is an often quoted law of recruitment advertising which states that the ideal advertisement attracts only one applicant and that this applicant will be successful. This is obviously overstating the case but it does illustrate the need to think carefully about the media and the message. After all, money wasted on ineffective advertising could well have been spent on new equipment, redecorations or even increases in salaries, and other employees in the organization will not be slow to point this out.

The chef's position described in Figure 3.3 could be advertised in the form shown in Figure 4.6. This illustrates an advertisement for a skilled person. Advertising for unskilled people needs a different approach; for example, if advertising for a barman/barmaid it may well be that the person appointed will need no experience, but some personal qualities instead, such as 'good appearance and personality'. For this reason the headline could be directed at unqualified but enthusiastic people, not experienced bar staff (Figure 4.7).

Figure 4.6 Display advertisement for a chef de cuisine

Figure 4.7 Display advertisement for a barman or barmaid (local press)

There are three main ways of inserting advertisements in newspapers: display, semi-display and classified. The examples in Figures 4.6 and 4.7 are display; because this form of advertisement takes up the most space and involve the most work, it is the most expensive.

The second method is semi-display, which gives the advertiser some prominence in the classified section. Often this is all that is required to attract applicants. An example of semi-display is shown in Figure 4.8.

Classified advertising is the least expensive and can be the least effective. This is because a large number of job advertisements are lumped together and consequently are less likely to catch the reader's eye. This is most likely to be the case when trying to recruit unqualified part-timers, because these are often recruited from normal readers who are not looking for jobs and consequently they will not look up the classified columns. On the other hand, a good display advertisement may well attract their attention and prompt them to apply. Many people, after all, have never thought of themselves working in a bar or restaurant, but the advertisement in Figure 4.8 would probably prompt several to apply. Figure 4.9 shows a typical classified advertisement.

In preparing recruitment advertisements it is useful to draw from product-selling techniques and to use the acronym AIDA which stands for:

Attract	ATTENTION
Create	INTEREST
Stimulate	DESIRE
Lead to	ACTION

WORKING HEAD CHEF

required

for busy 60-bedroomed Hotel.

Large banqueting suite, 100-cover restaurant and pub food operation.

Ideal candidate will be required to form five commis into a cohesive team, maintain strict food cost control and attain percentages.

Candidate will be totally responsible for kitchen cleanliness.

Apply in writing to:
Managing Director
Osterley Hotel
764 Great West Road
Isleworth, Middlesex

CVCR25-017

Figure 4.8 Semi-display advertisement

COOK REQUIRED at Sussex House Nursing Home for alternate weekends, hours 8 a.m.-1 p.m. If you are a kind, capable person interested in good home cooking then you may be the person we are looking for. Telephone for an informal chat on Horsham 12345.

Figure 4.9 Classified advertisement

Recruitment agencies

In large organizations where recruitment costs run into many thousands of pounds a year, it is often normal to retain a recruitment agency. Usually their services cost relatively little, since they receive a commission from the newspaper owners. Smaller firms, on the other hand, will not be able to offer recruitment agencies enough business for them to be interested, but in this case the media themselves will always give advice and guidance.

Increasingly, of course, the internet is being used, not just to advertise but also as an interactive means of processing applications. Reasons employers give for using the web include:

Reducing cost per hire (85%)
Increasing speed to hire (85%)
Strengthening the employer brand (65%)
Greater flexibility and ease for candidates (59%)
Broaden applicant pool (56%).

Source: Changeworknow/Lisa Astbury – published in People Management, July 2004.

One major hospitality employer, Whitbread, was quoted as saying that their development and use of the web resulted in their being able to recruit 60% of their managers directly and to improve the 90-day retention rate of starters from 85 to 95% (Smethurst, 2004).

The hospitality industry is now well served by a number of specialist executive selection and executive search (head-hunter) agencies.

Word of mouth

One particular method of recruitment has been purposely left in our discussion until last because of the unique and important part it plays in recruitment. People in the hospitality industry know well the value of word-of-mouth recommendation. Many highly successful hotels, restaurants and public houses do not need to spend a penny on attracting customers. Their reputation is enough. This applies equally to staff and there are many successful managers who never have to spend a penny to recruit new staff. Consciously or unconsciously, their existing employees recruit newcomers for them.

This method of recruitment is particularly good because of the two-way recommendation. An existing employee is recommending someone as a good employer and the applicant is being recommended as a suitable employee. Recognizing the value of this method of recruitment, some firms actually stimulate it by paying bonuses to employees who successfully introduce newcomers to the firm.

However, for large organizations there can be a risk of falling foul of race relations legislation, because word-of-mouth systems of recruitment have been found to be discriminatory.

Costs

Recruitment, like any other business activity, costs time and money. Most other business activities are measured in some way and standards or ratios are used to indicate the efficiency of the activity or otherwise.

This principle should apply equally to recruitment if it is a regular and substantial part of the running costs of the business. Where an agency is retained it will calculate the cost effectiveness of various media, but if an agency is not used this should be calculated internally. Figure 4.10 shows a simple form for the analysis of such costs.

	Daily Globe	Evening Star	Evening Star	Blue Agency	Job Centre
Job	Chef	Receptionist	Waiter	Waiter	Porter
Cost (£)	240	80	80	140	
Number of applicants	8	20	4	7	16
Number interviewed	5	12	3	6	9
Cost per applicant (£)	30	4	20	20	
Number of successful applicants	1	4	2	2	2
Cost per successful applicant (£)	240	20	40	70	

Figure 4.10 Recruitment costs analysis for various jobs and media

Analyses can be much more complex, but something along the lines of the form shown in Figure 4.10 will prove sufficient for the average organization to recognize which means of recruitment is the most effective and which involves the least interviewing, correspondence and other administration.

Recruitment code

Apart from costs, a manager also has wider responsibilities. As a result the Institute of Personnel Management (now the Chartered Institute of Personnel and Development) drew up the 'IPM Recruitment Code', the main points of which are as follows:

1 Job advertisements will state clearly the form of reply desired (e.g. curriculum vitae, completed application form) and any preference for handwritten applications.
2 An acknowledgement or reply will be made promptly to each applicant. Where consultants are acting mainly as forwarding agents for companies, the parties will agree who will acknowledge applications.
3 Candidates will be informed of the progress of the selection procedure, what this will be, the time likely to be involved and the policy regarding expenses.
4 Detailed personal information (e.g. religion, medical history, place of birth, family background) will not be called for unless and until it is relevant to the selection process.
5 Recruiters will not take up any reference without the candidate's specific approval.
6 Applications will be treated as confidential.

The future of recruiting in the hospitality industry

Traditional forms of recruitment and sources of labour, it appears, are not going to be sufficient to provide the necessary number of people required by the hospitality industry over the next few years. Instead new methods and sources are going to be needed. For example, much more effort will be needed to create a positive awareness of the industry among young school children, not just those about to leave school. Another measure that can be developed is to recognize that, already, large numbers of young people work in the industry on a casual and part-time basis and more effort needs to be devoted to converting a proportion of these into permanent workers in the industry, by offering real career prospects involving training and personal development. One employer of a large number of casual workers, in 1995, won a human resource award (awarded by the Hotel and Catering Personnel and Training Association) for the approach it adopted to making casual workers become an integral part of the employing organization. Effort is also needed to develop more family-friendly policies in order to attract and retain more women returners and to assist them through the provision of crèche facilities, etc. These could be organized by employers on a cooperative basis. Apart from these sources of labour, employers could also consider targeting older people. Age discrimination, according to the Institute of Personnel Management (*IPM Digest*, June 1989), affects not just those over 50; women can start to experience age discrimination from the age of 35 onwards and men from 40 onwards. Other sectors of the population include people who have been unemployed for a long period and various minority groups. These are in addition to the many millions of young people in continental Europe who are keen to work in Britain for a period to improve their English.

Further Reading and References

Armstrong, M. (1999) *A Handbook of Human Resource Management*, 7th edn, London: Kogan Page.

Beardwell, I., Holden, L. and Claydon, T. (2004) *Human Resource Management—A Contemporary Approach*, 4th edn, Harlow: Prentice Hall.

Commission for Racial Equality (1991) *Working in Hotels*, London: CRE.

D'Annunzio-Green, Maxwell, G. and Watson, S. (2002) *Human Resource Management— International Perspectives in Hospitality and Tourism*, London: Continuum.

Goss-Turner, S. (2002) *Managing People in the Hospitality Industry*, 4th edn, Kingston-upon-Thames: Croner Publications.

Hall, M. (1989) *Great Expectations*, Brighton: Brighton Polytechnic.

Hoque, K. (2000) *Human Resource Management in the Hotel Industry*, London: Routledge.

Plumbley, P. (1993) *Recruitment and Selection*, 5th edn, London: Institute of Personnel Management.

Pratt, K. J. and Bennett, S. C. (1990) *Elements of Personnel Management*, 4th edn, Wokingham: GEE.

Riley, M. (1996) *Human Resource Management in the Hospitality and Tourism Industry*, Oxford: Butterworth-Heinemann.

Sisson, K. (ed.) (1989) *Personnel Management in Britain*, Oxford: Blackwell.

Smethurst, S. (2004) *People Management*, July, p. 38.

Storey, J. (ed.) (2001) *Human Resource Management—A Critical Text*, 2nd edn, London: Thomson Learning.

Torrington, D., Hall, L. and Taylor, S. (2002) *Human Resource Management*, 5th edn, Harlow: Pearson Education.

Questions

1 Describe the objectives of recruitment and the various steps you would normally expect to find in a systematic recruitment procedure.

2 Discuss which you consider to be the most important steps in recruitment and why.

3 Discuss what changes are likely to be made in the future to improve recruitment.

4 Evaluate the approach to recruitment used by an employer you know well.

CHAPTER 5

Selection

A key feature of the labour market of the current era is its competitiveness, caused by a rise in the number of jobs and a decline in the traditional sources of labour. For the hospitality industry it is likely to be extremely competitive as other service industries expand or emerge and compete for labour.

The consequence is that organizations will have to put much more effort into designing attractive jobs and conditions, using effective recruitment methods and developing applicant-friendly selection techniques. These techniques will have to serve the dual purpose of ensuring that the proper candidates are selected and also that the employing organization is sold effectively, remembering always that many candidates may also be customers of the enterprise.

The selection process

One of a manager's major responsibilities is to initiate action but to do this he or she has to receive and interpret information in order to arrive at conclusions that will lead to the right action. The further up the hierarchy of management that people move the more they exercise skills of judgement and the less they carry out routine and supervisory tasks. In fact, a senior manager's job should normally be devoted almost entirely to making decisions that implement action and to designing systems that enable better decisions to be made. The skill of selecting staff is concerned entirely with this same process. In filling a vacancy a manager obtains information, sorts it, compares it, makes conclusions and implements action. This is illustrated in Figure 5.1.

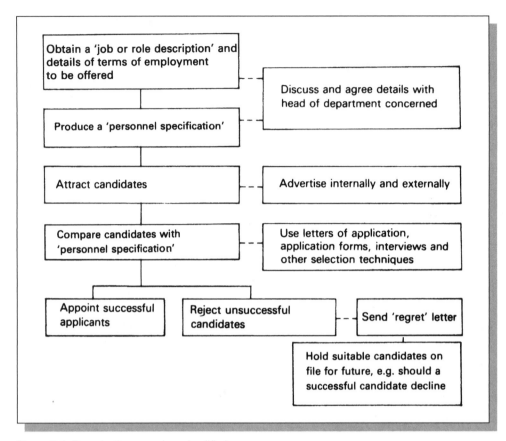

Figure 5.1 The selection procedure simplified

A manager will use the selection procedure normally for three different occasions:

1 To choose the most suitable person from several applicants to fill one vacancy.
2 To choose the right job from several for an applicant or several applicants.
3 Where there is only one applicant for a vacancy, to decide whether to appoint that applicant and, if so, to know his or her strengths and weaknesses so that additional supervision or appropriate training can be given, or so that the job can be modified.

In order to do this the manager should go through the procedure (described in Chapters 3 and 4) of preparing a comprehensive job or role description and personnel specification. Correct advertising will attract candidates and it is then the manager's job to ensure that information is obtained from candidates in a way that enables a comparison to be made with the personnel specification. From this procedure the most suitable applicant will emerge.

To assist in selection a variety of tools are available to the manager, including letters of application, application forms, interviews, group selection procedures, assessment centres and a range of tests sometimes referred to as psychometric tests.

Selection procedures attempt to predict, as accurately as possible, a person's likely performance in a particular job or, where there are several vacancies, the job in which he or she is most likely to be successful. Most selection methods are of a 'historical' nature, i.e. they base their predictions about future performance on a person's past performance. Other methods, such as group selection procedures, set out to predict future performance by simulating the type of work the candidates will have to perform. However, most people accept that, economic and human considerations apart, the best method is to employ a person for a period of time and then, if they prove satisfactory, to offer them the job. This is obviously not a practical method, although trial periods are used both consciously and unconsciously in most industries. Selection procedures, however, need to be designed in order to elicit the most useful and appropriate information in the most economical way.

The personnel specification

In attempting to assess or to measure a person's suitability for a job it is important to know what characteristics are to be measured. The range and description of these characteristics can be vast and in many cases almost meaningless to the uninitiated. Some interview assessment forms contain a long list of items including charm, punctuality, honesty, integrity, ability, etc. Many of these are supposed to be assessed (or guessed) at an interview.

Most characteristics or patterns of behaviour, however, can be grouped under several broad headings and two methods of assessment in particular are of interest. The National Institute of Industrial Psychology (NIIP) system uses seven broad headings and J. Munro Fraser's plan uses five (Figure 5.2). The fivefold system is a system for measuring to what degree an individual possesses each of

THE SEVEN-POINT PLAN (NIIP).

The seven-point plan covers:

1 Physical make-up — health, physique, appearance, bearing and speech.
2 Attainments — education, qualifications, experience.
3 General intelligence — fundamental intellectual capacity.
4 Special aptitudes — mechanical, manual dexterity, facility in the use of words or figures.
5 Interests — intellectual, practical: constructional, physically active, social, artistic.
6 Disposition — acceptability, influence over others, steadiness, dependability, self-reliance.
7 Circumstances — domestic circumstances, occupations of family.

THE FIVEFOLD GRADING SYSTEM (MUNRO FRASER).

The fivefold grading system covers:

1 Impact on others — physical make-up, appearance, speech and manner.
2 Acquired qualifications — education, vocational training, work experience.
3 Innate abilities — natural quickness of comprehension and aptitude for learning.
4 Motivation — the kinds of goals set by the individual, his consistency and determination in following them up, his success in achieving them.
5 Adjustment — emotional stability, ability to stand up to stress and ability to get on with people.

Figure 5.2 A summary of two approaches to staff selection

five points or groups of characteristics. Most managers will not wish to use rigidly such systems, instead they may wish to develop their own. It is important, however, to be consistent and to ensure that such specifications are not discriminatory in any way.

In producing a personnel specification, therefore, inclusion of such aspects with indications of desirable characteristics or precise requirements creates a 'pen picture' of the person required. During the subsequent selection procedure, candidates should be assessed or measured in the same way, making it a relatively simple task to identify the person with the assessment nearest to the personnel specification. He or she should be the most suitable of the candidates.

Letter of application

Generally, it is not advisable to use letters of application as a selection method, any more than the telephone, without the support of an interview or other method. However, well-designed advertisements can ask applicants to give sufficient information from which some candidates can be chosen for interview. A typical sentence at the end of an advertisement would read: 'Kindly write giving details, include education, training, experience, and earnings to . . .'

The main occasion when selection will depend only upon an application letter is when applicants live at some distance, usually overseas. In such cases the cost of travel excludes the possibility of interviewing. Previous empoyers' references then become extremely important.

To attempt to make an appointment purely on the strength of information contained in a letter is very risky but if done, references and a full curriculum vitae should certainly be obtained first.

Telephone and internet applications

Some employers have developed methods for using the telephone and the internet systematically as the first step in the selection procedures. When an applicant telephones he or she is interviewed via the telephone, the interviewer using a telephone interview questionnaire. The employer is able, as a consequence, to decide on the next step in the process. The internet is used in a similar way.

Application forms

The application form is used primarily to gather together relevant details so that the selector has this information at his or her fingertips and can make fair comparisons with the personnel specification and with other candidates' applications.

When designing an application form it is important to remember that it may have to serve several purposes such as

1 deciding whom to invite for an interview
2 being used as an interview assessment form
3 documenting employees and obtaining referees' names and addresses

4 providing a reserve list of potential employees
5 measuring the effectiveness of various recruitment media
6 analysing the labour market
7 obtaining agreement for medical examination, reference enquiries, etc.

The information required on an application form will, therefore, include some or all of the following:

1 position applied for
2 personal data – name, address, telephone number, nationality
3 education – schools, subjects studied, exams passed and further education
4 professional qualifications
5 experience – jobs, duties, responsibilities, employers, earnings, reasons for leaving
6 skills – e.g. word processing (which applications?), PBX, languages
7 military experience – branch of the service, rank attained, experience
8 personal circumstances – when available, prepared to travel or to move, current holiday plans
9 medical history
10 interests – hobbies, sports, other activities
11 record of offences. *Note*: This is subject to the Rehabilitation of Offenders Act.

Note: Questions relating to sex, marital status, children, age may be discriminatory and have to be considered very carefully (usually after legal advice). If asked, the purpose should be for discrimination monitoring purposes i.e. to demonstrate that no discrimination occurs.

The exact nature and extent of the information asked for will depend on the type of job and the employer's administrative requirements, but it should be confined to information necessary for sound assessments to be made. It is not appropriate, therefore, for one blanket-type form to be used for all job categories. The type of form used for senior executives, which asks about professional qualifications and total employment history, would not be suitable for an unskilled worker such as a room attendant, where the last five years' work history may be quite sufficient.

In the design of an application form, legal aspects also have to be considered, particularly discrimination legislation. Questions about marital status and number of children, for example, may be permitted so long as everyone, regardless of sex, is asked such questions, and decisions are not based on this information to the exclusion of other information. See Figures 5.3 and 5.4 for examples of application forms.

The interview

The next step after candidates have completed and submitted their applications, or discussed their qualifications on the telephone, is to invite selected candidates in for interviews. The interview is the most commonly used method of selection. It is also considered by many to be one of the least effective, largely because it bears no resemblance to what a person is likely to be employed to do and also because few managers are properly trained in interview techniques. In one survey of graduate recruits, 52% reported that their selection interviews had left them with a poor impression of the company, due to lack of skill on the part of the interviewer (*Personnel Management*, October 1989). Consequently, many bad appointments are made because the candidates have not had the opportunity to show their paces,

AFFIX PASSPORT PHOTOGRAPH HERE IF AVAILABLE

Comfort Quality Clarion
CHOICE HOTELS
EUROPE

EMPLOYMENT APPLICATION FORM
If attaching a CV, please ensure in addition that all sections are fully completed in BLOCK LETTERS

HEAD QUARTERS ADDRESS:
112 - 114 STATION ROAD
EDGWARE, MIDDX HA8 7BJ
Tel: (44) 181 233 2001
Fax: (44) 181 233 2080
Internet: http://www.choicehotelseurope.co
Email: hr@choicehotelseurope.com

Hotel/Inn applied for:........ **Position applied for:**........

Date available:........ **How long available:**........

PERSONAL DETAILS **Do you prefer to**........**LIVE IN/OUT***

Surname (Mr/Mrs/Miss)........ **First Name:**........

Full Address:........ **Tel No:**........**Date of Birth:**........

.... **Nationality:**........**Place of Birth:**........

Name & Address of next of kin (to notify in case of accident or illness) **Marital Status: Single/Married/Widow/Widower**........

.... **Have you any dependants YES/NO*** **If so, number***........**Ages***........

.... **Do you require a work permit YES/NO* If YES; duration of permit**........

........**Tel No:**........ **NHI No:**

Have you had any serious illness/operation in the past five years? YES/NO*

If so, please provide details........

(Delete as necessary)** **Have you any un-spent criminal convictions: YES/NO

DETAILS OF PREVIOUS POSITIONS
(References will be applied for, unless otherwise requested.)

PRESENT OR LAST EMPLOYER:
1) Company Name:........
Address:........
....
Position:........Rate of pay:........Employed from:........To:........
Reason for leaving:........

PREVIOUS:
2) Company Name:........
Address:........
....
Position:........Rate of pay:........Employed from:........To:........
Reason for leaving:........

PREVIOUS:
3) Company Name:........
Address:........
....
Position:........Rate of pay:........Employed from:........To:........
Reason for leaving:........

SERVICING EUROPE
HUMAN RESOURCES
CHOICE HOTELS EUROPE

Choice Hotels Europe is operated by Friendly Hotels Plc

Figure 5.3 Application form for non-management positions
Source: Reproduced by courtesy of Choice Hotels Europe.

EDUCATION:

Name and Address of School/College:..

Qualifications:...

Professional Qualifications Passed:...

....

....

TRAINING: (Details of Courses/Industrial Release)

OTHER EXPERIENCE OR QUALIFICATIONS:

INTERESTS/HOBBIES:

ACHIEVEMENTS:

AMBITIONS:

To comply with the Working Time Directive, I agree to advise the Company in writing, prior to any other work being undertaken, or if currently employed elsewhere, to confirm the number of hours and days involved.

I declare that the above is a true representation of the facts given and that employment, or continuity of employment will be subject to satisfactory references.

APPLICANT'S SIGNATURE: **DATE:**

FOR OFFICE USE ONLY

Date of commencement:..................   Position:...Rate of Pay:.............................

(Weekly/4 Weekly)*

References: SENT   SENT   SENT

1 [   ]   2 [   ]   3 [   ]

INTERVIEWER NAME:...   SIGNATURE:...DATE:....................

C:\GENERAL\HR\REF55B2\04\99

Figure 5.3 *continued*

or because the interviewer could not interpret rightly the available information. It is not possible in this book to discuss interviewing in depth, but excellent books have already been written on the subject (see the further reading at the end of this chapter). In conducting an interview, however, it is important to keep to a plan (see Figure 5.5 for an example), and the simplest method is to follow chronological order – starting at childhood and working up to the present day. Questions normally become more searching as one approaches current or more

WHITBREAD
HOTEL COMPANY

CONFIDENTIAL APPLICATION FOR EMPLOYMENT

Please complete this form clearly in ink and in your own handwriting

Position applied for:

| Full time ☐ | Part time ☐ | Location: | Temporary ☐ |

Personal details

Forenames _____ Surname _____ Title _____

Address _____

_____ Postcode _____

Age _____ Date and place of birth _____

Home telephone no. _____

Education

Schools	Dates (approx)		Examinations (subjects/results)
	From	To	

Further education and training	Dates (approx)		Examinations (subjects/results)
	From	To	

Employment: 1

For school leavers and college leavers

Please provide details of any paid employment you had while you were at school/college.

Please provide details of any Youth Training Scheme (YTS) courses you completed.

Employment: 2

Have you ever been employed by Whitbread PLC?
If Yes, please give details.

| From/To | Whitbread Division | Position Held | Reference Contact | Reason for Leaving |
| | | | | |

Employment: 3

Please complete if you are currently in employment, or have previous work experience.
Please give details of your work history beginning with your most recent job.

| From/To | Whitbread Division | Position Held | Reference Contact | Reason for Leaving |
| | | | | |

Which job have you enjoyed most and why?

Interests/hobbies (Give details of pastimes, sports etc.)

Offices held in social/sports clubs etc.

Have you ever been convicted of a criminal offence?   Yes ☐   No ☐
Details   (Declaration subject to the Rehabilitation of Offenders Act)

If offered the position will this be your only form of employment?   Yes ☐   No ☐
(if no, give details)

How will you get to work?

Please give the name of one work related referee from your last or current job and one personal referee
(not a member of your family) who has known you for at least two years.

Name: _____   Name: _____
Address: _____   Address: _____
Occupation: _____   Occupation: _____
Telephone no: _____   Telephone no: _____

Please give details of next of kin who can be contacted in an emergency:

Name: _____
Address: _____
Telephone no: _____ (business)   Relationship: _____   (home)

Please state your National Insurance Number:

Britains favourite Hotel Company

MARRIOTT HOTELS   • COURTYARD BY MARRIOTT   • TRAVEL INN   • THE BREWERY

Figure 5.4 A typical extended application form
Source: Reproduced by courtesy of Marriot Hotels.

Please complete the following three questions, with reference to either work or social situations. When completing, please include detail about how you went about it, what happened, how you felt at the end of it.

1. An example of the greatest challenge you have achieved.

2. An example of a time when you had to achieve something working with a group of people.

3. An example of a time when you were asked to do something you have never done before – how did you go about it.

WHITBREAD
HOTEL COMPANY

	Yes	No			Yes	No
Interview Comments	☐	☐	Reference taken up	☐	☐	
Reject letter sent	☐	☐	Reference OK	☐	☐	
Offer letter sent	☐	☐	Proof if details seen	☐	☐	
Job offered			Driving licence	Yes ☐	N/A ☐	
Start date			Other (specify)			
Pay			P45 or P60 provided	Yes ☐	No ☐	
Hours						
Job accepted	Yes ☐	No ☐				
Work permit seen	N/A ☐	Yes ☐	No ☐			
Number		Expiry date				
Notes						

MARRIOTT HOTELS • COURTYARD BY MARRIOTT • TRAVEL INN • THE BREWERY

Managing Diversity

The Whitbread Hotel Company is committed to an equal opportunities policy in employment and will assess applicants for jobs without regard to sex, marital status, race, disability, age or sexuality. To enable the company to monitor this policy please indicate to which ethnic group you belong. These are the approved categories from the Commission of Racial Equalities.

Single ☐	Married ☐	Separated ☐	Divorced ☐	Widowed ☐

Number of children: _____ Male ☐ Female ☐ Ages _____

Nationality _____ Do you need a work permit to work in this country? Yes ☐ No ☐

White ☐	Indian ☐
Irish ☐	Pakistani ☐
Black African ☐	Bangladeshi ☐
Chinese ☐	Black Caribbean ☐

Black Other (Please specify) _____

Other (Please specify) _____

Are there any disabilities which may affect your application? Yes ☐ No ☐

Describe disabilities _____

Are you registered disabled? Yes ☐ No ☐ RDP No. _____

Declaration

The contents of this form are confidential. If you are successful it will form the basis of your records held by the Company. You should understand that if at a later date it is discovered false information has been given, this could lead to your dismissal.

I authorise the Company to obtain references to support this application once an offer has been made.

Declaration: I confirm that the information on this form is, to the best of my knowledge, true and complete. Any false statement may be sufficient cause for rejection or, if employed, dismissed.

Signature _____ Date _____

Figure 5.4 *continued*

Interview plan

Part 1
Introduction | Introduce oneself, describe position held and responsibilities, give brief description of unit, company, job, conditions, prospects, reasons for vacancy, hours of work, rate of pay. Format of interview.

Part 2
Facts | What made applicant decide to come into the industry?
Any connections with the industry, e.g. brought up in hotels?

Life | Where did applicant go to school, college, university?
What qualifications did he or she attain?
Special interests at school, college, both academic and non-academic.
What was the first job after leaving school?

All jobs | Reasons for joining. Reason for leaving. Responsibility when first appointed and upon termination.
Earnings when appointed and upon termination.
What did applicant think of employer, manager?
What was the most important lesson learnt there?
What changes could be made? Main problems there. Main achievement there.

General | What is applicant's most important achievement?
Hobbies and interests. What is ambition in life – next year, five years, ten years?

Technical expertise | A series of questions to test an applicant's technical knowledge should be asked.

Attitudes | Towards, e.g., recent legal changes. Unions, customers, work, management, college training/informal training.

Achievements | Greatest personal achievement. Greatest work-related achievement.

Family | Any domestic responsibilities at home? When available to start?
What hours/days prepared to work? Mobility.

At present | Working? Type of job, duties, progress made in that job. Prospects, wages, benefits, reason for leaving, reason for coming to this position. Health, personal and of family. Criminal convictions.

Part 3
Close | Answer applicant's questions. Explain next step in selection procedure. Check on travelling expenses.

Figure 5.5 An example of what can be included in an interview plan

recent experiences, and these later questions must therefore be designed to test fully a person's claimed level of competence and likely level of achievement.

Main types of interview

The most common method is the individual interview, i.e. one interviewer interviews one candidate at a time. Although this method usually enables the candidate to relax more quickly, there is the risk of bias or preference – particularly if the interviewer's decision is made independently of other colleagues.

The second method is a panel interview or selection board – very common in the public sector. This will usually consist at least of the line manager concerned and a personnel specialist. This approach reduces the risk of bias, particularly as the panel increases in size. However, for many candidates a panel interview can be a daunting experience, particularly as some panels are constituted more for political reasons than for expertise. The format of the panel interview can be varied by candidates being seen individually in turn by each member of the selection panel.

There is one type of interview sometimes referred to as a 'stress' interview. The intention is to create a stress situation to see how an applicant reacts. It is only valid if a person is likely to encounter stress situations (e.g. difficult customers) regularly and such interviews should only be administered by trained interview specialists. Even so, there are serious doubts about the ethics of conducting such an interview without giving the candidate prior notice – in which case much of the effect of the stress interview will be lost. The methods of selection used by the armed services tend to create such situations but this is because the military are likely to be subjected to severe stress.

Some do's and don'ts

The following do's and don'ts should be useful.

Do

1 Have a clear job or role description, personnel specification, details of conditions, and an interview plan that contains prepared technical questions.
2 Use a quiet, comfortable room.
3 Suspend all phone calls and other interruptions.
4 Introduce yourself, be natural and put the candidate at ease.
5 Explain clearly the job, conditions of employment and prospects.
6 Ask questions that begin with when, where, why, who, what and how. This avoids receiving 'yes' and 'no' as an answer and encourages the candidate to talk.
7 Avoid asking unnecessary questions already answered on the application form.
8 Listen and let the candidate talk freely, but at the same time guide and control the interview.
9 Encourage the candidate to ask questions.
10 Close the interview firmly and explain the next step in the procedure.
11 Treat all candidates as though they are potential employees and customers.
12 Write up your assessment immediately after each interview (see Figure 5.6 for an example).

If necessary make notes during an interview, but do explain to the candidate that this is necessary so that nothing of importance will be forgotten.

Don't

1 keep the candidate waiting
2 oversell the job
3 conceal unpleasant facts about the job
4 interrupt or rush the interview

NAME .... AGE .... APPRAISED FOR ....

INTERVIEWED BY .... DATE ....

1 PRESENT CIRCUMSTANCES:

Firm .... business .... size ....

Position held .... location ....

Salary .... benefits .... pension .... holidays ....

Availability .... preferred location ....

Notice given/received .... other appointments pending ....

Salary expectation ....

Responsible to: ....

Responsible for: ....

a) no. and type of staff ....
b) duties ....

Prospects: ....
....

Reasons for leaving: ....
....

Reasons for wanting this appointment: ....
....

2 PERSONALITY AND APPEARANCE:

Appearance: ....

Dress: ....

Self-expression, accent, voice: ....

Manner: ....

Acceptability: ....

3 FAMILY BACKGROUND:

Origins .... married/single .... children ....

Views of candidate   and his/her spouse on conditions of employment, including travel:
....
....

4 EDUCATION:

Type of education .... achievements ....

5 PROFESSIONAL QUALIFICATIONS:

Type .... place ....

Method of achievement; number of attempts:
....
....

Figure 5.6 Selection interview appraisal report (for a senior appointment)
Source: Croner's Personnel Records, with kind permission of Croner Publications.

```
  6  EXPERIENCE:
     ..............................................................................................................................
     ..............................................................................................................................
     ..............................................................................................................................
     ..............................................................................................................................
     ..............................................................................................................................
     ..............................................................................................................................

  7  APPRAISAL

     Intelligence and ability
     ..............................................................................................................................
     ..............................................................................................................................
     ..............................................................................................................................

     Knowledge and experience:
     (breadth and depth) ..................................................................................................
     ..............................................................................................................................

     Career development — salary progression:
     ..............................................................................................................................
     ..............................................................................................................................

     Motivation, personal relationships, adjustment, stability:
     ..............................................................................................................................
     ..............................................................................................................................

     Health, outside interests, etc.:
     ..............................................................................................................................
     ..............................................................................................................................
     ..............................................................................................................................

  8  RECOMMENDATION:
     ..............................................................................................................................
     ..............................................................................................................................
     ..............................................................................................................................
     ..............................................................................................................................
     ..............................................................................................................................
     ..............................................................................................................................
```

Figure 5.6 *continued*

5 preach to the candidate

6 read out to the candidate what is on the application form: he or she filled it in and knows it already

7 ask questions that indicate the answer

8 ask questions that only get 'yes' or 'no' for an answer

9 allow the first impression to influence the whole interview

10 ask unnecessary personal questions

11 raise hopes unnecessarily

12 leave candidates with a bad opinion of your organization; they may be potential customers in other contexts.

13 wait until the end of the day or even till the following day to write up your assessments.

The three C's – contact, content, control

There are many different approaches to developing and practising interview technique; readers interested in taking the subject further should read the books listed at the end of this chapter. One simple approach for the non-specialist HR or personnel manager to use as a guide is one referred to as the three C's – contact, content, control.

'Contact' refers to the ability to make contact with the candidate, to develop a rapport. This is achieved by setting out to enable the candidate to relax so that the real person comes through. This is a difficult situation to achieve because for many candidates the interview can be very nerve-racking. However, a number of techniques, usually combined, can help, such as those listed below:

- Interview in an informal setting, but where there are no risks of disturbances or of being overheard.
- Avoid having a desk between the interviewee and yourself – a desk creates a psychological barrier.
- Offer a cup of tea or coffee.
- Invite a candidate to smoke if he or she wishes.
- Discuss common ground, e.g. a hotel, company, manager, town, football team, known to both of you (this information is easily found in a good application form).
- Use body language, e.g. move towards the candidate to emphasize that you are interested in what is being said.
- Use encouraging statements such as 'That's interesting', or 'Tell me more about that'.

'Content' is concerned with the two most important issues of selection – competency and compatibility. Can the person do the job, i.e. will he or she be competent? Secondly, will he or she fit into the team, i.e. be compatible? Thus the interview must cover all the important ground, including a person's technical competence, ability to get on with others and maybe their ability to take on increased responsibilities. It is particularly difficult to judge a person's future potential but one useful piece of information can be provided by a person's perspective of what is challenging. The question 'What is the biggest work-related responsibility you have ever had?' can be very informative. One person may answer, 'To have catered for 5000 at an agricultural show', whereas another candidate may answer, 'To have prepared a cold buffet for 200.' Such answers enable the interviewer, having checked the facts, to determine which of the applicants is more likely to fit in with the employer's scale of expectations.

Another important piece of information useful in predicting a candidate's growth potential is their career progression chart. From this, one can look for growth in responsibility, such as size of establishment, number of subordinates, standards (e.g. star rating) and earnings over a period of time. Figure 5.7 shows three hypothetical career paths.

Manager A (aged 33) has had an erratic career, manager B (aged 33) appears to be on a growth path and manager C (aged 40) has plateaued out. If all three were applying for a position with, say, around 150–200 subordinates, everything else

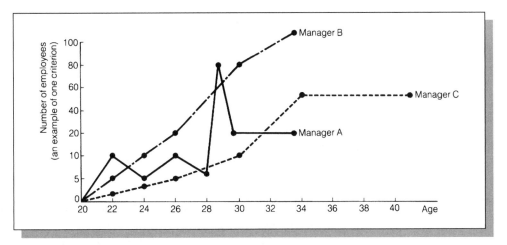

Figure 5.7 Comparative career progression chart

being equal, then manager B appears to be most likely to be suited for the position. Obviously, many other factors have to be considered such as the number of job changes or promotions in each person's career and the reasons for the changes.

Another important aspect of 'content' is to ensure that the interviewer communicates all the necessary information to the candidate, pleasant and unpleasant (e.g. unsocial hours). The interview is, after all, a two-way process.

'Control' refers to the interviewer's ability to ensure that the interview plan is completed in the time allocated. This will require the skill to guide the candidate through the career and technical questions and to bring the candidate back if he or she begins to wander from the subject – without changing the 'contact' or rapport being built up.

One final rule and a useful one by which an interviewer's skill can be measured is to estimate the amount of time devoted by the interviewer to listening and to talking. Generally, the less the interviewer talks the better he or she is at formulating questions, listening and making the right assessment.

Group selection procedures and assessment centres

The main weakness of the interview is that it relies on one technique only. This weakness can be compensated for to some extent by training and by involving a number of people in the process. One way of improving the reliability of a selection method, however, is to introduce more techniques so that the combination of techniques exposes more of a candidate's skills, personality traits, etc. to scrutiny. This is increasingly done through assessment centres or group selection procedures, which trace their roots back to methods used to select officers for the armed services.

These are specialized techniques and should always be conducted by people trained in their design, operation and interpretation. The purpose of a group selection procedure is to observe candidates' behaviour in a situation or in a variety of situations similar to those they would have to face in the organization. A group selection procedure could include

1 analysis of problems with reports and presentations
2 group discussions and debates
3 business games and in-tray exercises
4 individual interviews
5 tests – aptitude, personality, interest
6 informal drinks and dinner
7 simulating an element of the job for which the candidate is applying, e.g. selling conference facilities.

Group selection procedures and assessment centres are normally used to identify personality traits, skills, etc. and to predict behaviour that is difficult to assess in an interview or from personal history. These traits may include leadership ability, persuasiveness, self-confidence, ability to stand up to pressure, and mental flexibility. Such procedures are used both for recruiting new employees (usually senior) and for assessing the promotion potential of existing employees.

Psychometric tests

The testing of individuals in education, at work and in other aspects of their lives has been going on in various forms for many years. Its main industrial purpose is to help to predict future performance in particular fields by understanding individual and group behaviour. As with other selection procedures, testing assists in identifying the most suitable person for a job and in identifying the most suitable jobs for individuals.

Claims are made that well-constructed tests predict performance better than most other selection measures (*Best Test Practice*, 1991). It is reported that 85% of organizations now use tests (IPM/Mori, 1994), although such a percentage in the hospitality industry is most unlikely due to the large number of small employers.

Most tests can normally be administered only under the supervision of a trained person. The five main groups of tests are as follows.

Intelligence (IQ) tests

These measure the stage of development of intelligence in children and the intelligence of adults relative to the general population. The mean score is 100. Such tests are commonly used to determine whether a person will be able to cope with certain intellectual tasks.

Attainment tests

These measure the degree to which a person has acquired knowledge or skill. Applicants for jobs such as cashier, book-keeper or other clerical positions could be given simple attainment tests which could easily be devised by supervisors along with a personnel or training specialist. But it is important, in designing such tests, to recognize that failure to do the test may not indicate total unsuitability, but only a need for training. Many more skill or attainment tests, including those shown in Figure 5.8, could be used in this industry.

Example of category of employee	Nature of test
Chefs and cooks	Demonstrate knowledge of recipes and practical skill in making up certain dishes
Waiters and waitresses	Demonstrate knowledge of recipes, the accompaniments for certain dishes, and the service of some complex dishes
Barmen and barmaids	Demonstrate knowledge of and ability to prepare certain of the more popular drinks Demonstrate the ability to compute the cost of rounds of drinks
Cashiers and receptionists	Demonstrate knowledge of some common reception routines, the ability to operate appropriate office machines and to compute typical cash transactions

Figure 5.8 Attainment tests – examples of uses

Aptitude tests

This group of tests identifies an individual's innate suitability for particular types of work and can indicate whether a person would be more suited to one type of work rather than another.

Interest tests

These tests indicate broadly which type of work an individual would prefer, such as: indoor, outdoor, computational, gregarious, individual, routine, creative. It is important to stress that an interest in, or preference for, particular work need not indicate an aptitude for that work. However, where an aptitude for a certain type of work is supported by an interest in the same type of work, the chances of that individual succeeding are likely to be much higher.

Personality tests

These tests determine an individual's reactions to different situations, from which general conclusions can be drawn about likely future behaviour. They are concerned mainly with measuring non-intellectual characteristics. In particular most attempt to measure how a person relates to the world around him or her and they do this by measuring the degree to which the person possesses certain personality traits, such as drive, stability, persuasiveness, self-confidence, introversion and extroversion. Some personality tests, such as Raymond Cattell's 16PF (Sixteen Personality Factor Questionnaire), are claimed to be extremely comprehensive, covering most aspects of personality encountered in normal individuals.

In some countries, France for example, graphology is used. Graphology is the study of handwriting in order to determine personality. In the UK and many other countries it is, however, not considered to be a reliable method of testing for employment purposes.

Test batteries

It will be clear that each of the groups of tests mentioned above, with one or two possible exceptions, attempts to measure limited aspects of an individual. These are intelligence, attainment, aptitude, interests and personality. Each individual employed, however, needs levels or aspects of each of these characteristics and using one type of test only may not do the person justice. As a result some selection specialists use a battery or variety of tests that measure several of those aspects of a person that may be considered of importance. Additionally, a test battery may be only part of an overall procedure incorporated, for example, in a group selection procedure or assessment centre.

There is concern that tests may have a disparate impact, i.e. their use may result in discriminating against, or in favour of, one or more groups. Codes of practice concerning the use of tests have been produced by the Institute of Personnel and Development and by the Commission on Racial Equality.

References

It is important to remember that references are only as reliable as the judgement of the person giving them, and because of the fear some employers have of putting a bad or indifferent reference in writing, many written references are worthless. The best procedure for obtaining references, therefore, is to telephone referees and to discuss a candidate's application on the telephone. This discussion should be written up afterwards so that it can be put into a person's file (remember that under the Data Protection Act the subject may have the right to see this). Alternatively, a standard letter or questionnaire asking previous employers to confirm certain details can be used (Figure 5.9).

References must only be sought after candidates have been offered an appointment subject to references, since they may not have informed their current employer of their plans to move – unless, of course, they have given specific permission for references to be applied for before an offer of appointment is made (which is common in the public sector).

Successful selection, i.e. placing suitable people into the right jobs, is vital to the prosperity of an organization. But selection can only be successful if it is carried out methodically, and this requires a clear job description and personnel specification, plus a system that ensures that the most suitable candidates are attracted and identified. This will require well-designed advertisements and application forms that elicit appropriate information. Interviews and other selection techniques, as outlined above, will then have to be conducted enabling the assessor to predict, as accurately as possible, a candidate's performance if he or she were to be appointed. This will involve knowing which characteristics are desirable and it will also involve using techniques that identify or measure those same characteristics.

REQUEST FOR REFERENCE

CHOICE HOTELS
EUROPE
Headquarters Address:
112 - 114 Station Road, Edgware, Middx. HA8 7BJ
Tel: 0181 233 2001 Fax: 0181 233 2080
Internet: http://www.choicehotelseurope.com
Email: hr@choicehotelseurope.com

To:

PLEASE REPLY TO: _____

Re: Mr/Mrs/Miss: _____
Position Applied for: _____

Dear Sir/Madam

The above named has applied to work for us and I will appreciate you completing the reference request and returning it to me as soon as convenient.

We shall gladly reciprocate at any time, and of course, you are assured that all information that you give will be treated in the strictest confidence.

Thank you for your help.

Yours faithfully

WITHOUT PREJUDICE

Date of Study: From: _____ To: _____
Course: _____

Kindly rate the Student for:	EXCELLENT	GOOD	AVERAGE	POOR	*COMMENTS
JOB KNOWLEDGE					
CAPABILITY - OVERALL					
ATTENDANCE/TIMEKEEPING					
CO-OPERATION					
CONDUCT					
TEAM WORK					
OPERATIVE SKILLS					
LEADERSHIP QUALITIES					
ENTHUSIASM					
WORK RATE					

WOULD YOU EMPLOY?   YES/NO   * More details will be appreciated

Do you have any additional information regarding the suitability of the applicant for the position applied for   YES/NO
(If YES, please advise). _____

or: I would prefer to discuss this reference request over the phone, and my telephone number is: _____

DATE: _____   SIGNED: _____   POSITION: _____

Figure 5.9 A reference enquiry letter
Source: Reproduced by courtesy of Choice Hotels.

Future trends

For the industry's smaller employers the need to adopt more effective selection techniques, or at least to apply commonly used ones more effectively, is vital. Larger organizations need to examine not only the techniques they use but also where the emphasis is placed. Currently, for example, most applicants are eliminated before interview on the basis of their application form – among the least reliable of the selection tools. The most systematic methods are used on the smallest number, those who remain after the first screening. Maybe more effort needs to be devoted to ensuring that the good candidates who currently are lost through the initial screening are not lost, by using more systematic methods in the earlier stages of the process such as through telephone or internet interview. This would require considerably more thought in designing recruitment literature, so that self-selection plays a bigger part in bringing forward a smaller number of candidates, who are better candidates, followed maybe by self-administered tests. It is very likely that the internet will help this process.

Careful selection is an investment in team building and though it is more time-consuming and hence more costly than haphazard recruitment, the reduction in labour turnover which normally results, together with the consequent improvement in efficiency and customer satisfaction, should make it worthwhile.

Further Reading and References

Armstrong, M. (1999) *A Handbook of Human Resource Management*, 7th edn, London: Kogan Page.

Beardwell, I., Holden, L. and Claydon, T. (2004) *Human Resource Management—A Contemporary Approach*, 4th edn, Harlow: Prentice Hall.

Best Test Practice (2001) London: Savill & Holdsworth.

D'Annunzio-Green, N., Maxwell, G. and Watson, S. (2002) *Human Resource Management—International Perspectives in Hospitality and Tourism*, London: Continuum.

Eder, R. W. and Ferris, G. R. (1989) *The Employment Interview*, London: Sage.

Goldsmith, A., Nickson, D., Sloan, D. and Wood, R. C. (1999) *Human Resource Management for Hospitality Services*, London: International Thomson Business Press.

Goss-Turner, S. (2002) *Managing People in the Hospitality Industry*, Kingston-upon-Thames: Croner Publications.

Institute of Personnel Management (1991) *Best Test Practice*, Wimbledon: Institute of Personnel Management.

Institute of Personnel Management/Mori (1994) *Recruitment Methods*, Wimbledon: Institute of Personnel Management.

Lucas, R. (2004) *Employment Relations in the Hospitality and Tourism Industries*, London: Routledge.

Pugh, D. S. and Hickson, D. J. (1997) *Writers on Organizations*, 5th edn, London: Penguin.

Rae, L. (1991) *The Skills of Interviewing: A Guide for Managers and Trainers*, 2nd edn, Aldershot: Gower.

Riley, M. (1996) *Human Resource Management in the Hospitality and Tourism Industry*, Oxford: Butterworth-Heinemann.

Sisson, K. (ed.) (1989) *Personnel Management in Britain*, Oxford: Blackwell.

Torrington, D., Hall, L. and Taylor, S. (2002) *Human Resource Management*, 5th edn, Harlow: Pearson Education.

Questions

1 Describe the objectives of selection, the alternative methods and the various steps you would normally expect to find in a systematic selection procedure.

2 Discuss which you consider to be the most effective selection method and why.

3 Compare and contrast interviews, psychological tests and group assessment procedures.

4 Discuss what changes are likely to be made in the future to improve selection procedures.

5 Evaluate the approach to selection used by an employer you know well.

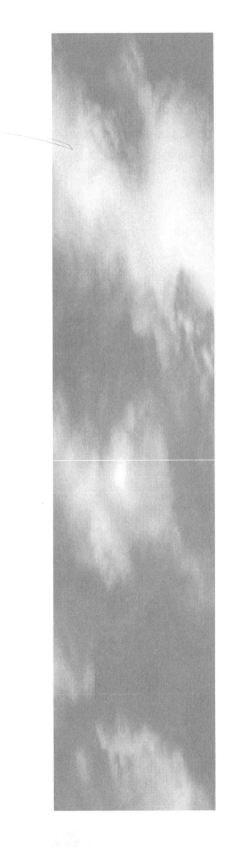

Appointment
and induction

First impressions are often the most lasting impressions, and the first impressions formed by many employees upon starting employment with a new organization may not be good ones. Although these may become false, the employee is not to know this. Impressions have been shaped by the advertisement, the interview and interview arrangements, treatment of travel expenses, etc., and new employees arriving to start work are in many cases thrust straight into the job without even minimal introduction to the employer's methods and rules, let alone introductions to colleagues and management. The first hours and days are critical and if properly dealt with can create the right relationship that contributes to employees staying with an employer.

Induction has been defined by the Department for Education and Employment as, 'Arrangements made by or on behalf of the management to familiarize the new employee with the working organization, welfare and safety matters, general conditions of employment and the work of the departments in which he is to be employed. It is a continuous process starting from the first contact with the employer.'

As this definition shows, the process of correctly inducting an employee starts even before the formal offer of employment. When the employer has made a decision, the successful applicant should be told immediately that the employer wishes to make an offer. This should be done, if possible, at an interview (not at the selection interview) or by telephone so that agreement can be reached about details such as starting date and outstanding holiday arrangements.

Letter of appointment

A formal letter should then be sent off incorporating all conditions of employment and also the job description. An example of a typical letter of offer is shown in Figure 6.1. Figure 6.2 shows a North American example.

Such letters of offer should incorporate several requirements:

1 It gives the new employee full details concerning the job and conditions.
2 It demonstrates an efficient, businesslike and, by its tone, sympathetic approach that should make the person feel he or she is joining a worthwhile organization.
3 It obtains written acceptance of the offer and also written permission to write off for references.
4 It states exactly when and where the person is to come, and what to bring on the first day.

Note the approach of the American employer (Figure 6.2) who asks for a US$25 dollar commitment fee which will be returned once employment has started.

PRIVATE AND CONFIDENTIAL

Dear

Following your recent interview, I am pleased to offer you the position of Terms of employment are as follows –

Salary	**£ per hour**
Start Date	
Contracted Hours	hours per week, worked over days
Pension Scheme	After six month's service you are entitled to join either the Whitbread Group Pension Fund or the Personal Pension Plan. Please speak to Human Resources for further details.
Incentive Scheme	You will be entitled to participate in the Whitbread Hotel Company reward scheme called PRIDE. Full details will be given when you join.

Figure 6.1 Example of a letter offering employment
Source: Reproduced by courtesy of Marriott Hotels.

Staying for Pleasure	You are entitled to two weekends at our UK hotels each year, after completion of one years' service. Full details will be given when you join.
Staff Discount Scheme	After three months service you are able to participate in the staff discount scheme. Full details will be given when you join.
Uniform	We will order your uniform and name badge on your first day. However, we would be grateful if you would wear smart attire for your arrival at the hotel. You will need to supply black shoes and socks (Males), and either flesh coloured tights 15 denier or less (Female supervisors, managers and administration staff) or navy tights 15 denier or less (all other associates). **Navy** court shoes need to be worn by all female members of staff. A temporary name badge will be given to you on your first day.

Although you are employed as   , you may be required to work in other areas of the hotel to meet the needs of the business.

You will be required to serve a 90 day probationary period, at the end of which time, provided that your progress in the job is satisfactory, you will be appointed to the permanent staff.

This offer is subject to:

1 Our receipt of two satisfactory references. I would, therefore, be grateful if you would let me have the names and addresses of two referees whom we may approach on your behalf.
2 Medical clearance by our Occupational Health Department. I would, therefore, be grateful if you would complete the enclosed questionnaire and return it to me as soon as possible.

The Company reserves the right to vary the Terms and Conditions of your employment relating to your working hours to give effect to the Working Time Regulations 1998. This may involve varying the numbers of hours you work and when you work, even though you may or may not be directly affected by the details of the Regulations.

We have enclosed two copies of this letter and would be grateful if you would sign and return one copy as soon as possible to the Human Resources Department at the Leeds Marriott Hotel. Also, I would be grateful if you would complete the enclosed New Starter Form and return it to me as soon as possible. Please note that until I receive this form, I cannot set you up on Payroll.

Please could I ask that on your first day you arrive at 9 am for your induction. Please ask for me at the reception desk.

Finally, I would like to take this opportunity of welcoming you to the Whitbread Hotel Company and the Leeds Marriott Hotel and I hope that your career with the Company will be a long and happy one.

Yours sincerely,

Michelle Walton
Human Resources Officer

I have read and agree to the above terms and conditions of this offer of employment. I confirm that my start date is

Signed ....   Date ....

Figure 6.1 *continued*

FLAMINGO LODGE
Marina & Outpost Resort
IN EVERGLADES NATIONAL PARK
Flamingo, Florida 33034

Dear Katherine:

Congratulations! You have been selected from among several hundred applicants to fill an important position at Flamingo Lodge for the winter season. You were chosen because we felt you stood out as an individual who shares our commitment to quality guest services. Working together, I know we can be the best concession operation in the National Park system. I look forward to having you as part of our team.

Please review your employment agreement and dates. Contact me directly if you have any questions. Return one signed copy of your employment agreement, the Employment Fact Sheet, and a $25.00 check or money order by the date indicated in order to secure your position. Your $25.00 deposit is used only to establish your commitment to be with us this winter. It will be returned upon your arrival.

If, for any reason, you cannot accept our offer for employment we would appreciate your letting us know so that we can offer the position to another individual.

I look forward to meeting you soon.

Julie Fondriest

Julie Fondriest
General Manager

JF:ml
enc.

(305) 253-2241 • (813) 695-3101 • FAX: (813) 695-3921

TW RECREATIONAL
SERVICES, INC.
CANTEEN CORPORATION

Figure 6.2 An alternative letter offering employment

From a legal point of view such letters may be structured to fulfil the requirements of the Employment Rights Act 1996. This Act requires that a written statement of the main terms of employment is given to all employees within two months of starting employment. These include

name of employer and employee
date employment began (including continuous employment)

job title
place of work
scale or rate of pay
pay intervals (e.g. weekly, monthly)
working hours and patterns of work
if not permanent, the date of termination
holiday and public holiday entitlements
any sick pay schemes, other than Statutory Sick Pay
any pension scheme rights
length of notice
any collective agreements
disciplinary and grievance procedures.

Note: some of these conditions may be contained in separate documents but should be referred to.

Documentation

The first step when the employee arrives is to arrange that all documentation proceeds smoothly. This includes obtaining the P45 (record of tax and National Insurance paid to date) and, where the employee is to be paid through a bank, the bank's address. A personal file or dossier will have to be opened, which will contain all relevant correspondence and documents including the application form and acceptance of offer, and in time a variety of other documents such as maximum working hours opt-out agreements.

In larger companies an engagement form should be completed to ensure that no documentation procedures are missed out. This could look like the one illustrated in Figure 17.5 and would be produced with sufficient copies for each interested department, including the wages department.

Introduction to workplace, colleagues, rules, etc.

The second part of inducting new employees is concerned with ensuring that they know and understand what is required of them in order to do their jobs satisfactorily. This includes telling them or preferably showing them the layout of the place of work, introducing them to colleagues and explaining to them the function of other relevant departments. It will also be necessary for them to know about house rules such as 'no drinking' and relevant laws such as licensing hours and 'no smoking' in food areas and what the disciplinary procedures and consequences are.

Training needs

The third aspect is concerned with determining the employee's ability to do the job itself effectively and this will depend upon the person's training and experience. On the one hand no training may be needed, or merely working under close guidance and supervision for a few days may be adequate. On the other hand, detailed training may be required and this is often the case in larger organizations that are prepared to employ untrained people and have standard methods common to many branches.

Induction checklist

Whatever the level of competence, however, it is advisable to use a checklist to ensure that an induction procedure deals adequately with all necessary aspects of induction. In this context it is important to remember that what may not appear important to the employer may be very important to employees. Figure 6.3 shows the checklist used by a hotel.

Each employee is an individual

Introducing staff into an organization inevitably involves some of the mechanistic processes just described, but it has to be remembered that each member of staff is an individual. Precisely how one introduces or inducts each new individual to an organization depends upon many factors, such as the newcomer's experience and knowledge and the type and level of job he or she is to undertake. It is vital, however, if induction is to be successful, to try to put oneself in the new employee's place. As Rafael Steinberg (1977) writes, 'He arrives unknown. His face is not recognized. His interests and idiosyncrasies are ignored by people he meets. He has suddenly become a number, an anonymous replaceable cog. Quite naturally, without thinking about it, he resists this depersonalization and strives to introduce a measure of humanity to his strange new world.'

Probably the simplest and most common method of induction is a short discussion in a supervisor's office followed by informal chats. This may be quite practical where a person's superior is readily available. However, where this is not the case, unless a checklist is used, many points may remain unclear for a considerable time.

Another method is the 'sponsor' or 'mentor' method in which a newcomer, after an initial talk with their own supervisor, is introduced to an established employee who will show them the ropes. This should not be confused with 'sitting next to Nellie', which is concerned primarily with training and not induction. If this sponsor technique is used, however, the sponsor should be carefully selected to ensure that he or she knows what the duties are and has the necessary knowledge to carry them out. These would include many of the items listed on the induction checklist. In addition, however, a well-chosen sponsor will introduce the new employee to the inner face of the organization, i.e. informal systems, unwritten rules, etc. A copy of this list should be given to the sponsor, to be returned to the newcomer's supervisor once everything has been completed. The process might take as little as a few minutes, or could be spread over several days.

Finally, some induction programmes make use of formal training techniques in classroom situations. This is normally only used by larger employers that can afford the facilities, and these programmes, apart from the initial documentation, may include talks, discussions and films on the company's history, organization, rules and regulations. In addition, a large part of the programme may be devoted to job training.

The advantage of formal systems such as the sponsor and classroom methods is that because one person is clearly responsible for the induction of newcomers it is more likely to be organized and conducted properly.

Induction can be considerably simplified by the preparation of clear handouts or manuals elaborating aspects of employment that may need some explanation. Pension schemes and grievance procedures, for example, are ideally explained in written form owing to the amount of detail involved. Many other subjects, too, can be included in manuals such as trade union or staff association agreements, suggestion schemes, holiday arrangements, sick leave and fringe benefits.

NEWPORT
Marriott,

_____   _____   _____
Name of Employee   Department   Hire Date

Manager, please check each item as it is covered with the employee and return to personnel by_____

1. **INTRODUCTION**
    Department Head/Supervisor/
    Co-workers

2. **EXPLAIN WORK SCHEDULE**
    Work schedule (posted as soon as business for following week can be forecasted)
    Changes must be approved by manager

3. **EXPLAIN ATTENDANCE REQUIREMENTS**
    Attendance (Mandatory on scheduled days)
    Punctuality (Must be on time)
    Reporting absences (Phone supervisor/manager at least 2 hours in advance of scheduled time and if unable to reach, leave a message with Security)
    Punch own time card
    Punch in in uniform at shift starting time.
    All work must be on the time clock & a mgr. must approve any overtime before it is worked.

4. **EXPLAIN GENERAL RULES**
    Employee entrance/exit (by Security)
    There is no employee parking
    No return after work policy
    Red sticker policy (items subject to inspection by Security or Management)
    No personal phone calls & employee pay phone
    Hotel telephone number and department extension
    Groom standards (dress code & hygiene)

Professional conduct/behavior required
Smoking policy
No gum chewing
Uniforms (includes name tag)
Employee restrooms (uniformed employees use locker rooms)
Employee cafeteria (time card stamped/wear name tag)
NOTE: Proper behavior is required in the Cafeteria; including cleaning up after eating—emptying trash and ashtray. No food/beverage is to be taken out of the Cafeteria.
Use service elevators
No eating in areas outside cafeteria without management approval
Notify supervisor before leaving at the end of your shift
No wandering out of work area without management approval
Phone answering procedures (give name, do not screen calls)
Employee lockers (unauthorized substances or materials)

5. **EXPLAIN TRAINING PROGRAM**
    Who will train
    90-day probation period
    Encourage asking questions

6. **MEAL**
    30 minute meal period (punch in and out for meal)

7. **EXPLAIN RELATION OF WORK TO OTHERS**
    Chain of command
    Guarantee of Fair Treatment
    Relation of job to other jobs
    Relation of department to other

Figure 6.3 Orientation checklist for new employees at Newport Marriott Hotel (USA)
Source: Reproduced by courtesy of Marriott Hotels (USA).

departments and to hotel
Individual responsibility to guests
(Aggressive Hospitality/Customer
Concern)

8. **EXPLAIN IMPORTANCE OF JOB**
Employee's contribution to job
Rewards of enthusiasm, job
satisfaction, advancement
(Promotions based on qualifications)

9. **QUALITY/QUANTITY OF WORK**
Importance of accuracy/speed when
experienced
Importance of courtesy and smile

10. **SAFETY**
Fire/emergency procedures
Nearest fire extinguisher (location)
Report ALL accidents IMMEDIATELY
(no matter how minor) to your
supervisor/manager
Clean as you go policy
Job safety analysis

11. **EXPLAIN PAY POLICIES**
Starting pay rate/performance
reviews/increases (PAF)
Pay periods (Sat.–Fri.) payday/time
Thursday
Accurately report all tips on tip sheet
each week and sign name

12. **EXPLAIN BENEFITS**
NOTE: Full time is 30 hours or more
per week

Vacation policy (eligible if full-time
after 1 yr., part-time after 2 yrs.)
Sick leave (for full-time employees,
after 6 months)
Holidays (full/part-time)
Medical Insurance (full-time; if not
enrolled within 1st 30 days there is a
90 day waiting period before
insurance is effective! May also have
to take a physical exam)
Group Term Life Insurance (additional
life insurance; same enrollment
requirements as Medical Plan)
Dental Plan (full-time/after 6 mos. in
Medical Plan sign up at hire or at
change from PT-FT)
Credit Union (full-part-time
employees)
30% Gift Shop discount

13. **DISCIPLINARY PROCEDURES**
Verbal Warning
Coaching and Counseling
Written Warning
NOTE: Policies on this list with an (*)
are important. When not followed an
automatic written warning may result.
Suspension pending termination

14. **REVIEW POSITION DESCRIPTION**

Initial

I have received the Newport Marriott Hotel Handbook and understand that it is my
responsibility to study and use the handbook as a reference to the benefits and rules of
the company. If I have any questions I will ask my manager or the Human Resources
staff.

I understand that the Human Resource Director is my Equal Employment Opportunity
representative, and that he/she will insure my rights under the Marriott Guarantee of
Fair Treatment.

Regarding medical, dental, group term-life, and disability insurance coverages, I
understand that I must see the human resources representative and complete the
enrollment forms within 21 days of hire, or eligibility, to assure full coverage without
an additional waiting period.

FOR EMPLOYEES WHO HAVE BEEN ISSUED UNIFORMS AND/OR EQUIPMENT: The
uniforms and/or equipment issued to you are to be used only while performing services
for Marriott Corporation. In the event you leave the Corporation, you must return the
uniforms and/or equipment in good condition minus normal wear and tear. Also,
uniforms and/or equipment damaged due to normal wear and tear shall be returned for
replacement and, if lost, you will be personally responsible to accept the expense of the
uniforms and/or equipment. Marriott Corporation will be authorized to deduct (by your
signature below) from any of your earnings, present or future, the value of said
uniforms/equipment.

I have read, or have had read to me, the items listed above. The items on the other side
have been explained to me and I understand and agree to abide by these and all other
rules of this hotel.

Employee's Signature:_____   Date:_____

Explained by (Mgr/Supervisor):_____   Translator:_____

Figure 6.3 *continued*

What a job consists of

Induction is not something that takes place on the first morning of a new job; it can be a relatively long process, with some people taking many weeks to settle in. This is because every job has two elements. First there is the work itself and second there are all the peripherals to the job, including conditions and social contacts, which go to make up the work community in which the work is performed.

People will not be able to cope with the work part of their job unless they understand and are familiar with the surrounding elements. These include

- location and physical layout
- colleagues and informal relationships
- management, supervision and formal relationships
- customers
- conditions of employment and contracts
- company and house rules.

The induction process is concerned with introducing an employee to all these elements as quickly as possible so that he or she can concentrate on the work, which is the main purpose of the job, rather than having to learn and worry about all the elements surrounding the work (Figure 6.4).

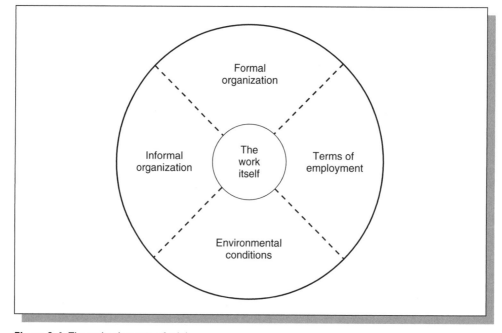

Figure 6.4 The main elements of a job

Benefits of induction

The employer benefits from effective induction by

1 reducing staff turnover
2 improving staff efficiency, work standards, revenue and profits
3 improving staff morale
4 meeting a number of legal obligations.

The employees benefit by

1 fitting in and feeling part of the team
2 being accepted as part of the team
3 becoming competent and hence confident in the shortest possible time.

Measuring the effectiveness of induction programmes

The purpose of induction procedures is to introduce new employees into the work-force and, with most employers, to reduce the likelihood of the new employee leaving. The effectiveness of induction can be measured by measuring labour turnover in three specific ways. These are

1 the survival curve, which measures an employer's ability to retain its entrants. It shows employee wastage as a curve which can be divided into the induction crisis, differential transit and settled connection.
2 the labour turnover and retention rates, which measure leavers as a proportion of the labour force, and the average length of service.
3 the length of service distribution, which shows the employer's ability to build a stable team.

These are discussed in more detail in Chapter 14.

In meeting the individual's needs it is important to recognize features of the employer's organization and the industry. The hospitality industry has a number of features that distinguish it from many other employers and these should be borne in mind when induction programmes are being prepared:

1 The industry employs a large number of people from the secondary labour market, i.e. people such as housewives who have not trained specifically for employment in the industry and who may not want a career.
2 The industry has its own traditions and jargon, much of it either based on a highly specialist use of normal words or, in the case of kitchen work, based on French.
3 Immediate customer contact, frequently with little, if any, supervision.
4 Complex interdependent operations which can be seriously interrupted by one person not performing his or her role properly.
5 Many units employ a high proportion of foreign workers, often from different cultures, with different values, expectations and behaviour.

Effective induction is important also because of the wide range of responsibilities imposed on employers by various national laws. At the least, effective induction can demonstrate that the employer has exercised 'due diligence', i.e. all reasonable precautions have been taken to prevent a breach of the law, such as health and safety or food safety law.

In the obviously difficult field of managing people, comparing human beings with machines should be avoided, but in the case of induction a very useful parallel can be drawn. Time spent in carefully installing and running in a new piece of machinery usually results in that machinery giving long reliable service.

Further Reading and References

Armstrong, M. (1999) *A Handbook of Human Resource Management*, 7th edn, London: Kogan Page.

Department for Education and Employment (1991) Employment, *Glossary of Training Terms*, 3rd edn, London: DfEE.

Goss-Turner, S. (2002) *Managing People in the Hospitality Industry*, 4th edn, Kingston-upon-Thames: Croner Publications.

Lashley, C. and Best, W. (2002) Employee induction in licensed retail organisations, in *International Journal of Contemporary Hospitality Management*, Vol. 14, No.1, pp. 6–13.

Pugh, D. S. and Hickson, D. J. (1999) *Writers on Organizations*, 5th edn, London: Penguin.

Riley, M. (1996) *Human Resource Management in the Hospitality and Tourism Industry*, Oxford: Butterworth-Heinemann.

Steinberg, R. (1977) *Man and the Organization*, London: Time-Life International.

Storey, J. (ed.) (2001) *Human Resource Management—A Critical Text*, 2nd edn, London: Thomson Learning.

Torrington, D., Hall, L. and Taylor, S. (2002) *Human Resource Management*, 5th edn, Harlow: Pearson Education.

Tyson, S. and York, A. (2000) *Essentials of HRM*, 4th edn, Oxford: Butterworth-Heinemann.

Wood, R. C. (1997) *Working in Hotels and Catering*, 2nd edn, London: ITB Press.

Questions

1 Describe the objectives of induction and the various steps you would normally expect to find in a systematic induction procedure.

2 Discuss which you consider to be the most important steps in job induction and why.

3 Describe also who should be involved in the procedure and what they should be responsible for.

4 Discuss what changes are likely to be made in the future to improve induction procedures.

5 Evaluate the approach to induction used by an employer you know well.

Developing the Human Resource

Performance management

The great majority of organizations today, in order to prosper or even to survive, are obliged constantly to seek ways of improving their performance. In some cases this may be merely through fine tuning existing performance. In other cases it may involve fundamental changes to policy, market positioning, objectives, structures, sourcing materials, human resources and even organizational culture. Many different approaches to achieving these ends are used by organizations, with greater or lesser effect. These include performance-related pay (PRP) systems, performance management systems (PMS), empowerment and various forms of management by objectives (MbO). Figure 7.1 summarizes what many would consider to be the essentials of effective performance management. How each of these is dealt with will vary from one employer to another. In some cases staff will be fully involved in decisions. In other cases senior management take all the decisions and communicate them to supervisors and staff.

It can readily be seen that there are consistent linkages between the factors highlighted in Figure 7.1 and

Standards of performance for the manager and/or departments or functions are established (see Chapter 3).

Standards of performance for individuals and groups are established (see Chapter 3).

Policies, objectives, targets and plans are communicated to appropriate people (see Chapter 3).

Individuals and teams are involved in work organization and allocation, with clear targets, roles and responsibilities set.

Appropriate human resources, in numbers and skills, are made available (see Chapters 3, 18 and 19).

Resources and support are made available to support the achievement of the policies, objectives, targets and plans (see Chapters 2–9).

Problems and opportunities are identified through proper communication and consultation (see Chapters 7, 19 and 20).

Individual and group training and development needs that match the employer's, individuals' and groups' objectives are established (this chapter and Chapters 8 and 9).

Monitoring and evaluation systems are set up and operated to provide accurate and timely information on performance (see Chapters 3 and 18).

Opportunities for individuals and groups to participate in their own performance reviews are provided (this chapter and Chapters 3 and 15).

Appropriate feedback is provided and development plans are reviewed (this chapter).

Causes of conflict and instances of actual conflict are identifed and procedures are developed for their resolution (this chapter).

Legal requirements are met such as the need for health and safety consultation and grievance procedures (see Chapter 16).

Similar elements are to be found in the 'performance criteria' listed in NVQ/SVQ Key Role C, Manage People, Hospitality Training Foundation, 1998.

Figure 7.1 Managing performance – some key elements

the defining characteristics of HRM as discussed in Chapter 2 earlier. Indeed, one aspect considered to be an essential element of HRM in contrast to earlier versions of the so-called personnel or people management is its concentration on individual and organizational performance. Holbeche is unequivocal in supporting the notion, arguing that HR helps to implement high-performance work practices, 'by creating a culture which is supportive of high performance . . . conducive to productivity and quality improvement' (2001: 123). She stresses the importance of issues such as communication between management and staff, the trust factor, and productivity measurement. Beardwell, Holden and Claydon (2004) also point to performance management being a crucial aspect of the 'HRM Mantra', which consists of cohesive cultures, flatter structures, a customer focus, productivity through people and a strong leadership. With a planned and direct correlation to contingent pay and rewards systems, performance management can be seen as a bridge between HRM and the achievement of strategic goals of organizations.

At the heart of performance management in practice lies the need to evaluate or appraise the performance of the people concerned. Each time a supervisor praises, counsels or disciplines a subordinate, some form of performance appraisal has almost certainly taken place. From time to time, however, it may become necessary for a supervisor to get away from the hurlyburly of the workplace and to examine objectively the performance of his or her subordinates. The supervisor needs to do this because the employer should know the strengths and weaknesses of the employees and because employees need to know how they stand. The supervisor should examine each employee's performance against expectations and at the same time consider the person's potential as well. He or she should then decide what steps should be taken in both the employer's and the individual's best interests. This process has several titles but is commonly called 'performance appraisal'. This important procedure, often formalizing the ongoing feedback to the employee, is normally carried out annually, though some companies have felt the need for a more regular occurrence.

The Chartered Institute of Personnel and Development reported that performance appraisals 'are a definite motivating factor . . . with over 60% of workers feeling positive and only 11% feeling demotivated' (*Employment News*, March 1996). In an earlier publication the Institute identified a number of different reasons why employers review the performance of their employees (Institute of Personnel Management, Fact Sheet No. 3, 1988). These are shown in Figure 7.2. From this it is apparent that performance appraisal is aimed at improving performance both of the individual and of the employing organization. This is achieved by

1 identifying both individuals' and group's weaknesses and strengths so that weaknesses can be corrected and strengths developed and built upon
2 identifying each individual's hopes and aspirations so that, where these do not conflict with the organization's objectives, they can be satisfied.

From a properly conducted appraisal programme an employer should obtain the following:

1 Commitment to a 'performance contract'.
2 An analysis of development needs which enables individual competencies to be extended and group or employment category training needs to be identified.
3 A succession plan and management development programme that earmark individuals for promotion and identify their particular development needs.

To assess training and development needs	97
To help improve current performance	97
To review past performance	98
To assess future potential/promotability	71
To assist career planning decisions	75
To set performance objectives	81
To assess increases or new levels in salary	40
Others – e.g. updating personnel records	4

Figure 7.2 Reasons for reviewing performance (% of respondents)
Source: IPM Fact Sheet No. 3 (1988).

4 A reasonably objective basis for allocating rewards.
5 Improved communications.

The individual also benefits by knowing

1 how he or she stands and what help is to be given to improve performance and competencies
2 what his or her career prospects are.

There are three main steps in conducting appraisals correctly:

1 Having an up-to-date and objective job description, and performance targets or performance contracts.
2 Comparing the person's performance with the job description and targets or performance contracts.
3 Communicating and discussing the supervisor's and the person's views regarding his or her performance, and recording both the supervisor's and the subordinate's views (but see 360-degree approaches below).

Job descriptions have been discussed in Chapter 3; it now becomes apparent why they should contain as many objective, measurable items as possible; for example, if the word 'satisfactory' is used, superior and subordinate may interpret the word differently. On the other hand, if an objective term such as '60% gross profit' is used, neither person can dispute the interpretation of this figure so long as each is clear about what is included in the calculation. In comparing a person's performance with his or her targets, therefore, it is necessary to bring together as much relevant information as possible, such as budgets, forecasts and other records.

The approach to appraisal

There are many different approaches to appraisal but it is possible to divide schemes into those concerned mainly with

- outputs, i.e. results orientated
- inputs, i.e. job behaviour or personality traits–orientated
- a combination of the two.

The IPM (CIPD) Fact Sheet No. 3 survey referred to above identified a number of different approaches:

Results-orientated	63%
Job behaviour–orientated	52%
Personality trait rating	29%
Alphabetical/numerical rating	28%
Narrative – free essay	2%
Controlled writing	44%
Forced distribution global rating	10%

From the above it is obvious that there are many different approaches to assessment; as organizational types become more diverse, so do approaches to assessment. Ian Roberts (in Beardwell and Holden, 1997) reports a number of different approaches, which include the following.

Absolute methods

In such methods individuals are assessed relative to an absolute standard.

Comparative methods

- Ranking whereby individuals are assessed and placed in a hierarchy using certain criteria as a benchmark.
- Paired comparisons whereby each individual is compared with each other individual until everyone has been compared with everyone else, from which a ranking scale may be produced.
- Forced distribution whereby individuals' performances are ranked and then allocated to some predetermined distribution point.

Critical incident techniques

Assessment is based upon positive and negative behaviour in the employee's performance.

Results-orientated methods

Assessment is based upon results and not upon behaviour.

Pratt and Bennett (1990) describe three commonly used techniques for rating performance. The first is the 'linear rule', which requires the appraiser to place a tick along a numerical scale or in a box to represent ratings for the characteristics. They point out the distinction that needs to be made between measuring results, such as quantity of work, and traits, such as reliability. The second technique is known as BARS (behaviourally anchored rating scale). In this technique people familiar with a job select appropriate aspects of it and describe examples of behaviour ranging from ineffective to effective along a scale for each aspect. An appraiser can then identify individual performance on the scale. Third, Pratt and Bennett describe MbO, which is discussed in Chapter 3 of this book.

Some schemes require the manager making the assessment to place ticks in graded boxes, or to award letters, grades or points, as judged appropriate. They are relatively easy to operate, but just how reliable or fair they are is very debatable. They are particularly difficult to use for the assessment of unquantifiable factors such as personality traits. The British Psychological Society was reported to have found that such schemes were less popular because of the difficulties associated with them.

In written assessment schemes much greater importance is attached to a freely written report. These types of schemes have the advantage of encouraging the manager making the assessment to think broadly rather than having to use preselected labels.

There are systems that compromise between these two extreme types and which ask the manager to fill in boxes and to write a broad statement as well. One such scheme is shown in simplified form as Figure 7.3.

Performance review: Part 1   Confidential

Name of employee ———   Job   ———   Branch   ———
Completed by   ———   Name   ———   Position ———

Overall assessment *Put tick in*   Whichever grade you award please
appropriate boxes   elaborate here on this person's performance:

Excellent ☐   Satisfactory ☐
Good   ☐   Poor   ☐

Detailed assessment

	Excellent	Good	Satisfactory	Poor	Remarks
For all staff					
Technical competence	☐	☐	☐	☐	
Application	☐	☐	☐	☐	
Initiative	☐	☐	☐	☐	
Relations with:					
Supervisor	☐	☐	☐	☐	
Colleagues	☐	☐	☐	☐	
Customers	☐	☐	☐	☐	
For supervisory staff					
Ability to direct others	☐	☐	☐	☐	
Planning and organizing ability	☐	☐	☐	☐	
Expression:					
Written	☐	☐	☐	☐	
Oral	☐	☐	☐	☐	

Performance review: Part 2   Confidential

Is this person promotable, and if so, what type of job would most suit his/her abilities and aspirations?

List what training can be given, of other action taken, to assist in improving performance or preparing for promotion

Figure 7.3 Example of an appraisal form

What salary increase would you recommend? Give reasons

High   ☐   Low   ☐
Standard   ☐   None   ☐

Have you discussed this appraisal with your subordinate? Yes/No

If no, why not?

If yes, what were his/her comments?

Figure 7.3 *continued*

Who should be appraised?

These days where appraisal schemes are operated, most managers and supervisors are included. The IPM (CIPD) survey showed the following participation by percentage of those employed by responding companies:

Directors (board level)	52%
Senior management	90%
Middle management	96%
Junior management	92%
First-line supervisor	78%
Clerical/secretarial	66%
Skilled/semi-skilled	24%
Knowledge workers, e.g. those who provide professional, scientific and advisory services	55%
Others, e.g. graduate trainees	7%

Who appraises?

As organizations reduce the number of layers of management, as more organizations adopt more flexible hierarchies and practices such as matrix management, the question of who appraises becomes more difficult in some cases. Traditionally a person's superior was responsible for assessing a person's performance, usually moderated by the assessor's own superior and sometimes a personnel officer. This has been modified by the adoption by many organizations of self-assessment methods in which a subordinate has a role in assessing his or her own performance. Nowadays it is increasingly common for an employee's peers and even subordinates (upward appraisal) or clients (like students reporting on a teacher's performance) to be involved. In some cases, outside agencies are also being used.

Most organizations in recent times have been through fundamental changes: they have become less hierarchical, more flexible and structurally flatter. Methods of evaluating performance have, as a consequence, had to change.

The 360-degree feedback method

According to a Towers Perrin survey, the use of 360-degree feedback is on the increase (reported in *Management Consultancy*, September 1998). The system sets out to assess employees' performance based on feedback from a wide circle of work contacts including superiors, subordinates, peers, customers and, in some cases, suppliers. The survey found that 94% of firms use it for training and management development, 31% use it to assess potential, 27% use it for succession planning and 13% for promotion. One of the reported advantages is that 'it crosses the cultural divide – the tool will work in any country' (*Management Consultancy*, September 1998).

There is further evidence in recent commentaries that 360-degree appraisal techniques are being used more widely (see Armstrong, 2002), particularly regarding behavioural aspects such as communication skills and teamwork capabilities. Robbins (2005) reports that following a survey in the USA, 21% of US organizations are utilizing 360-degree formats and that sophistication of technique is growing within consultancies. More generally a linkage has been established between such systems and the increasing usage of a balanced scorecard approach to management, strategy and performance measurement. In this process, organizations set specific objectives or targets (directly related to overall strategy) for the business and evaluate performance against these defined aims (Norton and Kaplan, 1992). These objectives normally fall within a matrix of four key imperatives, such as financial/shareholder value performance, employee-focused elements, customer-perspective issues and, for example, innovations in products or service delivery concepts/systems. Individual performance targets would therefore need to be set and appraised with a direct linkage to these elements of the balanced scorecard. This approach has been found to be an important and successful part of the performance management system of Marriott Hotels, as reported in a study by Millett (2002).

The appraisal interview

The crucial aspect of appraisal is the conduct of the interview itself. Some managers find that asking their subordinates to examine and complete an appraisal report themselves makes the situation easier. This is sometimes known as 'self-appraisal' and enables a supervisor to study beforehand a person's views concerning his or her own performance. This obviously means that the supervisor is better equipped to get the best results from the interview, as he or she knows where the person is likely to be most sensitive. At the same time, if the person has identified known weaknesses, the supervisor can concentrate on means of improvement and on the future without dwelling on shortcomings and the past.

Some schemes are now going even further and allow the appraisee to actually design the basis of the performance review – selecting what he or she thinks is relevant to a review.

The appraisal form

The type of form used to record the appraisal should be incidental to the interview itself although a well-designed form can help in preparing for and conducting an interview. In cases where the form itself is of more importance than the interview, the approach to the management of people is likely to be mechanistic. It enables employers to achieve some of their objectives without fully considering the individual's own needs and aspirations.

The contents of the form therefore should be dependent upon the purpose of the appraisal scheme and the nature of the approach. One concerned with 'inputs' would include the following type of information:

1 personal details, e.g. name, length of service, job
2 performance report covering
   - knowledge
   - skill
   - application
   - initiative
   - expression – written and spoken
   - ability to plan and to organize
   - ability to work with others
   - ability to direct others
   - specific job targets or objectives and the measure of achievements.
3 training needs in present job
4 potential
5 training or development needs if promotable
6 general salary recommendation
7 employee's comments.

One concerned with 'outputs', on the other hand, would be more likely to look like Figure 3.7, a typical MbO format.

Appraisal styles

Pryor and Mayo suggest that there are six styles on a continuum consisting of dominating, telling, advising, joint, self-assessment and abdicating. These relate to the interaction between the appraiser and the appraised and can be seen on the appraisal interaction model in Figure 7.4.

Effective appraisal interviews – some tips

As with selection interviewing, appraisal interviewing is a skilled technique and those responsible for conducting these interviews need training and practice, along with the ability to examine and criticize their own performance. Here are some useful rules to follow:

Do

1 Plan the interview by obtaining all necessary information and by giving the person to be interviewed prior notice of the interview and its purpose.
2 Remember that interviews are a means of two-way communication and that the best interviewers do little talking themselves.
3 Suspend phone calls and other interruptions and allow plenty of time for the interview.

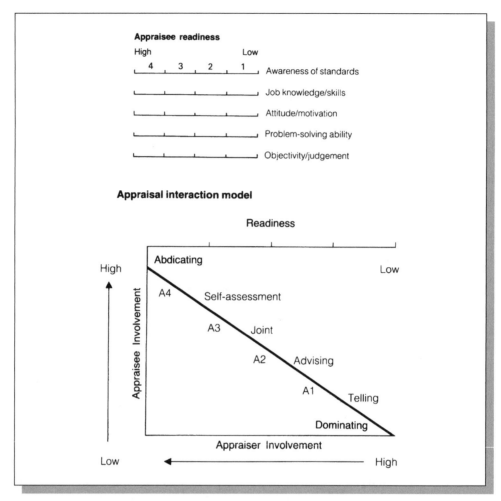

Figure 7.4 Appraisal styles
Source: Personnel Management, June 1985.

4 Put the interviewee at ease and try to make the occasion an informal one. For example, avoid having the desk between yourself and the interviewee.

5 Make the interviewee feel that the main purpose of the interview is to benefit him or her.

6 Start by praising strong points. Remember a person's ego and that any subsequent criticism will be rejected as unfair or even untrue unless the balance is maintained by acknowledging good points.

7 Ask the interviewee their reasons for any shortcomings and ask for suggestions for improvement.

8 Finish the interview firmly on a positive note by reiterating what performance has been agreed and what assistance the employee can expect in the form of training or other help.

9 Remember always that giving a person a poor appraisal can be a reflection on the manager's own ability.

Don't

1 rush the interview. It is one of the most important occasions in a person's working year.
2 prejudge the outcome of the interview; and therefore don't finalize the form until afterwards.
3 read out the printed form. Your appraisal should come over in your own words.
4 preach or be pompous. This is an occasion to discuss how a person's performance targets may be achieved.

Salary reviews and performance appraisal

There is constant debate among HR specialists as to whether salary reviews and proposals should be part of performance appraisal systems. The IPM 1988 survey showed that 40% of employers used performance appraisal for salary purposes. The IPD 1996 survey reported that less than one third of appraisees had their appraisal linked to their pay. This suggests there has been a reduction in the number of companies directly linking pay to appraisals. The debate, however, is bound to continue because, after all, it would be manifestly unfair if poor performers were rewarded to the same level as exemplary performers. More recently, notable management consultancies such as McKinsey and Hay have certainly promoted the line of direct relationship between performance and pay. This approach is in line with the conceptual models of HRM which consider that there is a 'bundle' of HRM practices, including performance management and reward systems for example, which will lead to performance enhancement, the so-called normative perspective (see Guest, 1997).

Small organizations

In the smallest organizations, with no more than a few employees, a formal approach may be unnecessary and could even disrupt some healthy superior–subordinate relationships. Even so, employees with potential and prospects should be told of this so that they will be less likely to go to another employer for advancement.

Appraisal is one of the most personal and potentially unsettling situations that occurs in a working person's life. It can be, after all, an examination and judgement of their main role in life and consequently it can be very damaging to the ego. It must therefore be positive, constructive and helpful. It should not be an occasion for apportioning blame or responsibility for past shortcomings or failures. If these are discussed, they should be used as examples to illustrate points from which both sides can learn in order to take steps to build for the future. Appraisal must be creative and must result in new objectives and in agreement on the means by which these objectives can be achieved.

Further Reading and References

Armstrong, M. (1999) *A Handbook of Human Resource Management*, 7th edn, London: Kogan Page.
Armstrong, M. (2002) *Employee Reward*, London: CIPD Publications.
Beardwell, I. and Holden, L. (1997) *Human Resource Management*, 2nd edn, London: Pitman.

Beardwell, I., Holden, L. and Claydon, T. (2004) *Human Resources Management—A Contemporary Approach*, 4th edn, Harlow: Prentice Hall.

Guest, D. (1997) Human resource management and performance: A review and research agenda, in *International Journal of Human Resource Management*, Vol. 8, No. 3, 263–290.

Holbeche, L. (2001) *Aligning Human Resources and Business Strategy*, Oxford: Butterworth-Heinemann.

Hospitality Training Foundation (1998) NVQ Managing People, London: HTF.

Institute of Personnel Management (CIPD) (1988) Fact Sheet No. 3, Wimbledon: CIPD.

Jones, P. and Lockwood, A. (1989) *The Management of Hotel Operations*, London: Cassell.

Millett, B. (2002) Performance management in international hospitality and tourism, in D'Annunzio-Green, N., Maxwell, G. and Watson, S. (eds) *Human Resource Management—International Perspectives in Hospitality and Tourism*, London: Continuum.

Norton, D. and Kaplan, R. (1992) The balanced scorecard: Measures that drive performance, in *Harvard Business Review*, Jan./Feb., 71–79.

Pratt, K. J. and Bennett, S. C. (1990) *Elements of Personnel Management*, 4th edn, Wokingham: GEE.

Pugh, D. S. and Hickson, D. J. (1997) *Writers on Organizations*, 5th edn, London: Penguin.

Robbins, S. (2005) *Organizational Behaviour*, 11th edn, New Jersey: Pearson Education Inc.

Sisson, K. (ed.) (1989) *Personnel Management in Britain*, Oxford: Blackwell.

Torrington, D., Hall, L. and Taylor, S. (2002) *Human Resource Management*, 5th edn, Harlow: Pearson Education.

Questions

1 Describe the objectives of a performance appraisal scheme and the various steps or phases that you would normally expect to find.

2 Discuss which you consider to be the most important steps in a performance appraisal and why.

3 Discuss what changes are likely to be made in the future to improve performance appraisal procedures.

4 Discuss the relationship between performance appraisal and approaches to management, such as management by objectives (see Chapter 3).

5 Evaluate the approach to performance appraisal used by an employer you know well.

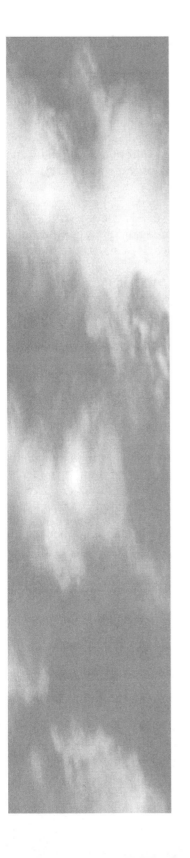

CHAPTER   8

Training

One of the features of working life today is that whatever education and training is obtained at the start, it will almost certainly become redundant or obsolete during one's working lifetime. The need to train, and to acquire new knowledge, new skills and new attitudes has become an everyday aspect of each individual's working life. In some cases this may merely be an updating process, but in others it will require a complete change from one occupation to another.

Some jobs and whole industries will disappear and others will emerge. Fortunately for the hospitality industry, there is no likelihood of the main services it provides becoming redundant in the immediate future. Some types of jobs will disappear either through technological change (e.g. telephonists) or through outsourcing. Other jobs within the industry will change, but the industry itself is predicted to continue to flourish.

The responsibility for ensuring that working people are equipped to cope with these changes is threefold. First, the state carries part of the responsibility, particularly in providing education and training for school leavers and for those who need retraining due to the decline of their own industries, nationally or regionally.

From the hospitality industry's point of view the government was instrumental in a number of important initiatives aimed at improving the industry's standards. The most important probably was the establishment in 1966 of the Hotel and Catering Industry Training Board (HCITB), now known as the Hospitality Training Foundation (HTF). Though many industrial training boards were disbanded in the 1980s, the government decided for a number of reasons to retain the hospitality industry's training board. These reasons included the obvious growing, even vital, importance to the economy of tourism, and also the tremendously fragmented and still predominantly untrained workforce in hospitality generally. The Education and Training Advisory Committee for the hotel and catering industry demonstrated that less than 40% of the workforce, including management, had any appropriate training and that the output of all the college courses would not keep pace with replacement needs, let alone the needs generated by the growth of the industry. This shortfall persists today with a 2001 estimate by the HTF that 21% of the hospitality workforce hold no qualification of any sort. In April 2002, there were 93,360 reported vacancies across the industry (HTF, 2003).

Apart from the traditional training work of industry training providers, the government also set up a national scheme for the development of open access and distance learning programmes, such as Learn Direct, designed for anyone wishing to acquire technical expertise without having to have prior qualifications and without having to attend conventional college courses. A number of courses have now been developed for the industry. Secondly, employers, too, have their share of responsibilities and they discharge these by providing training intended to suit their individual needs. Some employers provide excellent training, whereas others are quite content to recruit trained individuals from the labour market without putting any trained people into the market themselves.

Within some sectors of the hospitality industry staff training is steadily becoming more effective. However, the generally high labour turnover still reduces the effectiveness of the training effort, although companies such as several of the branded fast food operators cope well with the challenge of high labour turnover. They do this by using extremely well-thought-out and well-supervised training programmes. In addition, like many of the best of the large retailers, they budget for and plan training time into all recruits' work. Their 'crew members' only progress to more responsible roles when they have satisfactorily completed the preceding training.

In addition, the industry's leading trade body, the BHA, has taken a lead in a range of training initiatives including the Excellence through People scheme. The BHA has also taken a lead in consultation with government on a range of human resource issues. The Hospitality Network is a forum for various of the industry's sectors to influence the future provision of hospitality training and education.

Many of the industry's traditional employers, particularly the smaller, privately owned businesses, do not implement proper training for a number of reasons:

1 Many proprietors and managers have had no formal training themselves and, therefore, are unaware of the standards that can be achieved and of the benefits of training.
2 Many employers are concerned constantly with immediate operational problems and do not plan ahead.

3 Many are undercapitalized and cannot afford the investment.

4 Many believe that it is the responsibility of others, such as colleges, to provide them with trained staff.

At the same time, however, there is a constant upgrading in the industry and a move towards both 'high tech' (modern technology and costly capital investment) and 'high touch' (high customer contact and high wage costs), each demanding more training, with the leading employers now putting more resources into training.

The third part of the responsibility rests with individuals. No amount of training will be effective unless an individual wishes to make the most of what is available. The state and employers may provide facilities, but it remains ultimately for individuals to make the most effective use of these facilities for the benefit of themselves, their employers and the community.

A fourth participant in training and development are the professional bodies. These, such as the Hotel and Catering International Management Association (HCIMA) and the British Institute of Innkeeping (BII), take responsibility for setting professional standards and today many such professional bodies expect their members to participate in continuous professional development (CPD), which can involve annual attendance at various forms of professional updating.

Industrial training is concerned primarily with bridging the gap between individuals' and groups' actual performance and the performance required to achieve an undertaking's objectives. These objectives may include such things as expansion, obtaining repeat sales, increasing sales, increasing profitability and improving standards. On other occasions training may be needed merely to maintain the employer's position in the market. However, there are some useful signs, or symptoms, that may indicate a need for training and these include

1 failure to attain targets such as gross profit on food or liquor, turnover and net profit
2 dissatisfied customers
3 slow service
4 high labour turnover, low morale
5 friction between departments such as restaurant and kitchen, or housekeeping and reception
6 high accident, breakage and wastage rates
7 staff unable or unprepared to adapt to changes.

In one case, the then Forte Hotels, a survey conducted by Mori showed the following (*Caterer and Hotelkeeper*, December 1998):

1 Guests recommending the hotel brand to others:
   Meridien   82%
   Heritage   71%
   Posthouses   68%
2 Staff recommending the hotel brand as an employer to others:
   Meridien   61%
   Heritage   51%
   Posthouses   41%

The managing director of the company stated that he wanted a 95% 'advocacy' or recommendation rate. The findings led to the development of the company's Commitment to Excellence programme, a 16–20 week training programme for all staff including temporary staff. This illustrates how training should be developed in order to achieve companies' objectives.

It is not suggested that training alone can solve all problems. If a hotel or restaurant is badly planned or wrongly situated, no amount of training (apart from training the executive responsible) can rectify this. However, training can often provide the solution or part of the solution.

Training should also consciously try to help individuals to extend their competencies to reach the limits of their capabilities and realistic aspirations – so long as these do not conflict with organizational goals.

The main components of training

There are three main components that an individual requires in order to do a job effectively: knowledge, skills and attitudes. Each of these can be developed or improved upon (from the organization's point of view) by effective training. Each component, however, needs a different training approach. Knowledge, for example, can be imparted by talks, lectures and films, but these techniques would prove almost valueless in imparting the second component, skills such as handling a knife. In this case, practice is necessary. The third component, a person's set of attitudes, is the most difficult to impart or to change, even with soundly based training, and it requires deep understanding of human behaviour among those responsible for training. Training techniques in this field may include discussions, case studies and role playing. It is agreed, however, by many behavioural experts that because attitudes are extremely difficult to modify, it is better to select people with the right attitudes rather than attempt to train people who have attitudes that conflict with those of the employer.

In order to design effective training programmes the following principles should be known and understood:

1 Training can only be successful if it is recognized that learning is a voluntary process, that individuals must be keen to learn and consequently they must be properly motivated; for example, if trainee waiters are losing earnings in the form of tips in order to attend a course, they may well begrudge the time and therefore may be unwilling to participate actively.
2 People learn at different rates and, particularly in the case of adults, often start from different levels of knowledge and skill and with different motives and attitudes.
3 Learning is hindered by feelings of nervousness, fear, inferiority and by lack of confidence.
4 Instruction must be given in short frequent sessions rather than a few long stints; for example, if a trainee is being instructed in the use of kitchen equipment, ten lessons lasting forty-five minutes are obviously far better than one lesson lasting seven and a half hours.

5 Trainees must play active roles – they must participate; for example, lecturing puts the trainees into a passive role, whereas discussions or practical work gives them active roles.

6 Training must make full use of appropriate and varied techniques and of all the senses, not just one, such as the sense of hearing.

7 Trainees need clear targets, and progress must be checked frequently.

8 Confidence has to be built up by praise, not broken down by reprimand. Learning has to be rewarding.

9 Skills and knowledge are acquired in stages marked by periods of progress, standstill and even a degeneration of the skill or knowledge so far acquired. Instructors must know about this phenomenon (the learning curve), as it can be a cause of disappointment and frustration for many trainees.

These principles of learning illustrate and emphasize that it is both difficult and wasteful to treat individuals as groups. So far as possible, training needs to be tailored to suit individual needs. The techniques to be used depend on a variety of factors, including whether it is knowledge, skills or attitudes that are to be imparted and whether individuals or groups are to be trained. The two main approaches are 'on the job' and 'off the job' training.

'On the job' training

In the hospitality industry much of the staff's work is performed in direct contact with customers. For this reason much of the training of new staff has to be performed 'on the job' so that experience of dealing with customers can be obtained. 'On the job' training, therefore, plays a vital part in the industry's approach to training. In one large survey conducted in the USA 'experiential learning' was ranked as the most effective form of training. If handled correctly, it can be very effective for the teaching of manual and social skills, but it requires that training objectives are clearly defined and that those responsible for instruction are proficient in training techniques.

Unfortunately, newcomers are often attached to experienced workers who are not in any way equipped to train others. This is often referred to as 'sitting next to Nellie'. Apart from not having a suitable personality, the trainer may not even have been told what to instruct and what not to instruct. Instead, if experienced workers are to be entrusted with the training of newcomers, they should be chosen because of their ability to deal sympathetically with trainees, not just because of their knowledge of the job itself. They should then be given appropriate instructor training before being asked to train newcomers. The progress of trainees should be checked from time to time by the person responsible for training. Responsibility for training should not be abdicated to the instructor. An example of an 'on the job' training programme for a cocktail bartender is shown in Figure 8.1.

Note that the programme in Figure 8.1 is in progressive stages. It requires each phase to be completely covered before the next is started. In addition, this particular programme is only a checklist and therefore presupposes that the instructor already has the detailed knowledge. Because of this, in many cases it will be necessary to expand this type of list by specifying in a document such as a training manual exactly what has to be instructed under each new heading.

First stage

1 Bar preparation and cleanliness
- (a) Washing down of bar counter, bottle shelves
- (b) Polishing of mirrors, glass shelves
- (c) 'Bottling up'
- (d) Use of counter towels, drip mats and trays
- (e) Preparation of accompaniments including lemon, olives, cherries
- (f) Use of beer dispense equipment

2 'Cash'
- (a) Price lists
- (b) Use of cash register
- (c) Cheques and credit cards
- (d) Charging to customer accounts
- (e) Computation of costs of rounds and 'change giving'

3 Main points of law
- (a) Licensing hours and drinking-up time
- (b) Hotel residents and guests
- (c) Adulteration
- (d) Weights and Measures Act

4 Service of simple orders
- (a) Beers, wines by the glass
- (b) Spirits and vermouth with mixers
- (c) Use of accompaniments such as ice, lemon, cherries
- (d) Cigarettes, cigars

Second stage

1 Bar preparation and cleanliness
- (a) Requisitioning of stock
- (b) Cleaning of beer dispense equipment
- (c) Preparing weekly liquor and provisions order

2 'Cash'
- (a) Checking float
- (b) Changing till roll
- (c) 'Off sales'

3 Further law
- (a) Betting and gaming
- (b) Young persons
- (c) Credit sales of intoxicating liquor

4 Service of simple mixed drinks
- (a) Shandies
- (b) Gin and Italian, gin and French

Third stage

1 Bar preparation and cleanliness
- (a) Rectification of faults such as 'fobbing beer', jammed bottle disposal unit
- (b) Preparation for stock taking

2 'Cash'

Cashing up

3 Service of all drinks contained in house list
- (a) Knowledge of recipes
- (b) Use of shaker and mixing glass

Figure 8.1 Example of an 'on the job' training programme for a cocktail bartender – basically a list of duties and tasks

'Off the job' training

'Off the job' training takes place away from the working situation. A variety of methods and techniques may be used but the particular choice will depend on what is to be imparted. The main methods are listed below:

1 Talks are best used for imparting knowledge such as company history and policies, legal matters, regulations, recipes, and outlines of methods and procedures. In giving a talk, progress must be checked frequently by the use of questions and answers.
2 Discussions are best used to elaborate on and to consolidate what has been imparted by other techniques.
3 Lectures often mean little more than talking at trainees and are therefore to be avoided, as there is usually little trainee participation.
4 Case studies, projects and business games are best used to illustrate and to consolidate principles of management such as planning, analytical techniques, etc.
5 Role playing is best used to develop social skills such as receiving guests, handling customer complaints, selling, interviewing or instructional techniques. Ideally this should be supported by tape recordings and closed circuit television recordings.
6 Films, charts and other visual aids should not normally be used as instructional techniques by themselves, but should support talks, discussions, case studies and role playing. Films on a variety of hotel and catering subjects are obtainable from several training organizations.
7 Programmed texts, interactive videos, CD-ROMs and internet-based on-line programmes satisfy many of the principles of learning. In addition, they can be used by individuals at any convenient time – not requiring the presence of an instructor. They cannot, of course, be used to teach something such as manual skills, and they can be very expensive to design.

An example of a fairly typical 'off the job' programme for cooks is shown in Figure 8.2. Figure 8.3 ranks the effectiveness of different forms of training.

Training-needs analysis

Having looked at what training attempts to do, the main principles of learning and the main techniques available, the next step is to consider the design of training programmes. Figure 8.4 gives a simple overview of the complete process. This starts with an identification of training needs, sometimes referred to as a 'training needs analysis', which is conducted by the person responsible for training in consultation with line management. It should attempt to identify those problems and opportunities that line management could solve and exploit with the assistance of appropriate training. It should be produced by studying the training needs of individuals as identified in 'appraisal reports', and by detailed discussions with the line managers. The individual's job description, actual performance and potential should be the basis for these discussions, together with organizational plans for the future. One useful approach is to adopt the 80/20 principle, e.g. What is causing most problems? Which is the largest category of staff? In the commercial context it is always vital to concentrate limited resources on areas that will give the biggest rewards.

Time	Subject matter	Method of instruction
9.00–9.45	Company history Present organization and objectives Personnel policies	Talk, discussion and film
9.45–10.30	Kitchen equipment; cleanliness, safety, uses	Demonstration and discussion
10.30–11.00	Hygiene	Film and discussion
11.00–11.15	Coffee	
11.15–12.00	Principles of cookery; grilling	Demonstration and discussion
12.00–1.00	Portioning, preparation and presentation	Demonstration and practical work
1.00–2.00	Lunch	
2.00–4.00	Practical cookery	Practical preparation of simple dishes
4.00–4.15	Tea	
4.15–5.00	Costing and portion control	Talk and discussion
5.00–6.00	Clearing up	

Figure 8.2 Example of first day of an 'off the job' training programme for cooks employed by a firm, with many establishments, offering standardized service

1 Personalized experiential learning; e.g. on job training, 'mentor' supervision
2 Textual material; e.g. text books, manuals
3 Self-directed learning resources; e.g. resource area, programmed learning
4 Observational learning; e.g. exhibits, working models
5 Interactive simulations; e.g. games, role play
6 Visual lecture aids; e.g. flip charts, OHPs
7 Expert formal presentations; e.g. lectures, panel presentations
8 Impersonal passive electronic media; instructional TV and radio

Figure 8.3 Rank order of training effectiveness for non-supervisory jobs
Source: CHRIE conference paper 1988, Dr R. Foucar-Szocki, Syracuse University, USA.

From the consolidation of individual training needs will emerge organization or corporate training needs. Some will be 'essential' and some 'desirable'. These priorities should be laid down by the senior management and will consequently fit in with the undertaking's business objectives.

In the case of an industrial catering contractor or a group of restaurants, for example, there may be plans to expand the number of units and in order to do this a variety of key staff for the new units will be needed over a given period of time. It will be important, therefore, to identify those people who can be

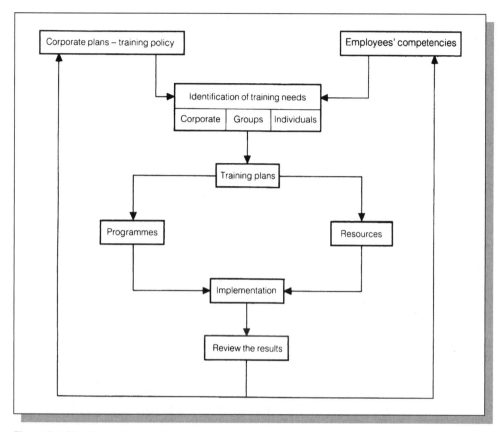

Figure 8.4 Meeting training needs

transferred or promoted and the training that will be needed in order to pre-pare them. This may range from preparing some assistant managers for full management, to preparing junior kitchen hands to take over more skilled responsibilities such as cooking.

The question of having sufficient trained personnel to fit into expansion plans is a critical one to the successful growth of an organization and it is one area where the training function together with effective recruitment can prove to be of considerable value to a company.

Obviously not all training needs emerge from the annual training-needs analysis. They also arise from unexpected changes in trading conditions or business emphasis; for example, many restaurant operators do not pay sufficient attention to the profits that can be generated by liquor sales. In this case, if a company decides that sales of drinks are to be promoted, effective training of waiters and waitresses in product knowledge, service and selling techniques can play a big part in boosting sales and profits. Likewise, a brewery may change its emphasis from running tenanted houses to running managed houses. In this case it will have to recruit and train managers to run the public houses; it will also have to train district managers in the supervision of managed houses.

Training needs may be identified in three broad areas. The first is the organization's needs; for example, improved customer relations. Such a need may affect all employees. The second need is a group need; for example, a particular group of employees such as receptionists may need training in yield management techniques. The third is that of individuals; for example, the proposal to computerize the payroll could result in the need for the payroll clerk to be trained in appropriate computer skills. Figure 8.5 shows one company's off-job annual training plan.

GROUP TRAINING PROGRAMME FOR 1999

COURSE NAME	J	F	M	A	M	J	J	A	S	O	N	D
FRONT OFFICE INDUCTION	✓	✓	✓	✓	✓	✓	✓	✓	✓	✓	✓	✓
RECEPTION SALES				✓			✓				✓	
RESERVATIONS MANAGEMENT			✓			✓				✓		
CRAFT TRAINER AWARD	✓	✓	✓	✓	✓	✓	✓	✓	✓	✓		
GROUP TRAINING TECHNIQUES		✓		✓		✓	✓		✓		✓	
HEALTH AND SAFETY NETWORK		✓		✓			✓	✓		✓		✓
SALES AND MARKETING			✓				✓			✓		
ASSERTIVE COMMUNICATION				✓								
THE EFFECTIVE MANAGEMENT OF TIME		✓				✓				✓		
NEGOTIATION TACTICS					✓				✓			
SERVICE EXCELLENCE WORKSHOP	✓		✓			✓			✓			
CONFLICT AND CONFRONTATION					✓				✓			
LEADERSHIP AND MOTIVATION		✓				✓			✓		✓	
COMPANY OPERATING PROCEDURES				✓	✓		✓			✓		
F.A.D.S.1 FURTHER ADVANCEMENT		✓				✓		✓			✓	
F.A.D.S 2 FURTHER ADVANCEMENT				✓					✓			
INTERVIEWING TECHNIQUES		✓				✓		✓			✓	
APPRAISAL SKILLS				✓					✓			
PERSONNEL OPERATING PROCEDURES				✓								

Figure 8.5 Example of a company's off-job annual training plan
Source: Reproduced by courtesy of Choice Hotels.

Effectiveness of the different forms of training

A survey conducted by Syracuse University in the USA on the effectiveness of different forms of training in the hospitality industry found that the most effective form of training for both management and non-supervisory staff was 'personalized experiential learning'. The next most effective in the case of management grades was self-directed learning and in the case of non-supervisory staff it was textual material, e.g. books. The fuller findings are shown in Figure 8.3.

An article states that 'the two most effective activities of management development are planned experience and performance management' (Robert Craven, *Management Consultancy*, March 1998).

Line management support

It is vital that line management is seen to support training by participating in it as far as possible, because if all training and instruction is left to the training staff an undesirable gap can develop between the line management and the trainers. The best way to overcome this is to ask line management, such as unit and departmental managers, and the most skilled operators, such as chefs and wine waiters, to be trained in training skills to take some training sessions. This ensures that the instruction given is in line with working requirements, practices and conditions, but, of more importance, it persuades line management that training personnel are working with and for line management.

Training is one of the tools of management that should be used to increase an employer's efficiency. It enables the undertaking's goals to be achieved by properly equipping its personnel with the competencies, knowledge, skills and attitudes necessary to achieve those goals. But at the same time training should also enable individuals, through increased competence and confidence, to achieve whatever realistic aspirations they have in their work.

Further Reading and References

Armstrong, M. (1999) *A Handbook of Human Resource Management*, 7th edn, London: Kogan Page.

Beardwell, I., Holden, L. and Claydon, T. (2004) *Human Resources Management—A Contemporary Approach*, 4th edn, Harlow: Prentice-Hall.

Boella, M. and Calabrese, M. (1994) *Effective Staff Training*, Brighton: University of Brighton.

Gode, W. (1989) *Training Your Staff*, 2nd edn, London: Industrial Society.

Goss-Turner, S. (2002) *Managing People in the Hospitality Industry*, 4th edn, Kingston-upon-Thames: Croner Publications.

Hospitality Training Foundation (2003) *Labour Market Review (Hospitality)*, London: HTF and VT Plus Training.

The Hospitality Training Foundation, London publishes a large number of useful publications.

Kelliher, C. and Perrett, G. (2001) Business strategy and approaches to HRM: A case study of new developments in the UK restaurant industry, in *Personnel Review*, Vol. 30, No. 4, 421–437.

Lucas, R. (2004) *Employment Relations in the Hospitality and Tourism Industries*, London: Routledge.

Storey, J. (ed.) (2001) *Human Resource Management—A Critical Text*, 2nd edn, London: Thomson Learning.

Torrington, D., Hall, L. and Taylor, S. (2002) *Human Resource Management*, 5th edn, Harlow: Pearson Education.

Questions

1 Describe the objectives of systematic training and the various steps or phases that you would normally expect to find in its operation.

2 Discuss which you consider to be the most important elements in training and why.

3 Discuss what changes are likely to be made in the future to improve training and what areas employers are most likely to concentrate on.

4 Discuss the relationship between training and approaches to management, such as management by objectives (see Chapter 3).

5 Evaluate the approach to training used by an employer you know well.

Management development

In the preceding chapter it was seen that training focuses very much on developing competencies needed to perform particular tasks and roles. It is concerned, in the main, with the present and the immediate future, with meeting customers' immediate needs. However, organizations also need people, the managers, who are able to interpret external environmental influences, plan ahead, organize resources, develop and interpret control information and motivate the workforce. To ensure that such people are available when and where needed, organizations operate, explicitly or implicitly, management development systems. Some systems are sophisticated, involving the constant monitoring of individuals' performance, progress and careers. There are other systems, however, consisting in the main of poaching managers from other organizations.

Whichever approach is adopted, management development is likely to become more challenging in the near future – for various reasons. These include

1 increased competition between employers
2 increased development needs and expectations of management
3 flatter organizations with fewer promotion opportunities
4 internationalization of markets and operators
5 shortage of younger people; more older people
6 the role of Continuing Professional Development (CPD)
7 the expectations of those available to join or rejoin the labour market, e.g. women returners, ethnic minorities, retired people.

In particular, a further issue needs to be confronted by employers. Management in the UK is among the least qualified when compared with major competitors abroad. The 1995 Grant Thornton European Business Survey showed that 56% of the UK's managers had some formal business education compared with an EU average of 72%. Within the hospitality industry literature, there has also been criticism of the offering of management training and development, much of it being reactive and unplanned responses to difficulties rather than linked closely to business objectives (see McGunnigle and Jameson, 2000). It is also true, however, that major hospitality chains are amongst those service businesses to have developed 'management academies' or management training centres, in an attempt to inculcate management training and learning into a clearly developmental culture. The importance given to corporate culture within multi-site companies has also been a boost to the significance of strategic-level management development plans and activities, exemplified by the recent programme of training and development within the Compass Group, impacting on all its 400 000 worldwide workforce.

Management development may be defined as those activities designed to provide the organization with a competent management team which is able to meet its short-, medium- and long-term objectives. In particular, management development has been defined as 'the intersection of three variables – individual career, organizational succession and organizational performance' (Lees, 1992: 91). Again we see the strong threads to business strategy and performance management (see Chapters 2 and 7), where the planned training and development, such as executive courses, events and mentoring, attempt to satisfy the strategic aim of merging the career development aspects of HR with the priorities of the business, including frequently in an ever changing environment a major component of change management processes (Mabey and Salaman, 1995).

To achieve this an organization needs to plan for natural replacement caused by retirements, resignations, deaths, etc., and it needs to ensure that sufficient competent management is available for expansion plans. However, in a healthy organization these plans must also extend to satisfying each individual's reasonable aspirations; for example, if an employer stands in the way of an employee's trying to obtain a recognized qualification, by not allowing adequate time-off, the employee will almost certainly place his qualification before his job and seek an employer who will assist him. Plans that accommodate only the employer's needs may result in dissatisfaction, frustration, low morale and high labour turnover.

The senior management of an organization must therefore ensure that adequate plans and resources exist to recruit, motivate, train, develop, obtain commitment from and retain its existing and future management. This is all part of management development, but in this chapter only the planning of management succession and the development of individual management skills will be discussed. Other aspects of the full management development function, such as recruitment, induction and appraisal and reward systems, are dealt with in other chapters.

Succession plans

In larger organizations management development and succession plans will be interdependent. The approach to succession planning itself will vary according to an organization's own needs. In an organization that operates within one large homogeneous market (McDonald's, for example) it may be possible to develop all an organization's management along similar lines. In another organization, operating in very different markets with very different products (Whitbread, for example), it may be necessary to develop managers specifically for particular market segments – the managers of Whitbread's Marriott hotels may need very different development and succession plans compared with managers of their David Lloyd Sports Clubs or their Brewer's Fayre Pub chain.

Succession planning has two main elements. First, there have to be decisions regarding the sources of future management. These may be all home-grown or developed internally, or they may be recruited from other organizations or there may be a mixture of both sources. Secondly, there is the process needed to identify management needs and the individuals to fill these needs. In small organizations this will be a simple informal system because senior management is likely to know everyone with potential. In large organizations complex, formal systems may be needed because of the large number of job opportunities, managers and potential managers involved. There will also be a need to manage the entire process so that an appropriate management team results.

A succession plan is produced by comparing future management requirements with currently available management. In order to do this, organization charts may be drawn up, which show the structure of the undertaking at the present time and at various future dates; e.g. in three months, one year, three years or five years. Each job shown may have two boxes immediately next to it or under it in which the names of suitable successors can be inserted. A replacement form is shown in Figure 9.1, and a succession chart in Figure 9.2.

Position	Present job holder	Most suitable replacement Put present job in brackets	Second recommendation Put present job in brackets
Hotel Manager (Splendide)	J. Jones	A. Smith (Food and Beverage Manager, Splendide)	R. Barker (Front Office Manager, Grand)
Promotion potential		Ready for promotion	Promotable with training
Training and/or development needed		None	Food and beverage experience needed
Signed by	J. Jones	Date	20/1/96
Approved by	J. Walker	(Area Manager)	

Figure 9.1 A management succession or replacement form

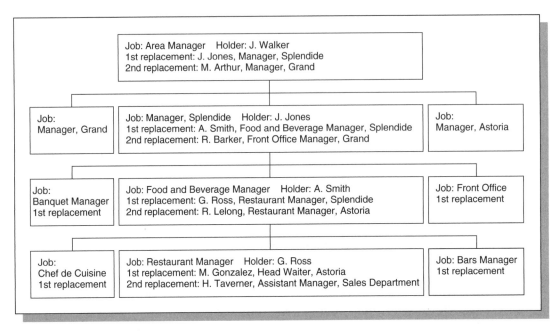

Figure 9.2 A succession chart

The names shown in Figures 9.1 and 9.2 would result from discussions between the most appropriate levels of management, using appraisal reports as a basis. This emphasizes the need for a section on promotion potential to be included in the appraisal report. Increasingly, promotion potential is being assessed through the use of assessment centres (see Chapter 5).

So long as the basis for discussion is that replacement will be due to normal retirement, accident or the voluntary departure of the incumbent, the most appropriate levels of management to be involved in discussions will be:

1 The present holder of the job for which a replacement is being discussed.
2 The present jobholder's superior.
3 The superiors of those proposed as replacements.
4 A member of senior management who is fully aware of future plans.
5 A personnel specialist (if one is employed).

In some cases one person will fulfil more than one of these roles. The final plan, particularly for the more senior levels, must carry the approval of senior management.

In order to identify likely successors in the first place it is common practice to ask each member of management to nominate those he or she considers to be the most suitable as successors. However, where this is done it must be recognized that there may arise a danger of rigid departmental career paths, whereas in some cases inter-departmental transfers and promotions will be more desirable in order to broaden the experience of individual managers.

In the largest organizations, which break down into regional or functional operating companies, the danger of sitting on talent, consciously or unconsciously, has to be avoided. This can be achieved by all management above a certain level of seniority being dealt with as a group resource, in which case appraisals and other management development processes will be monitored by a central department.

Increasingly in multinational companies such approaches to management and staff development make use of interactive computer-based systems.

What do managers do?

Before designing detailed management development plans it is important to consider what managers do so that the development plans meet the needs of the organization and of the individual. The Council for Management Education and Development suggested that there are a number of management competences which fall into three main levels. These are concerned with different issues according to the seniority of the managers concerned. An example is shown in Figure 9.3.

Management level	Management competences				
Supervisory/ operational/ junior					
Middle/tactical	Managing systems	Managing people	Finance management	Changing systems	Political sensitivity
Senior/strategic management					

Figure 9.3 Competences needed by middle management

This can be expressed in other ways. As a person moves up the organizational hierarchy, tasks will change from mainly routine ones, concerned with supervising operations, to non-routine interpretation of management information and organization of change. The question of management competencies also needs to be seen in the context of the international, multi-cultural nature of many hospitality firms, though such competencies could be seen as essential in any environment. The CIPD (1999) findings in this area are instructive, with key competencies required being summarized as: people or relationship skills, perception skills, ability to tolerate ambiguity, ability to demonstrate flexible behaviour, clear goal orientation, sociability and interest in people, empathetic and non-judgmental, and good communication skills. Some larger firms have analysed their own desired set of management competencies, and based personnel and job profiles upon the competencies identified (see also Chapter 22).

Development of managers

In accordance with the succession plan, individual training and development programmes have to be designed. It is here that an understanding of how a manager acquires his or her knowledge, skills and attitudes is vital. Although some management knowledge, skills and attitudes may be learned through training and courses, much comes from experience. Professor Wild of Henley Management College writes, 'The most effective and enduring executive-level management development is not simply provided by courses – it is a product of experience' (*Management Today*, October 1994). From this it is apparent that people do not become managers in a classroom, although they can acquire much of the necessary knowledge and basic skills there. Most of their expertise is obtained in the hard practice of managing people in the workplace.

As Robert Craven, of Warwick Business School, writes, 'It is by learning through experience (also known as experiential learning) that the best and most effective learning takes place . . . the really powerful learning comes when we are an involved partner in the process' (*Management Consultancy*, March 1998). He goes on to say that 'the most effective activities of management development is perform-ance management. It is a way of obtaining better results by understanding and managing performance . . . finally the glue that binds experiential learning and performance management is coaching.'

A management development programme must therefore contain a balance of formal training and planned experience (Figure 9.4 shows a rank order of the different forms of training). It is not something that operates for one period only of a manager's life. It should be updated constantly to continue throughout a manager's working life. Over a period of years, therefore, a programme may include spells in line management and in various specialist departments; for example, a young executive's first ten years with a company could be as shown in Figure 9.5.

1 Personalized experiential learning
2 Self-directed learning resources
3 Interactive simulations
4 Visual lecture aids
5 Textual material
6 Observational learning
7 Expert formal presentation
8 Impersonal passive electronic media.

Figure 9.4 Rank order for effectiveness of training of management grades
Source: 'A Model of Excellence of Training Managers and Non-supervisory Employees in the Food Service Industry', CHRIE Conference Paper 1988. Dr Reg Foucar-Szocki, Syracuse University, USA.

During this period the executive may also attend a dozen 'off the job' courses on such subjects as

- supervisory skills
- budgetary control and forecasting
- techniques of instruction
- interviewing and selection techniques
- project planning
- finance for non-financial executives.

Year	Approximate age	Position
1	21	Trainee management programme, various departments and establishments
2–3	22–24	Junior supervisory position, e.g. assistant manager/manageress of a hotel or restaurant
4	24	Specialized function, e.g. new projects department, sales office, training department
5	25	Line management, e.g. unit management, food and beverage management
6	27	Specialist function, e.g. sales management, training officer
7	28	Assistant to area manager
8	30	Line management, e.g. manager of medium to large unit, area manager

Figure 9.5 Example of a career path for a young executive

Whether these are internal or external courses depends on the needs of the organization and the individual. Generally, internal courses are more precisely designed to satisfy the needs of the organization, whereas external courses have to be broadly based to appeal to a wider market.

The value of external courses lies to a great extent in the opportunity to exchange views with managers from other organizations, but this only has value if those attending can bring about organizational changes. This prerogative normally lies only with more senior managers and therefore the value of external courses probably increases with the seniority of those attending (so long as they are geared to their needs).

Research from the USA showed that the most effective management training, not surprisingly, was 'on the job' training (Figure 9.4).

Trainee management courses

Within the hospitality industry the approach to trainee management courses varies considerably. In some cases they will consist of job rotation through a variety of jobs for a sometimes indeterminate period of time, the length of time in each department being more dependent upon business needs than upon those of the trainee. In other cases programmes will be individually designed, taking into account previous experience such as industrial release, and the trainees' progress will be carefully monitored by the managers responsible for them.

As the first step in a young manager's career, the design of trainee managers' courses is critical. It is in the first months that the basis of knowledge and skills and, in particular, an understanding of the employer's policies, attitudes and values will be formed. During this period, however, unless worthwhile targets are set and some experience of supervision is obtained, most trainees will feel frustrated. For this reason there are many critics and opponents of the traditional 'Cook's tour' involving spells of training in the most important departments. In some cases this criticism is well deserved because no objectives are laid down and the trainees are merely used as cheap labour, or not used at all.

However, in order to be a successful manager, knowledge and experience of certain departments are vital and the well-designed 'Cook's tour' serves this purpose; at the same time objectives must be agreed with departmental supervisors, and trainees should be given their training objectives preferably in written form. They should not move from one department to the next until departmental training objectives have been attained. Trainees should maintain training logs or diaries and, in addition, they may be given projects. Regular progress interviews should be held to ensure that the trainees' objectives are being achieved.

In considering an individual's development programme, which is updated and modified year by year, it is vital to examine both strengths and weaknesses, remembering that they may well be strengths and weaknesses only so far as the employer is concerned. In another type of organization the same characteristics may be seen in a completely different light. Ideally the weaknesses should be corrected and the strengths built upon. However, this will not always be possible, because some 'weaknesses' may not be merely lack of knowledge or skill but rather may be of a personality or attitudinal nature and these are often very difficult to correct even if it were in the individual's interest to do so. For example, a highly creative person may prefer to work as an individual. He or she may not enjoy or wish to work with others, nor to control them. The 'weakness', so far as the employer is concerned, is that he or she cannot direct or lead others, so the employer decides to give the individual 'a spell managing others' to make him or her into an all-rounder. In some cases this may work out, but in others it could have disastrous results, with the person concerned eventually leaving. Equally damaging, the individual could unsettle subordinates whom, it must be remembered, he or she may not have wanted to control in the first place. As Robert Craven writes, 'we often attempt to play at Pygmalion. We select individuals, whom we believe to have the talent and potential, and we try to make them into something which they are not (or at least not yet).'

A major research report conducted by the Council For Hospitality Management Education (CHME), *Getting ahead: Graduate careers in hospitality management* (2001), revealed interesting features regarding the growing demand for hospitality qualifications within the sample of leading firms across all sectors of the hospitality industry. Key findings included a confirmation of the importance of qualifications for career development to senior managerial roles; the developing need for management qualifications and competencies at unit manager level; the linking of in-house development to externally awarded qualifications; and the preference of the major companies for hospitality graduates because of their industry understanding and enthusiastic commitment to the sector.

The future of management development

Until recently management development in Britain was a largely uncoordinated set of dispersed activities which depended upon initiatives coming from individuals or employers or education and training institutions. The Management Charter

Initiative and other related activities are an attempt to bring some order into the present situation. They are based upon certain key principles:

1 Open access, enabling many more to benefit from management education.
2 Flexible and innovative forms of education, including distance learning and in-house projects.
3 Corporate and individual development plans.
4 A shift towards work-based assessments rather than end-of-course exams.
5 Credit accumulation which may also recognize learning acquired through experience.

In the hospitality sector, there are the professional qualifications of the HCIMA and its Advanced Certificate course, as well as a range of HCIMA-accredited programmes at universities and colleges throughout the UK, from higher national diplomas and foundation degrees to BA undergraduate and Masters level postgraduate courses. Human resource management qualifications and CPD in HRM are guided by the CIPD, and an increasingly professional HRM function within hospitality companies is leading many individuals to seek CIPD membership and professional status. The HCIMA website (accessed November 2004) includes a section on CPD, the basic principles seen as a means to

• update knowledge and skills on existing and new areas of practice
• keep professional qualifications up to date
• raise profile through certification and networking, thus increasing employability
• gaining recognition for informal CPD activities
• increasing competence in a wider context
• demonstrating commitment to the profession and feel empowered.

In the hospitality industry, in most cases, management development will remain the personal responsibility of individual managers. A number of employers, particularly the larger ones, are now offering a comprehensive range of management development options ranging right up to the MBA. The industry, however, consists, in the main, of small privately owned enterprises, and their perceptions and financial resources are likely to limit the extent to which they fund the development of their management, irrespective of the need to do so.

Further Reading and References

Armstrong, M. (1999) *A Handbook of Human Resource Management*, 7th edn, London: Kogan Page.

Chartered Institute of Personnel and Development (1999) *The IPD Guide to International Recruitment, Selection and Assessment*, London: CIPD Publications.

Council For Hospitality Management Education (2001) *Getting Ahead: Graduate Careers in Hospitality Management*, London: CHME/HEFCE Publications.

Lees, S. (1992) Ten faces of management development, in *Management Education and Development*, Vol. 23, No. 2, 89–105.

Mabey, C. and Salaman, G. (1995) *Strategic Human Resource Management*, Oxford: Blackwell.

McGunnigle, P. and Jameson, S. (2000) HRM in UK hotels: A focus on commitment, in *Employee Relations*, Vol. 22, No. 4, 403–422.

Torrington, D., Hall, L. and Taylor, S. (2002) *Human Resource Management*, 5th edn, Harlow: Pearson Education.

Questions

1 Describe the objectives of management development and the various steps or phases that you would normally expect to find in the operation of an effective management development programme.

2 Discuss which you consider to be the most important steps in management development and why.

3 Discuss what changes are likely to be made in the future to improve management development procedures.

4 Discuss the relationship between management development and approaches to management, such as management by objectives (see Chapter 3).

5 Evaluate the approach to management development used by an employer you know well.

PART 4

Rewards and Remuneration

Job evaluation

The following four chapters look at the major management tools used to develop and administer reward systems. These are concerned with two absolute essentials in reward systems: external competitiveness and internal equity or fairness.

One of the major causes of friction between employers and their employees, between individual employees and between groups of employees is a real or perceived lack of fairness in the distribution of wages. For many years British industry was bedevilled with industrial strife caused by 'pay differentials'. Today we have two extreme approaches to the determination of wages. At one extreme we have total transparency in which every employee can know what everyone else earns, e.g. in many public sector organizations. At the other extreme are employers who not only keep secret what they pay each employee but also make it a condition of employment that salaries are not to be discussed between staff.

If dissatisfaction is to be avoided, or if equal pay for work of equal value disputes are to be avoided, a methodical, fair and transparent approach to the award of wages and salaries is essential for harmonious relationships to exist at all levels within an enterprise. In organizations of any reasonable size, this can probably be achieved only if the relative value of each job is recognized; to do this, a system of ranking jobs in order of importance needs to be used. It is important that a person, such as a chef, who has completed a relatively long and formal training and has acquired knowledge and skill should be paid more highly than a person whose job needs little knowledge or skill. It is simple to distinguish between jobs with skill and those without, but the problem arises when comparing jobs that are less easily differentiated; for example, when comparing those of a cook and a waiter. Both demand particular skills and knowledge but management has to decide whether to award more, and how much, to one than to the other. A system of comparison which embraces all jobs within an enterprise needs to be adopted to ensure that wages are distributed fairly. Such a system, usually called 'job evaluation', provides a sound basis for comparisons to be made. Some systems attempt to be objective and analytical, whereas others are somewhat subjective, but if managed properly they can be equally successful. Job evaluation may, therefore, be defined as the process that establishes the relative value of jobs in a job hierarchy.

Not all employers are in favour of job evaluation. One criticism is that it evaluates a job rather than the person's contribution to the employer. This criticism can be met, however, through merit awards in a well-designed salary structure. Figure 10.1 gives some reasons for the use of job evaluation.

	Existing schemes	New schemes
Fair pay	54%	49%
Company pay	16%	11%
Performance pay	9%	16%
Pressure	7%	–
Management information	6%	16%
Explain job Relatives	5%	6%
Other	3%	2%

Figure 10.1 Reasons for using job evaluation
Source: Personnel Management, January 1990.

The Institute of Personnel and Development (now the CIPD) together with The Advisory, Conciliation and Arbitration Service (ACAS) in 1996 reported that job evaluation was on the increase. Three reasons are behind this growth: legal issues of equal pay for work of equal value, the simplification of pay structures through the growth of flatter organizations, and the introduction of competency-based approaches to reward systems.

An earlier survey conducted jointly by the IPM and the Wyatt Company found that the following symptoms can indicate a need for methodical job evaluation:

1 Employees leaving because wages are not awarded fairly and, in particular, because some newcomers earn more than long-serving employees.
2 No formal periodic review of wages or salaries.

3 Difficulties, due to wage levels, in transferring and promoting employees.
4 A need to pay extras or bonuses to get people to do what is, or should be, part of their normal job.
5 Some employees working excessive overtime.

In order to carry out effective job evaluation, precise job descriptions and even job specifications are required because without these the comparison of jobs becomes difficult, if not meaningless. Also, because comparisons of jobs are to be made, the preparation of job descriptions must be standardized throughout the undertaking, and the actual evaluation should be conducted by one specialist or the smallest possible number of people to ensure a consistent result.

As Figure 10.2 shows, there are many different job evaluation techniques. The first type – the non-analytical – considers the whole job when jobs are being compared.

Title	Broad description	Advantages	Disadvantages
Non-analytical methods			
Ranking	A simple method whereby the relative importance of the total job is assessed. Jobs are put in order of importance and may then be divided into groups.	Very simple to use.	Assessors need to know all jobs in some depth.
Grading or classification	A simple method in which a grading structure indicating relative job values is designed. Each job is then placed within the most appropriate grade.	Very simple to use.	Assessors need to know all jobs in some depth. Marginal jobs may be placed in higher or lower grade because system may not be sufficiently discriminating.
Analytical methods			
Points assessment	A commonly used and very acceptable method. Factors common to most jobs in the organization are identified such as knowledge and responsibility. Maximum points are allocated to each factor weighted according to importance. Each job examined is broken into the various factors. Each factor is then awarded points between zero and the maximum. The total of points awarded will give the score for the job and thereby its standing relative to other jobs. Benchmark jobs will be used to assist in allocating points.	Simple to understand and operate.	Takes longer to implement than ranking or grading. It can lead to considerable discussion on weighting of factors.
Factor comparison	Similar in some respects to points assessment but in some cases monetary values are used instead of points. Fewer factors, also, will normally be used than in points assessment. Benchmark jobs will normally be used.	Simple to operate once it has been designed.	Difficult to arrive at monetary values.

Figure 10.2 Job evaluation

Title	Broad description	Advantages	Disadvantages
Direct consensus method or paired comparisons	A complex technique where evaluators representing all interested parties are asked to indicate which job of a pair or which factors within pairs of jobs they consider more important. The evaluators will probably deal with several or even many jobs. The paired comparisons of all evaluators may then be fed into a computer which will produce the ranking of all jobs considered.	Reduces individual subjectivity to a minimum.	Complex, usually needs a computer.
Time span of discretion	This technique measures one factor only: the length of time in which an individual's work or decisions remain unchecked, e.g. a typist four hours, a managing director four years.	Simple, once the concept has been fully understood.	Sometimes difficult to determine true discretion span.

Figure 10.2 *continued*

For ranking, jobs are placed in order of importance. They may then be placed in clusters of closely ranked jobs.

For grading or classification, a number of grades will have been decided upon. A typical job illustrating the grade will be chosen, known as a 'benchmark' job. All other jobs are then placed into the most appropriate grades using the benchmark job for guidance. Figure 10.3 shows a typical approach – the system devised by the Institute of Administrative Management – and demonstrates its application to jobs in the hotel and catering industry.

The other approach consists of analytical methods. Most of these involve some form of point scoring of job elements or factors such as level of responsibility (e.g. sales volumes or number of staff managed) or competencies such as technical skills needed.

Points assessment

This method allocates points for each factor of a job. The points for all factors are added up and the total indicates the job's relative position in the job hierarchy.

The type of factors evaluated in each job may include the following:

Knowledge – This may be simple knowledge acquired in a few days or, at the other extreme, may be knowledge acquired by several years of study and application.

Skills – This refers mainly to manual skills. These may be acquired within a very short period, such as the skills needed to operate a limited range of equipment, or they may take many weeks, even months of practice, as in the case of keyboard skills or the varied skills needed by a competent cook.

Grade	Definition	Example
A	Simple tasks requiring little training; closely supervised or controlled through self-checking	Cleaner
B	Simple jobs that consist of standard routines and require a short period of training	Room attendant
C	Some experience or aptitude needed; standardized duties; little room for initiative	Assistant waiter Clerk
D	Considerable experience; limited degree of initiative but mostly within predetermined procedures	Receptionist
E	Technical or specialist knowledge or both; Supervision of up to five other workers	Head waiter Head hallporter
F	Technical or professional operations at intermediate membership level of a professional institute; performance or control of complex work; supervision requiring leadership skills and training of others	F & B manager Bars manager
M1	Professional or specialized knowledge up to professional institute membership level; performance or control of work of wide complexity; management of sufficient staff to need grade F subordinates as supervisors	Hotel manager
M2	Jobs requiring the final qualification of a professional institute or university degree; regular non-routine decision making; use of judgement and initiative; assistance in policy making; management of specialist functions involving more than one level of supervision	Group human resource manager
M3	Jobs requiring the final qualification of a professional institute or university degree plus several years' experience of wide-ranging authority; performance or control of work over several functions, demanding general as well as specialist expertise and policy making at the highest level; management of a series of specialist functions where management level jobs report in for guidance, control and monitoring	Group chief executive

Acknowledgement to Institute of Administrative Management.

Figure 10.3 A job grading or classification system (based on the Institute of Administrative Management grading scheme)

Responsibility – This may be of the type in which a person makes important decisions that are not checked for a long period; alternatively they may be simple decisions that are checked immediately. This factor may include responsibility for people, equipment or cash.

Physical demands – Some jobs, such as cooking, are physically demanding, or they may make little physical demand, as in book-keeping or typing.

Mental demands – All jobs, to a greater or lesser extent, make demands on a person's mental abilities including the abilities to concentrate and to apply oneself; for example, a senior receptionist's job will be much more demanding mentally than a porter's.

Social skills – Some jobs require more social skills than others. A restaurant manager, for example, will require a high degree of tact and patience, whereas a chef may require little or no social skill.

Working conditions – This includes physical and social inconveniences such as heat, long hours and whether one sits or stands while working. This may also take into account hazards such as risk of burns, cuts or even physical violence.

These seven examples give a broad indication of the types of factors considered. Others may be used and, in addition, a breakdown into subfactors may also be desirable.

The normal method of awarding points for each factor is to have a scale with benchmark jobs on it. When evaluating a particular factor of a job it will be placed at or between what appears to be the most appropriate benchmark job or jobs; i.e. in evaluating one factor, such as knowledge, the list of benchmark jobs is examined and the job being evaluated is then placed in the most appropriate position on the scale (Figure 10.4).

Points	Benchmark jobs for knowledge: maximum points – 30; minimum points – 0
30	Hotel manager
24	Front office manager
18	Restaurant manager
12	Station waiter
6	Hall porter

Figure 10.4 Example of benchmark jobs (for one factor only)

The knowledge required of a head waiter, for example, would fall between the station waiter and the restaurant manager in Figure 10.4, consequently being awarded about 15 points. The same procedure would then be adopted for all other factors to be evaluated. The benchmark jobs will not necessarily be the same for each factor. After this has been done for all factors, the points are totalled and the job grade should be determined by reference to a grade table such as that shown in Figure 10.5.

Grade	Points (Total of all factors)	Example of job
7	121–140	Chef de cuisine
6	101–120	Restaurant manager
5	81–100	Senior receptionist
4	61–80	Waiter
3	41–60	Clerk
2	21–40	Hall porter
1	0–20	Kitchen porter

Figure 10.5 Example of a grade table

Figure 10.6 shows the technique applied to two jobs: a restaurant manager's and a commis waiter's. In this example the factors outlined above are used but in designing a scheme entirely other factors may be considered. After the points have been totalled, a look at a grade table will indicate the grades of the two jobs – refer back to Figure 10.5. The commis waiter's job, therefore, is Grade 3 and the restaurant manager's is Grade 6.

Factor	Maximum points	Example evaluation of two jobs	
		Commis waiter	Restaurant manager
Knowledge	30	5	18
Skill	20	10	20
Responsibility	30	3	24
Physical demands	10	5	4
Mental demands	20	8	15
Social skills	20	12	18
Working conditions	10	5	3
Total	140	48	102

Figure 10.6 Example of a points assessment system showing the evaluation of two jobs

This is a very simplified example of a points assessment system. Some systems may be much more complex than this, but no matter which technique is used, the principles of job evaluation are as follows:

1 Job descriptions must be precise and up to date.
2 Because wages and salaries depend on the results, evaluation must be scrupulously fair and consistent.
3 It is the job, not the jobholder, that is being evaluated.

People at work tend to measure the value their employer places upon them by reference, among other things, to how much they are paid, relative both to their own colleagues and to the outside market. If they perceive their level of pay (and other conditions) as inferior to that of their colleagues and of similar workers elsewhere, the relationship with the employer may well be affected adversely. This could take a number of forms, including absenteeism, pilferage, theft and even vandalism.

Arriving at a fair system for awarding wages and salaries is not easy and too often is a matter of expediency. Ian Kessler (1995) writes, 'pay systems have been used in an ad hoc manner to address specific managerial problems or goals'. The hospitality industry is no exception. Too often in the hospitality industry, wages and salaries are the result of expediency rather than methodical planning and application. It is vital, however, to recognize the relative importance of each job and to remove any potential causes of dissatisfaction. In order to do this it is vital, therefore, to adopt a methodical system of evaluating jobs so that wages and salaries are fairly distributed to all.

Having said this, the IPM–Wyatt (Spencer, 1989) survey found less than full satisfaction with job evaluation among those employers using the process. They found

1 the process is time consuming and inefficient, and demanding of resources
2 it is difficult to ensure high quality results
3 the centralized process runs counter to the current trend in employee relations, i.e. it tends to be unitarist rather than pluralist in approach.

For these reasons some employers have dropped job evaluation in favour of market pricing or competency awards.

Job evaluation in the hospitality industry

Job evaluation is commonplace in the public sector of the hospitality industry. Many jobs are evaluated using one or other of the job evaluation methods. It is also used by a number of larger operators, who use companies such as Hay-MSL (a specialist management consultancy) to determine pay rates and scales for their managers. Otherwise job evaluation is not very common, owing to the large number of small employers. Instead wage levels are frequently determined by expediency rather than by a methodical approach.

Further Reading and References

Armstrong, M. (1999) *A Handbook of Human Resource Management*, 7th edn, London: Kogan Page.

Armstrong, M. and Baron, A. (1995) *The Job Evaluation Handbook*, London: IPD.

Armstrong, M. and Brown, D. (2000) *Paying for Contribution*, London: Kogan Page.

Beardwell, I., Holden, L. and Claydon, T. (2004) *Human Resource Management—A Contemporary Approach*, 4th edn, Harlow: Prentice Hall.

Kessler, I. (1995) Reward Systems, in Storey, J. (ed.) *Human Resource Management*, London: Routledge.

Lucas, R. (2004) *Employment Relations in the Hospitality and Tourism Industries*, London: Routledge.

Matthewson, J. (1995) *Flexible Grading Systems*, Croner's Pay and Benefits Briefing No. 87, Kingston-upon-Thames, Surrey: Croner Publications.

Spencer, S. (1989) Devolving job evaluation, *Personnel Management*, London: January.

Storey, J. (ed.) (1995) *Human Resource Management*, London: Routledge.

Questions

1 Describe the objectives of job evaluation and the alternative approaches to implementing it.

2 Discuss what you consider to be the most important elements in job evaluation and why.

3 Discuss in which sectors of the hotel and catering industry job evaluation is most likely to be found and why.

4 Evaluate the approach to job evaluation used by an employer you know well.

Administration of wages and salaries

Wages and salaries in the UK hospitality industry have long been a focus of criticism of the industry as an employer.

One of the problems for the hospitality industry and its pay levels is that, relatively speaking, each employee does not generate large sums of revenue for the employer. In hotels, for example, a Plimsoll analysis (*Hospitality*, February 1998) showed that hotel and restaurant staff on average generated around £50,000 per annum per employee. Using BHA figures the actual figure in 2004 was around £36,000 including part-timers (*Trends and Statistics 2004*, BHA, 2004). From this the employer has to pay all costs, including materials, labour, debt financing and tax. Such levels of sales per employee do not leave much room for significant increases, particularly when compared to other industries where each employee may generate hundreds of thousands of pounds each year.

Many organizations have wage and salary systems that have evolved over time and which in many cases have not really addressed the crucial task of matching an organization's goals closely to its reward systems. This is particularly so in the hospitality industry, where the majority of enterprises tend to be small and where there is a lack of professional management expertise. In order to be effective, a remuneration policy and its dependent package needs to be aimed at achieving the owner's overall business objectives. For example, if an owner's business policy focuses on quality, the rewards system must not conflict with that policy by focusing staff effort on other objectives such as sales volumes per se. From the human resource policy perspective, if an employer's policy is to encourage long service and career development among most of its employees, the employer may offer an incremental payment system that rewards long service in itself. If the employer chooses to recruit from a volatile, young and relatively cheap labour market, it will probably offer low rates of pay with little room for significant increases. Some employers will mix their policies, encouraging managers to make careers with them whilst not encouraging long-serving operative staff. Obviously, wage payment is a highly charged subject and in the hospitality industry it is a very contentious one owing to a variety of complications. Apart from the lack of method in setting basic rates, in some sectors other factors such as tipping, service charges and the provision of meals and living accommodation all have to be taken into consideration. Within a single establishment it is quite possible to find a complex range of permutations of all the various benefits received by employees. Some live in and earn tips, some live out and do not earn tips; some are provided with meals and some are not. In addition, in the largest organizations, some subsidiaries encourage tipping, whereas others do everything to eliminate it and also levy service charges. This may be even further complicated by some executives being provided with company cars and other benefits. On closer examination, however, it may well be found that these same executives are worse off (in cash and kind) than their own residential managers.

In the contract catering field the problems can be exacerbated by other factors. The client's employees, for example, may enjoy extremely high rewards (e.g. in the City of London) which make the catering staffs' rewards look very insignificant.

Mars, Mitchell and Bryant (1979) claim the payment system in hotels has particular problems because it consists of

- basic pay and subsidized lodging and subsidized food
- tips and service charges (where applicable) and fiddles and 'knock-offs'.

Although Mars and Mitchell wrote this 25 years ago, regular surveys among returning industrial release students indicate that little has changed in this respect. Mars and Mitchell attached particular importance to the fiddles element because of the power it provides to management. They suggest that management lays down parameters within which fiddles are acceptable, but at the same time if someone displeases them for other reasons they can dismiss the person for fiddling. Undoubtedly, whether fiddling is institutionalized or not, it is a major source of income to employees, and causes headaches to the industry's employers.

Types of employees

Within the hospitality industry, irrespective of any legal definitions (see Chapter 16), there are four main types of employee. From a payment or earnings point of view these are

Salaried employees: usually paid monthly by cheque or credit transfer and usually consisting of managers and senior supervisors.

Full-time employees: usually working around 30–45 hours a week and who know from week to week that they have guaranteed work; paid usually weekly in cash.

Part-timers: usually working fewer hours than a full-timer and who generally know from week to week that they have guaranteed work. Usually paid by the hour. As a result of the EU decisions most part-timers qualify, pro rata, for the same fringe benefits, such as holidays, as the full-time members of staff.

Casuals: normally working on a session-by-session basis (e.g. one evening) with no guarantees about future work. Usually paid by the session in cash.

Most pay systems are based on two principles: to reward for time or for performance. In the first case, obviously, there is also an element of performance – one is not paid indefinitely for time if the performance is not satisfactory. In the second case, however, payment for performance, there are a number of questions that have to be addressed, e.g. is it the individual's, the group's or the enterprise's performance that is rewarded, or is it the inputs or the outputs that are rewarded? In some cases performance-related schemes have been introduced in order to strengthen the employer–employee link at the expense of the trade-union–member link.

Formal wages administration

In the hospitality industry a major responsibility of owners and their managers is to decide how to distribute fairly among all employees the money set aside for payment of staff. This may range from as little as 10% of revenue in some efficient public houses to over 40% in top-class hotels. This money may derive from normal revenue or may also come from retained service charges. Managers may decide by looking at what competitors are paying, what has been historically the employer's practice and, in many cases, what is necessary to overcome a current crisis. The result is that considerable anomalies exist in many hotels, catering establishments and, indeed, whole firms. As mentioned in the last chapter, newcomers may be paid more than similar staff with long service and more-senior staff may earn less than some juniors.

The exact policy to be adopted by an employer with regard to wage and salary systems will depend to a great extent upon the business objectives, human resource policies and style of management; for example, in organizations where labour turnover is not considered to be important, there may be little method or formality in setting rates of pay. In other organizations, however, where it is recognized that a stable labour force is a valuable asset, much more method will be applied to wage and salary matters. This is typically so in the public sector, where for many years employers set out to be exemplary.

Where there are many employees with differing levels of skills, fair salary administration may depend upon job evaluation, which measures the relative importance to the organization of different jobs. But after jobs have been evaluated, rates will have to be set for each grade to ensure that there are realistic differentials between grades so that more senior jobs and promotions are rewarded by worthwhile differences in earnings; promotion then becomes something to aim for. This is illustrated in Figure 11.1.

Grade	Basic wage (£ week)
1	200
2	220
3	240
4	265

Figure 11.1 Example of a grade and wage table

Determining the rate for each job or for key jobs depends on many factors, including the make-up of the workforce, statutory requirements, competitors' rates of pay, other industries' rates of pay, cost of living and the location of the employer. Because of this, in order to establish or to maintain competitive rates of pay, it will be necessary to study advertisements in the press and to keep in touch with staff agencies, the local Job Centres and the local associations of hoteliers and caterers. In making decisions as a result of this research, it is vital to ensure that all factors affecting rates of pay are taken into account, such as tips and service charges, actual hours worked and the provision or otherwise of meals and accommodation. Some employers with units in different regions may, in addition, require different rates or even entirely different structures for each branch or region.

Increments – merit and service

In some situations, in order to encourage good performance and long service, it may be appropriate to provide merit and service increments and where this is done there will normally be overlaps between grades, enabling someone in a low grade, but with long service or high merit, to earn more than someone in a high grade with short service. This recognizes that a person's competence and value to an organization may increase with service, and because of this the increment is granted both as an increased share of the employee's overall contribution and to encourage them to stay. Figure 11.2 shows a scale for such a scheme.

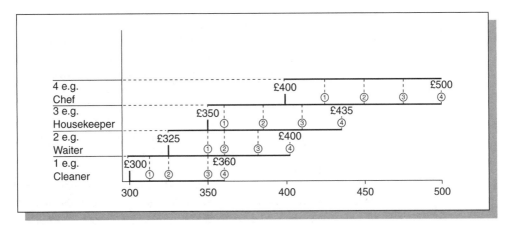

Figure 11.2 Example of an incremental pay scale

In the example shown in Figure 11.2 an employee could anticipate, with satisfactory service, to move from the minimum to the maximum in a period of about four years, giving an average annual increase of about 6–7%. The exact rate might be determined by performance appraisals and by the employer's financial policy. The advantage of this system, if publicized, is that employees know what they can expect to earn by gaining promotion or by staying with an employer. In addition, some employers have age-related scales or rates of pay, usually for employees up to about 21 years of age. Increases in these cases would normally be granted on each employee's birthday.

In some cases starting wages or salaries offered to newcomers may not normally be more than 20% above the minimum and this would only be permitted where appropriate experience in the type of job justifies it. Some trade unionists are opposed to incremental scales, saying that every job should have a set rate and that age and service are irrelevant if the job is performed satisfactorily. Furthermore, they claim that such systems can have an adverse effect on staff turnover because management, in order to keep payroll costs down, will encourage labour turnover, thus retaining a high proportion of employees at the lower end of the scales.

Reviews should take place regularly and should fit into the employer's budgetary and financial cycle. In seasonal establishments reviews may take place towards the end of the season in order to retain those employees management wants to keep.

Apart from increases for merit, service and promotion, some systems also allow for cost-of-living increases to be made from time to time. These will probably be related to government data such as the retail price index, but where such increases are granted it is important to bear in mind that they have little positive motivational effect – unlike a promotion or merit award. That is because they are usually granted to all employees without discriminating between the good and the not so good. On the other hand it is important to keep in mind that the absence of cost-of-living increases may have a negative effect – i.e. the employees' relative level of earnings may fall and force them to seek employment elsewhere. It can be said that although cost-of-living awards have little positive motivational effect, their absence may have a negative effect such as a higher labour turnover.

In the last twenty years, changes in approach, from salary administration to reward management, have been observed. More and more senior executives are trying to turn their employees into entrepreneurs – people who earn a direct return on the value they help create. 'The shift towards contribution-based pay makes sense on grounds of equity, cost, productivity and enterprise.' Such changes to salary systems have continued since Kanter was writing in 1989, encouraged by various changes such as delayering, restructuring, the competitive environment and changes to taxation.

As Ian Kessler (1995: 255) writes, 'the search for the perfect pay system has assumed something akin to the search for the holy grail and has been reflected in pay fads, fashions or cycles'. In spite of this comment, which suggests that the perfect system has yet to be developed, most experienced managers would probably support the view that once a systemized salary system is operational the whole question of pay issues such as differentials or 'equal pay' becomes easier to manage effectively.

Further Reading and References

Armstrong, M. (1999) *A Handbook of Human Resource Management*, 7th edn, London: Kogan Page.

Armstrong, M. and Brown, D. (2000) *Paying for Contribution*, London: Kogan Page.

Armstrong, M. and Murlis, H. (1991) *Reward Management: A Handbook of Salary Administration*, 2nd edn, London: Kogan Page.

Beardwell, I., Holden, L. and Claydon, T. (2004) *Human Resource Management—A Contemporary Approach*, 4th edn, Harlow: Prentice Hall.

British Hospitality Association, *Trends and Statistics 2004*, BHA 2004.

Cole, G. A. (1997) *Personnel Management—Theory and Practice*, 4th edn, London: Letts.

Kanter, R. M. (1989) *When Giants Learn to Dance*, London: Simon and Schuster.

Kaye, M. (1995) *Employee Motivation and Effective Rewards*, Croner's Pay and Benefits Briefing No. 77, London: Croner Publications.

Kessler, I. (1995) Reward systems, in Storey, J. (ed.) *Human Resource Management*, London: Routledge.

Kessler, I. (2001) Reward system choices, in Storey, J. (ed.) *Human Resource Management—A Critical Text*, 2nd edn, London: Thomson Learning.

Mars, G., Mitchell, P. and Bryant, D. (1979) *Manpower Problems in the Hotel and Catering Industry*, Farnborough: Saxon House.

Torrington, D., Hall, L. and Taylor, S. (2002) *Human Resource Management*, 5th edn, Harlow: Pearson Education.

Tyson, S. and York, A. (2000) *Essentials of HRM*, 4th edn, Oxford: Butterworth-Heinemann.

Questions

1 Describe the objectives of a systematic wage and salary administration system.

2 Discuss in which sectors of the hotel and catering industry systematic wage and salary administration is least likely and most likely to be found and why.

3 Discuss what you consider to be the most likely consequences of a lack of systematic wage and salary administration and why.

4 Discuss what changes are likely to be made in the future to improve wage and salary administration procedures.

5 Discuss the relationship between salary administration and performance appraisal (see Chapter 7).

6 Evaluate the approach to wage and salary administration used by an employer you know well.

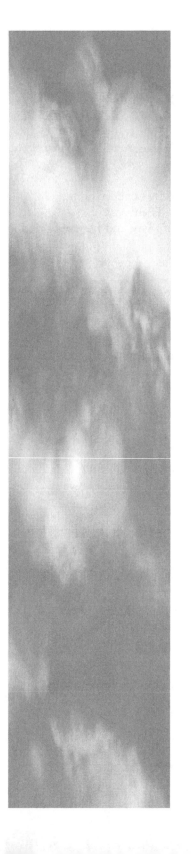

C H A P T E R

12

Incentives

Competition among employers to attract and motivate effective employees, and other factors such as the nature of the taxation system have obliged employers over the years to seek ways and means of making the total remuneration package more attractive to employees. In some cases benefits, such as free health care insurance and airmiles are offered, often because other competitors do so. In other cases, incentives are offered in order to focus the employee's attention on the business objectives of the employer, e.g. to support a yield management system or to increase the number of contracts run by a contract caterer.

What motivates?

In Chapter 2 the contributions of a number of different theorists were considered. Most of these are crucially concerned with what motivates people to work. In spite of the vast body of knowledge coming from people like Taylor, Mayo, McGregor, Maslow and Herzberg, there is still no consensus. Many managers still hold to the belief that money, because of what it can buy (including security and status), is a major motivator. Others tend to the more complex views of Maslow and Herzberg, arguing that people work for a composite package, including money, security, self-esteem, esteem of others, job satisfaction, etc. At a practical level this discussion obviously concerns the merits or otherwise of reward systems and incentive schemes. Some people argue that employees should be given an adequate wage or salary and that so long as other conditions and prospects are adequate, such as regular review of earnings and the likelihood of promotion, people will give what they consider to be a fair day's work. The prospect of incentives will not spur them to continued greater efforts. It is also argued, on the other hand, that incentive payments are most effective when people are dependent upon them, i.e. the nearer the basic pay is to subsistence levels, the more effective an incentive scheme.

In works of a highly creative nature the prospect of incentive payments is considered unlikely to stimulate greater creativity. There are others, however, who argue that incentives will certainly influence productivity, saying, for example, that in a selling situation the prospects of earning commission will definitely stimulate greater selling effort. It is also argued that because of the growing interdependence of working people they can no longer increase their own earnings without the involvement of their colleagues. In many cases nowadays this is true, and this is recognized in various schemes that reward teams as opposed to individuals.

In the hospitality industry, because of its nature, there are many opportunities for individuals to increase their earnings considerably – particularly in the selling areas, such as waiting, bar work, hotel reception and function catering. Within the scope of this book it is not possible to consider further the arguments for and against incentive schemes. There are unfortunately innumerable examples supporting both viewpoints. It is intended here to look at the main forms of incentives operated in the hospitality industry, including tips, the 'tronc', service charges, bonuses and commissions. Other financial incentives such as profit sharing are considered in the next chapter.

In other industries other forms of incentive payments are used. These include methods such as payment by results (PBR), piece rates or measured day work, which are usually based on work measurement techniques, whereas those commonly used in the hospitality industry are more normally related to financial targets such as gross profits, turnover and variable costs (e.g. gas, electricity). In some cases they may be entirely discretionary.

Although tipping and the tronc were mentioned along with other forms of financial incentive, it is probably better to think of them as part of normal earnings. Financial incentives are normally intended to stimulate and promote extra productivity, whereas tips, the tronc and service charges are considered by many employees as a matter of right and something without which they could not have a reasonable living standard.

Tipping is a form of payment that originated when many workers in the old inns were not employed by the innkeeper but were retained by guests to do particular jobs such as carrying bags, cleaning garments, etc. Many consider it an anachronism in this day and age, and a view that has been expressed by many people for many years is that it needs to be eliminated as rapidly as possible. Professor Nailon of Surrey University, however, wrote in 1978 that it is not necessarily a bad practice but that it may have profound effects on interdepartmental relationships. Also it removes from management an important area of personal control by making the customer, rather than the employer, the paymaster (Nailon, 1978).

Service charges, many argue, on the other hand, are quite acceptable methods for an undertaking to use to raise revenue, so long as the sum allowed for distribution to the workforce is distributed on a fair basis. In many tourism-based economies it is common to find that tariffs are inclusive of taxes and service charges, and tipping is being eliminated, although in some countries where service charges are included staff still expect some tip, if not the traditional 10–15%. Sometimes where a service charge is included in the bill, tipping may be discouraged, and notices on bills, menus, brochures and in guest rooms discourage guests from giving tips in addition to paying the service charge.

Principles of incentive schemes

In designing an incentive scheme, whether for the hospitality industry or any other, there are several principles that should be adhered to for it to be effective in the long term:

1 Take into account cultural differences – some forms of incentives just do not work in some cultures.
2 The undertaking's major business objectives should be promoted and their achievement assisted by incentive payments. These payments should enable individuals to identify with the success of the undertaking; for example, if food gross profit is vital, the chef and maybe his staff as well should be rewarded for achieving gross profit targets. But only elements over which a person exerts control should be included. A chef, for example, has no control over the rent and the rates, so there is no point in including these in a scheme for the chef.
3 When an incentive scheme is to be introduced, all workers should be considered because of the effect the scheme may have on existing earnings differentials and the possibility of creating friction between staff.
4 Payments should be related to results by comparing actual performance with forecasts, targets, standards or budgets. This may be done individually or on a group basis.
5 Targets should be realistic, i.e. achievable with reasonable effort and agreed with the person or group concerned.
6 Targets should be reviewed regularly, and at least annually, so that payments are something to be earned with effort rather than something that becomes a matter of right. They should also be reviewed if circumstances change considerably; for example, if a vast new office block opens next door to a snack bar, trade will probably increase greatly, through no effort of the manager. The turnover and other targets should, therefore, be reviewed at the same time, bearing in mind that extra work will be created and that wages and salaries may have to be increased.
7 An incentive scheme should be simple and clearly understood by those within the scheme.
8 Payment of the incentive should be made as near as possible to the period in which it was earned. Long delays in payment cause irritation and reduce the incentive element.
9 All elements of a scheme and any rules should be objective. Management should not incorporate discretionary rules such as 'management reserves the right to withhold payment without giving a reason'. Incentives, if earned, should be a matter of right, not for management to dispense on a discretionary basis, and the terms of the incentive scheme should become part of the contract of employment.

1 *Job*   Chef

2 *Commission*   1 per cent of all 'gross profit' (for this purpose revenue less purchases and labour costs) in excess of £2000 per week, after achieving the following targets

3 *Targets*   1 Purchases not to exceed 45 per cent of revenue
                     2 Kitchen labour not to exceed 15 per cent of revenue

4 *Example of calculation*
  Period 7

Food cost	£6000	(37.5%)	Revenue	£16000
Labour cost	£2200	(13.75%)		
	£8200			
'Gross profit'	£7800	(48.75%)		

Gross profit £7800 − £2000 = £5800 × $\frac{1}{100}$ = £58.00

Commission to be £58.00

Figure 12.1 Example of an individual incentive scheme (chef)

Incentives are normally used to stimulate performance and particularly to increase sales and control costs. Figures 12.1–12.3 are included as examples. Having looked at these examples, which are intended to illustrate principles only and which demonstrate that incentive schemes can be designed for many departments in an organization, it is vital to bear in mind that their introduction may have undesirable consequences which could exclude their being used; e.g., the chef may well place commission above customer satisfaction and buy cheap materials or keep labour costs too low for efficient service; the receptionists may overbook (more than is desirable) and consequently lose customers for the future. On the

1 *Department*   Front Office

2 *Commission*   £120 for every 1 per cent in excess of occupancy targets, distributed to all front office staff pro rata to salaries

3 *Target*   85 per cent occupancy

4 *Examples of calculation*
  Period 7
Actual occupancy 90.0% therefore 5.0 × £120 = £600 to be distributed

Salaries: Head receptionist	£14,000
2 Senior receptionists @	£13,000
2 Cashier/receptionists @	£10,000
Total salaries	£60,000
£600 commission	
£30,000 salaries =	£0.01 per £ salary

Therefore the following commissions will be paid

Head receptionist*	£14,000 × £0.01 = £140
Senior receptionists*	£13,000 × £0.01 = £130
Cashier/receptionists (part time)	£10,000 × £0.01 = £100

* live in staff

Figure 12.2 Example of a group incentive scheme

1	*Job*	Restaurant manager		
2	*Commission*	5 per cent of net profit up to budget		
		10 per cent of net profit between 101 per cent and 130 per cent of target budget		
		20 per cent of net profit in excess of 130 per cent of target budget		
3	*Target budget*	£40,000 net profit		

4 *Example of calculation*
Year ended 31 December 2005   Actual net profit = £56 000

Commission rate	Qualifying net profit	Commission
5%	£40,000	£2000
10%	£12,000	£1200
20%	£4000	£800
Total	£56,000	£4000

Note: In this example it is interesting to note that although the top rate of commission is 20 per cent and consequently well worth striving for, the actual rate of total commission is only just over 7 per cent.

Figure 12.3 Example of an individual incentive scheme (manager)

other hand, from the restaurant manager's scheme it can be seen that, because the commission is related to net profit, the manager has an interest in successfully controlling all aspects of the business, including turnover, purchases, wages, variables and, of course, customer satisfaction. In designing an incentive scheme, therefore, one has to ensure that the benefits to the individual do not stimulate him or her to take measures that may not be in the employer's interests. Incentives can cover such things as sales, gross and net profits, occupancy, average room rates, suggestion schemes, new staff introduction bonuses and new business introduction bonuses.

Financial incentives can reward individual employees or groups of employees through increased payment for their increased contribution to the enterprise. However, they can achieve little on their own. They should be part of a comprehensive, well-balanced human resource policy that is based upon achieving the employer's main objectives.

Further Reading and References

Armstrong, M. (1999) *A Handbook of Human Resource Management*, 7th edn, London: Kogan Page.

Armstrong, M. and Brown, D. (2000) *Paying for Contribution*, London: Kogan Page.

Goss-Turner, S. (2002) *Managing People in the Hospitality Industry*, 4th edn, Kingston-upon-Thames: Croner Publications.

Kessler, I. (2001) Reward system choices, in Storey, J. (ed.) *Human Resource Management—A Critical Text*, 2nd edn, London: Thomson Learning.

Nailon, P. (1978) *HCIMA Review*, Vol. 2, No. 4, London.

Roots, P. (1989) *Financial Incentives for Employees*, London: BSP Professional Books.

Tyson, S. and York, A. (2000) *Essentials of HRM*, 4th edn, Oxford: Butterworth-Heinemann.

Questions

1 Describe the objectives of incentive schemes and the various alternatives in regular use.

2 Discuss which you consider to be the most important principles if incentive schemes are to be effective. What do you understand by 'effective'?

3 Discuss what external factors influence the nature of incentive schemes.

4 Discuss the relationship between incentive schemes and alternative methods of wage and salary administration.

5 Discuss the role played by wages, salaries and incentives in implementing an employer's human resource policy.

6 Evaluate the approach to incentive schemes used by an employer you know well.

CHAPTER 13

Fringe benefits

The range, variety and importance of fringe benefits in employment policies have grown in recent years, partly because of the nature of personal taxation and partly because of pressure from other sources such as the rapidly increasing competition for employees. Fringe benefit packages have been adopted in order to motivate employees to enhance their performance and to encourage them to maintain and extend their continuity of service with their employer. They include benefits that attract little or no tax, such as meals and holidays, and deferred earnings such as pensions. Fringe benefits have considerable value to many employers in that they represent a form of reward that does not necessarily have progressive or long-term effects in the way that a salary increase does. A salary increase is usually for all time. It affects all future settlements because most settlements are percentage based. Also a salary is the basis for settlements such as redundancy and pension rights whereas many fringe benefits may not have such long-term effects.

The total list of benefits offered today is considerable and is continually growing as employers look for new ways to woo employees. They can be divided into three main types: financial, part-financial and non-financial.

- Financial benefits include commissions, bonuses, profit sharing, share options.
- Part-financial benefits include pensions, meals, cars, subscriptions.
- Non-financial benefits include holidays, sick pay, medical insurance.

See Figure 13.1 for a list of fringe benefits selected from various companies' information.

Staff restaurant, free meals	Company newspaper, staff newspaper
Luncheon vouchers	Discount buying
Living-in accommodation, staff hostel	Discounted holidays
Assistance with finding accommodation	Familiarization weekends
Training and educational fees	Discounted meals in company hotels or restaurants
Use of customers' facilities	Savings schemes, loans, house purchase assistance, relocation grants
Free uniform, laundry services	
Paid holidays in excess of statutory minima	Long service awards
Pension scheme, sickness leave	Christmas bonus, birthday gift/cards
Company car – personal use, fuel for private use	Suggestion bonus, language proficiency, employee introduction bonus
Mobile phone – personal use	
Maternity leave, paternity leave	Jury service pay
Medical services, private medical insurance	Share option scheme
Social and sports clubs, cinema and theatre passes	Volunteer reserve paid time-off.

Figure 13.1 Some fringe benefits offered in the industry
Source: Company induction material.

In considering fringe benefits it is vital to recognize that what may be considered an 'incentive' or 'motivator' today may lose its motivating effect with time. This may be because what is offered by only one or two employers to start with will be offered by many employers as they follow suit. Alternatively, what may have been offered as a reward for exceptional services one year becomes expected and a 'matter of right' within the next two or three years.

Having made this point, it is necessary to bear in mind also that, although the presence of many fringe benefits in a remuneration package may not be a positive incentive to work harder or to perform better, the absence of fringe benefits, on the other hand, may be a disincentive and will put an employer at a disadvantage in recruiting or retaining staff.

In some cases, offering high salaries, commissions or bonuses may compensate for lack of fringe benefits, but owing to the fact that non-cash benefits may be taxed lightly or not at all, these have been playing a bigger part in employee compensation in recent years. They can add another 25% to the total payroll costs but a similar increase to salaries, due to personal tax, would almost certainly not enable employees to purchase the same type of benefits or to enjoy the same standard of living.

Fringe benefit programmes should be designed to further the employer's objectives and should, in particular, be designed to assist in human resource planning. Where, for example, it is desirable to have a stable, mature management team providing plenty of continuity, such as is required by many brewery companies, a very generous pension and life assurance scheme, along with loan facilities (e.g. for house purchasing among other things), will assist in retaining the management team. On the other hand a dynamic young organization may want a fairly steady flow of 'high flyers', the majority of whom will not want to stay for long because there will not be room for all of them. In this case high salaries and good incentives payments will be preferable, as this type of person will not be so interested in benefits such as pensions.

The differing needs of employers along with pressures exerted by competing organizations and by statutory requirements will all help to dictate what type of fringe benefits programme needs to be offered. There are many different components and the permutations can be numerous. Increasingly, fringe benefits are elements of a 'flexible' benefits scheme, which may consist of core benefits, core plus choice. Choice, in turn, can be limited or very open. In some cases, for example, an employee may be able to choose the type of car they would like, up to a limit. In a more open scheme an employee may be able to exchange the car benefit for an equivalent cash addition to salary. Such schemes recognize that each employee may have particular needs, which may vary at different points in their career. Figures 13.2 and 13.3 illustrate some fringe benefits offered.

Financial benefits

These were covered in more detail in Chapter 12; as was said there, they should be directly related, as far as possible, to performance. Discretionary handouts have little positive motivational value.

Profit sharing

Although many profit-sharing schemes may not be justified directly on motivational grounds, because individuals do not receive a commission or bonus related to their own efforts, and because these awards may be expected as a matter of right, profit sharing may well be justified for indirect reasons. Awarding a bonus of this kind may not assist directly in increasing profits, but withholding an award may have an adverse effect on employees' morale. Whether this share of increased profits should be in the form of a bonus or salary increase depends on current performance of the employer's business; for example, if there is a strong upward trend in profits an increase in salaries could be awarded, whereas if a year's performance was exceptional and not certain to be maintained, a bonus may be preferable from the employer's point of view, because it is a once-only payment and because it does not have a gearing-up effect on future wage increases, pensions, etc.

Share option schemes

These enable employees to buy options on company shares with loans provided by the employer. The better the company performs, the more the value of the shares increases. These schemes are strictly controlled by law; for example, they do not allow an employee to sell the shares until a certain number of years have elapsed. Once the prerogative of executives only, many organizations in the service sector are now offering such schemes to all staff with a certain length of service, full and part time. The supermarket chain Asda has had considerable success with its scheme and attributes a lowering of labour turnover to the scheme and the way it ties staff in to remaining with the company for a specified number of years, at least three years in the Asda, for example. Of course such schemes are only of real motivational value if the company is successful and its share price improves.

CHOICE HOTELS
EUROPE

HAVE YOU MANAGED TO EARN AN ADDITIONAL £5–£1000

many team members have already done so by taking advantage of the incentives offered such as:

❖ **NEW BUSINESS BONUS SCHEME**
by introducing new business to the Company,
you can earn yourself anything from **£25–£1000**

❖ **SUGGESTION SCHEME**
bright, fresh and new ideas could reward you from **£5–£250**

❖ **NEW EMPLOYEE INTRODUCTORY BONUS**
introduce a friend, colleague, relative or acquaintance
and receive for each person. **£50**

❖ **LONG SERVICE BENEFITS**
Those reaching 2, 5 and 10 years service with *'Friendly Hotels PLC'* receive *Free
Accommodation, a meal for two and a Bonus.*
For further details see the current Employee Long Service Benefits Booklet.

❖ **SPECIAL PRIVILEGE RATE OF £10.00** per person
bed and continental breakfast for all full-time employees with over 1 year service.

❖ **EMPLOYEE DISCOUNT RATE PROGRAMME INTERNATIONAL**
Worldwide discounts of at least 50% from rack room rate.
Maximum stay is seven days.

❖ **PROFIT SHARE SCHEME**
(**FREE** to all employees with over 3 years service) and become a part-owner of
Friendly Hotels PLC.

❖ **SAVE AS YOU EARN**
and acquire shares in the company in 3, 5 or 7 years time at discounted share prices.

❖ **'FRIENDLY' FACE and PERSON**
Monthly competition 'smiles all day bring clients your way'
and receive another award!

Full details of the schemes can be obtained either from your Manager or Headquarters and we will be circulating 'fliers'
regularly with your wage packets.

Do join in, or chase up your Employee Consultative Committee in arranging Social Events within your unit.

If you have any further ideas of Events; Competitions or Activities that you would like to either organise or join in, then
let your Manager know and we will see if they can be arranged.

For your own development, and no matter what your age, have you considered gaining additional qualifications such as
NVQ's? Contact your Personnel Manager for further information.

Please do check your employee notice board for more new ideas and incentives as they are introduced - for your benefit
so why not join in NOW...
"Applicable only to properties owned or managed by Friendly Hotels PLC"

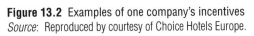

C:\GENERAL\REF034B\05\9!

Figure 13.2 Examples of one company's incentives
Source: Reproduced by courtesy of Choice Hotels Europe.

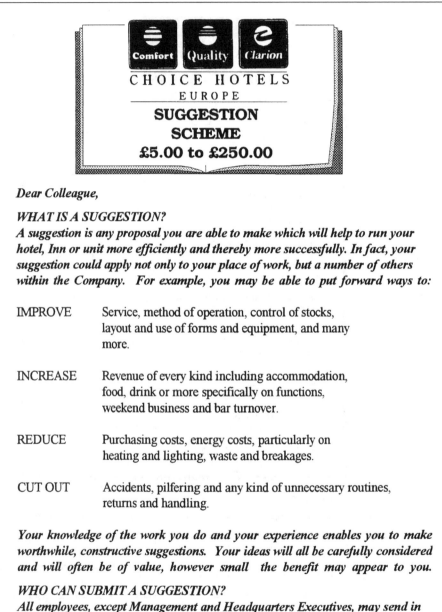

Figure 13.3 Example of one company's suggestion scheme
Source: Reproduced by courtesy of Choice Hotels Europe.

Part-financial benefits

There are many benefits that may be awarded which can be described as partly financial. These are benefits that the employee cannot normally dispose of in cash or kind, but which enable him or her either to avoid spending personal resources on these benefits or to enjoy a higher standard of living. These benefits include such things as pensions and life assurance schemes, company cars, expense accounts. The major part-financial benefits are as follows.

Pensions

Most schemes grant a fraction of final earnings for each year of service. The better schemes grant one sixtieth of final salary (sometimes the average of the last few years) for each year's service, thereby enabling a person with forty or more years' service to retire on forty sixtieths (or two thirds of final salary), the maximum pension currently permissible. Provision is also normally made for a person's dependants, whether he or she dies in service or in retirement. Some schemes are index linked; some are not.

One of the benefits to employers of comprehensive pension schemes is that they enable employers to retire their older employees, particularly for health reasons, replacing them by younger people, knowing that the older ones will be well provided for in retirement.

Life insurance

In itself this is hardly a benefit that will persuade a person to join one employer rather than another. From the employer's point of view, however, the major value is that it provides for the dependants of employees who die in service. Without this provision the employer may feel that there is a moral, if not a legal, responsibility to look after an employee's dependants, particularly if that person dies in the course of work. If no insurance is provided, some other provision may have to be made on a discretionary basis and, where large numbers of people are employed, cases may be treated inconsistently. Also, the burden may fall more heavily in one year rather than another and, worst of all, if the employer goes out of business the dependants of ex-employees may be completely unprovided for.

Company cars

Generally speaking, these are provided for one of two reasons. First, because an employee needs a car in order to do the job. This would include people such as regional or area managers, marketing and training staff, and stock takers. Second, cars are provided to improve a person's standard of living without incurring the full tax liability that paying an equivalent cash amount would impose.

The provision of company cars is a highly contentious benefit, however, for reasons such as these:

1 Cars are very nearly cash equivalent and therefore if a car is provided to one employee in a particular job grade because it is needed, another employee of similar grade but who does not need or receive a car may well expect a cash equivalent.

2 Cars are status symbols both within the organization and within the community at large and wherever status is concerned people are very sensitive and often irrational.

House purchasing

Purchasing a house is usually the biggest investment that a person ever makes and often moving house is one of the biggest obstacles to employee mobility. (The fact that labour mobility in the hospitality industry is high while home ownership by the industry's employees is relatively low is probably not unrelated.) By helping employees to buy a house, employers can increase the stability of their labour force. At the top of the scale this assistance can take the form of cheap loans, but, more practically, it can be confined to the employer acting as guarantor.

Removal or relocation expenses

These payments are intended to indemnify an employee for the cost incurred in moving home when being appointed, transferred or promoted by the employer. The amount allowed should be such that the employee is no worse off financially as a direct result of moving house. The expenses included in this, however, can be extensive, including estate agents costs, legal fees, furniture removal, new school uniforms, temporary accommodation, etc.

The employer's responsibility should be confined purely to indemnifying the employee for the actual costs incurred in the employee's transfer from one home to another. Considerations of capital appreciation should be excluded.

These are the major part-financial fringe benefits offered by many employers. There are many others as well which enable employees to enjoy a better standard of living and these include advantageous purchasing of food, insurance, furniture, etc. These can all be arranged through the employer's own suppliers or agents.

Non-financial benefits

Although the main benefits in this category can cost the employer considerable sums of money, they do not normally provide employees with any direct financial advantages. Instead they afford employees other benefits such as a degree of security or more time for leisure.

Holidays

Holidays can be used as a stimulus to labour stability; for example, extra days over the statutory minimum can be granted after a certain number of years' service. Extra holidays must be reasonably obtainable, however, because working for 15 years, for example, for extra holiday entitlement will contribute nothing to retaining staff. It is much better to grant two to four extra days after two to four years' service, leading up to an extra week after five years. Figure 13.4 illustrates one example.

Years of service	Holiday entitlement per annum
During 1st year	4 weeks (pro rata to actual service)*
2nd year	4 weeks and 2 days
3rd and 4th year	4 weeks and 3 days
5th and 6th year	4 weeks and 4 days
7th year onwards	5 weeks

*The statutory minimum paid holiday in the UK in 2005 is 20 days which may *include* public holidays hence the statutory right to paid holidays is actually 12 days!

Figure 13.4 Example of a service-related holiday entitlement scheme

Sick pay schemes

As with several other conditions of employment, details of pay during sickness have to be entered in the statement of conditions of employment. This is required by the Employment Rights Act 1996 and, in the absence of such details, an employer may have to pay a sick employee the full wage or salary until dismissal of the employee after giving full notice of termination.

It is for this reason as well as for normal human relations considerations that employers should formulate a sick pay policy that is consistent with their human resource management practices and which is affordable. It is important to recognize that in some employment situations sickness leave, with pay, can increase considerably the incidence of absence. This appears to be particularly so in the public sector, where sick leave may be seen as another form of holiday entitlement.

Statutory rights

Parliament has created certain rights to time-off and pay in the case of holidays, sickness and maternity. Many employers offer conditions additional to the minima laid down by Parliament.

Private medical treatment

Private medical treatment is one particular fringe benefit that is being granted to many employees these days. The direct advantage to the company is that employees can be treated at a time convenient to the company and not when it is convenient to the National Health Service (NHS). This is particularly appropriate for key members of the staff. Sometimes the cover provided by the company includes the employee's family as well.

Some employers may feel it is too expensive or even inappropriate to pay for this service, but even so employers can arrange 'group rates' and monthly deductions of premiums from salaries, enabling their employees to benefit from preferential rates at no cost to the employer. A combination of these two methods can be adopted in which senior employees are paid for by the company and the remainder of the employees have the option of participating in the group scheme. The HCIMA has negotiated a group rate with BUPA for members who may not have the benefit of a company scheme.

Tax pitfalls

Note that although some fringe benefits may offer tax advantages this is not always the case. The provision of company cars and fuel for private use creates tax liabilities. Various incentives such as foreign trips can catch the unwary. In one case a couple who benefited from a lavish holiday including seven nights in a five-star hotel received a tax bill for £4600 – the tax due on the value of the holiday. It is for the employer to account for any tax due on any fringe benefits that are taxable.

Concluding comments

This chapter has dealt with the major benefits that can be offered to employees. Employees will not qualify for all these benefits automatically. Some benefits should be incentives to stay with the organization and to seek promotion; therefore they should be granted only for service and seniority. On the other hand certain benefits may be offered to all employees upon joining, for example, discounted purchasing facilities.

Increasingly there is a trend to offer employees some choice over what and how they take such benefits, for example an employee may chose a smaller car in order to have more salary. One may describe such systems as *à la carte*.

Fringe benefits play a vital part in an employer's human resource policy, since the nature of all the benefits offered influences considerably the type of employees who will be attracted to the employer and who will stay. And since the cost of fringe benefits can add significantly to the payroll cost, it is essential that the range of benefits offered and their likely effects are fully considered.

Further Reading and References

Armstrong, M. (1999) *A Handbook of Human Resource Management*, 7th edn, London: Kogan Page.

Conoley, M. *et al.* (1993) *Flexible Benefits*, London: Croner Publications.

Goss-Turner, S. (2002) *Managing People in the Hospitality Industry*, 4th edn, Kingston-upon-Thames: Croner Publications.

Kessler, I. (2001) Reward System Choices, in Storey, J. (ed.), *Human Resource Management—A Critical Text*, 2nd edn, London: Thomson Learning.

Pugh, D. S. and Hickson, D. J. (1997) *Writers on Organizations*, 5th edn, London: Penguin.

Torrington, D., Hall, L. and Taylor, S. (2002) *Human Resource Management*, 5th edn, Harlow: Pearson Education.

Tyson, S. and York, A. (2000) *Essentials of HRM*, 4th edn, Oxford: Butterworth-Heinemann.

Questions

1 Describe the objectives of fringe benefits schemes and the various alternatives in regular use.

2 Discuss which you consider to be the most important principles for fringe benefits to be effective. What do you understand by 'effective' in this context?

3 Discuss what external factors influence the nature of fringe benefits.

4 Discuss the relationship between fringe benefits, incentive schemes and alternative methods of wage and salary administration.

5 Discuss the role played by fringe benefits, wages and/or salaries and incentives in implementing an employer's human resource policy.

6 Evaluate the approach to fringe benefits used by an employer you know well.

PART 5

The Employment Relationship

Labour turnover and termination of employment

The issue of unacceptable rates of labour turnover within the hospitality industry is a subject much considered by researchers, and features in every report or study conducted into the hospitality workforce characteristics or major challenges for the sector, not just in the UK but worldwide (see Lucas, 2004: 32–34). A government report into the industry in the UK (DfEE, 2000) points to the labour shortages and skill shortages across certain jobs within the sector, noting that, 'Best practice employers were able to keep turnover of full-time employees down to around half the industry norm of 48%.' In its 2003 report on UK industry levels of labour turnover, the CIPD considered that, 'highest levels (commonly in excess of 50%) are found in retailing, hotels and restaurants, (and) call centres'. These levels should be compared with a national UK average of 16% labour turnover per annum. There has been a significant amount of research into the causes and impacts of high levels of labour turnover, much of the discussion debating the advantages as well as the disadvantages or dysfunctionality of such levels. It is important to note that there can be some advantages of a healthy level of labour turnover, such as skills development, labour market regeneration and the 'fresh blood' argument. The causes of this turnover can be many in type, exemplified by pay and conditions, lack of job satisfaction, lack of commitment, lack of training and career development, work-related stress and the plain inevitability of high turnover due to the transient nature of many hospitality workers. Management, and their style and competencies, are not exempt from blame, although managers are certainly increasingly aware of the potential costs and service quality problems associated with high turnover (Rowley and Purcell, 2001). There is also evidence that rates of turnover vary between different sectors in the industry (Deery, 2002).

It is clear that rates of labour turnover and wastage are a problem for many businesses, especially in attaining the consistency in product and service quality so desired by hospitality firms in an evermore competitive market (Hoque, 2000; Tracey and Hinkin, 2004). A study in Australian hotels by Deery and Shaw (1999) linked the turnover issue with cultural perspectives, concluding that within the sector there has developed a phenomenon which is itself a culture, a labour turnover culture. They propose that a turnover culture is typified by the acceptance of labour turnover behaviour by peers, by management and by the organizations themselves. They assert that there is a relationship between an individual worker's values and norms and the propensity to leave employment, and that a turnover culture exists where turnover behaviour is regular, accepted as the norm and may be perceived as beneficial to both the employer and employee. Deery (2002) later reports that a set of variables influence the intention of an employee to leave their employment, such as their commitment to the organization, the promotional opportunities, work difficulties and job satisfaction. The relationship between organizational culture and labour turnover is an area which would warrant further detailed research, and as discussed in Chapter 2, the significance of culture in a contemporary definition of HRM is a major factor.

It is important to distinguish between labour turnover and stability rates. Labour turnover, defined very simply, is the total number of leavers expressed as a percentage of the total number of employees in a department, unit and/or organization. Stability is defined (Hospitality Training Foundation, 1998) as the proportion of employees who stay for more than one year. These figures show that almost 80% of employees have been in their job for more than one year. This is explained by the fact that certain jobs have very high turnover rates whilst others do not.

There are of course many factors influencing labour turnover. These include

1 the nature of the industry itself – e.g. seasonal, limited career structures, fragmented, large number of small units
2 the nature of individual units – e.g. location, size, staff/work ratios
3 the nature of individual managers – e.g. lacking formal management training, acceptance of high labour turnover
4 the high proportion of workers from the secondary labour market.

In 1998 the Hospitality Training Foundation (HTF) published *Key Facts and Figures* (Davie, 1999), which reported the statistics shown in Figure 14.1.

Sector	Full-time employees		Part-time employees	
	Labour turnover (%)	Staff stability (%)	Labour turnover (%)	Staff stability (%)
Hotels	50	76	42	66
Restaurants	55	71	80	52
Pubs and bars	40	66	75	49
Canteens and catering	25	77	58	71

Figure 14.1 Labour turnover and stability in the hospitality industry
Source: Davie (1998).

In order to understand and control labour turnover and staff retention rates properly at a unit level, not only is it important to analyse these rates by department (as illustrated in Figure 14.2), but also it is necessary to look at the 'survival curve'. This is a means of identifying when labour turnover is most critical; is it occurring during the early induction period, the subsequent settling-in period or after employees have become settled? Such an analysis (Figure 14.3) can indicate causes such as poor induction or a change of supervisor or manager. Regarding induction, it has been estimated that 20% of ALL leavers leave within 0 and 6 months in post (CIPD, 2003). With such information the employer may be able to take appropriate measures.

Whilst labour turnover is analysed both by department and by length of service, the actual reasons for employees leaving need to be determined also. Some employers do little or nothing about such an analysis whereas others obtain very detailed information. Figure 14.4 shows how one of the fast food companies analyses employees' reasons for leaving.

Sampled departments	Two large London hotels		Medium-sized county town hotel
	A	B	
Kitchens	140%	80% ⎱	47%
Wash-up, porters	550%	135% ⎰	
Coffee shop	125%	100%	17%
Hall porters	68%	105%	0%
Housekeeping	150%	146%	28%
Weighted average *all* departments	110%	105%	40%

Figure 14.2 Labour turnover in three hotels

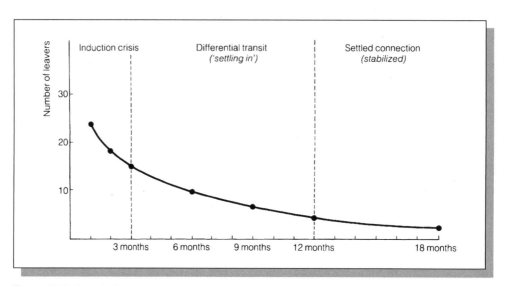

Figure 14.3 A survival curve

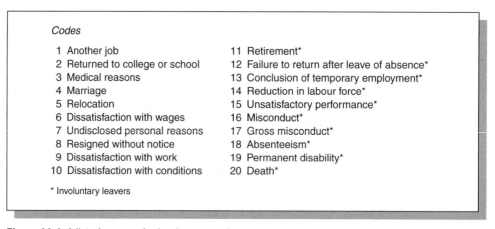

Figure 14.4 A list of reasons for leaving an employer

With such information, management may then be in a position to consider changes and improvements to their personnel practices in order to reduce labour turnover. Causes of turnover may include

1 wage and salary rates falling behind the rates offered by competitors
2 better conditions generally (such as reduction in split shifts) being offered by competitors
3 a decline in quality of supervision and departmental managers
4 recruitment, selection, induction and training practices needing improvement
5 unfair or uneven work distribution.

The statistical analysis of labour turnover is discussed further in Chapter 17. Both the staff turnover report itself and the information deduced from such reports are of a statistical nature, i.e. they are mainly concerned with groups and numbers of people.

The actual termination procedures adopted, however, are concerned with individuals and these are divided into two main types: voluntary, where the employees leave of their own free will, and involuntary, where the employer decides that employment should terminate. Retirement can fall into either category.

Voluntary termination

Most often this arises where an employee has the opportunity to take other employment that offers more attractive conditions. But, because employees leaving voluntarily have not been dismissed by the employer, they are probably the employees that an employer would most like to retain. It is for this reason that these employees should be interviewed to determine their reasons for leaving. The exit interview may reveal specific information regarding conditions of employment, competitors' conditions and the quality or otherwise of supervision, training and selection procedures. Finally, a well-conducted exit interview can ensure that employees leave on good terms. Ex-employees are, after all, to some extent an employer's ambassadors, broadcasting the employer's reputation among other potential employees. In some cases it may be advisable to supplement an exit interview by talking to a departing employee's past supervisor in order to check the reasons given by the employee.

Involuntary terminations

In this industry, along with some others, dismissal is often used as the first remedy for a variety of ills, rather than being used as the last. In fact, in some sectors of the industry dismissals may be quite indiscriminate; for example, it is common practice for the entire bar staff to be dismissed because of bad liquor stock results. The innocent suffer the same fate (dismissal) as the guilty.

One recognizes that pilferage in this industry is a serious problem, but other measures such as more methodical selection, checking of references, better conditions of employment and better career prospects, along with stricter and more accurate means of control, may be better solutions than indiscriminate sackings.

The dismissal of an employee is a very serious measure, particularly now that the law provides employees with protection against unfair dismissal. The law on dismissals is dealt with in more detail in Chapter 16. The most common reasons for dismissal are

1 lack of ability
2 conduct such as late arrival, absenteeism or disobedience
3 personality.

In all cases when dismissal is contemplated, other remedies should be considered first; for example, lack of ability may well be the fault of the employer because they did not select or place the employee carefully enough, or because they did not provide appropriate training. Secondly, tighter discipline could possibly overcome the problem and a discussion with the employee to discover the underlying causes would possibly be helpful (Figure 14.5). In the third case, if it is a clash of personalities, and if the organization is big enough, a transfer may be the solution.

On the other hand, once a decision is made to terminate employment it must always be borne in mind that the employer may have to prove in an industrial tribunal that the dismissal was 'fair' as laid down by the Employment Rights Act 1996. Documentary evidence, therefore, of unsatisfactory work or behaviour, and of warnings given may be vital in proving the case. It is important, therefore, to operate a formal system of warnings that can be used as a last resort by the employer should they be called to an industrial tribunal. Typical warnings could look like those shown in Figure 14.5.

RECORD OF VERBAL WARNING Disciplinary Procedure (Forte Hotels)

Employee's name: ....

Hotel: ....

Department: ....

Position: ....
I have had reason to issue a verbal warning to the above employee in respect of:
....

Signed: ....
                    Supervisor/Head of Department/Manager

Date: ....
To be retained on the employee's personal record file, and removed at the end of six months if there is no further offence.

FIRST WRITTEN WARNING – CONDUCT Disciplinary Procedure

Employee's name: ....

Hotel: ....

Department: ....

Position: ....
Further to your interview on .... (date), regarding the following offence, I have cause to issue you a first written warning as to your future conduct.
Details and date of offence..

In the event of a recurrence or continuance of the above, or any other breach of discipline within twelve months, you will be issued with a final warning and thereafter will be liable, should there be no improvement in your record, to disciplinary action, which could include dismissal.

Signed: ....
                    Manager
Date: ....
A copy of this warning will be retained in your personal file, but will be removed at the end of twelve months if your conduct has been satisfactory during that period.

I confirm that I have received a copy of this written warning.

Signed: ....

Date: ....

Figure 14.5 Examples of written warnings
Source: All examples reproduced by courtesy of Forte Hotels.

FIRST WRITTEN WARNING – PERFORMANCE Disciplinary Procedure

Employee's name: ....

Hotel: ....

Department: ....

Position: ....

I regret I have to warn you that considerable improvement must occur in your performance as set out below. Assistance and guidance will be given to you to achieve the required standard, but unless this is reached within the period specified, you will be issued with a final warning, and thereafter will be liable, should there be no improvement in your performance, to dismissal.

Area of sub-standard performance   Details of improvement required
....

Signed: ....
                                                        Manager

Date: ....

Date by which performance will be reviewed: ....

A copy of this warning will be retained in your personal file, but will be removed at the end of twelve months if your conduct has been satisfactory during that period.

I confirm that I have received a copy of this written warning.

Signed: ....

Date: ....

FINAL WARNING – PERFORMANCE Disciplinary Procedure

Employee's name: ....

Hotel: ....

Department: ....

Position: ....

I regret to have to tell you that following the written warning regarding your performance given to you on .... there has been no improvement in your performance. This is therefore a final warning and if there is no improvement by .... you will be liable to dismissal.

Signed: ....
                                                        Manager

Date: ....

A copy of this warning will be retained on your personal file but will be removed at the end of twelve months if your conduct has been satisfactory during that period.

I confirm that I have received a copy of this written warning.

Signed: ....

Date: ....

Figure 14.5 *continued*

FINAL WARNING – CONDUCT Disciplinary Procedure

Employee's name: ....

Hotel: ....

Department: ....

Position: ....

Further to your interview on .... (date), I have cause to issue a second and final warning as to your future conduct.

Details and date of offence ....

Any recurrence or continuance of the above, or any other breach of discipline within twelve months, will lead to disciplinary action, which could include dismissal.

Signed: ....

Manager

Date: ....

A copy of this warning will be retained in your personal file, but will be removed at the end of twelve months if your conduct has been satisfactory during that period.

I confirm that I have received a copy of this written warning.

Signed: ....

Date: ....

STATEMENT OF DISCIPLINARY ACTION Disciplinary Procedure

Employee's name: ....

Hotel: ....

Department: ....

Position: ....

Further to your interview on .... (date), it has been decided that the following disciplinary action will be taken (delete as appropriate).

1. Dismissal with .... weeks notice
2. Summary dismissal for gross misconduct

Details and date of offence ....

If you wish to appeal against this disciplinary action you have a right to do so in accordance with the Disciplinary Procedure. The Personnel Officer is available to advise you how to do this.

Signed: ....

Position: ....

Date: ....

TO BE SIGNED BY THE EMPLOYEE
Right of Appeal
I acknowledge that I have received a copy of this statement. I understand that I have the right of appeal against this disciplinary action which *I do/do not wish to take up. Any appeal must be made within 5 working days of the date of dismissal.

Signed: ....   Date: ....

*Delete as appropriate

Figure 14.5 *continued*

Redundancy

The other main form of involuntary termination is of course redundancy. This is where a job is eliminated owing to such things as changes in methods, or mergers. In this case the law lays down certain minimal payments to be made to the employee. In addition to this payment some employers, recognizing the inadequacy of the amounts awarded by the redundancy legislation, allow what is known sometimes as 'severance pay'. This is additional to redundancy pay and is usually calculated by using some formula that recognizes age, service and present earnings. Employers must recognize, however, that redundancies are sometimes the fault of their own lack of forward planning. If planning, and this includes human resource planning, is conducted thoroughly, many redundancies can be avoided by allowing natural wastage to reduce the labour force. But once it becomes apparent that redundancies are unavoidable this fact should be discussed with employee representatives so that plans for a properly phased rundown can be agreed (as laid down in employment protection legislation). This may include voluntary early retirements and compensation payments for voluntary terminations, and may also include special counselling and other services for the employees made redundant. In some cases it may be essential to keep employees working to a certain date, in which case special 'incentive payments' for them to stay in the job will have to be agreed.

Retirement

The last type of termination is, of course, when a person goes into retirement; and these days some of the more enlightened employers recognize that their responsibility extends beyond providing a pension and the proverbial gold watch. In fact, they provide some form of pre-retirement preparation that enables an individual to adjust to completely changed circumstances, because not only does he or she suddenly have greatly-increased free time but income may drop considerably and contact with friends and colleagues may be reduced. This preparation may take the form of a steadily reducing working week with attendance at a pre-retirement course. In addition, companies such as Granada run pensioner support schemes, whereby the company continues to maintain an interest in their pensioners through visits and other company benefits schemes.

Exit interviews

The importance of interviewing employees when they leave was touched upon briefly earlier in this chapter, but it cannot be overemphasized that the numbers and types of people leaving an organization are one critical indication of the success or otherwise of an employer's human resource policy. Employees leaving can be a valuable source from which to learn where improvements in personnel practice can be made. With few exceptions, therefore, all employees should be interviewed before their departure, in order to

1 learn the real reasons for their departure (unless these are patently obvious)
2 pinpoint trouble spots and causes of irritation and frustration

3 inform employees of all their benefits and rights, such as pensions and insurance. Pensioners will need to know what rights they retain, such as insurances, holidays and discount purchasing facilities.

4 explain the make-up of the final pay cheque, including such items as holiday pay

5 hand over the P45 or obtain a forwarding address

6 collect any company property that may be outstanding, such as cash advances, equipment, uniforms, protective clothing

7 part on friendly terms, if possible, so that ex-employees act as ambassadors.

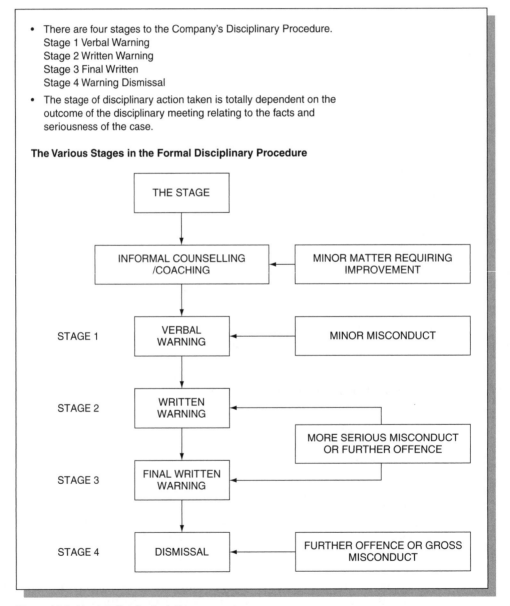

Figure 14.6 Marriott Hotel's disciplinary procedure
Source: Reproduced by courtesy of Marriott Hotels.

Who dismisses?

When the need arises to dismiss an employee, the question of who actually dismisses also arises. Many line managers feel that they need to have this right as a support to, and indication of, their authority. Others, on the other hand, would dearly like to abdicate the responsibility to someone else such as a personnel officer. However, because line managers, in the last resort, are responsible for the results of their departments, they should carry this burden and they should make the decision assisted and guided by specialists, where they are employed, such as personnel officers. In many circumstances it is best for the 'grandfather' principle to be applied to dismissals. This means that no person can dismiss subordinates without the approval of his own superior. Furthermore, in large organizations the approval of the personnel officer or department should also be obtained because they will know if any opportunities exist for an employee about to be dismissed or if legal consequences are likely. It has now become common practice in many companies for the right to dismiss to be held by the unit manager only, with the subordinate having the right to suspend and no more. Figure 14.6 illustrates one company's disciplinary procedure through its various stages.

Costs of labour turnover

Assessing the costs of labour turnover is extremely difficult. It is relatively simple to identify the factors that need to be taken into account but to put a cost to them is not so easy. For example, to include the costs of a manager's time is debatable because one has to know what they would have been doing if they had not been interviewing an applicant. Major costs can be analysed as including

1 costs associated with Leaving – personnel administration, payroll administration, exit interviewing
2 costs associated with Replacement – direct costs such as advertising and recruitment, selection processes including administration of applications, shortlisting and interviewing, agency commission if applicable, possibly travel expenses, postage and stationery
3 costs associated with Transition – direct and indirect costs such as relief cover and overtime payments, training costs, low productivity during training, possible wastage during training, induction time
4 costs of an indirect nature – such as management and supervisory time dedicated to the recruitment, selection and induction activities, and the potential loss in customer satisfaction and repeat business.

The CIPD (2001) estimates the overall average cost of turnover per employee to be around £4000, with naturally the highest costs being for managerial positions and skilled professionals such as highly sought-after heads of department with very special experience and competencies. Following a nationwide survey, the CIPD estimates that the labour turnover cost per leaver in the retail, hotel and leisure sectors to range from £5000–6000 for managerial/professional posts to £1500 for an operative. The report also highlighted that 68% of the sample (483 organizations out of the 605 surveyed) indicated that labour turnover had a negative effect on business performance. Note, however, that 5% of the companies actually declared a positive effect of some level of turnover, mainly due to the 'fresh blood' argument, as discussed in the introductory section of this chapter.

The HTF published the following data concerning the average costs of replacing hospitality sector employees (Davie, 1999):

Operative	£500
Craft and skilled	£1652
Clerical	£1746
Technical	£3671
Professional	£4861
Managerial	£5008

It would be a sanguine exercise for any business, large or small, to estimate the cost of replacing leavers and assess the impact on sales and profitability as a result. Each business is different and circumstances cannot be overgeneralized but often the cost of labour turnover is disregarded even by those managers who scrutinize in great detail their financial reports for every possible saving in operating costs. Labour turnover is undoubtedly a measure or barometer of the success or otherwise of HRM practices and line management approaches to employee relations and, where the rate is higher than is acceptable, can be of great concern to the customer and their desire for consistency in the quality of product and service and even the behavioural aspects of recognition being known by name by the employee in the service encounter. At the very least, management and HRM professionals must monitor and analyse the reasons for turnover and take action where discernible and negative trends are evident.

Further Reading and References

Armstrong, M. (1999) *A Handbook of Human Resource Management*, 7th edn, London: Kogan Page.

Chartered Institute of Personnel and Development (2001) *Labour Turnover Survey Report*, London: CIPD Publications.

Chartered Institute of Personnel and Development (2003) *Employee Turnover Survey Update*, London: CIPD Publications.

Davie, S. (1999) *Key Facts and Figures for the Hospitality Industry*, London: Hospitality Training Foundation.

Deery, M. (2002) Labour turnover in international hospitality and tourism, in D'Annunzio-Green, N., Maxwell, G. and Watson, S. (eds) *Human Resource Management*, London: Continuum.

Deery, M. and Shaw, R. (1999) An investigation of the relationship between employee turnover and organisational culture, in *Journal of Hospitality and Tourism Research*, Vol. 23, No. 4, 387–400.

DfEE (2000) *Employers Skill Survey: Case Study Hospitality Sector*, Nottingham: DfEE Publications.

Hoque, K. (2000) *Human Resource Management in the Hotel Industry*, London: Routledge.

Hospitality Training Foundation (1998) *Manage People*, London: Hospitality Training Foundation.

Lucas, R. (2004) *Employment Relations in the Hospitality and Tourism Industries*, London: Routledge.

Mitchell, P. (1995) *Disciplinary Procedures in the Hospitality Industry*, Brighton: Human Resource Management in the Hospitality Industry Conference Document, University of Brighton.

Rowley, G. and Purcell, K. (2001) As cooks go, she went: Is labour churn inevitable? in *International Journal of Hospitality Management*, Vol. 20, 163–185.

Storey, J. (ed.) (2001) *Human Resource Management—A Critical Text*, London: Thomson.

Tracey, J. B. and Hinkin, T. R. (2004) Accounting for the costs of employee turnover, in *Trends in the Hotel Industry*, PKF Consulting.

Wood, R. (1992) *Working in Hotels and Catering*, London: Routledge.

Questions

1 Describe how labour turnover may be measured, and discuss the different reasons for termination of employment.

2 Discuss the key ways in which labour turnover may be reduced.

3 Discuss what external factors may influence labour turnover, and the concept of a labour turnover culture.

4 Discuss the proposition that high labour turnover is not always a bad thing.

5 Evaluate the approach to managing labour turnover and terminations which is used by an employer you know well.

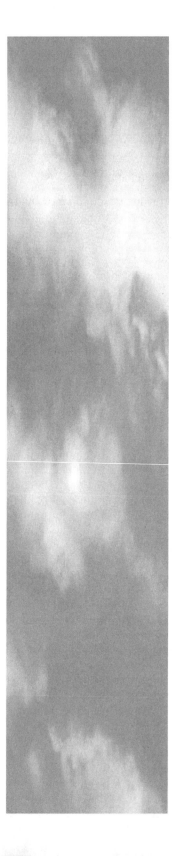

Employee relations

In many respects this whole book is concerned with the relationship between an employer and the employees. Whether one is considering recruitment, induction, discipline or reward systems all have important inputs into the employment relationship. However, all of these can be concerned with the relationship of an individual employee and the employer.

This chapter, instead, is to focus on the collective relationship traditionally referred to as 'industrial relations' but which, with the changed nature of trade union roles and power, is increasingly referred to as 'employee relations'. At one extreme, such relationships are seen as being concerned with purely economic issues, i.e. the 'pay for work' relationship. At another extreme are those who see industrial relations as being concerned with politics and as an extension of party politics.

The term 'employee relations' is generally used to describe the relationship that exists between the management of an undertaking and its work people in the collective sense. An important contributor to the subject of employment relations as it pertains to the hospitality industry is Rosemary Lucas, whose definition of the employment relationship also introduced the consumer within its scope:

> Employee relations in hotels and catering is about the management of employment and work relationships between managers and workers and, sometimes, customers, it also covers contemporary employment and work practices. (Lucas, 1995: 81)

In a later work, Lucas (2004) develops this important theme for service industries, where the role and behaviours of hospitality employees are impacted upon crucially by the organization, its management and the customer they are serving. The challenge for many hospitality employees is to satisfy the needs and demands of all these stakeholders, and this complexity of relationship can create significant problems for individual workers through the role conflict that can result. The hotel receptionist dealing with a stressed guest, disappointed and angry about the poor decorative order of a hotel bedroom, is in a parlous position, faced with the 'power' of the customer, and the 'power' of the organization and management that demands maximum occupancy and revenue from all rooms, including those not yet featuring on the carefully costed refurbishment schedule.

The traditional and collective term of industrial relations is still used in employment situations where employees are organized and represented within a trade union. In the hospitality industry the degree of organization of employees within trade unions varies considerably. At one end of the scale, in public sector and contract catering, it is possible for all employees' conditions of employment to be determined by collective bargaining and national agreements, hence a consequently high degree of union membership; yet at the other end of the scale, in most hotels and restaurants, trade union members are comparatively low, and often non-existent. Upon close examination it appears that there are certain factors that either contribute towards or militate against strong union involvement. Bain and Price (1983) identified a number of determinants of union growth or decline, factors still relevant today. These include

1 industrial structure
2 government action
3 business cycle
4 composition of potential membership
5 employer policies
6 personal and job-related characteristics
7 union leadership

Using some of the determinants identified by Bain and Price, it is possible to conclude that union membership is low in the hospitality industry for the following reasons:

1 The large numbers of small establishments, which make it difficult for trade union officials to contact potential members and to organize meetings. Note, the average hotel has only about 25 bedrooms.
2 The highly dispersed and departmentalized labour force, even in the largest establishments, resulting in the absence of cohesive groups of workers with common interests.
3 The large number of part-time employees and also many young employees, who are not interested in belonging to a trade union. The high proportion of female employees may also be a factor (Stanev, 1999).
4 The large number of foreign employees who are in the UK for short periods of time.
5 Shift working, which makes it difficult to contact and organize employees.
6 Tipping, which introduces an entrepreneurial element into work, which many employees fear a trade union would try to eliminate.

7 Individual and secret contracts made between the employer and the employee.
8 No tradition of trade union membership within some sectors of the industry.
9 Employers' resistance, because employers fear that they have more to lose than to gain from the trade union movement.
10 High labour turnover in some sectors mitigates against membership, association and the ability of trade unions to organize.

Figure 15.1 illustrates how these can be applied to the hospitality industry.

Low union membership	High union membership
Small units – small workforces	Large units – large workforces
Many part-timers and casuals	Few part-timers and casuals
'Entrepreneurial' opportunities, e.g. tipping	No 'entrepreneurial' opportunities
Ownership and management combined or closely related	Management distinct from ownership
'Secret' contracts	No 'secret' contracts
Hostile ownership	
No other union involvement	Other unions involved in the enterprise
No tradition of union involvement	Traditions of union involvement
Some examples	*Some examples*
Restaurants, fast food, hotels, public house staff	Hospital catering, university and college catering, school meals, Civil Service catering, public house managers

In addition, recent research (Stanev, 1999) concluded that a major deterrent to high union penetration of the hospitality industry is the high proportion of part-time and women employees.

Figure 15.1 Factors contributing to low or high levels of union involvement

Development of the trade union movement

In order to see the hospitality industry's employee relations in perspective it is important to look at industrial relations generally and, in particular, to examine the development of organizations of work people and of employers.

The organization of employers and workers came about from the eighteenth century onwards with the emergence of modern industry. Before this time most conditions of employment had been regulated by the state, often through the local magistrate, and it was an offence in common law to do anything (even with the intention of improving one's own conditions of work) that might have been in restraint of trade. A combination of workers, therefore, to strike or to do anything else to improve conditions that adversely affected the employer's business was a criminal act of conspiracy. But at the same time it was illegal for employers to form such combinations. As industry became more complex, the state regulations of wages fell into disuse and employers themselves were able to fix conditions of employment. Legislation followed, banning combinations in one trade after another until the situation was made quite clear when the Combination Acts 1799–1800 provided for a general prohibition in all trades of combinations of employees or employers.

However, following the Napoleonic Wars there was an economic depression together with a movement to improve conditions, which resulted in the repeal, in 1824, of the Combination Laws. The effect of this was to allow workers to enter into combinations for the purpose of regulating wages and other conditions without committing the crime of conspiracy. This Act (the Combination Laws Repeal Act 1824) was followed shortly by another that somewhat circumscribed workers' rights, but still preserved the right to withhold labour by collective action and this right has never been withdrawn, although current legislation makes it more difficult to instigate certain types of industrial action without risk of penalties.

Subsequent acts, including the Trade Union Act 1871 and the Conspiracy and Protection of Property Act 1875, gave trade unions legal status and also permitted peaceful picketing. Then the Trade Disputes Act 1906 protected a trade union from being sued for alleged wrongful acts committed by it or on its behalf. Thus trade unions were freed of any risk of a civil liability arising from their actions. A variety of other legislation followed which repealed certain preceding legislation, covered the amalgamation of trade unions and tied up some other aspects that were not satisfactory.

However, the most notable legislation to date was the Industrial Relations Act of 1971, which replaced most preceding legislation regarding trade unions and followed both the main political parties' examination of the increasingly complex and potentially disruptive industrial relations scene. This Act granted to an individual the right to belong or not to belong to a trade union. This was subsequently repealed with many other provisions by the Trade Unions and Labour Relations Act 1974. Certain provisions particularly relating to 'unfair dismissal' remained to protect the individual, but have since been altered by subsequent employment legislation. Principal statutes enacted concerning employment rights and trade unions rights in the intervening period have been the Trade Union and Labour Relations (Consolidation) Act 1992, the Trade Union Reform and Employment Rights Act 1993 and the Employment Relations Act 1999.

Present position

The trade union movement, along with other sectors of our society, is undergoing a period of mergers and rationalizations. At the end of 1972 there were about 480 trade unions, whose members totalled about 11 million; in 1987 there were only 373 unions with 10.7 million members; in 1989 there were about 8.6 million members in unions affiliated to the Trades Union Congress (TUC). The number of union members was the same in 1993 (8.6 million) but the number of certificated unions had fallen to 267, of which 67 were affiliated to the TUC. Brown (2000) reports that the number of UK workers with trade union membership has decreased from 53% of the total workforce in 1979 to just 28% in 1999. The hospitality sector, as analysed by the Workplace Employee Relations Survey in 1998, had no members at all in 92% of establishments. Recent estimates of the percentage of the hospitality labour force who are members put the figure at as low as 4% (Brook, 2002 cited in Lucas, 2004).

The strength of the trade union movement obviously stems from its ability to present a united front, and therefore many individual unions join federations to further strengthen their movement. These federations are, however, in most cases rather loose, and the responsibility for action rests with the individual unions. There is no such strong federation in the hospitality industry. The trade union movement is united within the TUC, the aims of which are to promote the interests of all its affiliated organizations and generally to improve the economic and social conditions of workers.

Much of the TUC, as with the federations of unions, has little authority over individual unions, but it does oblige affiliated unions to keep its General Council informed of any trade disputes that may involve large numbers of work people.

The role of trade unions

Trade unions are primarily concerned with representing their members in order to obtain what is considered by their members to be reasonable conditions of employment. 'Reasonable' is, of course, relative; it may mean maintaining one's position in an earnings league or it may mean preserving one's purchasing power.

Although unions are concerned with obtaining increased earnings, they also strive to improve their members' other conditions of employment such as time-off, holidays, safety and status. They do, in addition, show particular concern over company ownership, job security, pensions and, very often, important political issues such as privatization. Their roles can be evaluated from a number of different perspectives that are set out below.

Economic–political

On the one hand, unions may be concerned only with improving their members' conditions and, at the other hand, unions may be an extension of a political movement. The Labour Party grew out of the British trade union movement. Some union leaders may use their unions in order to further their own political ends, which may have little relationship to the wishes of the rank-and-file membership.

Capital–labour

Another view is concerned with the relative rights of those who provide labour and capital. There are those who believe that ownership bestows certain inalienable rights, whereas others believe that those who provide labour have equal rights to those of the providers of capital.

Democracy–autocracy (pluralist–unitarist)

Related to the above is the argument about degrees of participation in decision making. There are those who believe that managers, because of training and experience, should be responsible for taking decisions, whereas others hold the view that decisions should be shared by all who are affected by them.

Rank and file versus union leadership

An important discussion is the extent to which union leadership is really representative of the membership. It is argued that the very process of moving up the union hierarchy separates leaders from their members. Many of the Conservative government's measures in the 1980s and 1990s were directed at reducing the power not just of trade unions, but of senior officers of trade unions.

Individual rights versus group rights

An important discussion, particularly where closed shops (compulsory 100% trade union membership) used to be involved, relates to the rights of individuals to choose whether to belong to a trade union or not. On the one hand it is argued that the rights of individuals must be upheld; on the other hand it is argued that the majority has greater rights. Certainly this would appear to be what democracy is about.

In essence, however, whichever perspectives are adopted, industrial relations is concerned, explicitly or implicitly, with the power of the participants to influence the distribution of the wealth they generate or the resources they have made available. Unions themselves claim to be democratic organizations – that the organization represents the wishes of the majority of its members. To what extent union leaders do represent their members', or their own, aspirations varies from union to union. Figure 15.2 illustrates the organization structure of a large trade union.

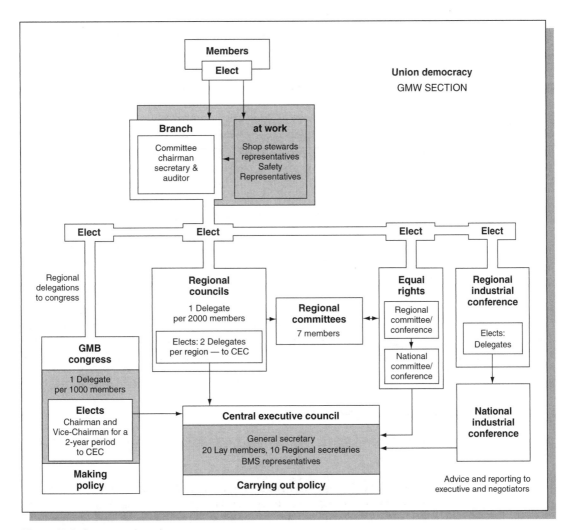

Figure 15.2 Structure of a union

Types of union

Over the years unions have evolved into four main types.

1 Craft unions – These usually consist of members with specific trade skills.
2 General unions – These unions consist mainly of members with little or no specific trade skills and they have no skill or training requirements. The general unions constitute the largest unions in Britain today (e.g. the Transport and General Workers Union). Some general unions, however, do incorporate specialist unions catering for workers with specialized skills.
3 Industrial unions – These unions consist of most workers in one industry or activity (e.g. the National Union of Teachers).
4 Whitecollar unions – These unions consist of administrative, clerical and managerial employees (e.g. Unison, a public sector employees' union).

Employers' associations

The first employers' associations of any importance were probably the merchant guilds and livery companies which existed throughout Europe from the early Middle Ages. They dealt with a variety of matters that affected trade and labour.

With the repeal of the combination laws and because of pressure from the growing trade union movement, employers' organizations grew rapidly during the nineteenth century. Nowadays they are, generally speaking, organized on a trade or industry-wide basis and because of this they deal with matters of trade, such as encouraging government to take defensive measures against foreign competition, and with matters of employment, such as negotiating industry-wide conditions of employment.

These employers' or trade associations come together in various national bodies, the main one being the Confederation of British Industries (CBI), which has individual employers, trade associations, employers' organizations and nationalized industries within its membership. In the private sector, the BHA and the BII are examples of the hospitality industry's principal trade or employers' associations. Figure 15.3 gives an overview of the industrial relations institutions which may impact upon employee relations.

The conduct of negotiation and consultation varies considerably from employer to employer and from industry to industry. In some cases all negotiations will take place at national level between the trade union concerned and the employers' association. This is sometimes referred to as the 'formal' system. In other cases all discussions and negotiations will take place 'informally' at plant level, i.e. between the local employer and their own employees.

Main types of agreement

There are several types of agreement normally entered into between employers and trade unions.

Recognition agreements – These are usually the first type of agreement entered into. Under such agreements the employer normally agrees to recognize the union in certain instances, such as representing members in grievance and disciplinary matters.

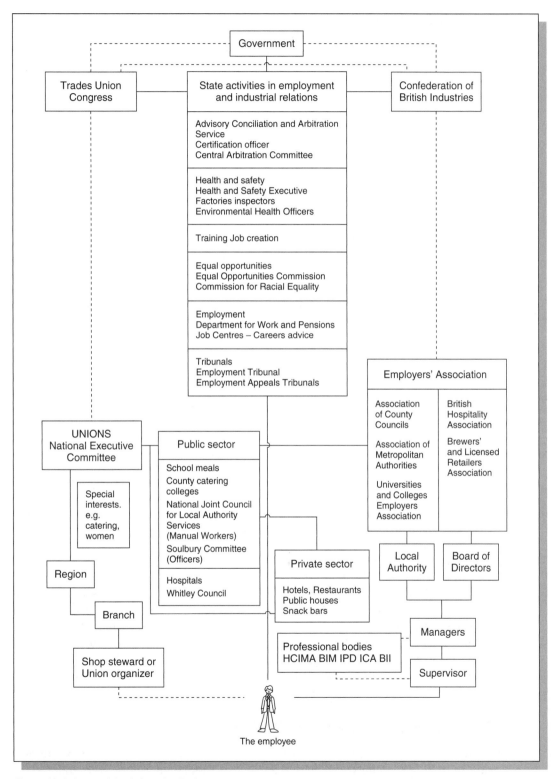

Figure 15.3 Industrial relations institutions

Negotiating agreements – Under a negotiating agreement, an employer agrees to recognize a union's right to negotiate on behalf of its members.

Substantive agreements – These contain the 'substance' of an agreement and include elements such as pay, hours and overtime rates.

Procedural agreements – These lay down various procedures to be followed, such as dates for agreements to be made, and procedures to be followed in the absence of agreements.

Individual contracts

A major feature of the employee relationship in the hotels sector of the industry is the secret and individual nature of contracts (Mars, Mitchell and Bryant, 1979). Because the vast majority of employers are small, with only a few staff, contracts are made between the employee and the employer, who offers terms that will solve the immediate staff problem. These terms may be better than those currently enjoyed by other similar staff. Consequently, an element of secrecy is expected. With some employers it is a dismissible offence to discuss remuneration. This system of individual contracts is made easier because a considerable proportion of recruitment is informal, on a person-to-person basis, and may involve undeclared cash payments. Although managers believe that this individual and secret contract works to their advantage, it creates ambiguity and confusion which causes grievances and high labour turnover.

Wages Councils

In 1945 with the enactment of the Wages Councils Act and the creation of wages boards it was recognized that where employees were not organized there was insufficient pressure on employers to ensure that wage levels and other conditions were kept up with those offered to other sections of the community. In the hospitality industry this had been recognized earlier and resulted in the Catering Wages Act of 1943, which created the Catering Wages Board. This board laid down minimum conditions of employment. However, this Act and others were superseded by the Wages Council Act 1959, which regulated wages and other conditions for employees in the industry until 1993.

The rates laid down by the various councils were considered by most employers and employees to be absolute minima and market forces generally obliged employers to pay above these rates. The value of wages councils was therefore questionable and they were eliminated in 1993. Furthermore they represented to the Conservative government an aspect of government intervention in the labour market which was inappropriate. However, since the election of the Labour Government in 1997, and under pressure from the EU, many of these issues have been impacted upon by regulation, most notably the National Minimum Wage and the Working Time Directive (see Chapter 16).

Employer/employee consultation

If good employment relations are to be achieved, many argue that discussion should take place between management and staff on all matters related to conditions and methods of work. The size of the organization does not affect this principle; the only variation to it is one of degree, since the actual size and nature of the organization determine the type and degree of formality of discussions.

Within this industry there are probably three main types of consultative procedure. The first and probably the least formal is found in the individually owned hotel or restaurant, managed by a proprietor who works in the establishment with a staff numbering up to about 20. In this case any formal joint consultation or negotiation may be unnecessary, since the employer is close to the employees and should be aware of their problems and views. It is the employer's job to keep informed of the employees' opinions and feelings and the employer may well hold informal meetings at regular intervals with all staff. Meetings may anyway be held to discuss menus, special functions, etc., and from time to time they should be enlarged to cover methods of work and conditions of employment.

The next level may be found in hotels or restaurants with groups of employees in several departments. Typically this would be a hotel or restaurant complex with from twenty to several hundred employees. In this case there may be small groups of people working together – each group with its own aims – often not the same as those of the organization as a whole. One only needs to think of the conflict between cooks and waiters in many hotels or restaurants to accept that this conflict exists. In this case it might be that each department should nominate a representative to meet management's representatives on a regular basis – probably between four and eight times a year. Some formality is needed, and agendas need to be circulated beforehand and minutes produced afterwards.

The level after this is the company or organization with several large units. Each establishment has its own joint consultative committee, and in addition it may find it worth organizing a company-based joint consultative committee where representatives from each establishment meet head office management. This system is most appropriate where a company is heavily represented in an area – London, for example – and where management might wish to discourage unnecessary movements between units caused by varying supervisory or personnel practices within the company's establishments. On the other hand it may not be necessary where an employer's establishments are located far apart in areas where conditions are different.

These are three examples of different levels of consultation (and possibly negotiation), but whether or not all three should be conducted with trade union representatives is generally for management and employees to decide.

Benefits of consultation

Managers may ask what benefits can result from their taking the initiative in establishing joint consultation and even bargaining or negotiating procedures with their employees. First, and most important, it must be recognized that although employees may have no negotiating machinery they still push up rates of pay and win other concessions by voting with their feet. They move from employer to employer continually looking for higher earnings and employers in turn have continually to increase their rates to attract replacement staff. Seasonal resorts will confirm that this practice is rife. The fear of runaway wage increases therefore is generally exaggerated. Instead, because of continuous collective pressure from the employees, through consultation, their conditions would steadily improve, and job security would become greater, with the result that the staff turnover rate would almost certainly drop to reasonable proportions. There are many cases in those sections of the industry where trade unions are strong where the annual staff turnover is not above 10% per annum, contracted food service units being one such example. As a result the economies to be made through not having to recruit and train a steady flow of replacement staff are considerable, apart from the benefits of being able to maintain consistent standards.

A second benefit of consultation is a more willing acceptance of change. By nature most people oppose change, but if they have been involved in discussing changes that affect them and they understand the underlying reasons, they will almost certainly be more prepared to make the changes work. A further benefit is that many people have ideas that can improve working methods, and by consultation, management can provide the opportunities for these to be expressed. A third view, however, is that whether these are measurable benefits or not, participation in decisions affecting working people is a right – not a privilege granted by management for instrumental reasons (see Chapter 20).

Disadvantages of consultation

On the other side of the coin there are disadvantages to be faced when entering into consultation with employees. First, management action will be open to question and discussion, with the consequence that management's decisions may take longer. Furthermore, even certain confidential information, by law, must be made available for discussion. Apart from this, it must be remembered that if trade unions are involved, the possibility of industrial action, such as working to rule, blacking, banning overtime and even striking, must not be ruled out when agreement on such things as pay, working conditions, methods or procedures cannot be reached.

Establishing consultation

Once the decision has been taken to establish consultation within an organization, the scope of any discussions may cover all matters of interest to both sides, including the total reward system, hours of work, working methods and company plans. It should be clear, however, that the purpose of such consultative committees is consultation and not negotiation.

Setting up a staff consultative committee sometimes presents problems, because it is essential that the employees' representatives are chosen, and seen to be chosen, by their colleagues and not by management. The outline of a constitution and rules for a staff consultative committee is illustrated in Figure 15.4. At an international level, it should be noted that following an EU directive in 1994, any company which has at least 150 employees in more than one country and at least 1000 employees within the EU must form a works council for information and consultation activities.

1 Objectives

The object of the Staff Consultative Committee is to provide a means of communication and consultation between the management and staff of the hotel on all matters of mutual interest, including:

(a) Explanation on general information concerning Company activities, policies and procedures.
(b) Business plans for the hotel and current results, expressed in broad terms as percentages, etc.
(c) Ideas for improving sales, standards of performance, efficiency and productivity.
(d) Discussion on staff rules and regulations, and discussion on security matters.
(e) Terms and conditions of employment, staff amenities and welfare facilities. Wage rates/Wage reviews may be discussed in general terms only. The wages or status of an individual member of staff may not be discussed.
(f) Training activities.
(g) Health and Safety at work, including hygiene and welfare. (The hotel Safety & Hygiene Officer should be in attendance during discussion on these items.)
(h) Organising of social, sporting and recreational activities.

2 Membership

The committee shall consist of:

(a) **A Chairman** who shall be the General Manager.
(b) **Another Management Representative** preferably the Personnel Manager or Assistant Manager responsible for personnel.
(c) **A Head of Department or Supervisor**: normally a different Head of Department or Supervisor attending the meeting in rotation.
(d) **Elected Staff Representatives** from each Department of the Hotel (normally there should be between 6 and 12 staff Representatives on the Committee depending on the size of the hotel). They will also act as Safety Representatives for their Departments — *see Guidelines for the duties of Staff Safety Representative*.
(e) **A Secretary** to record the minutes of Meetings of the Committee. Staff Representatives shall be chosen annually by election, other members of the Committee being nominated by management. Should members of the Committee cease to be employed by the Hotel, then membership shall immediately terminate.

3 Attendance

Any member who is absent without adequate reason for two or more consecutive meetings may, at the discretion of the Committee, be disqualified from membership.

4 Co-option

The chairman may invite additional members of management and/or staff to attend meetings to provide special information.

5 Election of Staff Representatives

All staff over the age of 18 years who have been employed for over three months by the hotel shall be entitled to stand for election which shall be conducted annually by Departments. Elections which shall normally be by secret ballot, shall be organised by the Head of Department in consultation with the Hotel Manager, and shall be held normally in January or as required if a vacancy arises during a term of office. All staff on the payroll at the time of the election shall be entitled to one vote. Staff Representatives are entitled to wear a special Company badge whilst they hold office. These badges will be issued by the Hotel Managers and must be returned if the person concerned is no longer the Staff Representative.

6 Officers

The officers shall consist of the Chairman, a Management and Head of Personnel Representative as referred to in Paragraph 2 (a), (b) & (c).

7 Retirement

Staff Representatives shall be elected for one year and may be eligible for re-election every year. Management members shall hold office at the discretion of their superiors.

Figure 15.4 Staff consultative committee constitution
Source: Reproduced by courtesy of Forte Hotels.

8 Meetings

(a) Ordinary meetings shall be held at least every two months during normal working hours if possible, and 14 days' notice of the meeting should be given. Items for the Agenda may be submitted to any member of the Committee and the Agenda should be distributed to members with a copy placed on the Staff Notice Board at least seven days before the meeting. Fixed items on the Agenda should be:

Minutes of last meeting
Matters arising
Training
Health & Safety
Business Results and Objectives
Security
Energy Conservation
Date of next meeting

(b) Special meetings may be convened at the request of any four members or the Chairman.

(c) The meetings shall conform to Committee procedure, members addressing the chair. Discussions shall be opened by the member in whose name the item on the Agenda stands. The first items of the Agenda should be the minutes of the previous meeting and matters arising.

9 Minutes

The Chairman shall ensure that accurate minutes of all meetings are kept which summarise the discussion and define clearly the action being taken and who is responsible for that action. (Minutes must always have an action column.) The minutes must be prepared and circulated within seven days of the meeting with copies distributed to all Committee members, all management and Heads of Department and all Staff Notice Boards.

Copies of the minutes are also to be sent to the Area/Operations Director, the Hotels Personnel Department and the Group Personnel Director.

10 Alteration of Rules

Additions or amendment to these rules may only be made by the Committee with the approval of the Company.

Figure 15.4 *continued*

Responsibility for good employee relations

The responsibility for good employee relations depends, within each undertaking, upon its management, and can only result from frank discussion between management and staff. The Industrial Relations Code of Practice places the responsibility for stimulating this dialogue squarely on management. In the section on communication and consultation it says:

Management in co-operation with employee representatives should

i) provide opportunities for employees to discuss matters affecting their jobs with those to whom they are responsible;

ii) ensure that managers are kept informed of the views of employees and of the problems which they may face in meeting management's objectives.

See also chapter 16 for information on union law.

Advisory, Conciliation and Arbitration Service (ACAS)

Advisory, Conciliation and Arbitration Service is the main state organization established to give advice on industrial relations and employment relations practices. They can also, as their title indicates, act as an intermediary in industrial disputes. In addition, of course, the industry's main trade bodies, such as the BHA, can be consulted by its members.

Further Reading and References

Armstrong, M. (1999) *A Handbook of Human Resource Management*, 7th edn, London: Kogan Page.

Bain, G. and Price, R. (1983) *Industrial Relations in Britain*, London: Blackwell.

Brewster, C. (1989) *Employee Relations*, revised edn, Basingstoke: Macmillan.

Brook, K. (2002) Trade union membership: An analysis of data from the autumn 2001 LFS, in *Labour Market Trends*, July, 343–356.

Brown, W. (2000) Putting partnership into practice in Britain, *British Journal of Industrial Relations*, Vol. 38, No. 2, pp. 299–316.

Cole, G. A. (1997) *Personnel Management—Theory and Practice*, 4th edn, London: Letts.

Farnham, D. and Pimlott, J. (1995) *Understanding Industrial Relations*, 5th edn, London: Cassell.

Joint Hospitality Industry Congress (1996) *A Vision for the Future*, Henley: Henley Centre.

Lucas, R. (1995) *Managing Employee Relations in the Hotel and Catering Industry*, London: Cassell.

Lucas, R. (2004) *Employment Relations in the Hospitality and Tourism Industries*, London: Routledge.

Mars, G., Mitchell, P. and Bryant, D. (1979) *Manpower Problems in the Hotel and Catering Industry*, Farnborough: Saxon House.

Stanev, P. (1999) *Why is Trade Union Membership so Low throughout the UK Hospitality Industry?* MA Dissertation, University of Brighton.

Storey, J. (ed.) (2001) *Human Resource Management—A Critical Text*, London: Thomson.

Torrington, D., Hall, L. and Taylor, S. (2002) *Human Resource Management*, 5th edn, Harlow: Pearson Education.

Tyson, S. and York, A. (2000) *Essentials of HRM*, 4th edn, Oxford: Butterworth-Heinemann.

Questions

1 Describe the structure of industrial/employee relations in the private (commercial) sector of the hospitality industry and also in the public sector of the same industry.

2 Discuss the factors contributing to high or low levels of union participation in different sectors or employers of the hospitality industry.

3 Discuss the external factors that influence the nature of employee relations.

4 Discuss the positive and negative contributions made to employment relationships by trade unions.

5 Evaluate the approach to employee relations used by an employer you know well.

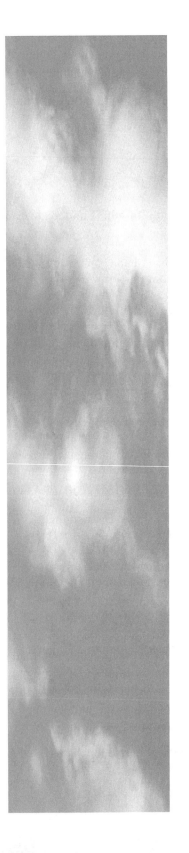

Law of employment

The evolution and development of our complex, modern, Western societies have been accompanied by the need to regulate many of the activities of various groups of people. Without this regulation, society would not be what it is today. In the case of employment, the activities of employees were long regulated by legal institutions such as magistrates, who had, among a number of powers, the power to set rates of pay. More recently, the activities of employers became subject to increasing regulation in order to provide employees with greater protection in economic and physical terms. Factories legislation is just one example. Up to the 1980s the increasing power of trade unions, as distinct from individual work people, caused concern, particularly to Conservative governments, with the result that the power of unions has been reduced by legislation.

As stated above, until fairly recent times in history the responsibility for regulating conditions of employment rested largely on Parliament and on local magistrates. This was relatively easy while the number of categories of workers was small. Gradually, however, as society became more industrialized it became increasingly difficult to exercise this control. The pendulum swung the other way. As was seen in the last chapter, various laws were passed that made it possible for both workers and owners to combine into trade unions and associations in order to bargain, until the stage was reached where the state appeared to avoid any direct involvement in the relationships between employers and employees. The whole system of bargaining and negotiation then rested on voluntary understandings between the workers and their employers. However, as industrial society developed even further, the power of trade unions grew and the concentration of certain vital resources and services into what became vulnerable positions made it possible for many groups of people to disrupt supplies to the whole community.

Before employment

Sex, race, age discrimination – e.g. advertising and interviewing
Rehabilitation of offenders – certain offenders do not have to reveal spent convictions
Employing overseas workers – work permits needed in certain cases
Employing children – local authority approval needed
Employing young persons – e.g. licensing law restrictions
Employment agencies – who is the employer? who pays the agency?
Disabled workers – physical impediments or obstacles to their employment to be removed
Trade union membership – free to belong or not to belong

On starting employment

Contract of employment – certain terms and conditions to be given in writing
Health and safety – e.g. induction, fire training, safety precautions
Employer's liability insurance – needed to indemnify employees in case of accidents at work

During employment

Maximum hours
Statutory paid holidays
Health and safety at work – range of health and safety measures
Disciplinary procedures – need to be communicated and fair
Time off – for sickness, maternity, jury service, etc.
Trade union membership – free to belong or not to belong
Harassment – employer to take reasonable measures to prevent harassment
Discrimination – e.g in promotion
Discipline and grievance procedures

Pay and other benefits

Minimum wages
Equal pay – pay to be equal for men and women doing work of equal value
Statutory pay for sickness and maternity
Taxation and National Insurance – who is responsible for collecting tax and deductions
Deductions – lawful and unlawful deductions

Termination

Termination procedures – resignations and dismissals
Written reasons for dismissal
Transfer of undertakings – protection of employment.

Figure 16.1 An illustration of the areas of employment regulated to a greater or lesser extent by the law (this is illustrative only)

The government therefore felt obliged to re-enter the field of relations between employers and employees by creating a legal framework for the conduct of what is called industrial relations or employee relations.

The role of the EU has become increasingly important also – not just to set out to improve employment conditions but also to ensure that all member states are competing on equal terms. The Social Chapter is a major EU initiative aimed at achieving this objective. Recent examples of such legislation include the introduction into the United Kingdom of the minimum wage, maximum hours and statutory paid holidays legislation.

Employment legislation is one of the more complex areas of legislation affecting employers so this chapter needs to be viewed as a very brief overview intended to illustrate its scope rather than its detail.

The law relating to employment is considerable now and it is only possible in this book to cover a small part of it. The major areas of employment law have been selected and summarized below.

Common law rights and obligations

Most aspects of the relationship between employer and employee are regulated by the contract of employment, much of which is now regulated by statute (i.e. Act of Parliament). Common law (judge made as opposed to Parliament made), however, also plays a part in setting minimum rights and duties.

The employer's duties are to pay the agreed wages, to provide work, to select and/or train competent workers, to provide adequate materials and to provide safe systems of work. Any breach of these common law obligations means that an employee could sue for damages, when an injury is sustained; or even to resign without notice and to sue for unfair constructive dismissal, when an employer creates circumstances in which an employee feels justified in resigning.

In turn, common law lays obligations upon employees as well. These include the duty to serve the employer according to the terms of the contract, to be obedient (i.e. to follow reasonable instructions), to work competently, to work for the employer in good faith – which includes not taking secret profits or commissions, to keep confidential information and not to set up in competition.

Contracts of employment

A contract of employment is the basis of the working relationship between employer and employee and is subject to the general principles covered by the law of contract. There are seven essentials for a contract to be valid. These are as follows:

1 *Offer and acceptance* – there must be an offer and an acceptance
2 *Intention to create legal relations* – each party must intend to create a legally binding contract
3 *Capacity* – each party to the contract must be legally able to make the contract
4 *Consent* – must be genuine and freely given
5 *Consideration* – something of value must be exchanged, e.g. money for work

6 *Legality* – the purpose of the contract must be legal

7 *Possibility* – it must be possible to perform the contact.

A contract of employment may be oral, written, or the terms may be merely implied. It consists of an offer by one of the parties and an acceptance by the other. A consideration – i.e. an exchange of promises to perform certain duties and to pay certain wages and provide certain conditions, is necessary to create the contract. The consideration, as with all contracts, must have an economic value. The offer is usually (but not necessarily) made by the employer and should contain details of remuneration, hours, location and holidays. The offer may refer to other documents such as pension scheme booklets. Not all conditions have to be included, as some may be implied by custom and practice. The contract comes into existence when the offeror receives acceptance from the offeree.

Although, in common law, contracts need not be in writing, it is advisable that all offers and acceptances are in writing in order to avoid misunderstanding and possible problems. Furthermore, because most employees are entitled to a written statement of the main conditions of employment (see below), there is no real reason today for not preparing a proper, written contract of employment.

The Equal Pay Act 1970

The purpose of this Act was to remove differences in terms and conditions of employment between men and women employed in the same or very similar work, or work rated as of similar value. Employment tribunals deal with any complaints and are able to award arrears of pay and damages. Job evaluation plays a part in determining pay differentials between jobs.

Discrimination in employment

Discrimination against applicants for jobs and those in employment can be directed at a range of different groups of people including women, men, people of some ethnic groups, people with certain beliefs or with disability, people of gay, lesbian or bisexual orientation, people with criminal convictions and older people. The UK legislation is directed at eliminating discrimination in the workplace aimed particularly at women, ethnic minorities, people with disability and those who may be discriminated because of their religion or beliefs (see the Employment Equality (Religion or Belief) Regulations, 2003).

Discrimination can take two main forms: direct discrimination and indirect discrimination. Direct discrimination consists of acts that discriminate against another on grounds of their sex, racial origin or disability. Indirect discrimination consists of applying conditions that make it more difficult for people of one sex or a racial group to fulfil the conditions.

Sex Discrimination Act 1975 and 1986

These two acts were introduced in order to grant equal opportunities to both sexes in the fields of employment, education and training and to make it an offence to discriminate against a man or a woman on the grounds of sex alone. The main provision of this Act is that if a job can be performed equally well by a man or a woman it is an offence to discriminate against a man or a woman on the grounds of sex alone. This applies to recruitment of new staff and also to promotion.

There are certain exceptions, of particular relevance to the hotel and catering industry, such as cloakroom attendants or where limited staff accommodation has to be shared. Positive discrimination may also be permitted in certain circumstances.

The Equal Opportunities Commission is responsible for ensuring that the provisions of the Equal Pay and Sex Discrimination Acts are implemented.

Race Relations Act 1976 • • •

This Act is directly analogous to the Sex Discrimination Act and was introduced to eradicate racial discrimination against ethnic minorities. The Commission for Racial Equality is responsible for ensuring that the provisions of the Race Relations Act are implemented.

Disability Discrimination Act 1995 • • •

This Act was introduced in order to prevent employers from discriminating against applicants and employees with disability. Disability also covers people with learning disability. Employers are expected to make reasonable alterations to working practices, layouts and equipment that might otherwise be barriers to the employment of people with disability. This Act also applies to other users of premises such as customers.

Rehabilitation of Offenders Act 1974

This Act permits people convicted of certain crimes to treat their sentences as 'spent' after a specified period of time has elapsed. Applicants for jobs do not have to reveal the conviction and sentence and the employer cannot dismiss the employee on the grounds of that conviction if they subsequently learn of the sentence. For example a sentence of up to six months in prison becomes spent after seven years.

The Employment Rights Act 1996

This Act provides the rights of employees, who work over a certain number of hours, to minimum periods of notice dependent on their length of service, and the Act also requires that employees are given written details of certain conditions of employment.

Where a contract provides for longer periods of notice the terms of the contract will apply, whereas contracts containing shorter periods are overridden by the periods laid down by the 1996 Act. Payment in lieu of notice may be made by the employer or the employee.

Written particulars

These must be given to people within two months of employment commencing. This does not apply to casual workers whose contract is for one session of work at a time.

Written statements need not take any particular form but the contents are prescribed and they can refer employees to other documents such as manuals and booklets, which must be reasonably available to them. There is no requirement in law for the employee or the employer to sign the statement. But it is advisable to issue all employees with a statement and to retain signed copies in the personal dossiers. The ideal procedure is to design letters of offer so that they satisfy the Employment Rights Act 1996 requirements. An example is shown in Figure 6.1.

Restraint on employees

In the case of some employees, such as chefs or managers, employers feel it necessary to include a clause in a contract which restrains an employee from divulging trade secrets, entering into direct competition by operating his or her own business, working for another person in the same line of business or using lists of customers prepared in the course of employment in order to entice customers away.

To obtain protection against such eventualities any terms in a contract need to be clearly stated and not implied. It is important, however, to make such a term reasonable in the circumstances, otherwise the right to any protection could be forfeited. At the same time such restraint clauses must be shown to be in the public interest and it is unlikely that such a restraint clause will be upheld.

Searching employees

It is always advisable to obtain an employee's permission before attempting to search his or her person or property. To search a person without permission, and without finding evidence of theft, can result in the employer being sued for assault and battery. In those cases where the employer's right to search is considered to be vital, such as in hotels and industrial catering organizations, a clause to this effect should be written into every person's contract of employment. Even so an employee cannot be forcibly searched if he or she refuses. Such a refusal instead becomes the subject of disciplinary or dismissal proceedings.

Dismissals

Under the Employment Rights Act (1996) there is protection for employees against unfair dismissal.

Until the 1960s, so long as an employer gave the agreed period of notice or money in lieu an employee had no recourse against the employer. The situation has changed and it is now necessary to show that reasons for dismissal were fair. Valid reasons include

1 lack of capability or qualification for the job for which an employee was employed
2 misconduct
3 redundancy, within the definition of the redundancy legislation
4 unsuitability due to legal restrictions (e.g. loss of Justice's licence)
5 some other substantial reasons (e.g. chronic sickness).

It should be noted that no complaint of unfair dismissal or of a worker's rights relating to trade unions will be heard by an employment tribunal until a conciliation officer has looked into the circumstances to see if a settlement can be reached without a tribunal hearing.

The 2002 Employment Act introduced very specific procedures for discipline and dismissal, with heavy penalties for employers who ignore them.

Instant or summary dismissal • • •

In certain instances an employer may be justified in dismissing an employee without giving the required period of notice or money in lieu. Although this may be permitted in such cases as an employee's permanent incapacity to perform his or her duties, in most cases it occurs where employees are guilty of serious misconduct. To dismiss a person instantly can have serious consequences for the employer if a dismissed employee sues him successfully for damages, so it is not a step to be taken lightly. Reasons for instant dismissal include

1 serious or repeated disobedience or other misconduct
2 serious or repeated negligence
3 drunkenness while on duty
4 theft
5 accepting bribes or commissions.

The argument underlying instant dismissal is that the employee, through serious misconduct, has repudiated the contract, and the employer chooses not to renew it.

An employer can normally only dismiss an employee for misconduct committed outside working hours and away from the place of work if other employees were involved, which could have an effect on the employer's business, or if the employee is in domestic service.

Where an employer dismisses a person instantly it should be done at the time of the misdemeanour or when it first comes to the attention of the employer. To delay may imply that the employer has waived his or her right to dismiss, but see the discussion of suspensions below. The reason for dismissal should be given at the time of the dismissal.

An employer may, in some cases, withhold money earned by an employee who has been instantly dismissed for good reasons, unless a contract states otherwise. However, legal advice should always be sought before taking such action.

Suspensions

In some circumstances, particularly involving alleged misconduct, an employer may wish to suspend an employee until the circumstances have been looked into and a decision has been taken regarding the employee's future. It is quite in order to do this so long as pay is not withheld – unless a contract specifically permitting the withholding of pay is in existence.

Maternity rights

The 1996 Act together with the Employment Relations Act 1999 provide for a framework of basic rights governing maternity rights and parental leave.

Transfer of Undertakings Regulations

Under these regulations employees of an undertaking that are transferred from one owner to another have their employment rights protected. Effectively this means that a new employer is required to treat all of an employee's previous service with the undertaking as uninterrupted. This is of crucial importance on matters such as redundancy, protection from unfair dismissal, etc.

Payment of wages

Employment Rights Act 1996 • • •

Generally speaking, arrangements for the payment of wages are regulated by the contract of employment. The 1996 Act, however, provides specific rules on deductions. These specify that an employer must not make deductions or receive payment (e.g. as a fine) unless

- the deduction is authorized by statute, e.g. National Insurance, income tax, court order
- the deduction is authorized in the contract of employment
- the worker has agreed in writing to the deduction.

Certain deductions are exempted from the above conditions, such as the recovery of an overpayment.

In the case of the retail trade, including catering, employees can be required, as a condition of the contract, to make good stock or cash shortages. However, such a deduction or payment must not exceed 10% of the gross pay due for the period. On termination of employment, however, such deductions may exceed 10%. They cannot be made retrospective for more than 12 months. Notice of intention to make such deductions has to be made in advance, and a written demand also has to be issued. Payment of wages may be in a form agreed in the contract. This may be in the form of cash, cheque or credit transfer.

Attachment of Earnings Act 1971 • • •

This Act enables a court to order an employer to make periodic deductions from an employee's earnings and to pay the sum deducted to the collecting officer of the court. The court specifies the amount and can make priority orders for payment of fines or maintenance of dependants, or non-priority orders for the clearance of civil debts. The court will also specify the protected earnings which is the level of income below which a person's earnings should not be reduced by these deductions. Any consequent shortfalls in payments will be carried forward.

Pay As You Earn (PAYE)

Employers are obliged to deduct tax payable on money paid to any of their employees' earning money falling under Schedule E (i.e. emoluments from any office or employment). Some items are not subject to deductions: business expenses, and rent-free accommodation or temporary accommodation allowances that are provided because of the nature of the employer's business.

This responsibility to deduct tax covers service charge earnings and tronc earnings where the employer is involved in their distribution. It is the duty of staff to declare tips where the manager or owner is not involved in their distribution.

Social security

The social security scheme provides a wide variety of benefits and welfare services such as benefits for unemployment, sickness, industrial injuries and retirement. Most people over school-leaving age and under pensionable age are insurable. Persons who are insurable must register and obtain a National Insurance number.

Employer's liability

There are two separate categories of liability that employers bear in relation to injuries suffered by their employees while in their employment. These are common law and statutory liabilities.

The common law responsibilities extend also to employees of other employers, such as contractors, while working on the employer's premises, and also to the employer's employees carrying out work for him or her on another person's premises, for example an outdoor caterer's staff.

In common law, employers are expected to provide protection that is reasonable in the circumstances. An employee will be compensated for injury if the employer was at fault in exposing the employee to unnecessary risk in the circumstances.

Unfortunately, common law is not able to provide for all developments in industry and therefore several statutes exist to specify the nature of protection to be provided and to lay down certain other regulations covering the working environment.

Health and Safety at Work Act 1974

The hospitality industry is not as dangerous as some other industries such as construction. However, there can be significant levels of risk to employees, managers and customers. These may include risks that are simple to recognize – such as falling on slippery floors, cuts and burns – through to less obvious risks such as damage to hearing due to very high noise levels, e.g. in discos, or violence from customers and other staff.

In 1975 the Health and Safety at Work Act 1974 came into force, which provides very flexible legislation protecting most employees at work. The Act is largely implemented through a number of different sets of regulations, including the Management of Health and Safety at Work Regulations 1992, amended by the Management of Health and Safety at Work (Amendment) Regulations 1994 and the Health and Safety (Young Persons) Regulations 1997. Other important regulations include the Manual Handling Operations Regulations 1992 and the Control of Substances Hazardous to Health Regulations 1994.

The Act, in principle, obliges employers to ensure the safety of their employees (and also the general public) at the employer's premises, by maintaining safe plant, safe systems of work and safe premises, and also by ensuring adequate instruction, training and supervision. This Act also covers such aspects as cleanliness, overcrowding, lighting, temperature, ventilation and sanitary arrangements for work people. Other people, too, such as designers, manufacturers, installers, importers and suppliers of goods for use at work, are to ensure, in so far as they are responsible, that any health and safety risks are eliminated. Employees also are made responsible for the safety of others.

Risk assessment

From a management point of view probably the most important issue is that of risk assessment. 'Risk assessment' is the term used to describe the process an employer uses to identify risks associated with a business's day-to-day operations. If risk assessment is carried out effectively it will almost certainly reduce the risk of injury, but should an incident occur which leads to litigation it can be used to demonstrate 'due diligence', a legal term used to demonstrate that an employer has taken all reasonable steps to minimize risk. Risks and the likelihood of occurrence are classified as follows:

Hazard severity	Likelihood of occurrence
1 Minor injury	1 Low – seldom occurs
2 Off work for three days or more	2 Medium – frequently occurs
3 Death or major injury	3 High – near certain

Multiplication of the two factors – to give, e.g. 2, 4, 9 – indicates the overall degree of risk. The HCIMA Technical Brief, 'Health and Safety at Work' is included in Appendix 4.

All employers, other than those with fewer than five employees, must have a health and safety policy statement. See Figure 16.2 for one company's approach.

Children (Employment of Children Acts 1933–1969)

Children are defined as being under the minimum school-leaving age. The principal Acts are concerned primarily with protecting the physical well-being of children and with specifying the hours that they are permitted to work. Children, for example, are not permitted to work during school hours and where a child is under 13 years of age the legal restrictions are particularly strict, for example, limiting their hours of work to no more than one hour per day outside of school hours. Restrictions on the working hours of young persons who have left school but are under the age of 18 are also included in the Working Time Regulations 1998. There are also safety reporting requirements for young people within the Management of Health and Safety at Work Regulations 1999.

The regulations regarding children are quite detailed but can vary in detail from one part of the country to another, as they are administered mainly by local authorities. Regulations cover the following points:

- hours of work
- hours on the employer's premises
- hours off duty
- frequency and duration of rest and meal breaks
- permitted overtime
- holidays
- medical examinations.

For details of the regulations as they apply to a particular area it is advisable to contact the local office of the Department for Work and Pensions.

CONTENTS

YOUR HEALTH & SAFETY

We want to make sure that our hotels and units are safe places for people to work and stay in. The Group fully appreciate the aims and provisions of the Health & Safety at Work Act & Regulations.

The Company recognises that one of its most important duties and responsibilities to its staff is to provide and maintain safe, healthy and hygienic working conditions and practices. We ensure, through regular training, that the management in your hotel/unit share this responsibility through the policy laid down and that all members of staff have an individual responsibility for ensuring that the Company safety rules and regulations are adhered to. All staff must co-operate with the management in maintaining a safe and healthy working environment, and if you do not understand your responsibilities or are involved in work that requires specific training, then speak to your Head of Department immediately.

OUR HEALTH AND SAFETY ORGANIZATION

The Managing Director has ultimate responsibility for the implementation of our Health and Safety policy, via the Regional Directors for ensuring that all Managers are made fully aware of, implement and regularly review the Company's Health and Safety policy.

Each individual *Manager*, with assistance of the hotel/unit *Personnel Manager*, has the responsibility for the effectiveness of Health & Safety training as well as drafting up and/or adapting the Health & Safety manual, to their own individual hotel/unit procedures; hazard analysis; and reporting structures. They are also responsible for ensuring that all the staff are aware of and trained in the relevant procedures and that records are kept of all training; accidents and health hazards. Each *Head of Department* is responsible for implementing the Company and hotel/unit policy within their own department.

The Company believes that its members of staff can make a considerable contribution towards achieving the Health & Safety objectives, and is keen to encourage all employees, and in particular staff representatives on the Staff Consultative and/or Health & Safety committee to make positive recommendations where applicable.

Figure 16.2 An example of some of the issues needing to be covered under health and safety law – one company's approach
Source: Reproduced by courtesy of Choice Hotels Europe.

Employment of non-EU subjects

The employment of non-EU subjects needs Home Office approval, through the granting of a work permit. Under the Asylum and Immigration Act 1996 it is a criminal offence to employ a person who does not have authorization to work in the UK. The penalty is £5000 for each offence. (Figure 16.3)

Trade union legislation

The main legislation currently covering trade unions is contained in a number of Acts, including the Trade Union and Labour Relations (Consolidation) Act 1992, the Trade Union Reform and Employment Rights Act 1993 and the Employment Relations Act 1999. These Acts contain legislation concerned with 'collective' employment issues.

PRIVATE AND CONFIDENTIAL   04 June 1999

Dear

Please find enclosed a letter confirming our offer of employment as a Food and Beverage Assistant in John T's Bar and I would be grateful if you could complete the enclosed forms and return them to me in the Human Resources Department as soon as possible.

Also, in accordance with the Asylum & Immigration Act 1996, all new employees are now required to provide proof that they are eligible to work in the United Kingdom. You should bring one of the following documents to the Human Resources Department on your first day:

- A document from a previous employer, the Inland Revenue, the Benefits Agency, the Contributions Agency, or the Employment Service, showing your name and National Insurance Number, e.g.
  - a P45
  - a payslip
  - a P60
  - a National Insurance Number Card
  - a letter from one of the agencies named above
- A passport confirming that you are a British citizen or European Economic Area National.
- A birth certificate confirming birth in the UK or Republic of Ireland.
- A letter from the Home Office confirming that you are allowed to work in the UK.
- A work permit issued by the Department for Education and Employment.

Please note that without these completed forms and proof of eligibility to work in the UK, we will be unable to process your details on our payroll system, which will delay payment of wages.

If you have any queries with any of the above, or your offer letter, please speak to me or any other member of the Human Resources Department.

Yours sincerely,

Michelle Walton
Human Resources Officer

Figure 16.3 An Asylum and Immigration Act statement
Source: Reproduced by courtesy of Marriott Hotels.

Recognition

To qualify for most rights under trade union legislation, trade unions have to be certified as independent by the Certification Officer. Employers themselves need only recognize trade unions if they themselves wish to do so. 'Recognition' means that the employer recognizes the right of the union to represent employees in membership of the trade union. Issues covered in such recognition can include terms and conditions of employment, recruitment and termination procedures, work allocation, discipline and negotiating procedures. The Act contains a 60-page schedule on recognition.

Information

Employers who recognize trade unions are required, by law, to disclose information that is necessary for collective bargaining. The Freedom of Information Act to be enacted at the beginning of 2005 was likely to pose additional challenges for HRM departments.

Trade disputes and immunities

Trade disputes only attract immunity from actions for damages if they are disputes between employees and their employer and are concerned with matters central to their employment relationship. In addition, any action must have been approved in a ballot by a majority of those voting.

Picketing

Picketing is only lawful if carried out as part of a trade dispute and should be at or near the place of work.

In 1999, the Employment Relations Act enacted improvements and new approaches to the statutory rights of trade unions such as recognition and made it a legal right for an employee to be accompanied at disciplinary or grievance hearings. There are also developments in the area of resolving disputes between workers and their employers, via the Employment Act, 2002, which has attempted to reduce the high number of Employment Tribunals by assisting the earlier resolution of such problems well before they get to Tribunal. This will extend the influence of the ACAS and the content of its codes of practice. The year 2004 had seen the implementation of the regulations regarding the non-discrimination of people at work because of their religion or beliefs.

Concluding statement

As stated at the start of this chapter employment is an extremely complex area of law so this chapter must be viewed as a simple introduction to some of the key issues.

Further Reading and References

Boella, M. J. (ed.) *Catering: Reference Book for Caterers*, London: Croner Publications, updated every two months.
Boella, M. J. (ed.) *Catering Records and Procedures*, London: Croner Publications, updated every three months.

Boella, M. J. (ed.) *Catering A–Z*, London: Croner Publications, updated every three months.

Boella, M. J. and Pannett, A. (1999) *Principles of Hospitality Law*, 2nd edn, London: Cassell.

Goss-Turner, S. (2002) *Managing People in the Hospitality Industry*, 4th edn, Kingston-upon-Thames: Croner Publications.

Guest, D. (2001) Industrial relations and human resource management, in Storey, J. (ed.) *Human Resource Management—A Critical Text*, 2nd edn, London: Thomson Learning.

Lucas, R. (2004) *Employment Relations in the Hospitality and Tourism Industries*, London: Routledge.

Sweeney, S. (ed.) *Reference Book for Employers*, London: Croner Publications, updated regularly.

Sweeney, S. (ed.) *Employment Law*, London: Croner Publications, updated regularly.

Tyson, S. and York, A. (2000) *Essentials of HRM*, 4th edn, Oxford: Butterworth-Heinemann.

Questions

1 Describe the main distinct areas of law affecting employment.

2 Describe the 'fair reasons' for terminating employment.

3 Describe a 'fair disciplinary' procedure (see also Chapter 14).

4 Discuss the proposition that a contract of employment is much more than the 'written statement' required by the Employment Rights Act 1996.

5 Evaluate the approach adopted by an employer you know well to managing their labour force as the law requires.

6 Discuss the proposition that government intervention through statute law has no place in the employment relationship.

Human resource planning, records and statistics

In recent years the importance of an undertaking's human resources has become much more apparent as employers look for competitive advantage through improved service and because of the considerable costs of labour and the growing staff shortages in some sectors of the hospitality industry. The 'demographic time bomb', i.e. the reduction in the number of young people available for work in the new century, will contribute to the scale of the problem for many employers. The arrival too of new employers on the labour market will create new demands on an evermore competitive labour market.

In many other industries and organizations these problems have led to much attention being paid to most aspects of human resource management. It has led, in particular, to accurate planning so that an employer has the right resources available when required and also so that labour costs are not unnecessarily high. Because of this, well-conceived human resource policies are now playing an increasingly important part in furthering many undertakings' business objectives. They translate the overall business plan, normally concerned in the private sector with competitiveness and profitability, into a detailed plan. Such policies and plans may be summarized in an enterprise's mission statement.

Sound human resource policies can only be achieved through a thorough understanding of the organization, its objectives, its management, its operating style and its social and political environment. Human resource planning can therefore be described as the process of interpreting the environment, predicting its effects on the organization, evaluating these effects and planning and controlling the appropriate measures in order that the right human resources are available when required.

Human resource policies must play a positive and creative role in the plans, developments and day-to-day activities of an undertaking. They must be designed to provide competent human resources when required. The need to plan on a sound basis of reliable information has been emphasized, and much of a manager's work revolves around certain basic and fundamental information; for example, precise job or role descriptions have been shown to be vital not only to recruitment but also to training, performance appraisal, job evaluation and salary administration.

Human resource planning is divided into two separate and distinct parts: strategic and operational. The strategic part of planning is concerned with ensuring that the right people will be available in the longer term, for example for hotels that are not even built.

Strategic human resource planning for larger organizations requires a thorough understanding of the organization and its environment. Figure 17.1 shows a 'systems thinking' diagram – how an organization's plan can be affected by its environment.

At the operational level, management needs to know precisely what staffing ratios are necessary. Each organization and each establishment will have its own, such as one waiter for ten covers and one room attendant for fourteen rooms (Figure 17.2).

At the strategic level, management needs accurate statistics in order to develop the undertaking's long-term plans. This is best illustrated by a real example with which one of the authors of this book was associated. A brewery company wanted to expand its number of managed public houses by 100. It needed to recruit at least 100 new husband-and-wife teams to run these public houses. In addition, if it had 100 managed houses already it would have to anticipate finding replacements for some of these existing 100 managers. If wastage rates are unknown, it is not possible to calculate accurately what numbers to recruit and train. On the other hand the company had kept records and these showed that wastage among established managers was 20% per annum and among trainees 30%. It was then simple to determine how many to recruit in a year.

Since 100 couples were required for new houses and 20 couples were required for existing houses, this indicated that a total of 120 couples were needed to complete training. However, as wastage during training is 30%, the number to be recruited had to be increased to compensate for this loss.

The brewery, therefore, knew on the basis of past experience that it would need to recruit about 172 couples to fill 120 vacancies likely to occur. The actual phasing of this recruitment depended on other factors such as the length of training, the availability of new public houses, the policy for retiring or replacing tenants, etc. This illustrates that plans for the future are difficult to implement effectively without adequate records and statistics. However, as was said much earlier, the individual's needs, as well as the employer's, have to be recognized – consequently any records and statistical data must serve the individual as well as the employer.

Personnel information and records are required for several reasons:

1 To provide detailed operational information such as monthly strength returns and payroll analyses.
2 To provide ratios or data such as wastage rates, age analyses and service analyses for planning purposes.

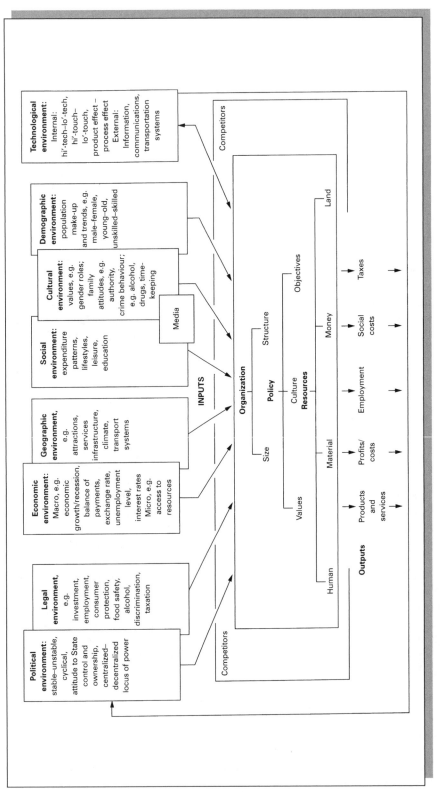

Figure 17.1 A 'systems thinking' diagram

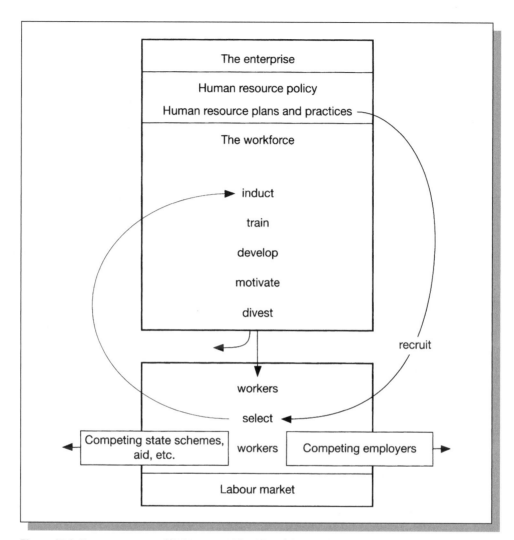

Figure 17.2 Human resource planning – matching labour supply to demand

3 To provide information on individuals for administration purposes such as salaries and pensions and to provide information for career development purposes.
4 To provide information for statutory purposes such as National Insurance, redundancy payment, minimum wage, maximum hours, etc.
5 To provide information for re-employment and reference purposes.
6 To provide information for discipline and possible employment litigation purposes.

The nature of records and statistics that may be maintained and produced by employers varies considerably. The largest organizations in the UK require highly sophisticated information using computer-based systems, whereas smaller organizations need only minimal information. However, the following systems are probably basic to most organizations employing more than a few people. It has to be borne in mind that all records including manual records are subject to data protection legislation (Data Protection Act 1984 and 1998) and may be affected by the Freedom of Information Act to be implemented in 2005.

Personal record

This is the backbone of a good records system. If both the contents and the layout are designed carefully, it can provide valuable information quickly and easily. Whether this record is a simple index card, a visible edge card or a computer file depends on the number of employees and the amount of detail required.

The record should contain concise information of a sort common to most employees, such as age, education, qualifications, training and marital status. It is used primarily for statistical exercises or for the speedy retrieval of information; for example, the record may be used to produce an age distribution of all management employees in order to assist with management development plans, or, alternatively, the cards may be used to discover French speakers or all those with 'instructor' training. The personal record does not replace the need for a personal dossier for each employee. The nature and purpose of personal information kept by employers now has to be carefully considered for a number of reasons. For example, to keep information that could be used in order to discriminate on grounds of sex or race may be illegal. A typical personal record card will look like the one shown in Figure 17.3.

Personal dossier

This should contain all documents relating to an individual employee. These may include

- copies of letters of offer and acceptance
- application form
- copy of engagement form
- various reports and correspondence
- performance appraisals
- changes of conditions, e.g. salary increases
- records of company property issued to the employee
- disciplinary measures.

The dossier is usually retained for a period of time (a year or two) after an employee has left, to assist in case of queries.

Employment requisition

This is a document produced by the heads of departments (in larger organizations) requesting authority to recruit a replacement or an addition to staff. The nature of this form varies considerably and depends on the degree of authority of individual heads of departments. In some cases, for example, heads of departments will need no special authority so long as the person to be recruited will be within the laid-down staff establishment or within authorized budget levels. On the other hand, there are chief executives even in some large organizations who insist on personally authorizing the recruitment of all new staff whether they are replacing leavers or exceeding the staff establishment. A typical form is shown in Figure 17.4.

Surname		Forenames		Clock/Staff no.
Home address				
1st change of address				Telephone no.
2nd change of address				Telephone no.
				Telephone no.
Sex	Date of birth	Nationality		Ethnic origin*
Marital status		No. of children		
Emergency contact (name, address, tel. no.)				Relationship

Employment

Work address				
1st change of address				Telephone no.
2nd change of address				Telephone no.
				Telephone no.
Start date		Work permit		Expiry date

Job History

Date	Dept.	Job title	Reason for change	Date	Dept.	Job title	Reason for change

Terms and Conditions

PT/FT	Temp/Perm	Working hours	Shift pattern	Hours pw
Holiday entitlement	Company sick pay entitlement	SSP qualifying days	Pension	
Other				

Pay History

Date	Current salary	Increase	Remarks	Date	Current salary	Increase	Remarks

*Such data may be needed to rebut accusations of discrimination.

Figure 17.3 A personal record card

Source: Croner's Personnel Records: reproduced with kind permission of Croner Publications.

Payroll

Payroll no.		NI no.		Tax code	
Bank (name and address)				Bank sort code	
				Account no.	

Health

RDP		Disability		RDP no.	
Medical restrictions					

Pension scheme/insurance etc.

Date	Comments	Date	Comments

Skills and qualifications

Educational achievements	
Work qualifications	
Languages and proficiency	Test scores
Other skills	Management experience

Miscellaneous

Professional bodies			Territorial army	
Public offices			Union or safety representative	
Union membership	Check off		Driving licence	
First aid certificate				

Previous Employment

Dates	Company	Position	Reason for leaving	Dates	Company	Position	Reason for leaving

Termination

Due retirement date		Termination date		Termination code	

Figure 17.3 *continued*

AUTHORITY TO RECRUIT

1. RECRUITMENT NEEDS ANALYSIS – Before completing the form:

a. Consider whether any of the following might provide a more cost-effective alternative to recruitment:
   — re-organisation of staff (duties/hours)?
   — contract labour?
   — mechanisation?
   — improved working methods?
   — revision of standards?

b. Consider whether business product changes might alter the situation.

c. Check whether recent exit interviews indicate a need to alter the job description, person specification or the reporting relationships.

Further guidance may be obtained from Personnel or by referring to the Recruitment and Selection Manual.

---

2. POSITION VACANT: ....

....

DEPARTMENT/LOCATION:...................

WAGE SCALE/SALARY RANGE: ....

HOURS OF WORK: ....

SPECIAL CONDITIONS:........................

Replacement/New Position*

Job Description

          attached/not attached*

Person Specification attached/
not attached*

*delete as appropriate

3. RECRUITMENT PLAN – indicate here which means of recruitment you intend to use or wish Personnel to use:

	tick
internal applications	
career development scheme	
holding file	
job centre	
schools & colleges	
mail shots	
advertising	
agencies	

---

4. NAMES OF AUTHORISED PERSONS

To authorise recruitment.......................

....

To recruit:...

To select: ....

To decide to make offer:........................

....

FURTHER DETAILS – e.g. media to be used if advertising:

ESTIMATED RECRUITMENT COST:

Figure 17.4 Example of an employment requisition
Source: Reproduced by courtesy of Forte Hotels.

```
┌─────────────────────────────────────────────────────────────┐
│  ┌──────────────────────────────────────────────────────┐   │
│  │ 5. I confirm that I have carried out a  6. AUTHORISED │   │
│  │    recruitment  needs  analysis  and                 │   │
│  │    wish to recruit as above.                         │   │
│  │                                                      │   │
│  │    Signed............................  Signed.............│ │
│  │                  (ORIGINATOR)           (DESIGNATED MANAGER)│
│  │                                                      │   │
│  │    Date............................    Date .............│ │
│  └──────────────────────────────────────────────────────┘   │
│  Completed form to be sent to the recruiter responsible for action.│
└─────────────────────────────────────────────────────────────┘
```

Figure 17.4 *continued*

In most of the larger well-organized undertakings, the personnel department also have to authorize the salary or wage to be paid in order to ensure that anomalies are not allowed to creep in.

Engagement form

This form should be completed when a new employee joins an employer. The purpose is to inform all the relevant departments so that appropriate action is initiated. These departments may include

- wages
- training
- pensions
- insurance
- personnel records.

The information contained on the form varies according to the system being used; for example, some employers may be able to use one engagement form for all departments and all levels of staff whereas other employers may need to use different forms for each. It is of prime importance, however, to ensure that the employee is paid and insured. Consequently information should include name, staff number, address, department, date of starting, rate of pay and bank address. Figure 17.5 shows one typical example.

Termination form

This form is necessary in order to fulfil several purposes:

1 To initiate documentation and administration procedures such as preparation of the P45 and the final wages payment.
2 To provide statistical information regarding labour turnover.
3 To provide information for reference or re-employment purposes.

NEW STARTER FORM (E)
FULL/PART TIME STAFF Only

CHOICE HOTELS EUROPE
Comfort Quality Clarion

To: SALARIES SERVICES   FROM:_____   DATE SENT:_____
                          (Personnel/Assistant/General Manager)

> **NEW STARTERS (Full/Part Time)**
> **WILL NOT BE PROCESSED BY SALARIES SERVICES UNTIL BOTH**
> **THIS PAGE AND THE REVERSE IS FULLY COMPLETED AND SIGNED**

SURNAME:_____ Mr/Mrs/Miss   HOTEL/UNIT:_____

FIRST NAME:_____   DEPARTMENT:_____

HOME ADDRESS:_____   JOB TITLE:_____

_____   START DATE:_____

_____   SALARY:_____

DATE OF BIRTH:_____   HOURS:_____ per week   LIVE IN/OUT*
                                                                          * (Delete as applicable)

NATIONAL INSURANCE NO:_____   P.45/46/38 ENCLOSED
(If **Temporary No.** attach benefit agency letter confirming   YES   NO
this has been applied for)   (Circle as applicable)

BANK/BUILDING SOCIETY DETAILS

BANK:_____   BUILDING SOCIETY:_____

ACCOUNT NO:_____   ACCOUNT NO:_____

SORT CODE:_____   SORT CODE:_____

                                         ACCOUNT REF. NO:_____

'I confirm that document numbers 1–6 & 13–16, as per the check list overleaf, have been duly issued, signed by the employee and filed, with document numbers 7–12 to be actioned on the specified date'.

A: Signed:_____   **Personnel/Assistant/General Manager**

As General Manager, I have authorised the *replacement/*increased establishment   (*Delete as applicable)

B: Signed:_____   **General Manager**

Figure 17.5 Example of an engagement form
Source: Reproduced by courtesy of Choice Hotels.

CHOICE HOTELS
EUROPE

THE FOLLOWING DOCUMENTS MUST BE COMPLETED
for all
FULL & PART TIME EMPLOYEES
(over 8 hours per week)
PRIOR
TO THIS 'NEW STARTER FORM' BEING FORWARDED TO
SALARIES SERVICES

(Tick or insert dates as applicable)

PHOTOCOPY OR FAX THE 'NEW STARTER DETAILS' ON THE REVERSE SIDE OF THIS FORM, AND FORWARD TO SALARIES SERVICES

THIS ORIGINAL COPY TO BE RETAINED IN THE PERSONNEL FOLDER.

---

1)	APPLICATION FORM	-	Completed in full and signed prior to interview
2)	JOB DESCRIPTION	-	Presented either **at interview** or **upon commencement**
3)	REFERENCES	-	a **minimum of 2**, preferably 3 to have been forwarded
4)	INDUCTION RECORD	-	complete within first **7 days**
5)	GUIDE TO HEALTH & SAFETY	-	complete within first **7 days** plus Dept. requirements
6)	HOUSE RULES	-	present and sign within **7 days**
7)	DEPT. TRAINING RECORD	-	to have commenced with **7 days**
8)	FOOD HYGIENE TRAINING	-	for all new Food Handlers within **7 days**
9)	3 WEEK APPRAISAL	-	indicate date
10)	CONTRACT	-	issue within **8 weeks** of commencement
11)	5 MONTH APPRAISAL	-	indicate date
12)	COSHH TRAINING	-	every **6 months** – indicate date to be arranged
13)	FOOD HYGIENE DECLARATION	-	issue **6 monthly** to all Food Handlers
14)	UNIFORM RECEIPT	-	where applicable	n/a _____ or
15)	LIVING IN RULES	-	where applicable	n/a _____ or
16)	LIQUOR RULES	-	where applicable	n/a _____ or

Figure 17.5 *continued*

Other forms

There is a variety of other information that may have to be kept for contractual, statutory or other purposes. This can include

- accident reports
- medical reports

- training reports
- absentee reports
- change of status, e.g. salary increases, promotions, transfers
- warnings.

From these various documents most of the statistical information required for the satisfactory planning and control of most undertakings can be produced.

Strength returns

This shows the numbers employed by departments and should show changes in numbers. It may also incorporate 'establishment' numbers, i.e. the agreed numbers to be employed in each department. Any variation from establishment will be shown.

Payroll analysis

This information (a development of the strength return) may be produced by a variety of departments including the wages department, the cost or management accountant's department and the personnel manager's department. It will include a breakdown, by departments, of labour costs. These may be shown in a great variety of ways including various ratios and percentages. The figures should always include a comparison of the actual and budget figures.

Both the strength return and the payroll analysis should be produced on a regular, periodic basis. Where there is strict control over wage and salary levels the strength return will be sufficient for most day-to-day management purposes, since cost variances will only arise where there are variances from the laid-down establishment. In any case the labour costs should show up elsewhere – in particular on periodic operating statements.

Procedures

Staff/labour turnover analysis

This has been discussed in Chapter 14. However, it must be stressed that regular production of this information can assist considerably in staff recruitment and retention, by identifying problem areas.

The turnover rate for each department and for the undertaking as a whole will make up part of this report. This can be arrived at roughly by the following formula:

$$\frac{\text{Number of employees who left during the period}}{\text{Average number employed during the period}} \times 100$$

Such data must be prepared and considered carefully, however. One company, for example, found that all in-company transfers had been included, thus distorting the turnover rate.

In itself the turnover rate may be of little value, since it gives no indication, for example, of turnover among long-serving employees, i.e. the 'retention' rate. This is a measure of the proportion of employees who have stayed for a specified period, e.g. one year. It may, therefore, be necessary to supplement labour turnover figures

Analysis of leavers for 12 months ending 31 December 2005		
Length of service (years)	Number of leavers	Percentage
More than 5	4	5.0
More than 2 less than 5	8	10.0
More than 1 less than 2	10	12.5
Up to 1	58	72.5
Total	80	100.0

Figure 17.6 An analysis of leavers by length of service, 2005

with further breakdowns. This may be done in a variety of ways including showing numbers of leavers by length of service, as shown in Figure 17.6.

Age and service analyses

For human resource planning and management development purposes it is important in the medium- and larger-sized organizations from time to time to look at the make-up of the labour force and in particular at the age profile of the workforce and management team. If this is not done, an unanticipated spate of retirements and resignations can leave an undertaking without the necessary trained personnel. It is useful, therefore, to produce an annual age profile of management, headed by those due to retire. In some cases it may be desirable to link this with service as shown above (Figure 17.7).

Age	Service									
	Under 1 year	1–5	6–10	11–15	16–20	21–25	26–30	31–35	36–40	41+
61–65			1		2		2			
56–60						1				
50–55		6	3	3		1				
46–50	3		2							
41–45	1									
36–40			1	1	2					
31–35	2	8	1							
26–30	8	7								
21–25	2	3								
under 21	1	2								

Figure 17.7 An age and service analysis

In examining the type of chart shown in Figure 17.7 one would hope to see the bulk of managers distributed fairly evenly through the chart, preferably slightly weighted towards the younger end. Where this is not the case, the management team may not have the necessary combination of age, experience and inbuilt continuity. Consequently senior management may wish to take steps to put this right by promotion, transfers, recruitment and appropriate training. However, because of age discrimination legislation this may be legally constrained.

Human resource audit

Some of the largest employers conduct detailed studies periodically which provide a complete breakdown of the labour force into various sections including job grades, age and service. They may also report on the quality of staff, their qualifications, performance and potential. The training plan, management development programme and manpower plan may be part of, or may be linked with, this audit.

Some organizations, the most sophisticated, may also set out to determine the 'economic' value of their human resources by placing values on the costs of recruitment, induction, training, development, wastage, etc. This is sometimes referred to as human asset accounting (HAA).

Apart from the records and data discussed here, there are many more that may be necessary for effective planning and control. However, it is important to bear in mind that although the production and interpretation of information and statistics can in itself be an attractive occupation, only those data that serve a useful purpose should be produced. They should clearly be aids to line management in providing an effective service. If they do not satisfy this requirement, the information being produced is almost certainly unwanted and consequently it is a waste of resources that could be employed more fruitfully elsewhere.

Computers and the personnel function

Computers have been used to a great extent for many years in business. Within the human resource or personnel function there are now many systems available, often known as computerized personnel information systems (CPISs). Major uses now include employee records, payroll, management reports, absence and holiday records and Statutory Sick Pay/Statutory Maternity pay (SSP/SMP) records. There are also software programmes for succession planning and management development purposes. CPISs will be integrated into the total management information system and accessed directly by line management. Line managers will not have their information filtered by personnel staff. Instead, personnel people will be more involved in designing CPISs. These predictions were made at the International Hotels Association (IHA) conference held in Tel Aviv in 1995. At this conference a speaker described the Federal Express personnel records system, which was already largely paperless and which was accessible to management and staff alike. Staff, for example, were able to search for internal transfer and promotion opportunities whilst supervisors and managers were able to access data instantly which previously was filtered by personnel staff. Another system reported at the IHA Human Resource Think Tank held in The Netherlands in 1999 described a system of self-rostering which, using a computer-based system, allowed (or empowered) staff to make decisions about where and on what shifts they worked.

Further Reading and References

Armstrong, M. (1999) *A Handbook of Human Resource Management*, 7th edn, London: Kogan Page.

Boella, M. J. (ed.) (2000) *Croner's Records and Procedures*, London: Croner Publications (updated annually).

Goss-Turner, S. (2002) *Managing People in the Hospitality Industry*, 4th edn, Kingston-upon-Thames: Croner Publications.

Jones, W. (1992) Labour control, *Caterer and Hotelkeeper*, 17 September.

Pratt, K. J. and Bennett, S. C. (1990) *Elements of Personnel Management*, 4th edn, Wokingham: GEE.

Richards-Carpenter, C. (1991) Towards 'On-Line' managers, *Personnel Management*, September.

Sisson, K. (ed.) (1989) *Personnel Management in Britain*, Oxford: Blackwell.

Torrington, D., Hall, L. and Taylor, S. (2002) *Human Resource Management*, 5th edn, Harlow: Pearson Education.

Questions

1 Describe the objectives of human resource planning and the various elements of an effective process.

2 Discuss what external factors influence the nature of human resource planning.

3 Evaluate the approach to human resource planning used by an employer you know well.

CHAPTER 18

Labour costs and productivity

In any industry in which labour is a significant cost, its monitoring and control is vital. This is certainly the case in the hospitality industry. However, labour costs in themselves do not give a full picture. A labour percentage or cost does not indicate whether an employer employs a few people at high rates of pay or a large number of people at low rates of pay. It is important therefore for a well-managed enterprise to monitor both its labour costs and its productivity.

In some industries it is reasonably simple to state with some degree of confidence what labour costs should be as a percentage of total costs, of revenue or of some other clear standard. However, hospitality enterprises often offer a service to other industries, apart from creating an end product in their own right, so no such simple yardstick exists; for example, labour costs in a modern, efficiently designed and well-managed public house may be as low as 10%, whereas in many sectors of institutional and industrial catering labour may cost 60–70% of revenue. In some clubs labour costs can approach 90% of trade done. In this case the apparently high labour cost is often caused by the very high level of subscription income not accounted for in trade revenue, and by the low level of price charged for goods and services.

Factors influencing labour costs

The factors that influence labour costs are numerous but probably what determines labour cost more than anything else is the precise nature of the enterprise, and the employer's particular policy; for example, if the business provides a subsidized service, with low selling prices to employees, then labour costs as a percentage of revenue will be high. If, at the other extreme, it wants to maximize profit in the short term, by providing a product involving minimum service from capital-intensive plant, using unskilled staff, as in many fast food operations, then the labour costs will be low. Figure 18.1 illustrates some factors influencing labour costs and productivity.

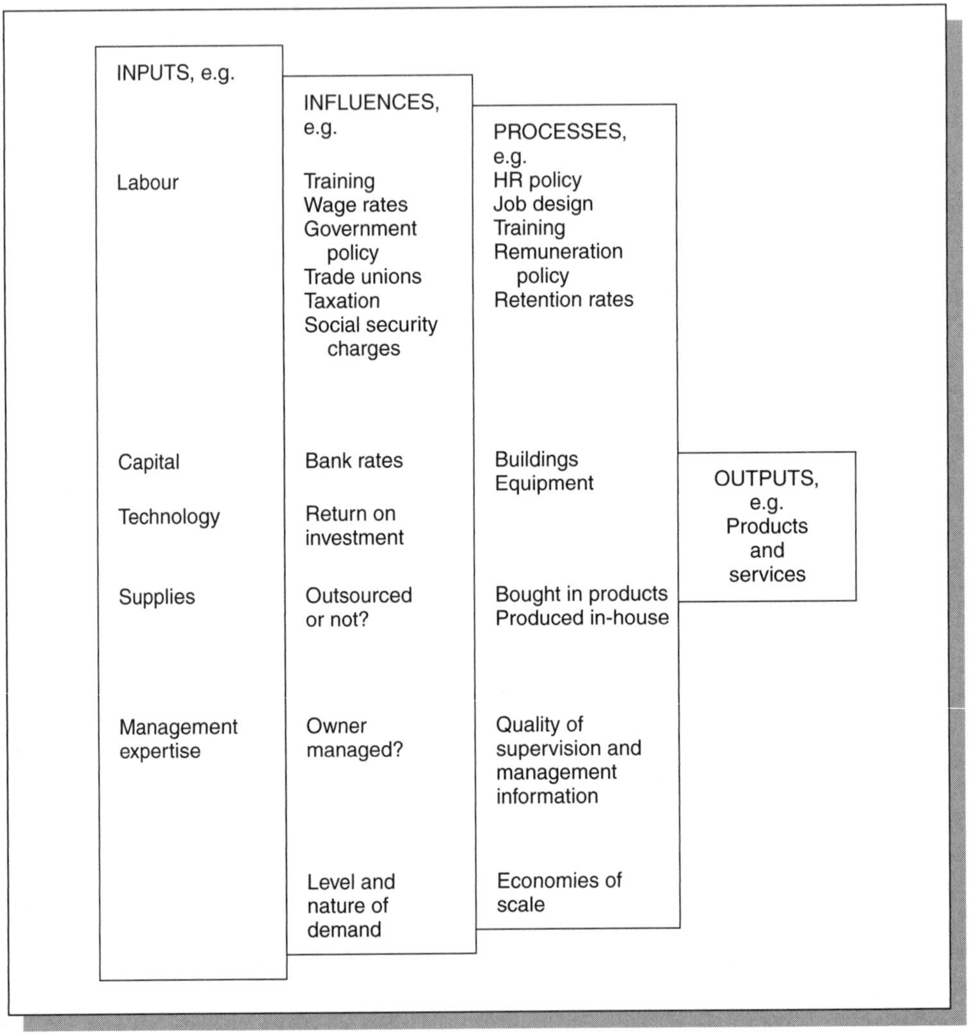

Figure 18.1 A simple 'input–output' productivity model

Another major factor is efficiency of design. Modern, carefully designed hotels can now expect room attendants to service around 17 bedrooms per section, in contrast to older hotels, where sections often have to be much smaller.

Equally important of course is the level of service provided. A fast food takeaway operation or a wine bar may operate with a labour percentage of around 15%, whereas a high-class restaurant offering skilled personal attention may need to operate at around 35% labour cost. Likewise a modern three-star hotel with minimal personal service can operate at around 18–20% labour cost while some five-star hotels may need to spend around 40% on labour. Such percentages also vary from country to country.

Trade unions

Trade unions can influence rates and labour costs in a number of ways. In the public sector they negotiate on behalf of catering workers along with many other workers. In the private sector some catering employees' rates are determined along with rates that unions have negotiated for another industry's primary workers such as motor manufacturers' or warehouse staff.

Owner managers

In establishments at the smaller end of the scale a vital factor influencing labour costs is whether an establishment is run by the owner or by an employed manager. Owners managing an establishment can influence labour costs in a number of ways. First, some owners pay themselves unrealistic wages for a variety of reasons, not least to minimize tax liability. Second, owners generally are much firmer in controlling costs and third, they avoid employing excess labour as cover for themselves and for other employees.

The labour percentages in Figure 18.2 are intended to indicate the approximate level of labour cost (as a percentage of revenue, net of value added tax) likely to be

Type of outlet	Percentage range (as a percentage of revenue) per annum	Factors which can affect labour percentage	
		low	high
Hotels		efficient design, limited menu, living-in staff, limited services	inefficient design, extensive menus, high level of service, e.g. room service
2–3 star	18–32		
4–5 star	25–35		
rooms division	12–20		
food and beverage	30–45		
Restaurants – waiter/ waitress service	25–35	as above	as above
Popular catering – waitress service	22–35		
Self-service	15–25	as above	as above
Wine bars	15–22	as above	as above
Fast food takeaway	11–18	as above	as above
Department stores	20–25	as above	as above
Kiosks, mainly confectionery and tobacco	around 6	very high tobacco element	
Public houses	10–20	efficient design, e.g. one bar, mainly liquor sales	high catering ratio, several bars/restaurants

This table is intended to be a guide only, and it must be recognized that businesses may still operate successfully outside of these. These should be viewed as the range within which most viable businesses operate on a long-term (e.g. annual) basis. There can be considerable fluctuation on a short-term basis as labour costs are not a completely variable cost. *Note*: Contract catering is not included as results are totally dependent upon client policy.

Figure 18.2 Labour costs as a percentage of revenue

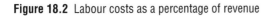

encountered in viable establishments. This does not mean that there are not successful establishments operating outside these ranges. Likewise, it must be recognized that labour costs are partly fixed and partly variable, so if trade drops dramatically there is a point beyond which labour costs can no longer be reduced to maintain them within the normally accepted percentages – a problem all too familiar to the management of seasonal establishments.

In some cases the wage percentage may well be reviewed on an annual basis. Most organizations, however, monitor labour costs on a shorter-term basis, monthly or maybe even weekly, with many of the fast food outlets now planning labour on an hourly basis.

Figure 18.3 illustrates a format used by some fast food operators. The consequence of this precise hour-by-hour planning is that labour costs are planned and controlled accurately to precise percentages. One of the international fast food chains operates branches at around an 11.5% labour cost, with management costs ranging from 2% for the most efficient and busy branches up to 6% for others.

Payroll burden

There are other factors to take into account, however, which influence labour costs. In particular there is what is often referred to as the 'payroll burden'. This consists of costs that are additional to the wages and salaries paid to labour and includes elements such as holiday pay, meals, uniforms, staff transport, etc. One key element is the extent to which an employer incurs tax or social security liabilities. In the UK the basic state social security cost (National Insurance) can be around 11%, which is relatively low compared with some other countries such as France or Sweden, where it can be as high as 40–50%.

Productivity measurement

As already mentioned, one of the problems of using labour percentage as the main means of labour cost control is that it does not indicate whether the cost is the result of employing a large number of low-paid people or of employing fewer people but paying them a higher wage. In addition, in many sectors of the industry, such as the school meals service, the hospital service and employee meal services, labour costs cannot be expressed as a proportion of revenue because there may be little or no revenue, or because subsidies distort the picture. Other measures, therefore, become necessary. Basically these are concerned with relating labour input to the various forms of output. Such measures include physical and part-physical, part-financial measures and they vary among the different sectors and also within departments. These may be based on some constant (i.e. a factor unaffected by inflation) such as time. Some examples are shown in Figure 18.4. It should be borne in mind, however, that straight comparisons can be dangerous; for example, in one contract-catering situation a 'main meal' may offer each customer a wide choice, whereas in another situation there may be no choice. Other factors such as shift work and night work also play an important part, as do national and international work patterns; for example, an Industrial Society survey (*Catering, Prices, Costs and Subsidies*) showed that for every individual catering worker employed, about 22 main meals were served. The author's own consultancy work shows that in some other

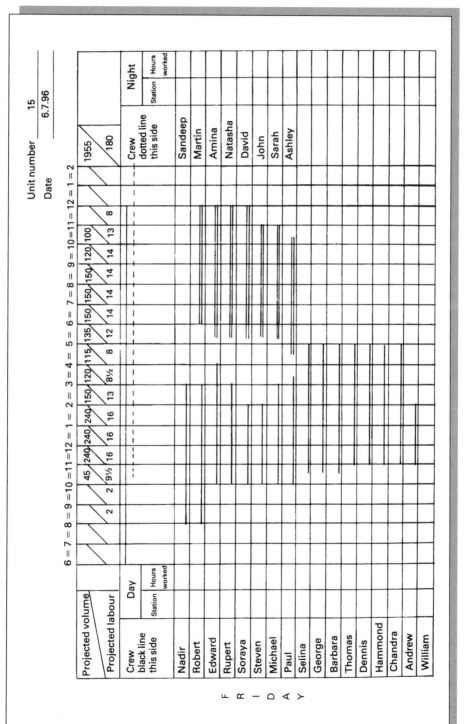

Figure 18.3 Employee's work schedule

Department	Description of productivity measure	Some examples
Catering		
Employee meal service	1 Number of meals served for each member of staff (full-time equivalent)	30 meals per day
	2 Covers served per paid hour	4.5 covers
	3 Paid minutes for each meal served	
	plate wash	7 minutes
	waiters	24 minutes
	cooks	15 minutes
	Coffee Shop	15 minutes
Hospitals	4 Labour as a percentage of direct costs $$\frac{Labour + Materials}{Labour} \times 100$$	e.g. 52%
School meals	5 Labour to materials ratio	£2 labour to £2 material
Hotels	1 Employees per room	e.g. 0.9 per room
	2 Number of guest nights for each member of staff (full-time equivalent)	21 sleeper nights for each member of staff
	3 Number of rooms served for each member of staff on duty	17 rooms to 1 member of staff
	4 Number of paid minutes for each sleeper night	
	room-attendants	27 minutes per room (attendants on duty only)
	reception	33 minutes per guest night
Public houses/bars	1 Barrels and barrels equivalent per full-time equivalent	3–7 barrels per week

Figure 18.4 Some examples of productivity measures

European countries the number of meals served is frequently between 50 and 60 for each industrial catering worker employed.

The list in Figure 18.5 is taken from one North American hotel. Not all items listed are direct measures of labour cost or productivity but they all inform management decisions, most of which will affect staffing.

Number of units sold per employee

A commonly used crude measure of productivity is that of the number of units produced/sold for each employee. This measure is frequently used, for example, to compare car-manufacturing productivity between nations. In order to make use of such a measure it is necessary to have additional information, e.g. how many components are outsourced. In hotels and restaurants one very simple measure is to relate the number of employees to the number of units of service, e.g. rooms, guests or meals served. These are usually extremely crude measures, since comparisons

Total food outlet sales

Breakfast, lunch, dinner 'capture'; number of hotel residents taking breakfast, lunch and dinner

Breakfast, lunch and dinner average checks, i.e. spend per head

REVPAR (Revenue per available room)

House profit PAR (per average room)

Rooms division hours per occupied room; total of rooms division hours paid divided by total of occupied rooms

Laundry hours per occupied room; similar to the above

Kitchen hours per cover; total of kitchen hours paid divided by total of covers served

Stewarding hours per cover; similar to the above

Beverage sales per hour paid; total of beverage sales divided by paid hours

Banqueting hours per cover; total of banqueting revenue divided by total of banqueting hours paid

Total of administration and general expenses per available room; total administration and general costs divided by total relevant labour costs including senior management.

Figure 18.5 A North American example of some key ratios

are rarely like with like. Some rooms may be larger than others, some meals may be more complex than others, some elements may be outsourced and some guests may stay for longer periods than others.

Number of employees per 100 rooms

This is a simple measure which can (but not always) indicate the level of service provided.

Sales to payroll index

This is another way of expressing the labour cost as a proportion of revenue. It indicates the amount of revenue in pounds generated by each pound spent on labour. For hotels in the UK, for example, the index for rooms was about £4.00 for every pound spent on labour (British Hospitality Association, 1999).

Sales and payroll cost per employee

Another method is to look at the sales per employee and, after deducting the employee cost, the net sales per employee.

Added value

This method assesses the value added by each pound spent on labour. It is calculated by representing the gross profit (sales less material costs) as a proportion of the labour cost.

Materials-to-labour ratio

In many catering operations where there may be little or no revenue, or where there is a subsidy element (e.g. hospitals, schools, employee meal services, clubs), expressing labour costs as a proportion of sales is either not possible or can be meaningless for comparative purposes. Other measures are, therefore, necessary – these can include the materials-to-labour ratio, i.e. how much labour is needed to process the materials required. In hospitals this can be around a 1:1 ratio, whereas in some school meals operations it can range from around 0.4:1.0 in centralized production operations to as high as 2.6:1.0 in some labour-intensive, localized production systems.

Effective use of available labour is obviously one of the key measures to controlling labour costs. Other factors to take into account include considering alternative ways of getting work done which can reduce the payroll burden. For example, many companies such as IBIS (part of the French Accor Group) use contract cleaners to service their hotel bedrooms. Whilst this may appear an expensive method in the short term, in the long term their labour cost is reduced and management can concentrate their efforts on the core business.

The international context

Costs of labour and productivity of the workforce vary considerably from one country to another for a whole range of reasons – to do with skill, training, government policy, management expertise and attitudes to work. Several of the leading specialist management consultancies produce regular reports on the worldwide hospitality industry and these show considerable differences in labour costs. Examples of these statistics are shown in Figure 18.6.

Bahrain	1.42	London (upper tier)	1.62
Berlin	0.68	London (lower-tier)	0.62
Brussels	0.51	London (all)	0.87
Cape Town	0.94	Moscow	1.20
Copenhagen	0.29	Paris (upper tier)	2.17
Helsinki	0.24	Paris (lower-tier)	0.62
Jerusalem	0.57	Paris (all)	0.95

Figure 18.6 Staff to room Ratio
Source: PKF 2003.

Good productivity measurement enables comparisons to be made between units or groups of workers employed on the same operations, or the same unit or groups of workers at different times. In spite of the many problems encountered in attempting to make comparisons, productivity measurement is a vital control tool for management, helping with budgeting, forecasting, human resource planning, incentive schemes and diagnosis of poor performance. Productivity measurement has the advantage over straight labour percentages of providing a constant measurement that is unaffected by inflation and changes in wage rates.

Further Reading and References

British Hospitality Association (1999) *British Hospitality Trends and Statistics*, London: BHA.

British Hospitality Association (2004) *British Hospitality Association: Trends and Statistics 2004*, London: BHA.

Catering Prices, Costs and Subsidies, London: Industrial Society, published annually.

PKF (2003) *City Survey*, London: PKF.

Ingold, T. and Yeoman, I. (2000) *Yield Management in the Hospitality Industry*, 2nd edn, London: Continuum.

Medlik, S. (1999) *The Business of Hotels*, 4th edn, London: Heinemann.

Questions

1 Describe the objectives of and alternative approaches to labour cost and productivity measurement.

2 Discuss the differences between labour cost measurement and productivity measurement.

3 Discuss what external factors influence (a) labour costs and (b) productivity.

4 Evaluate the approach to managing labour costs and productivity used by an employer you know well.

PART 6

HRM and Hospitality: Contemporary Issues

CHAPTER • • • • 19

Organizing human resources

The preceding chapters have concentrated largely on the various management techniques that are concerned with obtaining, training, motivating and administering staff. In addition to these various processes, however, managers also have to organize staff, i.e. to create groups of people who will meet the organization's objectives. This is normally one of the major responsibilities of line management who organize their work people into groups in the manner they think best, basing their organization usually on what they have observed or experienced elsewhere. Nowadays, however, there is a growing recognition that organizing people into the most appropriate work groups is a highly skilled and complex task, often referred to as 'organization development', which is concerned with 'improving an organization's ability to achieve its goals by using people more effectively' (French and Saward, 1977). A great deal has been written about organizing people at work. Major ideas on the subject range from the Scientific School of Management through the Human Relations School to current ideas on systems and contingency. Some of the relevant key writers' ideas are summarized in Figure 2.5.

The object of this chapter is not to give a history of the evolution of thinking on organization structures but to highlight some key issues and the factors that influence choice about the nature of an organization. Organizations exist principally to achieve certain goals. In the modern commercial world, put very simply, this is usually to achieve some form of competitive advantage. This usually means market share and sometimes even market domination. In the public sector the goal is to provide service.

In order to achieve these goals an organization will manage its work according to certain principles, including planning, organizing, commanding, coordinating and controlling (after Fayol, see Figure 2.5). In addition, work will be specialized (after Taylor, see Figure 2.5) in a number of different ways, for example, at the technical level and also at a hierarchical level, i.e. there are both horizontal and vertical divisions of work.

Lynda Gratton, of the London Business School, writing in 'Mastering Management' (*Financial Times*, 1995), states that an 'important issue for companies is to identify HR activities which link business strategy to performance. Key processes . . . include: reflecting business goals in individual and team objectives, and in performance measures; rewards and training; visualising the future; and identifying and encouraging individual talent.' As discussed previously in Chapters 2 and 7 the linking of human resource management and business strategy is a fundamental aspect of the developing concept of HRM and is particularly well articulated by Linda Holbeche (2001) in her book, *Aligning Human Resources and Business Strategy*.

Traditionally, the organizing of employees required that a structure exists in which lines of authority, responsibility and communication exist. Ideas about how these principles are achieved have evolved over time, but are summarized simply by Mullins (1996):

- *The Scientific School* – strict division of labour, formal hierarchy.
- *Human Relations School* – recognition of workers' social needs and the informal organization.
- *Systems* – recognition of the sociotechnical system, i.e. the need to integrate the benefits of both the Scientific School and the Human Relations School.
- *Contingency* – recognition that there is no one 'best' system for all management situations, e.g. managing the delivery of a fast food operation is very different from managing the planning of a new fast food restaurant.

Burns and Stalker (1961) identified two extreme types of organization – the 'mechanistic' and the 'organic'. The 'mechanistic' reflects the 'scientific school of management' in that it is very bureaucratic and has a hierarchical structure. The manufacturing sector of the mid-twentieth century particularly typified this approach with its emphasis on work specialization, the degree to which the organization's tasks are subdivided into separate jobs (see Robbins, 2005). The 'organic' organization, on the other hand, reflects the 'contingency' approach in that it is flexible and able to adopt new structures easily, where multi-skilled employees, for example, are more able to change their roles as situations demand. Most organizations come somewhere between the two extremes.

Handy (1989) writes of the 'shamrock' organization, which consists of the professional core, the flexible labour force and the contractual fringe. This closely reflects the reality of the modern labour force, which in many cases consists of managers, core workers and peripheral workers – in the hospitality industry examples would include the management team, full-time employed key workers such as chefs and receptionists, casual workers such as casual waiters, and a range of subcontracted functions such as cleaners, security personnel, musicians and drivers. Indeed, contemporary service sector organizations of all types consider outsourcing activities very carefully, with the underpinning philosophy being that the business should be concentrating on its prime purpose; many larger hotels, as an instance, are outsourcing their payroll administration rather than tie up the time and energy of the HRM department within the business.

Organization development (OD) is an all-encompassing term for planning organizational structures, relationships and change in order for maximum efficiency and well-being to be achieved for both the organization and the human resource. It must be based on a sense of involvement and collaboration between management and employees, and Robbins (2005: 558) points to the need for values such as respect for people, trust and support, the equalization of power (as in less hierarchical structures), confrontation (rather than problem-avoidance) and participation. The most common aims of OD are

- improvement in organizational performance, e.g. profits, cost reductions or service levels
- improvement in decision-making processes
- improvement in group or team work
- responding to change
- changing value systems and attitudes.

A whole range of factors influence organization structures, each factor having some effect on the final type of structure, which may be either the result of careful design, the result of evolutionary development or merely expedient.

The main options open to organizations are as follows.

Functional	Where different individuals attend to the main management functions, i.e. finance, marketing, human resources, operations, research and development.
Product/Brand	Where different managers manage different products or brands, e.g. hotels, licensed retail or quick service outlets.
Geographical	Where management attend to everything within a geographic region, e.g. Europe, Scotland, Manchester, the M1.
Project	Where groups are set up for specific projects and disperse upon completion, usually relying upon existing hierarchical roles.
Matrix	A loose form of the above where individuals may be members of a number of different groups, with leadership roles depending more on expertise than on hierarchical roles.

In the larger organizations it is possible to find a combination of the above. For example, some brewery companies are organized on both product and geographical bases. In recent years, companies have tended to flatten formerly hierarchical structures, reviewing the span of control (see below) of managers and supervisors, with the aim of developing a more responsive, effective organization where communication is more effective, and where perhaps the prevailing management style of the business, such as empowerment, may be more readily reinforced (Goss-Turner, 1999).

Power and the decision-making process

Driving the process of organization should be an overall philosophy of the senior management towards their workforce (see Chapter 2) and the principles of job design (see Chapter 3). Unitarist (or autocratic) managers will tend towards concentrating decision-making upon themselves, whereas a pluralist (or democratic) manager will be prepared to share decision-making and to empower the workforce. Public sector organizations tend to require committee decisions, made within a legislative or bureaucratic framework, whereas private sector organizations tend to have far fewer legislative or bureaucratic restraints and decision-making can be a simpler process, requiring fewer participants. Such differences in types of organization can influence quite considerably the formal and informal approaches to organizations.

Increasingly we hear of various approaches to management which are enabling or passing responsibility down the organization for a whole range of functions and decisions.

Organizational objectives

Each type of organization has particular objectives. In some cases the objective is, first and foremost, to make a profit, whereas in others it is to provide a service. These objectives obviously influence staffing levels because where profit is the main motive, staffing levels will normally be kept close to the most economic level, with attendant risks of occasional understaffing. Where service is paramount (e.g. on oil rigs), manning levels will normally be kept at safer levels because the cost of short staffing could be tremendous.

The market

The single most important factor is probably the type of market being catered for. Obviously not only consumer demands determine the type of staff required but also the degree of seasonal fluctuation influences organization structure. A hospital with predictable and stable levels of demand, where the catering service is ancillary to other services, will have staffing needs very different from those required by a highly seasonal resort hotel or holiday/leisure park where the accommodation and catering services themselves are the end product. The hospital will need a relatively stable and permanent labour force, whereas the seasonal hotel will probably need a small nucleus of permanent, key staff which is boosted by seasonal and casual labour as demand increases. The importance of the product market in the hotel sector of the hospitality industry in its impact on human resource management, in policy and practices, is well explored by Hoque (2000).

Technology

The technology of a particular sector is also important. One simple example is airline catering. In this sector of the industry, space is at a premium, weight carries penalties, and constant supervision is not possible. These factors obviously influence the product offered, the equipment used and the staff selected.

The role of technology in shaping organizations is consequently vital. One way to look at technology in the organization is to look at the 'tec-touch' matrix (Figure 19.1).

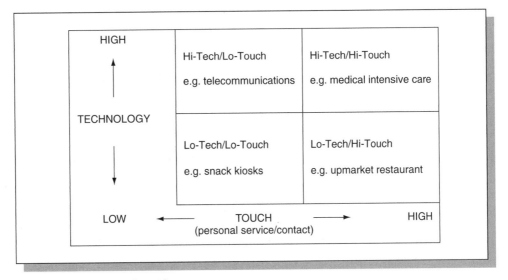

Figure 19.1 The tec-touch matrix

This diagram sets out to illustrate major approaches to the use of technology in industry. In some industries heavy investment in advanced technology is essential, such as in the information technology industries. Such technologies influence the hospitality industry mainly in an indirect way, for example through improved advance reservation systems. This influence may be known as the 'process' effect, i.e. the effect is mainly concerned with the process by which the customer receives or acquires the 'service' offering. Such advanced technologies may also enable a hospitality operator to offer enhanced 'service' products or offerings such as teleconferencing via satellite. This is known as the 'product' effect.

In other cases most reliance is based on the human touch elements of service. Where the human element is high this may be known as a 'hi-touch' offering. In some cases there is a combination of hi-tech and hi-touch – an example is intensive care hospital treatment. In many instances of hospitality offerings the technology used is relatively or very lo-tech and the human element of service is very low also – snack kiosks are examples of such lo-tech, lo-touch offerings. However, some developments in technology have seen a niche area of hi-tech infiltration, such as highly automated sushi bars with 'robotic' drinks trolleys, and almost employee-free hotels where credit cards rule, as in the capsule concept and other budget-hotel offerings.

Centralization and decentralization

The question of centralization and decentralization is at the heart of many organizational issues. In the hospitality industry this may focus on whether or not to centralize functions such as marketing and sales, reservations, financial management, purchasing, human resources, payroll and property management. In some cases, such as marketing or reservations, it is generally accepted that centralization can make good sense. In other cases, however, such as sales or personnel, unit managers often argue that they are better able to manage the activity.

Centralization of certain activities or functions has to address a number of different questions. Does centralization create opportunities to employ specialist skills, such as purchasing or marketing, which can bring significant benefits to the enterprise? Does it, on the other hand, create opportunities to reduce line management? A number of leading retail companies and hospitality companies have been developing 'cluster' management systems, by which one general manager is required to manage a number of outlets which were previously managed by their own managers. Arguably the increased expertise and skills of functional managers, supported by improved information technology systems, make this possible. It has to be seen, however, whether such approaches can work in those situations where the customer still expects to be received by a member of the senior management team, i.e. someone performing the role of 'mine host'.

The effect on employees also has to be considered. Centralization, whilst increasing some people's responsibility, may reduce another person's responsibility and hence job satisfaction. Decentralization, on the other hand, may well empower someone and hence give greater job satisfaction.

Size and diversity

Two other major influences on structure are the size of the organization and its diversity. However, there does seem to be some agreement among the largest organizations that they need to devolve responsibility to smaller, readily accountable units. This may be done on a geographic basis. An example is the way in which licensed retailers organize their pub outlet areas. Their management may be responsible for all activities in an area, such as managed houses, tenanted houses, catering and entertainment. Alternatively, an organization may prefer to make its management responsible for particular types of products or services. An example is how some companies may concentrate their restaurants into one division, their licensed houses into another and leisure into yet another. For the largest companies both 'regional' and 'product' organization structures will be necessary.

At the individual unit level the degree of specialization is an important question and of particular importance is the degree to which certain specialists such as sales executives and financial controllers may be responsible to the unit manager and to the head office specialist manager. Revenue control managers in hotels, for example, may be responsible for developing (and even imposing) capacity management (yield management) systems. This is a constant problem in hotels in particular, where revenue control managers and sales executives may see themselves as part of a head office team rather than part of the unit management. A consequence is that the sales staff often sell products the unit has difficulty providing.

Span of control

Something else discussed in the organizational context is the question of 'span of control', i.e. how many subordinates can each manager or supervisor successfully supervise. While most will agree that 'one over one' is rarely, if ever, justified, beyond this all the factors listed above play their part in resolving the question of how many subordinates one person can control. There are situations where one supervisor can quite successfully control a hundred or more subordinates. Likewise, however, there are many other situations where one person can successfully supervise, at most, a handful of subordinates. One very successful hotel executive who created at least three large, public hotel companies was reported to have over 20 executives reporting directly to him. One aspect of the hospitality sector where research has shown that the spans of control have steadily increased is that of area management or multi-unit management (Chapter 22), where, for example, some high-street, branded restaurant offerings have seen the area manager's responsibility level rise from about 8 units to around 15–20, with the consequent impact on levels of management (see below), unit management authority levels, management style and technology-enhanced control systems (Goss-Turner and Jones, 2000).

Levels of management

The number of levels of management (sometimes referred to as the 'scalar' chain) is another crucial element in any organization. Usually, this is a function of the size and diversity of the organization. Recent trends, however, have been to delayer, i.e. to reduce the number of levels of management, giving more authority to those who remain. Improved information technology makes such measures more practicable. One such example is Harvester Restaurants, who went through this process in the mid-1990s. The process was described as 'an approach to employee empowerment which is based on a flat organization and autonomous work groups at unit level' (Ashness and Lashley, 1995).

Outsourcing

'Outsourcing', as referred to earlier, is another influence. Outsourcing is the process by which an enterprise acquires products and services from outside suppliers rather than providing them internally using one's own employees. In the 1950s and earlier, many of the larger hotels were like small towns, employing many different trades, including upholsterers and silversmiths. Such practices have largely disappeared, it being thought more economic to buy in such expertise. Such outsourcing is now being extended into what may be described as pure management areas such as HR. One argument for outsourcing is that an enterprise should concentrate its management expertise on its core business. Examples include the purchase of many food and drink items and extend also to services such as maintenance, cleaning, vending, payroll and security.

The products and services

Obviously shaping all these factors is the product being provided. At one extreme there is the *haute cuisine* meal experience involving an extensive range of technical, social and organizational skills which have taken many years of experience and training to acquire. At the other extreme, nowadays we have fast food concepts and airline meals which involve very little craft skill but call upon management organization skills of a high order, exemplified by blueprinted service delivery systems in which every detail of operational design is considered. In between these two extremes are numerous types and styles of product and service which make differing demands on capital, craft skill, social skill, training and organization ability. Each combination creates a particular set of organizational needs and constraints which should be reflected in the consequent organization structure.

Age, size and culture

As successful organizations get older, so they have tended to become larger both through the natural or organic growth of their business and often also through mergers and acquisitions. Acquisition will bring problems both of managing the larger business and of integrating the differing cultures. One such case was the merger of Trust Houses with the Forte empire, which at the time created one of the world's leading hospitality companies. The merger was almost as famous, so it was reported, for the clash of cultures that emerged. Much later, in 1997, the then Trusthouse Forte was involved in an ultimately successful hostile takeover bid by Granada, the giant leisure and broadcasting firm, with much publicized culture clashes and personal acrimony between the Chief Executives of both companies. The subsequent organization was so large and disparate that it was eventually 'de-merged' into two, a hospitality company under the Compass banner, whilst Granada stuck to its original broadcasting expertise. Increasing size also creates subdivisions and problems of coordination. Large size consequently creates conflicting effects. On the one hand, size creates opportunities for economies of scale; on the other hand, increasing problems of coordination and control can add to the administrative burden – the law of diminishing returns?

Line managers and specialist managers

Once an enterprise reaches a certain size there will be a tendency for it to need to have specialist advice readily available. In the smallest organizations many specialist tasks will be performed by the owners or their managers. As the enterprise grows, the need for specialist advice grows and either this can be bought in from time to time – e.g. accountants or architects – or specialists may be engaged full-time. Human resource or personnel specialists are typical examples of the latter. Others include marketing, information technology and purchasing specialists.

The role of such specialists, usually referred to as 'staff' or 'functional' managers, varies considerably from one organization to the next. In some it will be, as the Human Resources Director of British Airways said, 'more strategic and less operational' (quoted from Goss-Turner, 1995). In any event, most believe that the role should be to advise and guide the line or operational managers, not to remove authority or responsibilities from them. In the larger organizations, distinguishing the roles and relationships of line and functional managers becomes quite difficult in some situations. This is particularly so where a hotel, for example, has a revenue management team that is responsible (or perceives itself to be) to the head office marketing department as much as to the hotel general management. There follow a number of sample organization charts of various different sizes of hospitality organization (Figures 19.2–19.6).

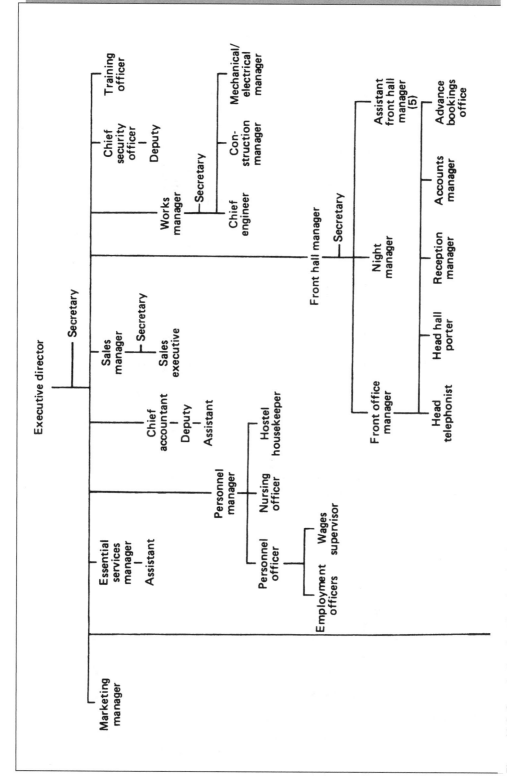

Figure 19.2 Organization chart for a large hotel

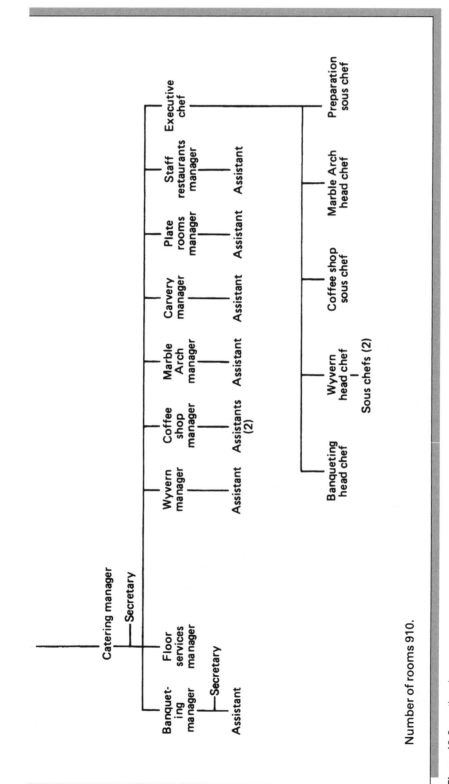

Number of rooms 910.

Figure 19.2 *continued*

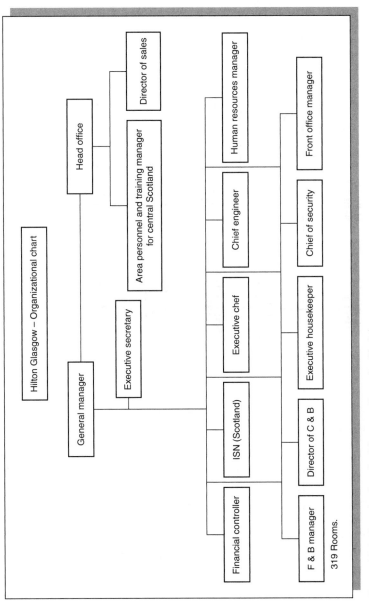

Figure 19.3 Organization chart for a medium-sized hotel
Source: Courtesy of Hilton Hotels.

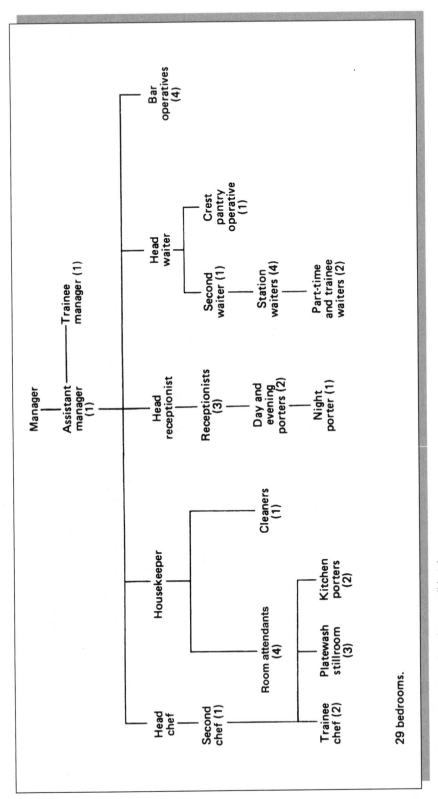

Figure 19.4 Organization chart for a small hotel

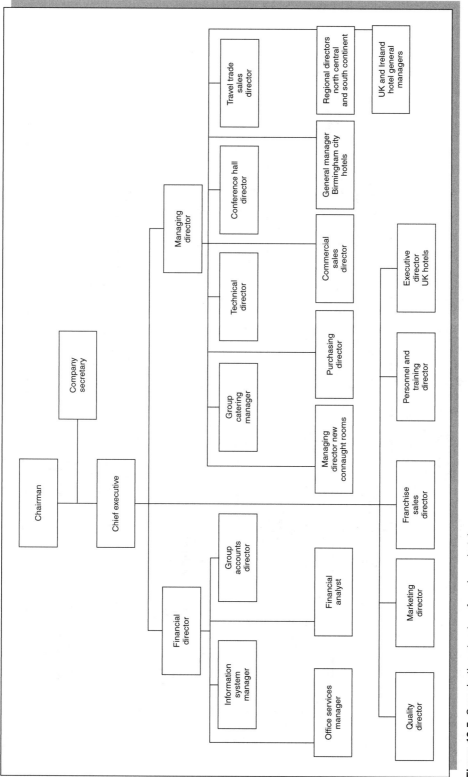

Figure 19.5 Organization structure for a large hotel company
Source: Reproduced by courtesy of Choice Hotels.

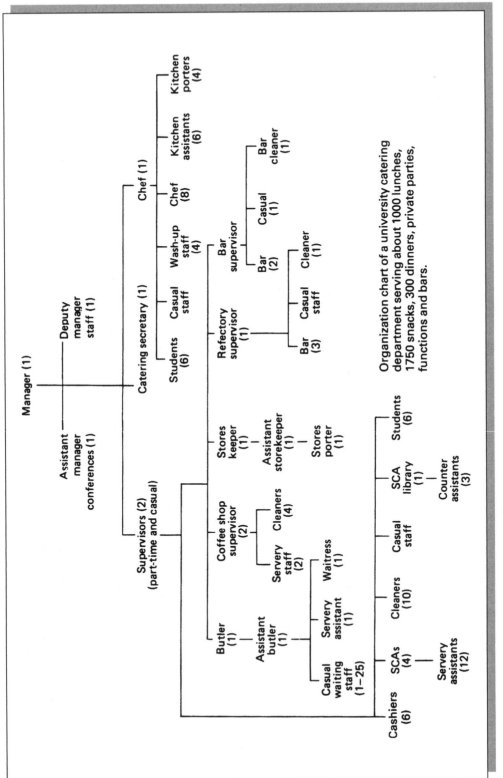

Figure 19.6 Organization chart for a university catering department
Source: Reproduced by permission of Sussex University.

Further Reading and References

Armstrong, M. (1999) *A Handbook of Human Resource Management*, 7th edn, London: Kogan Page.

Arnold, J. (2005) *Work Psychology*, 4th edn, Harlow: Prentice Hall.

Ashness, D. and Lashley, C. (1995) *Employee Empowerment in Harvester Restaurants*, Brighton: Human Resource Management in the Hospitality Industry Conference Document, University of Brighton.

Burns, T. and Stalker, G. M. (1961) *The Management of Innovation*, London: Tavistock Publications.

French, D. and Saward, H. (1977) *Dictionary of Management*, London: Pan.

Goss-Turner, S. (1995) *Human Resources and Line Management*, Brighton: Human Resource Management in the Hospitality Industry Conference Document, University of Brighton.

Goss-Turner, S. (1999) The role of the multi-unit manager in branded hospitality chains, in *Human Resource Management Journal*, Vol. 9, No. 4, 39–57.

Goss-Turner, S. and Jones, P. (2000) Multi-unit management in service operations: Alternative approaches in the UK hospitality industry, in *Tourism and Hospitality Research*, Vol. 2, No. 1, 51–66.

Handy, C. (1989) *The Age of Unreason*, London: Business Books.

Holbeche, L. (2001) *Aligning Human Resources and Business Strategy*, Oxford: Butterworth-Heinemann.

Hoque, K. (2000) *Human Resource Management in the Hotel Industry*, London: Routledge.

Huczynski, A. and Buchanan, D. (2001) *Organizational Behaviour*, 4th edn, London: Prentice Hall.

Medlik, S. (1994) *The Business of Hotels*, 3rd edn, London: Heinemann.

Mullins, L. (1996) *Hospitality Management*, London: Longman.

Robbins, S. (2005) *Organizational Behaviour*, 11th edn, New Jersey: Pearson Education Inc.

Sisson, K. (ed.) (1989) *Personnel Management in Britain*, Oxford: Blackwell.

Storey, J. (ed.) (2001) *Human Resource Management—A Critical Text*, 2nd edn, London: Thomson.

Questions

1 Describe the objectives of organization development and the various alternative approaches to organization structure.

2 Discuss the factors that influence organization structure.

3 Evaluate the approach to organization structure and development used by an employer you know well.

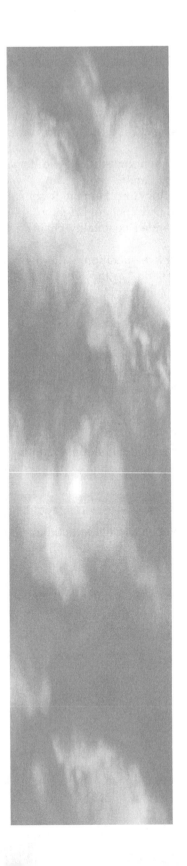

Managing people

Within the hospitality industry virtually everybody works in groups of interdependent individuals. A key feature of much of the industry is the fact that most work people are very dependent, in an immediate sense, upon the work of colleagues. It is this working of interdependent individuals, brought together as groups, which determines the success or failure of many enterprises. The success of the group in turn is dependent upon the ability of some individuals, the managers or leaders, to lead such groups to achieve desired results.

What makes a person a successful manager or leader of others has, no doubt, been a subject of discussion since the time people began to live in organized societies. At one extreme are leaders who are in positions of power and leadership as a direct result of their personalities. This is referred to by some as 'charismatic' leadership. At the other extreme are managers who rely on strict procedures and peer support in their approach to management. This is often referred to as 'bureaucratic' management. As mentioned in Chapter 2, there are other approaches too. Figure 20.1 identifies some of the more common approaches.

With such a variety of different approaches it is not surprising that people are constantly asking which of these is the most likely to be successful, and it is not surprising either that there is no clearcut answer. What may be successful in one situation may well prove a failure in another set of circumstances. For example, the type of leadership or management needed on the flight deck of an aircraft coming in to land will be very different from that needed in leading a team of architects designing a new building. Likewise the management skills needed to manage a fast food outlet will be very different from those needed to manage a small directors' dining room. Figure 20.2 illustrates some of the many factors that interact in any group/leadership situation.

Charismatic, Paternalistic, Bureaucratic	(Weber)
Theory X ——————— Theory Y	(Douglas McGregor)
Exploitive authoritative, benevolent authoritative, consultative, participative group	(Rensis Likert)
Autocratic processes, consultative processes, group processes	(Vroom)
Relationship motivated – task motivated	(Fiedler)
Concern for people – concern for production	(Mouton and Blake)
Sociotechnical system	(Trist et al)

Note: All of these are described in more detail in *Writers on Organizations*, edited by Pugh and Hickson; details in the reading list to this chapter.

Figure 20.1 Some of the more commonly described approaches to management

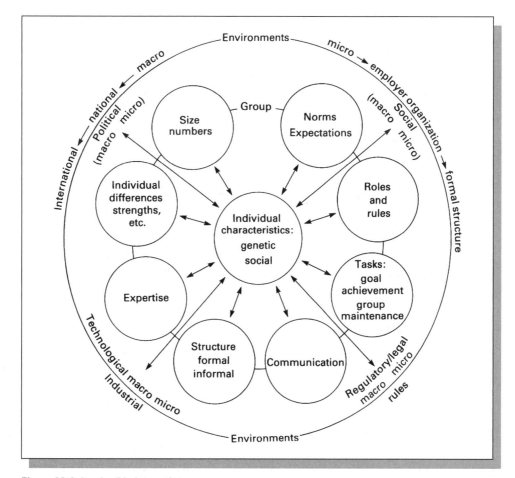

Figure 20.2 Leadership interactions

Individuals and leadership

Considerable research has been carried out to identify which traits contribute to an individual being a leader or a follower. One example is the work of the armed services, which subjects applicants for officer status to a series of tests lasting several days. The works of J. Munroe Fraser (five-point plan for interviewing) and the National Institute of Industrial Psychology (seven-point plan), discussed in Chapter 5, set out to evaluate both genetic and social or cultural factors, some of which may contribute to leadership abilities.

In looking at these different approaches it is apparent that a range of different characteristics are evaluated when individual potential is being considered. But in spite of there being a range of different methods of assessing leadership skills, many employers continue to devise their own methods of identifying and measuring management potential and performance (see Chapters 7 and 9). If, in fact, a single set of personality traits did make for successful management or leadership, it is probable that by now some agreement would have been reached, as is more the case with single and maybe simpler personality traits such as 'intelligence'. It would appear therefore that successful management or leadership may not be the result of a simple set of characteristics but is more likely to be dependent upon a whole range of interacting elements.

In looking at the many different contexts in which leadership functions, including business, government, the military, the church, etc., it is not surprising that many different types of approaches to leadership may be necessary. It is also not surprising that attempts to measure and to identify leadership characteristics have been so difficult and largely fruitless. Some of the key elements in Figure 20.2 are discussed more fully here.

The above division between genetic and cultural personality traits is illustrative only. There are conflicting opinions about many of the above traits, e.g. introversion and extroversion may be as much culturally influenced as genetically determined.

The individual

At the individual level there are two main aspects that have to be considered – each consisting of many different elements. First, there are innate characteristics such as intelligence, height and gender. Secondly, there are culturally acquired characteristics such as beliefs, attitudes and values. These are illustrated in more detail in Figure 20.3.

Genetic characteristics

What is inherited genetically may contribute to leadership in a number of different ways. Relevant characteristics include intelligence, gender, height, physical build and even the ability to be persuaded. For example, some research has shown that successful managers generally tend to have above average intelligence and to be above average height. Also males generally are more likely to hold senior management positions than females even when females make up the majority of the workforce. Whilst the reason for this may be more cultural than genetic, a person's sex (which is genetically determined) plays a significant part in determining whether a person will be more or less acceptable as a leader or manager.

Genetically determined characteristics	Culturally determined characteristics
Physical characteristics Gender, race, size, build, motor skills	Values, beliefs, attitudes, expectations, language, accent, behaviour, manners, perception of role, self-image, attitudes to work

Psychological characteristics
    Intelligence
    Introvert–extrovert
    Stable–unstable
    Creative	

Figure 20.3 Some individual characteristics

It may also be that male aggression or assertiveness contributes to male success in leadership in cultures where competitiveness is a key element in organization culture. Cattell (1957) identifies one factor, factor E, which is concerned with assertiveness, which, to some extent, may also be genetically influenced.

Cultural characteristics

Apart from the inherited characteristics, a society through socialization equips people with a whole range of beliefs, values, attitudes, prejudices and related behaviour patterns. For example, an individual's attitudes towards conformity, punctuality, honesty, work, the opposite sex, minorities, superiors and subordinates are all part of the individual's make-up and stem from the social context in which the individual has developed. For example, certain schools and types of schools build specific career expectations into their pupils, as do most higher education courses.

Groups

In any discussion on management or leadership it is essential to consider the nature of who or what is being managed. In most cases managers manage a range of resources including finance, equipment, buildings, land and a number of individuals, usually organized in a group or groups. Groups are the basic building blocks of society. Groups come in all shapes and sizes and have many different purposes and there are many different definitions of groups. For the purpose of this book, however, a group is defined as two or more people interacting together in order to achieve a common goal or goals.

Such a definition can include as few as two people working together and it can include an organization of many thousands of employees. For the purpose of this book the definition includes both the small group and the larger group, sometimes referred to as an organization, although some differences between groups and the organizations will be looked at later. The reason for this definition is that management, even that of large organizations, function through groups. Most chief executives of large organizations do not manage the organization, they manage a group of senior managers who in turn manage other groups.

Types of groups

The two most commonly distinguished groups are primary groups and secondary groups (Figure 20.4). There is another group called the reference group.

	Socioeconomic	Affiliative
Primary groups	A family	A group of friends
Secondary groups		
Formal	A Trading Company A District Council Trade Union	A sports club A professional body A charity
Informal	A neighbourhood protest group	A group of fellow workers

Figure 20.4 Some examples of groups

Primary groups • • •

Primary groups, of which the family is the best example, have few, if any, clearly written rules. The individual members are kept together through feelings for one another. Friendship groups are another example of a primary group. Objectives of primary groups generally are concerned with relationships between the members.

Secondary groups • • •

Most other groups are formed for social and economic reasons, e.g. profit, fundraising, education and employment. In general they are more formal than primary groups. As a consequence they have clearly articulated rules and procedures. Typical examples may include schools, employers, sports clubs and professional associations.

Primary groups, such as friendship groups, may form as a result of membership of secondary groups, such as attending the same school or college or working under the same employer. In some cases primary groups will devolve into secondary groups.

Reference groups • • •

A reference group (rather like a role model) is a real or imagined group that has attributes attractive to an individual who may aspire to becoming a member of such a group. Supervisors, for example, may aspire to becoming a member of the management group. The concept of the reference group can be used in a very manipulative fashion. Advertisers, for example, will suggest that the use of certain products will admit users to their reference group. Individuals may have several reference groups. Apart from the many different definitions, there are also many different features of groups which can be isolated for discussion, such as: why do groups form? how do they form? what effect does group membership have on the individuals making up the group? In order that a number of individuals may be described as a 'group' a number of elements have to be present to a greater or lesser extent. For the purpose of this book, only certain key issues will be discussed.

Features of groups

Shared goals

Ideally all members of a group share common goals. In work organizations the primary goals are likely to be task-orientated, with the making of profits and/or the provision of services as fundamental. The group is created or develops because it is likely to be more efficient than the individuals working independently. In non-work organizations, such as clubs, the goals are likely to be of a personal affiliation/fulfilment nature. In some situations, however, shared goals may hardly be present. In the work situation, for example, the sharing of goals can sometimes be minimal. Some trade unionists certainly do not share the same goals as their employers. Etzioni (1980: see Chapter 2) writes that some managers have a coercive attitude to their workforce and that the work people in such a situation are likely to have an alienative attitude to the management. In such a situation the only shared goal is likely to be to exploit one another to the full. At the other extreme, Etzioni identifies managers with a 'normative' attitude to their workforce, who in turn have a 'moral' attitude to their work. In such cases there is a sharing of common values.

Common values or norms

Ideally, members of a group should hold similar values. Employee selection and induction is largely concerned with identifying and developing individuals who share or will share the same values as the employer. To what extent, however, work people share values with their employers may be very questionable, particularly as a considerable proportion of the total workforce may be peripheral, i.e. drawn from the secondary labour market (see Chapters 1 and 2).

This question of the members of an organization needing to share common goals or values, and all that follows from this, constantly recurs as a major preoccupation of organizations. People with common interests and values alone do not make a group. The readers of a national newspaper, whilst probably sharing many interests and values, can hardly be described as a group. Cooks working thousands of miles apart for the same fast food chain can hardly be described as members of the same group. For a group to exist, there needs to be a common purpose, activity and a relational interdependence.

Communication between members

In order that individuals can work together to achieve their common goals, there will be a need for communication between some of, if not all, the members.

Group size – larger or smaller

Group size is a key feature affecting management. The smaller the group, the easier it is generally to coordinate its activities, and as membership increases so do the problems of coordination and control. Larger groups potentially, of course, can perform more work and have more skills available.

In employing organizations, because each member incurs costs, there is strong pressure to keep groups to a minimum size whilst aiming to have the number of individuals and skills necessary for the tasks to be performed. In other cases, such as trade unions, the pressure will be the reverse, to increase membership size because this increases economic and political power.

Group structure – formal versus informal

Because some individuals in a group will need to communicate – the leaders to exercise control – and because the individuals are interdependent, a structure will be developed. This may be very apparent and formal or it may be very loose, informal and changing.

Whilst larger organizations will set up formal structures that they believe will be most efficient from a task achievement, group maintenance and control point of view, other forces, informal ones, will be at work within the organization.

So, in any consideration of groups the two faces – the 'formal', as laid down by senior managers, and the 'informal', as determined by the emotional needs and the practical working circumstances – have to be considered.

Group development

A newly formed group of individuals are also subject to a process of development, as the members become acquainted, begin to formulate agreed approaches and develop norms and other shared values across the group. This process can also be difficult and lead to conflict and argument between members. Tuckman (1965) famously described the process as a series of stages, from 'forming' (finding out about each other and the task faced by the group), 'storming' (internal conflict and resistance), 'norming' (developing relationships and norms agreed across the members), 'performing' (effective teamwork phase), and perhaps 'adjourning' (group disperses, members change). The strength of the cohesiveness and association which can develop must not be underestimated by managers as a type of group culture forms. The power of a strong and effective group is considerable, and in HRM terms is a key factor in influencing reaction to change in the workplace. Another example of management recognition of the importance of groups is where some companies, including hospitality firms, are now involving the work group in the confirmation of appointment of a new colleague.

Group orientations

Groups, in the main, consist of both leaders and those being led, and each develops their own orientations or attitudes to work as well as towards those who work or organize their work. Etzioni (1980: see Chapter 2) describes both managers' attitudes to their workforce and the workers' corresponding attitudes to work:

Managers' power	Worker involvement
Coercive	Alienative
Utilitarian	Calculative
Normative	Moral

McGregor (1960: see also Chapter 2) describes theory-X managers who tend to expect the worst from their workers and theory-Y managers who expect the best. Schein (1965: cited in Pugh and Hickson, 1997) goes further than McGregor and suggests four main assumptions that managers make of their work people:

- *rational–economic* – workers motivated by money
- *social* – workers motivated by work-group relationships
- *self-actualization* – workers motivated by a need to fulfil their potential
- *complex* – other models are too simple; workers are motivated differently at different stages of life.

From these models of attitudes to workers and to work it is apparent that attitudes may be dynamic in the sense that managers can create policies, working environments and styles of supervision that shape the nature of the workers' own attitudes to work and the employer. Furthermore, one of the problems of attitudes (not just to work) is that they may persist long after the reasons that created them have ceased to exist, a phenomenon at the basis of much prejudice.

Communications

Groups exist because communication is possible between individuals. The communication process has important effects on group behaviour and leadership because if information itself is seen as a valuable asset, it is possible to use that asset as a means of exercising control. If, for example, groups are structured as illustrated in Figure 20.5 A, B or C, one person can easily monopolize information (whereas in D all have access to everyone in the group). The person can choose to pass it on or not. There are two consequences of such a situation. First, the person with the information can automatically acquire the role of leader or secondly, a person with certain personality traits, recognizing the power of the position, will move into the focal position.

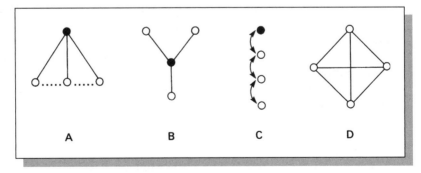

Figure 20.5 Different channels of communication

Communication is a complex subject and much has been written on it. In essence, however, the process consists of information to be transmitted, a transmitter of the information, a means of transmission and a receiver of the information, followed sometimes by feedback that demonstrates whether the process has worked or not. Obstacles to transmission arise, however, including language or cultural differences and attitudinal or emotional states. Such problems are common in the hospitality industry where managers, employees and customers often come from many different cultural backgrounds and may have very different perceptions. For the customer an undercooked steak may be a disappointment whilst the member of staff might be thinking that the customer is lucky to be able to afford a steak in the first place. Other problems may arise through lack of visual feedback (e.g. a telephone conversation), poor organization structure and timescale problems (e.g. communicating across time zones) (Figure 20.6).

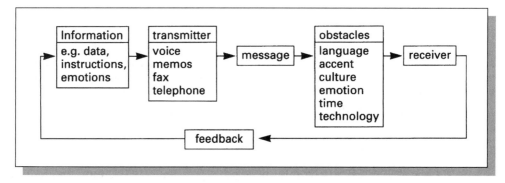

Figure 20.6 The communication process simplified

The hospitality industry depends largely on fast, accurate and reliable information, and many obstacles to such information exist. Managers therefore have to develop ways and means of ensuring that their communications are effective.

Group management

Where large groups of people have to be managed, as is the case with large enterprises, it is most likely that management will be, to a greater or lesser extent, of a bureaucratic nature. The word 'bureaucratic' is not meant in a pejorative sense but describes a particular approach to management, first described by Max Weber (1947). Procedures will be formalized. Decision-making is more likely to be a shared responsibility. Treatment of individuals will be based on clearly defined rules (as has been described in many chapters of this book). The key features of a bureaucratic approach to management include

- vertical authority structure
- maximum specialization
- close definition of duties, privileges and boundaries
- decisions based on expert judgement, technical competence and disciplined compliance with directives of superiors
- impersonal administration of staff
- employment consisting of a lifelong career.

The problem with Weber's view of bureaucracy is that it tends to imply that organizations are rational entities or systems, independent of the people who are the organization. Another view, that of Silverman, is that to understand organizations, it is necessary to view them from an 'action frame of reference', that is, as the product of the actions of the people who are the organization, pursuing their own objectives. This perspective, when contrasted with Weber's, indicates that organizations are not the rational system that many would like to believe they are, but are the results of the decisions of the leaders of the organization, pursuing their own ends.

Increasingly, however, some organizations are attempting to move away from the traditional hierarchical model so that creativity and innovation are released, rather than stifled by heavy bureaucracy.

Technology

Within an economy many different technologies are used to create goods and services. Different technologies create different organization structures and situations for managers. Joan Woodward (1965), in examining manufacturing industries, identified nine technologies grouped into three broad categories: unit and small batch, large batch and mass production, and process production. Each of these creates different management needs and structures.

Though not all hospitality operations fit into these categories, the industry does have many different market sectors with different technologies, ranging from the small, low volume (unit or small batch), top price restaurant through to high volume (large batch), low price fast food outlets and flight catering (mass production). Each of these creates different situations for management.

The nature of the task

In addition to the individuals and groups being managed, the nature of the task also has to be considered. In some situations, e.g. the reception/cash desk of an hotel at 8.30 a.m. or a busy kitchen at 1.00 p.m., there is little room for debate about how things may be done differently and therefore a strict hierarchical structure may be vital to success. Some of the variables concerned with the task itself include

- pressured – unpressured
- self-paced – externally paced
- skilled – unskilled
- hi-touch – lo-touch (e.g. level of customer contact)
- creative – non-creative
- difficult – simple
- group work – individual work
- perishable – non-perishable (e.g. if not sold today can it be sold tomorrow?)
- low risk – high risk.

Different combinations of the above variables should lead to different forms of management. Skilled tasks will need more investment in training. Group tasks will need more coordination. Perishable tasks (e.g. bedrooms unsold tonight can never be sold again) may need more complex communications and control. High-risk tasks (e.g. preparation of large numbers of in-flight meals) will need very strict systems of supervision and control.

Environment

As the leadership function can only function within groups of people, so too groups can only function within a wider environment. Groups are not closed, isolated systems. They draw from the environment. The environmental factors influencing management of the workforce are listed below (see also Chapters 17 and 19):

- economic
- politico-legal
- technological
- cultural
- demographic
- geographical
- demand for products
- employment legislation
- capital investment
- educational attainments of employees
- employee expectations
- labour supply.

What is a successful management or leadership?

Successful leadership should consist of the ability to achieve specified goals through the proper use of the resources available. For most managers this comprises at least two key elements.

First, there is the achievement of the specified goals, e.g. of a financial or service nature. To some extent the specification of goals and their achievement occurs through job design, performance appraisal and approaches to management such as MbO (see Chapters 3 and 7) and budgetary control.

The other key responsibility is the group maintenance and development role which has been the subject of most of the chapters of this book. Again the achievement of this dimension of management can be measured, but usually with more difficulty, through approaches to management such as performance appraisal and MbO.

Within the hospitality industry it could be argued that there appears to be more effort directed at the former goal than the latter – if the industry's high labour turnover is used as an indicator of the industry's managers' concern with group maintenance and development goals.

Many believe that successful management consists of achieving a balance between task achievement and concern for the group. This has been expressed by Blake and Mouton (1978; see also Pugh and Hickson, 1997), who developed the concept of the managerial grid, illustrated in Figure 20.7.

Other writers on management, including Fiedler, suggest that 'a group's performance will depend on, or be contingent upon the appropriate matching of leadership style with the group and the extent to which the situation provides the leader with influence over the group' (in Jones and Lockwood, 1989). In service businesses like hospitality, the task for leadership is crucial in declaring emphasis and reinforcing

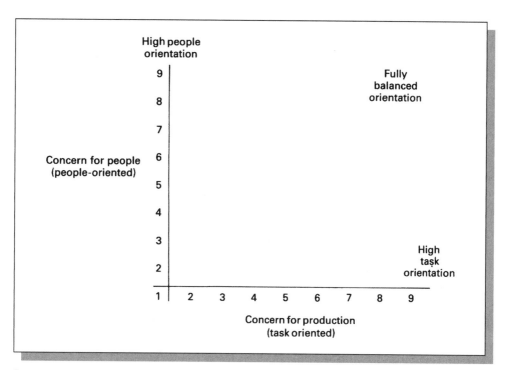

Figure 20.7 The managerial grid

the behaviours, values and culture desired by the business and HR strategy, such as customer care and service (Millett and Marsh, 2001). This may require the leader to be particularly charismatic or transformational (see Robbins, 2005), with a high level of personal credibility and influence over the employees, perhaps personified by the likes of Richard Branson (Virgin), Herb Kelleher (Southwest Airlines), Alan Parker (Whitbread), J. W. Marriott (Marriott Corporation) and Francis Mackay (Compass).

The process of managing groups

The process of managing groups at work has been analysed by many management writers in the past. One of the earlier writers, Henri Fayol (see Figure 2.5, Chapter 2), identified five key steps:

1 To forecast.
2 To organize.
3 To command.
4 To coordinate.
5 To control.

Another relevant writer is Peter Drucker (1969). Today it is possible to describe the process as a continuous, self-perpetuating process. Figure 20.8 illustrates this process.

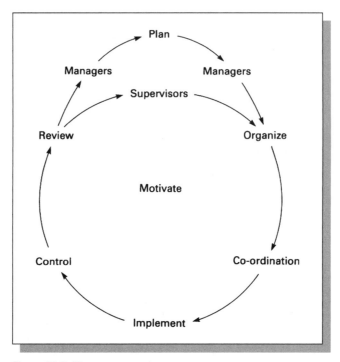

Figure 20.8 The management process

Managers and supervisors

Some argue that managers and supervisors are basically concerned with the same process and that there is no real distinction, apart from location in the hierarchy. However, from Figure 20.8, it can be seen that the main distinction, and an important one, is that managers are concerned with the planning function.

Differences between groups and organizations

Groups and organizations share many features in common. In order to be effective, members of both should have common goals and values. In many ways organizations are extensions of groups. Whereas groups consist of interdependent individuals, organizations consist of interdependent groups with overlapping memberships. Whilst all the individuals are members of the organization, they are also members of smaller groups. The board of directors of a hotel company, for example, makes up the group concerned with the overall direction of the company. Each director, apart perhaps from non-executive directors, in turn is a member, maybe the leader or manager, of specialist departments or groups. Figure 20.9 illustrates this.

From this it is apparent that, although the most junior members may be members of their own work group and of the organization overall, they are not members of 'similar interest' groups; most work people who have much in common, from a work point of view, are not members of a wider work people's group. One of the reasons for the emergence and development of trade unions was a response to the need for work people to form a group or organization with common interests. Some enlightened

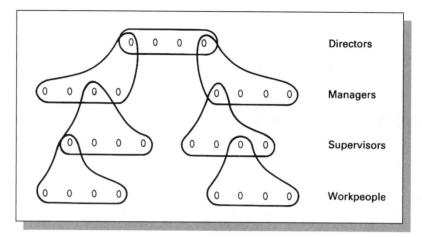

Figure 20.9 Organization and group membership

employers also set out to develop ways and means of making every employee, including even their part-time and casual employees, feel an integral part of the wider group or organization. Such techniques include induction, internal transfers and promotions, joint consultation, staff exchanges, company newspapers, staff parties and dances, staff guilds and interunit competitions of a work or social nature. Some differences and similarities between groups and organizations are summarized in Figure 20.10.

	Groups	Organizations
SIMILARITIES	Members may share common goals and values	
DIFFERENCES	Small	Large
	Simple structures	Complex structures
	Informal	Formal
	Emotional bonds	Economic/social bonds
	Simple decision-making	Complex decision-making
	Short-lived	Long-lived?
	All members know one another	All members do not know one another

Figure 20.10 Groups and organizations compared

Conclusion

Most of this book has been devoted to the various processes used by employers to attract, retain, develop and motivate their workforces. This chapter has focused on considering what is involved in actually managing the workforce and what influences that process. It has suggested that managing work people successfully depends upon a complex consisting of the make-up of the individuals involved, the nature of groups (which is different from the sum of their members), the nature of the work performed by the work people, and the environment in which the performance of the work takes place. The conclusion of this author is that there is no simple explanation of successful management or leadership, but that, using an analogy that it is hoped will be meaningful to most readers, success in this area is more like a successful meal. The component parts should always be of good quality but the recipe can be different for different situations.

Further Reading and References

Armstrong, M. (1999) *A Handbook of Human Resource Management*, 7th edn, London: Kogan Page.

Blake, R. R. and Mouton, J. S. (1978) *The Managerial Grid*, Houston: Gulf.

Cattell, R. (1957) *Personality and Motivation Structure and Measurement*, New York: World Books Co.

Drucker, P. (1969) *The Practice of Management*, London: Heinemann.

Etzioni, A. (1980) *Modern Organizations*, New Jersey: Prentice Hall.

Handy, C. (1993) *Understanding Organizations*, 4th edn, London: Penguin.

Huczynski, A. and Buchanan, D. (2001) *Organizational Behaviour*, 4th edn, London: Prentice Hall.

Jones, P. and Lockwood, A. (1989) *Management of Hotel Operations*, London: Cassell.

Koontz, H., O'Donnell, C. and Weinrich, H. (1993) *Management*, New York: McGraw-Hill.

McGregor, D. (1960) *The Human Side of Enterprise*, New York: McGraw-Hill.

Millett, B. and Marsh, C. (2001) The dynamics of strategic learning in an era of industry restructuring, in Wiesner, R. and Millett, B. (eds) *Management and Organisational Behaviour*, Brisbane: John Wiley & Sons.

Pugh, D. S. and Hickson, D. D. (1997) *Writers on Organizations*, 5th edn, London: Penguin.

Robbins, S. (2005) *Organizational Behaviour*, 11th edn, New Jersey: Pearson Education Inc.

Sisson, K. (ed.) (1989) *Personnel Management in Britain*, Oxford: Blackwell.

Torrington, D., Hall, L. and Taylor, S. (2002) *Human Resource Management*, 5th edn, Harlow: Pearson Education.

Tuckman, B. (1965) Developmental sequence in small groups, *Psychological Bulletin*, Vol. 63.

Weber, M. (1947) *The Theory of Social and Economic Organization*, New York: The Free Press.

Woodward, J. (1965) *Industrial Organisation: Theory and Practice*, Oxford: Oxford University Press.

Questions

1 Describe what you consider to be the key features that contribute to effective management of people at work.

2 Discuss the proposition that leadership is an 'innate' characteristic.

3 What relevance does the 'informal' group have to the manager?

4 What effects does the 'nature of the task' have on the management of groups and organizations?

5 What effects does the 'environment' have on the management of groups and organizations?

6 Design a procedure for selecting individuals with management potential.

7 Describe the 'process of managing' and discuss how a manager should relate this to the task and to the people being managed.

8 Compare and contrast 'groups' and 'organizations'.

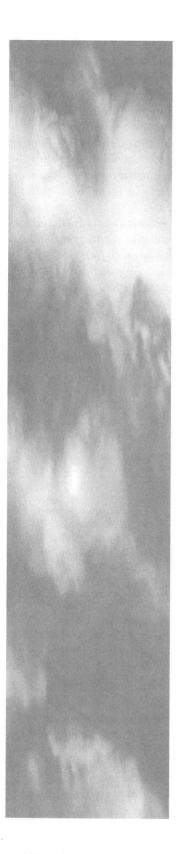

CHAPTER 21

Managing in an international context

Much of the world's economy is now transnational, international or global by nature. Several of the hospitality industry's major companies have long been large-scale international players. Specific sectors of the hospitality industry have, for many years, been international by nature. Most deluxe hotels and many top restaurants anywhere in the world expect that a significant proportion of their visitors will be foreign. Much of the industry in Britain, as it is today, has been significantly influenced by overseas managers and staff. Some of Britain's top hotels and restaurants of the last hundred years, such as the Savoy and the Ritz, were designed and run from over the Channel – by people such as Cesar Ritz. The former Forte plc, one of the world's foremost hospitality companies of the twentieth century (taken over by Granada in 1997), was founded by Charles Forte, of Italian origin, and the Stakis group (now part of Hilton) was formed by Reo Stakis of Cypriot origin. Significant companies and also small independent businesses in the hotel, restaurant, brewery, fast food and takeaway sectors are run by people of Asian origin. Furthermore, many of the managers and staff in certain sectors of the industry are of foreign nationality or origin. In turn, leading British-based hotel companies such as Hilton International and Holiday Inn run hotels throughout the world. One crucial point about the industry which has made this possible is that the knowledge and skills necessary to work in the industry are readily exportable or importable. As a result, most people joining the industry can anticipate working with people of nationalities and cultures very different from their own – be they customers, staff, managers or, increasingly, owners – in their own countries or abroad.

The globalization of the marketplace, which the hospitality industry serves, will accelerate this process even further and have far-reaching implications for HRM (see Baum, 1993: also Lashley and Watson, 1999), as will the establishment of the single market within the EU, together with its expansion into Central and Eastern Europe. In addition, the growth of tourism, estimated to triple around the Mediterranean basin alone over the next 25 years, as just one example, will increase the demand for staff with international capabilities, such as those with cultural awareness and an ability to adapt to different environments.

The range of issues that differ from one country setting to another is vast, and it is beyond the scope of this book to go into any detail. However, the major differences can be identified and evaluated using a systems thinking approach (see Chapter 17). Figure 21.1 illustrates some of these points with a few very simple examples, intended to highlight some dimensions on which countries differ in ways significant for HR management. Figure 17.2 can be used to identify and evaluate a full range of dimensions on which countries differ.

Figure 21.1 is intended to emphasize that when people go abroad to manage businesses the challenges they face are not just cultural. There are likely to be many very obvious differences, such as those of a legal nature. There are also likely to be some very subtle ones as well, many of a clearly cultural nature, such as attitudes to authority or the opposite sex. This chapter therefore concentrates on cultural differences likely to be encountered by hospitality managers. An understanding of such cultural differences may well provide the competitive advantage that many companies seek.

Political	Stable/unstable? Business friendly/unfriendly? The UK attracts substantial inward investment because the UK has a reputation for being a stable economy and business friendly, which results in job creation. Some countries deter investment because of government policies, particularly on taxation, sometimes encouraging their own domestic companies to consider moving abroad (e.g. Sweden).
Legal	Business friendly/unfriendly? Compared with countries such as France it is easier to set up and to run a business in the UK. From the human resource viewpoint some countries are extremely protective of working people (e.g. France), which tends to slow down job creation, whereas other countries will adhere to free-market principles (e.g. UK), believing that a healthy market economy will result in job creation.
Social	The social environment, generally speaking, shapes the attitudes and behaviour of the workforce. Attitudes to work, to religion and to authority derive from the social environment, as Hofstede has shown. Western companies entering Central European markets have encountered serious staffing problems because of the lack of a service culture.
Technological	The level of development of technology and attitudes to its adoption and use vary widely between countries. Some countries have a well-educated and developed workforce, so the adoption of new technology is relatively simple, whereas some other countries have attitudes towards machines and technology which will slow down their adoption. For example, when McDonald's entered the Russian market a major challenge to be overcome was the lack of suitable suppliers plus a lack of staff adapted to a service culture.

Figure 21.1 Some dimensions for evaluating differences between countries

As a leading authority on intercultural management, Geert Hofstede (1989) states, 'cultural awareness is one of the subtle features of competition in world markets, and firms which are better at it have a distinct advantage over their competitors'.

Cultural awareness is much more than the ability to speak a foreign language or two, although this in itself may be vital. In Britain now, efforts are being made through the national curriculum and the design of many higher education courses to improve the overall foreign language ability of the British. In this respect Britain compares unfavourably with some of its continental partners and competitors. In Belgium, for example, it is estimated that around 90% of hotel managers can work in four languages. In several European countries it is a requirement of all higher education courses, and the Baccalaureat ('A' level equivalent), that at least one foreign language is studied.

Cultural awareness is the ability to anticipate, to recognize and to respond to cultural differences. This may include not only the ability to communicate correctly with staff, customers or potential customers in both written and spoken form but also to anticipate and to meet their particular cultural expectations.

Besides language there are many other differences that exist between cultures. These may include differences in values, attitudes, behaviour, communication, personal space, technical differences, dress, religion, etc. Hofstede, in a study of over 1000 IBM employees employed in over 70 countries, identified 4 key dimensions that help to distinguish one culture from another. These are shown in Figure 21.2. (Although IBM is not a hospitality company it has many features that are similar to those of multinationals operating in the hospitality sector, including Accor, Sheraton, Holiday Inn, Marriott and Hilton.)

The power-distance dimension sets out to differentiate to what extent a country's organizational culture encourages supervisors to exercise power. France, for example, was found to have a high power-distance culture. This explains to some extent why many British students, accustomed to relatively close relationships with English managers or lecturers, when on industrial placement in France, have difficulties with French managers. Conversely, French students sometimes have difficulty adjusting to the relatively relaxed, first-name style of lecturers in English colleges and universities.

The uncertainty-avoidance dimension is concerned with the degree to which people in a country prefer structured or unstructured situations. Where uncertainty-avoidance

Dimension	High	Low
Power-distance	Supervisors are distant from their staff	Supervisors are close to their staff
Uncertainty-avoidance	High risk taking is encouraged	Risk taking is discouraged
Individualism	Individual initiative/and private life valued	Individual initiative discouraged, collectivist culture significant
Masculinity	Assertiveness valued	Warm, caring values significant

Figure 21.2 Dimensions for comparing cultures
Source: Hofstede (1991).

is strong (e.g. Japan, Greece), people need clear guidelines and support. In weak uncertainty-avoidance cultures, structures and rules are less important.

The individualism dimension is concerned with the degree to which people in a culture learn to act as individuals as opposed to as members of a group. Britain, Australia, Canada, New Zealand, Ireland and the USA are described as being high on individualism. This encourages personal initiative and achievement and a right to a private life. Countries low on the individualism dimension tend to have collectivist cultures where the extended family and the clan are more significant than the individual.

The masculinity dimension is concerned with values such as assertiveness, performance and success as opposed to feminine values such as warm personal relationships, quality of life and caring for others. Countries high on the masculinity dimension include Italy and Australia, whereas those at the other extreme include the Scandinavian countries and The Netherlands.

Hofstede analysed each country using these four main dimensions and then grouped countries with similar sets of dimensions into eight clusters which tend to have historical developmental similarities rather than simple geographical connections. These are shown in Figure 21.3.

Fons Trompenaars

Trompenaars, another Dutchman who has contributed considerably to the literature of international business culture, writes that 'culture' comes in layers like an onion (Trompenaars, 1998). He suggests that the outer skin is the observable, such as buildings, language, dress and food. The middle layer consists of norms (what is right and wrong?) and values (what is good and bad?); When norms reflect values, a society can be described as stable. The innermost core contains the assumptions about existence which he describes as the 'unquestioned reality'.

Trompenaars writes that cultures distinguish themselves by the way they solve particular problems. He groups the problems under three main headings: relationships with others, treatment of time and relationship with the environment as given below. He then divides these three into a total of seven dimensions, as follows.

Relationships with people

Universalism versus particularism. This dimension contrasts those cultures in which there is an abstract notion of what is good and right to those cultures where relationships and unique circumstances may come before abstract societal codes. In many Latin countries, for example, obligations to the family will override any obligations to adhere to strict legal or societal codes.

Individualism versus collectivism. This dimension is concerned with how people perceive themselves; as individuals or as members of a wider social group.

Neutral versus emotional. This dimension is concerned with how people behave in their interactions. Is it permissible to express emotions? In northern European cultures the whole purpose of business is about achieving objectives whereas in many other cultures business is about relationships – expression of emotions in such cultures is quite in order.

Diffuse versus specific. This dimension is concerned with the extent to which the business relationship is concerned only with achieving the narrow business objective or is concerned with a wider-ranging relationship.

I: More developed Latin
high power-distance
high uncertainty-avoidance
high individualism
medium masculinity

BELGIUM
FRANCE
ARGENTINA
BRAZIL
SPAIN

II: Less developed Latin
high power-distance
high uncertainty-avoidance
low individualism
whole range on masculinity

COLUMBIA
MEXICO
VENEZUELA
CHILE
PERU
PORTUGAL
(former) YUGOSLAVIA

III: More developed Asian
medium power-distance
high uncertainty-avoidance
medium individualism
high masculinity

JAPAN

IV: Less developed Asian
high power-distance
low uncertainty-avoidance
low individualism
medium masculinity

PAKISTAN
TAIWAN
THAILAND
HONG KONG
INDIA
PHILIPPINES
SINGAPORE

V: Near Eastern
high power-distance
high uncertainty-avoidance
low individualism
medium masculinity

GREECE
IRAN
TURKEY

VI: Germanic
low power-distance
high uncertainty-avoidance

medium individualism
high masculinity

AUSTRIA
ISRAEL
GERMANY
SWITZERLAND
SOUTH AFRICA
ITALY

VII: Anglo
low power-distance
low to medium uncertainty-
avoidance
high individualism
high masculinity

AUSTRALIA
CANADA
BRITAIN
IRELAND
NEW ZEALAND
USA

VIII: Nordic
low power-distance
low to medium uncertainty-
avoidance
medium individualism
low masculinity

DENMARK
FINLAND
NETHERLANDS
NORWAY
SWEDEN

Figure 21.3 Country clusters and their characteristics
Source: Reproduced by courtesy of G. Hofstede.

Achievement versus ascription. This dimension is concerned with the way society ascribes status. Does status derive from what you have achieved or gained from class, birth, gender and age?

Attitudes to time

Trompenaars writes that the way societies perceive time varies considerably. For some societies what was achieved in the past may be more important than what is achieved now or will be achieved in the future. Links between the past, the present and the future are also perceived differently, so such things as forward planning and strategy may present serious problems for managers in cultures with which they are unfamiliar.

Attitudes to nature and the environment

Trompenaars also identifies very different approaches to the environment. He writes that in some cultures individuals are very concerned about their impact on others and the environment and will take measures to reduce their impact. For example, the Japanese wear face masks in winter, not to protect themselves from infection but to protect others from being infected. In other cultures, in contrast, individuals take measures to protect themselves from the effects of the environment.

Using these seven main dimensions Trompenaars shows how societies differ and that preconceptions about a universal science of management ignore one major element – the culture within which management functions or attempts to function.

John Mole

Another writer, John Mole, identifies two main dimensions, organization and leadership, as cultural differentiators.

The organization dimension is based on the degree to which rational order is imposed. At one end of the dimension, the systematic end, is the belief that organizations 'are coordinated by well-defined, logical relationships' whilst at the other end of the same dimension, the organic end, 'is the belief that organizations are like living organisms growing out of the needs of their members, their environment and the circumstances of the moment'.

The leadership dimension has at one end the individualistic (even absolutist) approach and at the other end the group (even collectivist) approach to leading others. At the 'individual end of the dimension is the belief that individuals are intrinsically unequal'. The group end of the same dimension is based on the belief that 'everyone has a right to be heard and to contribute to all decisions that affect them' (ibid.). The two dimensions are then divided into subdimensions. Some examples from Mole are shown in Figure 21.4.

The main conclusion from research is that even if business practices within one type of business or company are similar across international boundaries there may be significant differences in culture. It follows that if countries have different values, then similar management styles used across different cultures will not necessarily work. For example, MbO, which involves managers negotiating targets and taking personal risks, may well succeed in Britain or the USA but not in France, Spain or Portugal.

In human resource policy terms the different approaches have been categorized by Watson and Littlejohn (1992) into three broad categories:

- *ethnocentric* – in which all strategies and practices are the same in all countries, based on head office's own national practices
- *polycentric* – HR strategies and practices are decentralized on a country-by-country basis
- *geocentric* – HR strategies and policies are managed on a global basis.

Human resource policies are shaped as indicated earlier in this chapter by the environments in which an enterprise operates. These push policies to emphasize particular issues. Figure 21.5 illustrates how particular environments shape human resource policies.

	Organic	Systematic
The organization dimension		
Forecasting	Plans based on hunches	Plans based on analysis
Decision-making	Decisions evolve	Decisions are made
Supervision	Who you know?	What you know?
Control	Criticism is personal	Criticism is objective
Communication	Informal	Goes through the formal hierarchy
Reward	Success depends on luck	Success depends on skill
Motivation	Pride in status	Pride in achievement
Style	Rules are to be circumvented	Rules are to be obeyed
The leadership dimension		
Forecasting	Plans made by those involved	Plans made at the top
Decision-making	Made by groups	Made by individuals
Supervision	Leaders are one of us	Leaders are different
Control	Groups are accountable	Individuals are accountable
Communication	Meetings are for sharing	Meetings are for briefing
Reward	Teams strive	Individuals strive
Motivation	Individuals work for the collective	Individuals work for themselves
Style	Hierarchy, status, titles are a convenience	Hierarchy, status, titles are essential

Figure 21.4 Mole's dimensions

Cultural differences, however, should not be seen as being confined to differences between nationalities. Obviously each country has its own cultural inheritance, which differs to a greater or lesser extent from other countries' cultures. However, cultural differences also exist within national cultures. Some socioeconomic groups from different countries have more in common, in some respects, than with different demographic or socioeconomic groups from their own country. For example, 20-year-olds from Britain are more likely to share tastes in music, clothes and leisure with 20-year-olds from other countries than with 50-year-olds from their own country.

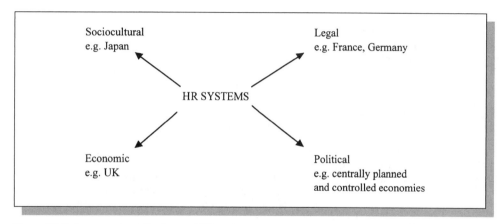

Figure 21.5 An example of the focus of HR systems

How individual hospitality companies demonstrate or develop cultural awareness varies considerably. In many cases nothing whatever is done to accommodate the needs of other cultures. For example, no staff may be able to speak another language and menus may not be translated even where significant numbers of foreign customers are served. At the most basic, it may be that brochures, tariff displays, menus, etc., are translated. At the next level, employers may translate important signs or at least use internationally recognized symbols. They may employ staff of appropriate nationalities or who are able to speak appropriate languages. Some employers will actively promote acquisition of language by paying 'language bonuses' and/or paying for or providing language tuition. Good language education not only equips people with basic communication skills but also introduces key cultural issues such as forms of addressing others. Some employers may go further by researching key cultural issues concerning potential and actual customers and setting out to meet these needs, such as the provision of a copy of the Koran in the bedroom rather than a Gideons Bible. Finally some employers train staff through role play, etc., in how to meet the needs of people from many different cultures.

The purpose of this chapter is not to produce a list of cultural differences. Instead it is intended to create the awareness that cultural differences do exist, that they are important, and that they are ignored at the risk of giving offence at the very least and of losing business at worst. When working with people of other cultures, whether as managers, employees, customers or owners, the relationship is likely to be more successful if cultural differences are anticipated and accounted for. Figures 21.6 and 21.7 illustrate some of the areas where significant differences are likely to be encountered.

Aspects of culture	Some dimensions	
Values, e.g.		
individual's place in society	autonomy valued	collective effort valued
social status	material wealth	social contribution
	ascribed at birth	acquired through personal effort
religion	restrictive	relaxed
	intolerant	flexible
concern for others	caring	unconcerned
Attitudes, e.g.		
towards work	economic necessity	personal identity
towards authority	formal, respectful	informal, unconcerned
towards those in subordinate social roles	demanding, superior	relaxed, egalitarian
towards the other sex	strong gender .... role differentiation	weak gender role differentiation
towards alcohol	alcohol consumed as .... adjunct to a meal	alcohol consumed in order to get drunk
towards food & meals	important, symbolic	unimportant, functional
towards time	punctuality	punctuality
	very important	unimportant
	one thing at a time	several things at a time

Figure 21.6 Examples of cultural differences

Behaviour, e.g.

relationship at work	formal .... informal
manner of dressing	formal .... informal
for work	important .... unimportant
personal space	close .... distant
forms of address	very formal .... informal
	important .... unimportant
non-verbal communication (e.g. gestures)	important .... unimportant
meals, eating habits	very formal .... informal
	important .... unimportant
meetings and conversations	only one person .... several talk at a time
	talks at a time

Figure 21.6 *continued*

Forms of greeting	Continental Europeans tend to be more formal than people from the UK or USA, and may address one another as 'Mr' or 'Mrs' throughout their working lives. First-name terms may be reserved for genuine friends or family. The familiar *tu* in France and its equivalents in other countries may have to be avoided.
	Some continental Europeans tend to shake hands the first time they meet each day and when they finish work.
Meals	In some cultures meals are extremely important; some cultures 'eat to live whilst others live to eat'.
	Staple elements of diet – e.g. rice, pasta, potatoes – vary between cultures.
	Courses may be in a different order. The French take cheese before dessert. Meals may consist of more courses, each of one item.
	Meals may contain different items. A Nordic breakfast may contain cheeses, hams, salami-type sausage. Asian breakfast may contain curry-like dishes.
	Table lay-ups may be different. The French may eat continental breakfast, using large cups, with no plate on the table. Side plates may not be used at other meals either. The same cutlery may be used throughout a meal.
	Many ingredients have local characteristics which can be important, e.g. the Latins drink much stronger coffee than do Anglo-Saxons.
	Meal times may be different, e.g. southern Europeans tend to eat for a longer period and later than the British.
	Children are not just tolerated but are welcome in most continental restaurants. Children tend to eat meals at the same time as their parents.
Drinks	Attitudes may be very different towards drink: in some cultures it is forbidden, other cultures view alcohol as an accompaniment to a meal, whilst other cultures may see drinking as an end in itself, with status connotations, e.g. a macho thing to do.
	Drinks may be used differently, e.g. port may be used as an aperitif, whisky as a digestif/liqueur.
Accommodation	Some nationalities prefer twin beds to doubles, showers to baths, duvets to blankets.
	Some ethnic groups require the Koran rather than the Bible in the bedroom.
Complaining	Some nationalities complain readily but are satisfied if the cause is rectified. Others, e.g. the British, tend not to complain but do not return.

Figure 21.7 Some examples of cultural differences of interest to the hospitality industry

How multi and transnational firms manage their human resources of course varies as much possibly as does their approach to marketing. Watson and Littlejohn (1992) write of alternative approaches adopted by such firms. The different approaches include Ethnocentric, Polycentric, Geocentric and Regiocentric.

An ethnocentric policy implies the same HRM strategies in all countries, a strong head office role and home country's managers occupying all key roles.

A polycentric policy implies that HRM is decentralised country by country, decision-making is devolved to local managers and local managers trained and developed.

A Geocentric policy implies that HRM is managed on a global basis, harmonises from the centre and allows for the best people to emerge irrespective of origin.

Finally a Regiocentric policy implies that HRM is managed on a regional basis.

Each of these approaches may be adopted in the hospitality industry.

Human Resource Management – the international context

The globalization of the hospitality industry and the development of worldwide groups such as Starwood Lodging and Accor have implications for the quality and effectiveness of HRM within an international context. At one level, there might seem little difference in that employees need to be resourced, trained, developed, managed and the like. However, there are serious and subtle questions for HRM practitioners to address. Cultural issues and national characteristics and regulations have been mentioned above and clearly these need to be considered. Some UK-based hospitality firms with little or no experience of dealing with trade unions have found that their expansion plans take them into countries where hotel and restaurant workers are 100% unionized. In other words, HRM needs to address all the particular factors prevailing on the workforce in each and every country in which the firm operates (see D'Annunzio-Green, Maxwell and Watson, 2002: also Beardwell, Holden and Claydon, 2004). Such firms need to be more aware of the salary and benefit packages expected by truly mobile international personnel, and need to plan issues not normally part of the host country operations such as language and culture training, schooling for management's families, taxation and legal aspects. There will be different types of employees with different terms and conditions and situations, such as expatriates, local workers and temporary secondments, and truly global, multi-site organizations will need to develop highly sophisticated succession planning systems in order to monitor and plan the future management of the business (see Goss-Turner, 1993, and Chapter 22 in this book).

Further Reading and References

Baum, T. (1993) *Human Resource Issues in International Tourism*, Oxford: Butterworth-Heinemann.

Beardwell, I., Holden, L. and Claydon, T. (2004) *Human Resource Management—A Contemporary Approach*, 4th edn, Harlow: Prentice Hall, Pearson Education.

D'Annunzio-Green, N., Maxwell, G. and Watson, S. (2002) *Human Resource Management— International Perspectives in Hospitality and Tourism*, London: Continuum.

Goss-Turner, S. (1993) Human resource management, in Jones, P. and Pizam, A. (eds.) *The International Hospitality Industry*, London: Pitman.

Hofstede, G. (1989) Organising for cultural diversity, *European Management Journal*, Vol. 7, No. 4.

Hofstede, G. (1990) *Culture's Consequences: International Differences in Work Related Values*, London: Sage.

Hofstede, G. (1991) *Cultures and Organizations: Software of the Mind*, London: McGraw-Hill.

Hofstede, G. (1994) *Cultures and Organizations: Intercultural Cooperation*, London: HarperCollins.

Jayawardena, C. (2000) International hotel manager, in *International Journal of Hospitality Management*, Vol. 12, No. 1, 67–69.

Jones, P. and Pizam, A. (eds) (1996) *The International Hospitality Industry*, London: Longman.

Lashley, C. and Watson, S. (1999) Researching human resource management in the hospitality industry: The need for a new agenda? in *International Journal of Tourism and Hospitality Research*, Vol. 1, No. 1, 19–40.

Mole, D. (1995) *Mind Your Manners*, 2nd edn, London: Industrial Society.

Tayeb, M. H. (2005) *International Human Resource Management: A Multinational Company Perspective*. Oxford University Press.

Teare, R. and Olsen, M. (1998) *International Hospitality Management*, London: Longman Publishing.

Trompenaars, F. (1998) *Riding the Waves of Culture*, 2nd edn, London: McGraw-Hill.

Watson, S. and Littlejohn, D. (1992) Multi and transnational firms: The impact of expansion on corporate structures, in Teare, R. and Olsen, M. (eds) *International Hospitality Management*, London: Pitman.

Questions

1 Describe, with examples, various ways in which one culture may differ from another. Apply your answer to the hospitality industry.

2 Describe different aspects of the hospitality experience which management needs to consider when providing for people from different cultures. Consider first customer needs, then staff needs.

3 Give examples of lack of cultural awareness which you have observed. Choose a particular setting such as at work, on holiday or at college.

4 Describe the measures that you believe would be necessary in order to develop an effective cultural awareness programme for a group of employees with whom you are acquainted. (You may find it useful to refer to Chapters 22 and 23.)

5 Discuss how cultural differences may lead to the need for different approaches to management style.

6 Discuss the proposition that cultural differences may be greater between socioeconomic groups within a country than between similar socioeconomic groups from different countries.

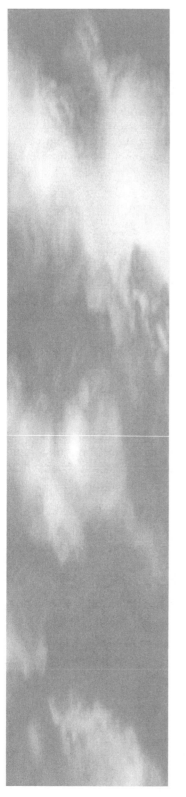

HRM and multi-site hospitality operations

In numerical and structural terms, the hospitality industry remains to this day one of predominantly independently owned enterprises, providing a particular locality with a range of appropriate food, beverage and accommodation services (Lee-Ross, 1999). These businesses are often small (Lucas, 2004), and may be considered family businesses or lifestyle choices regarding entrepreneurship. Many of these businesses stay the same size, whilst others grow and develop, the firm replicating the product or service in other locations further and further afield (Goss-Turner and Jones, 2000). In the past half-century a feature of the national and international industry has been the development of large hospitality chains, many emanating from US post-war prosperity and expansion, with brand extension strategies placing high in public consciousness company names such as Hilton, Holiday Inn and Pizza Hut. These large, multi-site, often multi-national corporations have unparalleled profile, and utilize their size and influence in areas such as economies of scale, quality assurance, customer recognition and standardization (Ritchie and Riley, 2004).

The expansion of service organizations like hospitality businesses has inevitable consequences for the organizational structure, reporting relationships and managerial competencies. Many such organizations adapted the principles of mass production and those of retailing services, consistent with the seminal work of Levitt (1972) and Schmenner (1986). This approach involves meticulous control and management of the supply chain from the sourcing of products, central purchasing and distribution to the operational elements of standardized menus, service delivery concept and system, pricing and uniforms. This chapter explores the employee development issues and challenges facing multi-site hospitality organizations as they continue to expand both nationally and internationally in a sector constantly subjected to the merger and takeover scenario of consolidation.

Much of the most pertinent literature on the subject of multi-site management and the service sector was developed by US researchers and writers. In view of the point raised above about the origin of many such multi-unit organizations, this is not surprising. Of notable relevance is the work of Olsen, Ching-Yick Tse and West (1992), which devotes considerable attention to the development of multi-unit hospitality organizations, including a review of the HRM implications. Their definition of a multi-unit (multi-site) firm is a useful starting point: 'an organisation that competes in the industry with more than one unit of like concept or theme'. Olsen, Ching-Yick Tse and West point to the problems of managing a dispersed operation across many geographical boundaries, and the subsequent challenges associated with quality control, in particular the supervision of the skills and attitudes of service delivery employees. They also raise the issue of the span of control, i.e. the number of unit managers reporting directly to a multi-site manager, their research indicating that this can vary between two and fifteen. There is also reference to the typical hierarchical structure and the position of the multi-unit manager within that structure. Literature on this subject focuses on the first-line area or regional management level, positioned between single-unit management and senior executive responsibility (see Goss-Turner, 1999: 39).

In reviewing the US literature, factors which emerge as significant include the link between HRM development in multi-unit firms and the organizational life cycle considerations of introduction, growth, maturity and decline, a link well established by Sasser, Olsen and Wycoff (1978), when extending the concept of the product life cycle into a service firm life cycle. The implication is that HRM will develop, either reactively or in alignment with business strategy and growth (Holbeche, 2001) in the areas of recruitment, selection, training and development, and in compensation and benefits. This concept gains insight when a new start business and its ensuing life cycle are considered (Tyson, 1995). The founding entrepreneur will be a dynamic, creative force behind the initial business, and will ensure that the other personnel involved are talented and enthusiastic, perhaps like-minded. The approach to HRM is likely to be ad hoc and without structure. Growth of the firm, including the opening of more identical concepts elsewhere, is associated with a need to develop more systematic HR approaches, and ultimately consideration of human resource planning, management development and succession planning. In the author's own research this proposition has been largely supported (Goss-Turner, 2002), with personnel documentation and techniques such as organization charts, job descriptions and appraisal systems often a later development as the multi-site firm develops.

Literature from the UK has focused on strategic and operational developments and service development issues connected with multi-site management, and there have been a number of studies covering the operational systems aspects of the contemporary hospitality industry, and about what hospitality managers actually do at unit level (Lockwood and Guerrier, 1990). The impact of empowerment has also been addressed in connection with multi-site firms, analysing the knock-on effects of the delayering of hospitality organization structures and therefore the nature of the roles of the different layers of management, including the impact on the multi-unit manager position. Lashley (1997) has contributed to the understanding of the concept of empowerment within a service industry context, relating particularly to research within the Harvester Restaurants chain. In Harvester, the empowerment of service employees via more self-managing work groups and the redistribution of responsibilities led to a delayering of two managerial levels. The removal of a layer above the regional/area manager and directly below the managing director increased the accountability of the regional management positions. More recently, Ritchie and Riley (2004) further stress the importance of the human capital inherent within the multi-unit manager role and the crucial aspect of organizational knowledge within a multi-unit structure, including a sense of the power of the hierarchy.

The implications of empowerment initiatives for the role of middle management is also considered by Simons (1995) who points to the need for robust control systems in order to avoid the danger of control failures due to a more remote management style, as in the situation often observed in delayered, decentralized organizations where the multi-site manager is made responsible for a span of control of 20 units when previously he or she had only 12 direct reporting unit managers. His framework, directly related here to the multi-unit manager role and the multi-site organization, consists of four dimensions. The first dimension concerns the need for diagnostic control systems, exemplified by the multi-unit management responsibility for checking that goals and targets have been achieved effectively and efficiently. The Second dimension is the dimension of beliefs systems or core values, such as the strong multi-unit manager influence in disseminating and re-enforcing corporate culture or preferred management style. The third dimension is boundary systems, providing clear parameters of the job and, finally, interactive control systems like regular face-to-face meetings or on-site business reviews to assess performance, issues and future plans and actions. The perspectives put forward by both Lashley and Simons impact on the topic of this chapter by assisting in the understanding of the role of the multi-unit manager within the wider managerial hierarchy, particularly focusing on the inherent tensions between the actual job and the range of tasks required, and as Ritchie and Riley (2004) vividly describe the resultant 'messiness' of the role.

The multi-site or multi-unit manager role is the most influential interface between corporate strategic management and the operational outlets in which the service encounter takes place. This manager, whilst responsible for unit managers across a particular region or brand, is only rarely present at the operation, is remote and yet a line manager of the unit manager, and direct control is only occasionally and briefly possible (Jones, 1999). Similarly the multi-unit managers themselves may well be located far from their peers and superiors. Coordination and collaboration is therefore relatively difficult. Goss-Turner and Jones (2000) conclude from their extensive research within multi-unit hospitality firms that there are four key aspects of the first-line multi-unit management level: job scope, organizational congruence, geographic density and unit conformity. Within job scope, i.e. the range of tasks and responsibilities, there was great variance, polarized between those with a very tightly defined set of tasks geared towards inspection and a broader concept within which the manager would have accountability for development of the business and innovation. International and mature restaurant chains with global brand significance tended towards the rigorous control aspect, in standardizing the offering and achieving high margins through control. Firms in earlier growth stages and less international were characterized by a broader range of duties. Interestingly, those with a strongly branded set of products, such as the major pubs groups, although national rather than international, also followed a pattern of evermore narrowly defined job scope.

For international firms, organizational congruence was important, i.e. the extent to which all managerial levels share a common vision and purpose. In global franchised hotel brands there were clear and formal systems of developing management and employees in the corporate culture and values of service inherent in the base company's strategic underpinning. Such international firms are also attempting a congruence of systems (such as information technology, appraisal and management development) and culture (such as values, beliefs and service). Geographic density, i.e. the number of units in an area or region relative to the size of the area, is again a key difference between large, mature multi-nationals and the developing, less mature nationals. For example, international hotel firms have a low relative density, requiring an even more mobile and experienced international manager to take on the area role. As for unit conformity, i.e. the extent to which units within an area are identical or not, there was a definite trend towards 'streaming' by brand rather than by geography due to the effectiveness and efficiency gains to be achieved from a regional manager always reviewing identical units.

In a study of further HRM implications of these characteristics of multi-site firms, Goss-Turner (1999) concludes that the multi-unit manager role is predominantly an implementer of policy, not a creator of policy. This is largely a function of the role being so clearly placed between the strategy-makers in the boardrooms and the operational front-line unit managers. It is also because all the companies in the research had strategic expansion plans, mostly involving international expansion, of their already tightly branded concepts, sometimes within strictly controlled global franchises. As a result such organizational development involving growth, consolidation and brand extension requires the implementation and maintenance of absolute standards. There is therefore a need for inspection, checking and systematic control, and contrary to some people's view of empowerment, the role has not necessarily become more strategic. From an overall HRM perspective, the aspect of the role which appears to give the multi-unit managers themselves the greatest satisfaction is their personal ability to 'make a difference', by motivating unit managers to achieve high performance. Elements of this aspect include also the beneficial outcome of their job in sharing good and bad practice across the area, often trying to combine high levels of brand prescription and company standardization with the need to encourage an equally high level of commitment to the values and philosophy of the company (Walton, 1985).

One hotel company regional manager interviewed during the author's own research study was typical of those managers who saw their job as a combination of the need to implement strategic imperatives with a need to motivate the managers in the units:

> The job entails firstly maintaining the brand – we do have an identity and maintaining that identity in terms of our standards in the customer's mind and in their perception. I also want to stretch the managers as much as I can by getting them to achieve, such as the 'Investors in People' in every hotel, giving them objectives, ensuring they are ambitious over their business plans. But of course you can never take your eye off the profit level, and implementing company policy.

In the larger, more complex and mature companies, a move towards more sophisticated human resource practices is evident, in line with the research of Doherty (1998). One national licensed retailer with more than 2000 outlets had carried out extensive analysis of the multi-site manager role and determined a set of competencies, which formed part of a detailed job profile which itself was a composite of job description, principal tasks, generic business targets and a review of key organizational relationships and meetings, both internally and externally. The competencies identified were then utilized in the recruitment and selection, whether via external or internal sources, for training and development, and for performance appraisal, ensuring that such managers were assessed against a range of results and abilities. Specifically, the company highlighted

- developing people
- commitment to results and standards
- business acumen
- objective analysis and decision-making
- planning and organizing
- maximizing business opportunities
- communicating
- influencing.

The wide range and scope of these managerial competencies and the tasks and activities within which the role-holder displays such competencies are in stark contrast to some companies' approach to multi-unit management. Where standardization is paramount, the multi-unit manager role can be a mere checker/inspector role, or if the company culture is dominated by a 'hands-on', almost egalitarian approach, area managers may sometimes be required to cover for absent restaurant managers and unit supervisors. In a typology of the multi-unit manager role, Goss-Turner and Jones (2000) suggest four main approaches. First, there is 'the Archetype' multi-unit management approach; a mature single brand organization, typified by McDonald's, with strongly branded identical units with tightly defined tasks for area managers, highly suited to international expansion strategies. The area manager would have narrow job scope; the firm, a high degree of organizational congruence with high geographic density so that area managers can visit regularly and control closely. The implications for human resource management are that most multi-unit managers of this type will have had in-depth unit level experience and be experts on the standards and procedures of the operation. They will be, in the main, inspectors of standards, ensuring consistency and replication of the product and service delivery system.

Secondly, there is 'The Multi-Brand Manager', with more than one concept, tightly branded, applying identical managerial systems in each brand. While the job scope is still narrow, there is more flexibility and variety as more concepts are involved in mature companies. High congruence is difficult to attain, and geographic density remains high as the firm's structure is predominantly region- or area-based on a critical mass of outlets rather than on streamed brands. This approach is difficult to position in the international marketplace. If selecting a manager for this role, there would be a need for an individual less deeply immersed in the detail of one particular brand, more an individual capable of understanding the differences and subtleties of the different brands, more general business management skills, as in an appreciation of merchandising and consumer behaviour rather than a concentrated focus on one set of standards or operational tasks.

Thirdly, 'The Business Manager' responsible for more than one brand and working within a more dynamic environment, with more opportunity for creative solutions and actions within broad policy guidelines and goals. This approach can be readily applied to international hotel companies for example. The personnel specification with regard to this role would be much wider in its requirement for managerial competencies. There would be a higher calling for large-scale business strategy skills, highly developed communication skills, possibly multi-cultural experience, and certainly an ability to motivate and direct other senior and experienced managers. A regional manager for an international hotel chain, for example, would be the line manager for perhaps 15 unit general managers who are themselves experienced hotel managers perhaps with international reputations.

Finally, there is 'The Entrepreneur' with each area manager responsible for one concept, tightly branded, but with an autonomy to develop the business, to be innovative where appropriate, and always within the cultural norms of the firm. Organizational congruence is driven by adherence to values and cultural issues, and job scope is relatively broad within a dynamic environment which eschews a global system of control. This approach will tend to be evident within fairly recently founded companies in the early stages of multi-site growth and expansion. The culture and drive behind the organization will still be linked to the personality and concept of the founder. The entrepreneurial area managers will have probably grown up within the company from the start, will be trusted acolytes of the founder and will be trusted implicitly to do the right thing. There will be no need for the paraphernalia of sophisticated HRM systems, and appraisal will be at most an informal if often extremely frank exchange of views.

The latitude of regional middle management is also determined by the size and stage of development of the firm's life cycle. It has been found that the larger, more mature companies display a control-oriented, structured approach, while smaller, more youthful, more entrepreneurial firms tend towards a strategy which emphasizes mission, values and culture. Organizational development in recent years is also directly affecting the role, as head office support has in many companies been diminished in downsized and delayered organizations. In the short term this may mean that the multi-unit managers need a broader range of management skills, and indeed it was found in the field research that such managers are much more involved with HRM issues than they used to be. Such managers will need more training and development in matters such as recruitment, selection and performance appraisal. Recruitment plans may be affected, with some hospitality and tourism firms perhaps having to recruit more from outside their firm, even the industry. There is evidence from the licensed trade that there are successful multi-unit managers joining the major pubs groups from high-street retailers.

One aspect that will need to be the focus of future research pertains to the longer-term career development and succession planning aspects of multi-site managers. Whilst there may be many more opportunities to become an area manager in the large branded chains, the decentralization of many such companies is leading to smaller head office support functions. This has a direct impact on future career development prospects, as many area managers in the past have aspired to more specialist, centrally-based roles. It is possible that such managers may have to stay in post longer than previously was the case, due to the flatter structure of such organizations. This clearly has implications for HRM, succession planning and indeed compensation and benefits if motivation is to be maintained.

With regard to training and development, the author's research has uncovered two significant challenges at crucial positions within the managerial succession. First, it is imperative that there is more systematic training of unit managers identified as possessing the potential for multi-unit management appointments, particularly in those competencies such as HRM, marketing and financial management which will be needed to a much greater extent in the multi-site role. Add to this the motivational ability required across a large number of units and unit managers in a geographically spread area, and it is clear that the skills of being a top-class unit manager are very different from those required in the area role. Yet many area managers in hospitality companies were identified and promoted because of being highly successful unit managers who experienced little developmental bridging to the new role with its very different set of required competencies. Secondly, it must be accepted in most firms that the multi-unit role is one of implementation of standards, and that positions higher up the organization will require additional and enhanced skills in the area of strategic formulation and corporate level decision-making. Some companies in the author's research sample were tackling this issue by introducing executive development programmes for high-potential managers, often utilizing universities and business schools as partners in such development activities. Succession plans must influence management development programmes to ensure that this gap in the training cycle is bridged.

This chapter has reviewed some of the HRM implications of an ongoing phenomenon, namely the continuing development of larger, multi-site firms within an evermore international and branded hospitality industry. It has been established that this has increased the need for, and significance of, a position of multi-site management, immediately above the front-line operations management and between operations and senior/strategic executive levels. As such it has been found to be a very important career development position for many unit managers, but essentially an implementer of strategy rather than a creator. Further, it has been discussed that the role in many strongly branded chains has the potential to be a largely controlling and checking role, with the proviso that there is still an opportunity for any area or regional manager to exercise their specific skills as a motivator and a coach to unit management. There is still the need to encourage and energize and to gain a high level of commitment to the values and beliefs of the company.

Further Reading and References

Doherty, L. (1998) What makes a successful influential human resource strategy? In *Proceedings of the EuroChrie/IAHMS Conference*, Lausanne, November, 123–131.

Goss-Turner, S. (1999) The role of the multi-unit manager in branded hospitality chains, *Human Resource Management Journal*, Vol. 9, No. 4, 39–57.

Goss-Turner, S. (2002) Multi-Site management: HRM implications, in D'Annunzio-Green, Maxwell, G. A. and Watson, S. (eds) *Human Resource Management – International Perspectives in Hospitality and Tourism*, London: Continuum.

Goss-Turner, S. and Jones, P. (2000) Multi-unit management in service operations: Alternative approaches in the UK hospitality industry, *Tourism and Hospitality Research*, Vol. 2, No. 1, 51–66.

Holbeche, L. (2001) *Aligning Human Resources and Business Strategy*, Oxford: Butterworth-Heinemann.

Jones, P. (1999) Multi-unit management: A late twentieth century phenomenon, *International Journal of Contemporary Hospitality Management*, Vol. 11, No. 4, 155–164.

Lashley, C. (1997) *Empowering Service Excellence*, London: Cassell.

Lee-Ross, D. (1999) *HRM in Tourism and Hospitality*, London: Cassell.

Levitt, T. (1972) The production line approach to service, *Harvard Business Review*, September/October, 41–52.

Lockwood, A. and Guerrier, Y. (1990) Managers in hospitality: A review of current research, *Progress in Tourism, Recreation and Hospitality Research*, Vol. 2, 151–167.

Lucas, R. (2004) *Employment Relations in the Hospitality and Tourism Industries*, London: Routledge.

Olsen, M., Ching-Yick Tse, E. and West, J. J. (1992) *Strategic Management in the Hospitality Industry*, New York: Van Nostrand Reinhold.

Ritchie, B. and Riley, M. (2004) The role of the multi-unit manager within the strategy and structure relationship; evidence from the unexpected, *International Journal of Hospitality Management*, Vol. 23, 145–161.

Sasser, W. E., Olsen, R. P. and Wycoff, D. D. (1978) *Management of Service Operations*, Boston: Allyn and Bacon.

Schmenner, R. (1986) How can service businesses survive and prosper?, *Sloan Management Review*, Spring, 21–32.

Simons, R. (1995) Control in an age of Empowerment, *Harvard Business Review*, March/April, 80–88.

Tyson, S. (1995) *Human Resource Strategy*, London: Pitman.

Walton, R. E. (1985) From control to commitment, in Clarke, K., Hayes, R. H. and Lorenz, C. (eds) *The Uneasy Alliance*, Boston: Harvard Business School Press.

Questions

1 Why has the position of multi-site manager become significant within branded hospitality chains?

2 What is the relationship between management style and the role of the multi-unit manager?

3 What do you understand by job scope, organizational congruence, geographic density and unit conformity?

4 What essential requirements would you include in the personnel specification for a multi-site manager within an international hotel chain?

5 What selection methods would you adopt when assessing the suitability of applicants for a multi-unit manager role in a fast food chain?

Customer care and quality

Customer care is nothing new. Top class nineteenth-century hotels and twentieth-century transatlantic liners were quite probably looking after their customers far better than most hotel guests are looked after today. What is new, however, is the 'industrialization' of customer care. As service businesses have become bigger, as more of the customers are dealt with by relatively untrained, perhaps uncommitted staff, frequently young and not particularly well versed in social skills, and as competition becomes more severe, the need arises for a systematic approach to ensuring that the target customers receive the service they expect.

Research by the University of Manchester Institute of Science and Technology (UMIST) classified organizations into

- uncommitted – Quality Initiatives (QI) not yet started
- drifters – QI started 18–36 months ago
- tool pushers – QI started 3–5 years ago
- improvers – QI started 5–8 years ago
- award winners – QI started probably some 10 years ago
- world class – QI started probably more than 10 years ago.

(source: Lascelles and Dale, 1993).

In the very best, the 'world class' organizations, customer care is clearly a responsibility of every single employee from the most junior to the chief executive.

In other organizations, however, customer care may be the responsibility of customer service or training departments, with little direct involvement of senior management. Many of the customer care initiatives of hospitality companies tend to fall into the 'tool pusher' category, at best. One indicator is that their quality initiatives, rather than being central to the company's policy, are given specific titles such as customer relations assistant.

In setting out to provide customers with what the operator thinks they expect, it is essential to recognize that the quality of service is influenced by a number of different factors. Some of these factors are only noticed by the customer if the factor is wrong in some way, as in the cases of room temperature and noise levels. Other factors contribute positively to the customer's experience, such as being recognized by the staff and being addressed by one's name. One can draw parallels with Herzberg's hygiene factors and motivators, which relate to employees' perceptions of their work experience (Herzberg, Mausrer and Snyderman, 1959; see Figure 2.5). In a seminal work regarding the development of service operations management, Gronroos (1994) indicates five characteristics of the subject area. First, the management of service quality and customer care must be a complete management perspective, impacting on the decisions and actions of all managers. Secondly, it must be driven by the consumer or the market in that the business needs to have a detailed analysis of the consumer demand and needs and expectations. Thirdly, it is a holistic approach, infiltrating all sections of the company from head office to unit management. Fourthly, that quality management and assurance is an integral feature of service management. Finally, that the human resource of the firm must be trained appropriately and motivated to be committed to the service quality strategy as part of the company's wider corporate strategy. Hence it is clear that there is a direct relationship between HRM and customer care, service and quality (see also Maxwell and Quail, 2002).

Today the majority of the British population experiences a wide range of service offerings, be they fast food, medical care, leisure or education. And the expectations of these consumers have been heightened, and are constantly raised, by these self-same service offerings. Concomitant with this has been the increasing similarity of many competing products, such as the basic similarity of features in a business class 4-star hotel, from satellite, interactive TV with internet access, to trouser press, hair-dryers, mini-bar and bathrobes. In many cases the search for product differentiation, the process by which a provider of a generic product makes the product different from competitors' products, has to be concentrated on the 'people interactions' involved. A classic example is the air transport industry, in which companies compete on similar, scheduled routes using similar aircraft. The main way by which such companies can gain competitive advantage and increase their market share at the expense of their competitors is to obtain the best flight slots and, increasingly now, to offer the best price, after which the only extra dimension they can add is that of better service; speedier check-in, better waiting arrangements and better in-flight food and cabin service.

Because 'customer care' has become fashionable, many organizations decide it is something they have to do. The problem is that, as Herzberg, Mausrer and Snyderman (1959) and many others showed with regard to employment, customer care is a highly complex issue. However, from the range of customer care programmes it is evident that many employers make assumptions about what the problem is. Very frequently it is apparent that the employer believes 'social skill' training is either what is required or is all that can be afforded, whereas the fundamental problem may be one of design, delivery or even product quality. What may not have been done is to analyse customer care needs systematically, e.g. through the use of 'critical incidence techniques', although most experienced managers and staff do know what the key issues are.

There are, however, organizations that do this. The Sheraton Hotel group (part of Starwood Lodging), for example, runs a very sophisticated programme which involves regular assessment of the standards being achieved. Other organizations run customer care audits, some of which are carefully structured and some of which are not. As discussed in Chapter 1, the Hospitality Assured scheme championed by the BHA and the HCIMA is especially geared towards benchmarking and setting standards for service quality and pays particular attention to customer needs and satisfaction.

SERVQUAL (service quality)

This is one of the most well-reported approaches to evaluating the effectiveness of service delivery. The approach has been developed since the 1980s by Parasuraman, Zeithasml and Berry (1988). A major thrust of their work has been that service providers must learn more about their customers through rigorous market research. These researchers believe that, in spite of the intangibility of services, their quality can be measured.

SERVQUAL is based on a generic 22-item questionnaire that considers five broad aspects of service quality:

- tangibles (appearance of physical elements)
- reliability (dependability, accurate performance)
- responsiveness (promptness and helpfulness)
- assurance (competence, courtesy, credibility and security)
- empathy (easy access, good communications and customer understanding).

Customers are asked to complete a questionnaire; the first part identifies their expectations and the second part identifies their perceptions of the actual offering. Using a value (Likert) scale the value gap between expectations and perceptions of the offering can be determined.

This process identifies a company's strengths and weaknesses. Different weightings can be given to the various elements. From the results can be derived a list of priorities needing attention through the most appropriate means such as training or investment in equipment.

SERVQUAL goes on to identify five key gaps:

Gap 1: A gap between consumer expectations and management perceptions. Managers think customers want one thing whereas the customers may prefer something else.

Gap 2: A gap between management perception and service quality specification. Management may not specify clearly what is needed or they may set unachievable quality standards.

Gap 3: A gap between service quality specifications and service delivery. Simply put, a service provider fails to meet the standards set.

Gap 4: A gap between service delivery and external communications. This may result from expectations being unrealistically raised through intermediaries such as sales offices, agencies or promotional materials.

Gap 5: A gap between perceived service and expected service. This gap is the result of one or more of the previous gaps. Basically the customer does not get what he or she expects.

The SERVQUAL method then goes on to identify a zone of tolerance, which is effectively the zone between what customers expect and what they consider to be the minimum acceptable service level.

The traditional marketing mix approach

Traditionally, most students of marketing (and customer care is one vital dimension of marketing) have thought in terms of four elements making up the typical marketing mix: product, price, place and promotion. Bitner *et al.* (1985, 1989, 1990) developed a seven 'P' mix for service industries:

1 product – range, quality, level, brand name, service level
2 price – level, discrimination, quality/price/perceived value
3 place – location, accessibility, environs
4 promotion – advertising, sales promotion, publicity, public relations
5 people – training, discretion, commitment, incentives, appearance, behaviour/attitude
6 physical features – environment, design, furnishings, colour, layout, noise
7 process – procedures, flow of activities, customer involvement.

The present author, over a period of time, and through many personal experiences and observations, has concluded that another element has to be added: method of payment. This appears to be at the centre of so many causes of dissatisfaction (e.g. hotel morning checkout, supermarket checkouts) and also at the heart of so many promotional initiatives (one shop in Edinburgh advertised no fewer than 14 different methods of payment) that it needs to be separated out for the purpose of analysing the service offering.

Eight 'P's of the customer care mix – the 'service offering'

A careful analysis of most service operations and the wide range of customer care programmes will identify between four (usually the classic four 'P's of the marketing mix) and eight key dimensions. The eight are: product, place, physical evidence, process, price, payment, promotion and people. In essence these are the seven elements identified by Bitner *et al.*, but with the payment method added.

Product

Obviously, in providing a service, the first thing to get right is the essential element, the core product. In a hotel, the beds have to be comfortable and clean. The room has to be in a comfortable temperature and it has to provide the services expected. In a restaurant, hot food has to be hot and tasty. Much research shows, however, that dissatisfaction with the core product is not a major cause of customer dissatisfaction. Rather the problems lie with one or more of the other 'P's of the mix.

Place

Paraphrasing the founder of the Hilton Corporation's famous dictum, 'There are three rules to success in the hotel business: location, location, location.' Although this may be a very sound advice, some very successful hospitality businesses have succeeded in spite of their location.

Place, or location, can embrace a number of different elements, including accessibility. Is the hotel or restaurant relatively easy to find and to get to? Is it by an airport, motorway junction or railway station? Does it have attractive features? Is it located in a place that people will want to visit? Is it located in an attractive town or rural setting? Is the location (e.g. a town or village) and the setting (e.g. a particular street) a strength or a weakness?

Physical evidence

Whilst the place itself might be an attraction and a strength, the actual physical ambience in which the core product is enjoyed may also be of crucial importance, e.g. the decor in themed restaurants. In other cases the physical ambience may be relatively unimportant when compared with the importance of the food on the plate.

In essence hoteliers or caterers can make decisions about how many senses they want to appeal to. This may be just the sense of taste or they can attempt to appeal to most, if not all, the senses of their customers through a combination of food, drink, decor, furnishings, air quality and music.

In addition customers may be seeking (sometimes subconsciously) clues about issues they consider important, such as hygiene, social recognition, esteem, etc. So, does the physical ambience meet these needs or expectations? Heskett (1986) strongly urges businesses to understand their customers and their needs in terms of not only the demographics but also their 'psychographics', how they think and feel about the product and service.

Process

The word 'process' is intended to describe all those experiences the customer goes through in order to enjoy the core product itself. Today, more than ever before, it is possible to acquire the same product through various different means. For example, it is possible to buy a product such as a pizza via restaurants, supermarkets, home delivery, telephone ordering and internet ordering. In all these cases the product might be the same or similar but the process itself may be an essential ingredient in the buying process.

In the case of hospitality products and services the 'process' can include elements such as reservation systems, car parking and signage. The process is distinct from, but closely related to, promotion, which includes advertising and merchandising. Sometimes the boundary will merge. As an example, an advertisement in a lift for a hotel's restaurant is not just providing the customer with useful information but is also promoting a profit centre.

For many people, the first step in buying a restaurant or hotel service consists of making a reservation. Is it as easy, efficient and friendly as possible? Is it easy to find the telephone number? Is it listed in an easy-to-find way in a directory? Is the telephone answered quickly and courteously? Are all staff trained to answer the phone and not leave it to someone else? How many people hesitate to telephone certain numbers because they know the number will be engaged? Some companies have a policy that the phone will always be answered within a certain prescribed time. Is the person passed from one to another before the booking is taken? Is there a set procedure for taking bookings, i.e. do all staff likely to take a booking, know what information is needed, e.g. a return telephone number, credit card number, table release time? Can staff quote with some accuracy the price of set menus or give indications of the cost per head of a meal? Do they understand the importance of making absolutely clear the prices quoted? Does a customer understand that the price quoted for a double room is a per-person price rather than a per-room price? Are they told of late arrival arrangements and room release times? Are customers told about extras; in buying holidays, for example, are all the extras quoted?

Arrival and access • • •

Is it easy for customers to find the establishment? Are they given a map or are they told of nearby landmarks? Are they told about car parking? Are the signs clear? Is international signage used? Are the 'Don't' signs friendly or are they aggressive? Is it easy to find one's way from the car park to the hotel, around the hotel, etc.? Is access safe and free of risk? Are car parks laid out so that ladies can park their cars close to the hotel reception?

Queuing • • •

If customers have to queue, there are some useful principles to know about queuing. If queuing is a 'lottery', i.e. some queues move faster than others, then customers are likely to feel very irritated if their queue is the slowest. Free-flow cafeteria systems have overcome some aspects of queuing problems. Hotels are introducing billing arrangements for the guest bedroom, i.e. the guest can view and check the bill on the bedroom TV, and use a fast check-out facility by simply leaving a completed form in a secure place at reception. Research has also shown that if customers are kept busy in the queue or whilst waiting, the waiting time is perceived as shorter. This is one reason why restaurants give customers menus to look at, bread rolls to eat and water to drink. It is not merely giving customers the sales catalogue to look at.

The increasingly common practice, in upmarket restaurants, of giving customers a tasty savoury before the hors-d'oeuvres also recognizes the importance of keeping customers busy. It may also help to 'exceed customer expectations'. If customers are acknowledged in a queue or whilst waiting, they are reassured and will find the queue less irksome. Good bar staff will acknowledge customers with eye contact, and maybe a short comment such as 'Be with you in a moment.'

Another fact known about queuing is that if customers know the likely duration of queuing this reduces a cause for irritation. The London Underground, rail networks and some bus companies have recognized this issue and now display the approximate waiting time for trains in many of their stations and bus stops. Likewise, customers do not feel that they are part of the process until they have been acknowledged by the staff or are clearly part of a queue – hence the considerable irritation felt by many pub customers.

Apart from the actual queuing there is also 'waiting time'. In a study ('Survey of good service in fine-dining restaurants', quoted in *Cornell Quarterly*, November 1988), it was reported that customers were prepared to wait for two minutes to be greeted. However, since waiting time is perceived as longer than occupied time the real time they are prepared to wait can be reduced dramatically to around 30 seconds. Effective service operators manage this element of the process. In a restaurant for example, 'waiting time' may be occupied by customers looking at menus and drinking an aperitif.

Some telephone waiting systems acknowledge this by repeatedly telling callers that they will be connected as soon as the line is free. Increasingly such telephone systems are telling the caller their place in the queue. Background music on telephones is there partly to let callers know that they are still connected. If the length of delay is known by the person waiting, it is less irksome than when the waiting period is unknown.

Menus • • •

Are these clear and easy to follow? Are foreign languages translated? Many ethnic restaurants, and many English ones as well, make it difficult for the customer to know what he or she is ordering. If a restaurant has a significant number of foreign customers, are the menus translated into their languages? In many continental restaurants the menus are available in three or four different languages, making it easy for customers to order what they want. Otherwise customers who cannot understand a menu may go for a safe universal word such as 'omelette' rather than risking something they may not want.

A key element in the 'process' is to ensure that when the process breaks down, e.g. because of a delay, an overbooking or the like, the customer is informed as quickly as possible and given information about what is being done to put things right. The customer should be given reassurance and solutions.

Price

In many service operations the price and the method of payment are crucial factors in customer choice and satisfaction. Price is often (but by no means always) an indication of quality to be expected.

First, is the price clear and unambiguous? Some of the continental countries have recognized the importance of this aspect and have legislated for all-inclusive prices. The French *prix net* system tells the customer that VAT and service charge are included and that no extra payments are needed, although tips may still be expected! English menus are sometimes less clear in this regard, but generally there is an improvement in the level of information given to customers about pricing, in line with industry codes of practice.

Discounting can be a major sales tool but it can also be a cause of dissatisfaction for customers when they discover that they may be paying a very different price for the same product compared with another customer. This can happen both in small country-house hotels and in the world's largest cruise liners. It can lead a customer who may well have been totally satisfied to feel dissatisfied merely because he or she has discovered that someone else got what he or she got for a cheaper price.

Having said that, there is also an increasing openness about variable pricing linked to yield management systems, such as the changing prices over time of flight tickets connected to the low-cost airlines. Some restaurants are openly promoting a similar approach, such as special prices at off-peak times of the day, especially where 'all-day' opening is a policy.

Payment

The method of payment also plays a crucial part in the service offering. This is evidenced by the number of traders who display that various credit cards and other forms of payment are accepted. Many customers will pay only by card and so traders may lose out by not accepting cards. Card companies estimate that spend per head is higher because customers can postpone or spread the day of reckoning by using their cards, as well as accumulating loyalty points or airmiles.

In the case of telephone bookings, are customers told that certain payments may not be acceptable?

Bill presentation is important too. Is it clear? Can the customer understand it? Is it properly itemized? Can customers get a receipt easily? Many caterers, particularly smaller ones, make giving a receipt a problem and yet for their business customers a receipt can represent a saving of around 35% of the cost of the meal, after VAT and income or corporation tax are taken into account.

In many cases customers want to have complete control over how much they spend. One of the reasons supermarkets are preferred by some customers to the local butcher shop, for example, is because the customer can look for a joint of meat that meets their budget precisely, rather than having to pay for what the butcher puts on the scales. Cafeterias and à la carte menus achieve this but sometimes set menus, the absence of half bottles on wine lists, etc., remove this degree of budget control from the customer.

Issues of importance in pricing include

- prices well displayed
- simple, easily understood prices
- clear, simple-to-understand bills
- easily obtained receipts
- easy methods of payment
- information about unacceptable methods of payment
- a simple approach to resolving payment problems
- ability of the customer to control spending
- value for money.

Promotion

Proper promotion depends upon a clear identification of the target market and use of the most appropriate media. The media may include various forms of advertising and merchandising. In some cases promotion may be an essential and significant item in the organization's budget. In other cases word-of-mouth recommendation may be quite sufficient to generate the required levels of business. Promotion is often the first contact a customer has with the enterprise. Does this contact contribute to customer satisfaction by creating the right level of expectations or is it the first step in creating dissatisfaction by creating unrealistic expectations? Is it helpful? Is it correct? Is the business's promotion a strength or a weakness?

People

Finally, the degree to which an employer succeeds in ensuring that staff give customers the standard of service desired varies from employer to employer. Some employers pay most attention to setting strict procedures and training, whilst others may rely more on selection and giving staff a free hand. Other employers arrive at a combination of both.

In businesses such as restaurants, hotels and holiday companies, social skills obviously play a crucial role in the success of the enterprise. Many managers argue that these cannot be easily taught or learned and that the ideal is to concentrate on recruiting people with the right attitudes to customers. To do this successfully means that employers need to develop effective selection skills and some of the industry's leaders now devote resources to training their managers in selection interviewing skills.

Some organizations (e.g. TGIF and Disney) look for the skills of entertainers rather than the more traditional skills associated with restaurants and hotels. Consequently they virtually audition their applicants rather than interviewing them.

In many cases it is vital that staff have a good understanding of what the customer expects. Some employers consider that the best way of achieving this is to recruit staff who share similar life experiences with their customers. In some cases employers encourage their employees to use their facilities as customers, maybe in other establishments owned by the employer.

Some employers (e.g. De Vere Hotels) set out to develop in staff the awareness that they must 'own' problems that affect customers. This means that they must seek solutions, not look for ways to avoid solving problems. No one should walk past litter in an establishment, even if it is not in their section. No one should leave a telephone ringing if there is no one else ready to answer it. No one should leave a customer with a problem, saying, 'Sorry, this is not my section.'

Some forms of training concentrate on teaching the staff certain 'scripts', such as 'Good day, how may I help you?' or teaching the staff to use a customer's name or to reply in a particular way to a telephone call. Others may be less prescriptive but may still require certain rituals to be observed. Sheraton for example sets a variety of 'Sheraton Guest Satisfaction Standards'. Figure 23.1 shows one such standard.

HANDOUT 1–1

Sheraton
Guest Satisfaction Standards

1 Every time you see a guest, smile and offer an appropriate hospitality comment.
2 Speak to every guest in a friendly, enthusiastic and courteous tone and manner.
3 Answer guest questions and requests quickly and efficiently, or take personal responsibility to get the answers.
4 Anticipate guest needs and resolve guest problems.

Figure 23.1 A Sheraton Guest Satisfaction Standard

Radisson Hotels run a 'Yes I Can' programme, which sets out to train staff so that they never say 'no' to a customer. Specific selling skills may also be developed. For example, one of the leading fast food chains trains staff to attempt to 'upsell' one item more than the customer has ordered but never two or more.

Transactional analysis

Other training will be concerned with developing attitudes and skills based on certain schools of psychology, such as 'transactional analysis' (TA; see Berne, 1976), which sets out to develop a person's ability to recognize a customer's personality state and to respond with an appropriate one. It has been used over many years as a form of customer care training by a wide range of organizations including many hotel and airline companies. It is described here in a little detail to illustrate one such approach – there are many others.

Transactional analysis sets out to analyse the nature of the individual personality states involved in transactions between people, and the nature of the transactions themselves. Each normal individual's personality consists of three separate but interacting personality states or elements: the Parent, the Adult, and the Child.

The Parent is derived from experiences of authority figures including parents and parent substitutes such as teachers, the police, etc.

The Child part of the personality draws upon the person's experiences, particularly the feelings and emotions, of childhood. For example the trepidation felt by many employees when the boss says 'I want to talk to you', may be to do with the memory many people have of how worried they were when their own father said just these words. There may be nothing to worry about but certain phrases and situations cause involuntary recall of certain experiences.

The Adult part of a person's personality functions rationally. It does not mimic parental attitudes nor does it react emotionally. The Adult part of the personality receives information from outside, from the Parent part of the personality and from the Child part of the personality as well. It questions the validity of the information from each source and it then attempts to produce a rational result. This is based neither on what is expected by the Parent nor on what is wanted by the Child.

A person with a strong Adult is often described as mature or well balanced. One with a strong Child may be described as immature and one with a strong Parent as too rigid.

When two people meet, therefore, the three parts of each person's personality are involved and the outcome of the meeting or transaction will be dependent entirely upon which part of each person's personality is involved. Every transaction is a two-way affair – with one person communicating in the first instance (providing the stimulus) and the other responding (making the response).

In the simplest transactions the arrows are parallel and these are called complementary transactions, as shown in Figure 23.2. If the arrows remain parallel – i.e. when the transactions are complementary – communication may proceed indefinitely.

Figure 23.2 shows a simple example of a Parent-type communication receiving a Child response. An illustration of such a transaction would be a domineering executive booking in at a reception desk manned by a receptionist who reacts as an obedient, submissive 'child' to the executive 'parent'. The interaction or 'transaction', as such processes are called, could continue for some time.

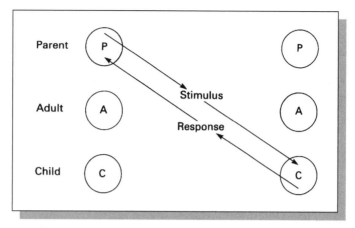

Figure 23.2 A complementary transaction

Figure 23.3 shows a crossed transaction – the type of transaction that apparently causes most trouble. An example of this is when a waitress asks (in Adult fashion) for the meals for a particular table and the chef replies that everyone is in a rush and that he needs more staff in any case, replying much as a child often does when irritated by a parent.

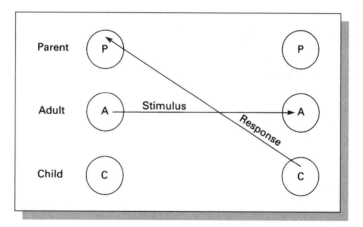

Figure 23.3 A crossed transaction

The transaction breaks down because the chef raised issues that were not relevant to the rational request of the waitress. It was not an Adult reply but a Child reply to an Adult request. The only probable solution to this Child response is for the manager (a Parent figure) to order the chef to produce the goods or for the waitress to switch on the chef's Parent. This would then keep the second part of the transaction upon parallel lines. These complementary and crossed transactions are simple one-level transactions.

But beyond these there are two types of ulterior or 'two-level' transactions. On the surface we see a complementary Adult-to-Adult transaction but the stimulus may be a sales hook appealing to the Child in the respondent. For example, to offer sweets from the sweet trolley or, at the other extreme, an executive jet to a chief executive can be made to sound very Adult, with Adult reasoning put forward in justification. But all along the offer – the stimulus – may really be appealing to the Child. In this case the respondent may respond to the stimulus in a Child way: 'I want it and I will have it' (Figure 23.4).

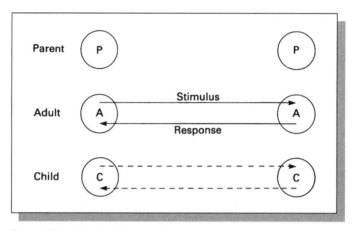

Figure 23.4 A two-level transaction

Types of transactions

The principal interactions or transactions that take place between people are divided into several basic types:

- procedures
- rituals
- activities and work
- pastimes
- operations
- games.

Procedures

The 'procedure' is a series of transactions between two people at an Adult level, and is concerned with achieving objectives as effectively as possible – objectives that are normally understood by each person. Booking a hotel guest into a hotel under normal circumstances is a procedure because one person wants a room and the receptionist wants to sell the room.

Rituals

'Rituals' consist of a series of stereotyped transactions, which may be informal or highly formalized. An informal ritual takes place when two close friends meet, shake hands and ask about one another's families. A more formalized ritual takes place between complete strangers and in many commercial transactions, e.g. when buying something in a shop. Rituals are the safest form of transaction because the outcome is predictable.

Activities or work

Activities or work transactions are programmed by the work itself, e.g. by the material or the system. During the activity there is no need for involvement with others – there may be a need, but it is not essential. The outcome again is predictable and therefore work is the next safest form of interchange between individuals.

Pastimes

After activities or work come pastimes. Pastimes are like social skirmishing – getting to know more about the other person in order to decide whether to proceed to 'games'.

Operations

An operation occurs when one person states his needs frankly and the other person, the respondent, satisfies these needs without taking advantage of the situation. Operations, no matter how often they are repeated, are to be distinguished from games and also from rituals and pastimes.

Games

'Games', though appearing to be operations, are ulterior transactions between people, which have psychological payoffs or rewards. They are normally repetitious but repetition in itself does not make the transaction a game. There must be a payoff. For example, if an employee regularly seeks reassurance that he or she is doing his or her job satisfactorily and when reassured goes away content, then there is no ulterior motive and therefore a game is not being played. But if after receiving several reassurances he or she were to say 'in that case I want an increase in pay', then there was an ulterior motive and he or she has conned his boss. He has played a 'game' with his boss, who probably now feels aggrieved that a normal human response – to give reassurance where it was merited – has been used against him for an ulterior or unexpected motive.

Within the hotel and restaurant world, where personal transactions are the very essence of the business, all of these types of transactions are possible and in many cases guests or staff will move rapidly from the ritual stage to the games stage. Once games are being played, unfortunately, either guests or a member of staff can suffer. As a consequence and to ensure that this does not happen, particularly to socially inexperienced staff such as young ones or newcomers from a business with less public contact, it is wise to build up a defence of rituals that will direct their social contacts with their guests. Some will argue that this will result in too much uniformity and lack of individual personality showing through. This could be the case if taken too far, but in the absence of rituals there is far too much game playing between guests and staff, leading to one or the other being hurt, so if rituals are designed carefully to meet all the more common, workaday transactions between staff and guests, a good deal of the hurtful game-playing that takes place will be eliminated.

Generally, the rituals need to be simple. Many socially aware managers have recognized the need and have ensured that their staff are trained to use them. There are, within a hotel context, two main types.

First, a regular ritual is one used when something normal and routine occurs. For example, when a guest arrives to book in, a strictly laid down script could be followed, which covers the various alternatives such as

- a guest with a confirmed booking
- a guest with a booking but no confirmation
- a chance guest.

The second ritual is one developed to deal with the non-routine events that occur from time to time – such as dealing with an overbooking or an incorrect booking.

In both cases one has to design a ritual that is acceptable to the Adult part of a person's personality. Frequently, particularly in the case of dealing with complaints, a situation immediately switches on the Child or the Parent in a personality. The Child has not got what they wanted. The consequence is that – as with dealing with young children – reason will not prevail in any event. And only when something switches on the Adult again will reason prevail. Frequently this occurs only after there has been a change of personalities involved – and the receptionist who has failed to placate an irate guest is surprised to see the manager deal with the situation very smoothly. It is not necessarily because of the manager's extra skill but only because the change of personalities enables the irate guest's Adult to be switched on again.

Different approaches to customer care

Frances Sacker, of the Industrial Society, in her article 'Customer service training in context' (*Personnel Management*, March 1987) divided training into two main types, the 'evangelical' and the 'exploratory' styles. This appears to be still relevant today. The evangelical style is aimed at creating 'a high degree of excitement and enthusiasm' whereas the exploratory style is concerned with giving individuals 'the opportunity, through discussion, video, etc., to make decisions about their own behaviour and about practical actions they can take to improve their own performance'.

The organization's needs, the resources they have available for training and the calibre of their staff all contribute towards decisions about the most appropriate approach to training. Obviously the question arises as to which is more important – the ability to select well or to train well. Many personnel specialists take the view, however, that training is only likely to be effective if the right calibre of person is recruited in the first place, and works alongside service-quality committed colleagues within an appropriately reinforced, service-oriented atmosphere and culture.

Selecting and motivating staff

In looking at the customer care mix it is apparent that there is considerable dependence between the separate elements of the mix (whether 4, 5, 6, 7 or 8). However, it is vital that the approach to staffing is correct as well, including recruiting staff with correct attitudes, training them and rewarding them appropriately. In the case of the Sheraton programme, employee recognition features as a key element (Figure 23.5).

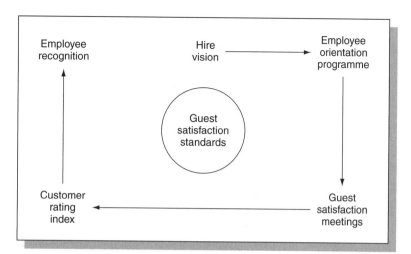

Figure 23.5 The Sheraton customer care cycle

In the case of Barclays Bank the fourth declared objective of their programme was 'to reinforce the objectives with accountability and recognition'. If an employer claims that customer care is so crucial to the success of the enterprise then the employer must demonstrate that commitment by developing proper rewards. This could be in the form of bonuses, but many programmes involving rewards appear to use other forms of employee incentive. Several of the large hotel groups and airlines, for example, select the 'employee of the month' from the workforce and reward accordingly. Sometimes these are selected by management, sometimes by customers. Unfortunately, many such schemes are known by the staff to be manipulated – the award going to each department in turn. It could be argued, however, that such approaches to motivation are external or extrinsic to a proper customer care programme. Instead a good programme, which is also concerned with recruiting the right staff, itself engages the interest of the staff and of itself provides the necessary motivation. Marriott developed a scheme whereby staff accumulated points for excellent service standards, customer complements and the like, and could exchange certain numbers of points for gifts from a glossy catalogue.

The need for a policy and diagnosis

An increasing number of companies have customer care policies, sometimes displayed in customer areas, e.g. in reception areas, on price lists, brochures and the like. Sometimes customer care plans derive from customer care analysis. The BHA Scher scheme gives participating companies important indicators of performance standards achievement. Sheraton Hotels (and many other companies as well) have a regular customer rating process (see Figure 23.5) which provides each unit with its own customer rating index and its rating relative to other similar Sheraton hotels. Some companies set out to measure accurately the cost of poor customer care. One measure used by a North American company is the number of abandoned telephone enquiries (their monthly target is 3% maximum) and what this represents as lost revenue to the company.

A diagnostic tool

One integrated approach (developed and used by the author and colleagues from the University of Brighton), called Bullseye, provided a flexible instrument designed specifically for each customer care situation. It consisted of a number of separate elements:

1 The initial research identified the organization's expectations. This research included management, operative staff and, of course, customers and potential customers of the organization.
2 Preparation of a questionnaire to be used for evaluation of the existing level of customer care (Figure 23.6A).
3 A Bullseye scoring sheet, which determined the actual level of achievement for each of the key elements (Figure 23.6B).
4 An 'improvement plan', which could be based on an MbO and/or quality circles approach.

Typically this approach fits well into Frances Sacker's 'exploratory' style – because it provides the basis for the participants to develop their own solutions to the problems they themselves have identified. Of course if an organization moves down the MbO, quality circles or empowerment route other issues emerge such as the need to train all management and operative staff in the effective operation of such an approach.

It should be evident from the above that effective customer care consists of a number of interdependent elements, some quite complex, some simple in themselves. In most cases effective customer care is likely to involve senior management commitment and the involvement of the whole workforce. It can also involve major investment in hardware such as buildings, equipment, etc. A simple outline of what can be involved is shown in Figures 23.7 and 23.8.

A. The questionnaire

	Positive +	Neutral	Negative –
Food temperature			
Signposting			
Value for money			
Sensitivity towards customers			
Drink temperature			
Menu information/explanation			
Payment system			
Ability to adapt			
Presentation			
Queuing			
Bill clarity			
Cleanliness of uniform			
Aroma of food			
Waiting time			
Price display			
Appearance			
Freshness			
Service			
Exchange of money			

Figure 23.6 A customer care evaluation scheme (Cross Channel Ferries)

	Positive +	Neutral	Negative −
Skill			
Taste			
Opening time			
Methods of payment (cheque, cash)			
Language			
Value for money			
Hygiene			
Usefulness			
Courtesy			
Appropriateness of dishes			
Ambience			
Dealing with a problem (payment)			
Understanding problems			
Product range			
Comfort			
Resolving complaints			
Shipboard knowledge			
Portion size			
Heating			
Budget control			
General knowledge			

Each item, to be evaluated, relates to one of the four 'Ps':

    product
    process
    price and payment
    people

B. Score sheet

	Question	P	Question	P	Question	P	Question	P
	1		2		3		4	
	5		6		7		8	
	9		10		11		12	
	13		14		15		16	
	17		18		19		20	
	21		22		23		24	
	25		26		27		28	
	29		30		31		32	
	33		34		35		36	
	37		38		39		40	
Total	(product)		(process)		(price/ payment)		(people)	

Figure 23.6 *continued*

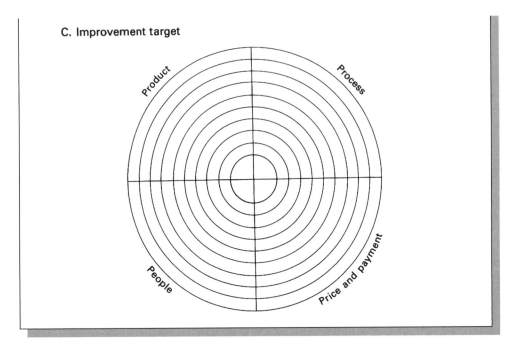

C. Improvement target

Figure 23.6 *continued*

What the customer wants	What the caterer or hotelier should do	How
Information	Inform the customer	Use positive, friendly helpful notice, **not** warnings and admonishments
Fairness	Design ordering procedures and queues to eliminate unfairness	Ensure that customer perceives ordering procedures and queues as fair, i.e. first come, first served
Activity	Keep customers actively involved in the 3 phases of a meal 1 pre-queuing 2 queuing 3 the meal	Involve customer as much as possible in the process, e.g. looking at menus
Attention	Greet and/acknowledge customer, top-up glasses, remove used plates	Use scripts, eye-contact, body language, develop perception skills
'Strokes'	Make each customer feel special	Use customer name, compliment
Reassurance	Keep customer informed, reassured	Devise scripts and/or procedures
Timely service (and an idea of the time he/she will have to wait)	Provide timely service and keep customer informed	Set standards, control standards, informing customers of waiting times
Courtesy	Provide courteous staff and service	Personal grooming, deportment, devise systems and routines and train staff Develop attitudes and empathy
Feedback system and ability to complain	Design an effective procedure for customer feedbacks, particularly complaints	Devise a policy and procedures provide training

Figure 23.7 Elements of a customer care programme

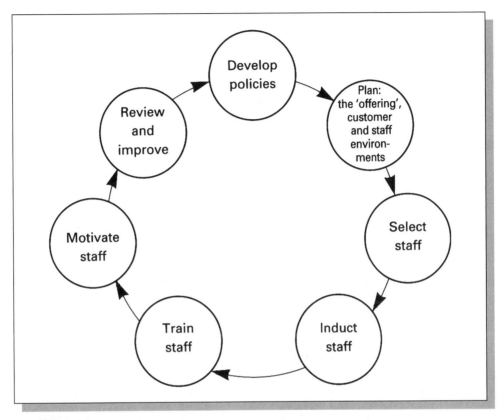

Figure 23.8 The customer care process

Further Reading and References

Berne, E. (1975) *What Do You Say after You Say Hello*, London: Corgi.

Berne, E. (1976) *Games People Play*, London: Penguin.

Bitner, M. J., Booms, B. H. and Tetreault, M. S. (1989) Critical incidents in service encounter, in Bitner, M. J. and Crosby, L. A. (eds) *Designing a Winning Service Strategy*, American Marketing Association.

Bitner, M. J., Booms, B. H. and Tetreault, M. S. (1990) The service encounter: Diagnosing favourable and unfavourable incidents, *Journal of Marketing*, Vol. 54, January, pp. 71–84.

Bitner, M. J., Nyquist, J. D. and Booms, B. H. (1985) The critical incident as a technique for analysing the service encounter, in Block, T. M., Upah, G. D. and Zeithaml, V. A. (eds) *Services Marketing in a Changing Environment*, American Marketing Association.

East, J. (1993) *Managing Quality in the Catering Industry*, London: Croner Publicatons.

Gronroos, C. (1994) From scientific management to service management: A management perspective for the age of service competition, in *International Journal of Service Industry Management*, Vol. 5, No. 1, 5–20.

Herzberg, F., Mausrer, B. and Snyderman, B. (1959) *The Motivation to Work*, New York: Wiley.

Heskett, J. L. (1986) *Managing in the Service Economy*, Mass.: Harvard Business School Press.

Johnson, R. (1989) Operations management issues, in Jones, P. (ed.) *Management in Service Industries*, London: Pitman.

Jones, P. and Lockwood, A. (1989) *The Management of Hotel Operations*, London: Cassell.

Lascelles, D. and Dale, B. (1993) *The Road to Quality*, Bedford: IFS.

Lucas, R. (2004) *Employment Relations in the Hospitality and Tourism Industries*, London: Routledge.

Maxwell, G. and Quail, S. (2002) Human resources strategy and development for quality service in the international hotel sector, in D'Annunzio-Green, Maxwell, G. and Watson, S. (eds) *Human Resource Management*, London: Continuum.

Parasuraman, A., Zeithasml, V. and Berry, L. L. (1988) Servqual: A multiple item scale for measuring consumer perceptions of service, *Quality Journal of Retailing*, Vol. 64, No. 1.

Teare, R. and Olsen, M. (eds) (1998) *International Hospitality Management*, London: Pitman Publishing.

Zeithaml, V. A. and Bitner, M. J. (1996) *Services Marketing*, McGraw-Hill International.

Questions

1 Describe the key elements that need to be considered relative to customer care.

2 What constitutes the service offering from a customer care perspective?

3 What can be done to minimize dissatisfaction caused by queuing?

4 Discuss the value of transactional analysis to a work organization.

5 Evaluate the effectiveness of the customer care approach of an employer with whom you are familiar.

6 Design a customer care programme for an employer with whom you are familiar.

7 What issues will need to be considered in designing customer care programmes in the future?

Business ethics

Business essentially consists of economic relationships concerned with the exchange of goods and services. But managers of businesses function within a more complex cultural environment. Key elements within that environment, as Trompenaars (1998; see Chapter 21) wrote, are what cultures consider to be right and wrong and good and bad – issues at the heart of ethics. This chapter sets out to discuss approaches to considering ethical issues and behaviour in business. It does not attempt to state what 'good' or 'ethical' behaviour is. This would lead into the realms of philosophy, which would pose such questions as who and what determines what is right and wrong. Instead, this chapter sets out a way of evaluating an enterprise's or an individual's behaviour in business so that the reader can arrive at his or her own judgements.

Ethical issues are of concern to all managers within an enterprise but particularly to the most senior managers because it is they who create and control the whole environment in which their enterprise functions. At the same time ethical issues are of particular concern to human resource managers because many of the roles of human resource managers are concerned with ensuring that an enterprise functions ethically through the recruitment of the right people, training them in the norms and values of the employer and, particularly, motivating employees in such a way that the employer's ethical position is not compromised.

The definition of ethical behaviour is very difficult, since it depends upon each individual's own perceptions of issues within the broader social/moral context.

As Mole (1990; see Chapter 21) writes, 'There are different degrees of belief as to what constitutes actual wrongdoing. What is illegal need not be unethical and vice versa.'

Some will argue that the law defines what the limit of business behaviour is, whereas others argue that the law merely provides a safety net to prevent the worst excesses only. Some business people will argue that their sole responsibility is to their shareholders and so long as what they do is no different from what their competitors do then nothing is wrong.

At the other extreme are owners and managers who apply very strict ethical standards to everything they do in business, showing consideration for all stakeholders, e.g. owners, managers, employees, customers, suppliers and the wider community. Recent developments here have seen many organizations include statements of corporate responsibility and ethics within mission statements and annual reports. If anything, the public is evermore aware of issues such as ethical or fair trade (the non-exploitation of supplying nations), as it is about financial accounting scandals such as Enron, and other well-publicized cases which brought the topic of managerial ethics and legality to the forefront. The hospitality sector has seen a massive increase in interest in the sourcing of foods, from the organic farming debate to the humane rearing of beef cattle and chickens to supply the huge fast food market.

Hoffman and Frederick (1995) define business ethics as 'the study of what is good and right for business' and they suggest three questions. What is the better decision for the business? What is the better decision from a legal point of view? What is the better decision from a moral point of view? This last question, however, poses difficult value judgement questions. In order to determine what is moral or good and right, Steven Hall (1992) of the International Institute for Quality and Ethics in Service and Tourism (IIQUEST) has devised a number of questions which test a manager's or an organization's ethical behaviour. These seven questions can be applied to all aspects of running a business.

Seven tests for ethical business behaviour

These are taken from *Caterers Briefings*, 1994 by permission of Croner Publications.

1. Is it legal?

The first question to ask, 'Is it legal?' Relevant examples in the catering industry include common sharp practices such as short measuring of drinks, substituting products and misleading customers by false descriptions (e.g. 'frozen' for 'fresh'). Overcharging is common as well. How many price lists are hidden so that customers cannot check what a round of drinks should really cost?

2. Does it hurt anyone?

Many business decisions may be legal but they may hurt people. Obviously some actions will hurt the competition – they are designed to do just that. The mere decision to open a unit somewhere is almost bound to hurt the neighbouring competitors. It is an overt action and it could be argued that if the benefits to the consumer through lower prices, better service, etc., outweigh the damage done to a few competing traders then the behaviour is justified.

Some other activities, however, may be less ethical. Acquiring others' mailing lists is an example. Spreading damaging rumours about a competitor is another.

Breaching copyright on business products, be they recorded music or computer programmes, is another example.

In some respects this question 'Does it hurt anyone?' may be more valid than the first question, 'Is it legal?' Some activities may be illegal but may not hurt anyone (the concept of the victimless crime). Serving drinks after hours in a small village pub may hurt no one, but it is illegal.

3. Is it fair?

Whether something is fair or not depends upon a person's own perception of fairness. But probably a good test would be to ask what the other person would think if he or she knew the full facts (see also Question 6). For example, what would customers think if they knew that they were being sold wine, mixers or food left by previous customers?

Other aspects of being fair could include how the business is promoted. For example, is the price list clear? Are there hidden extras so that customers spend much more than they may have expected to spend? Unadvertised hotel telephone charges are an example.

4. Am I being honest?

Again, honesty, like fairness, is dependent upon a person's own perception of 'honest behaviour'. Honesty may be defined, among other things, as not being deceitful. It is in this sort of area that there are many ethical problems.

How many business people try to close a sale by falsely boosting the scarcity of something – 'we only have one left', 'someone else has already offered so much for it', etc. Such phrases are built into the normal vocabulary of many people concerned with selling, so that additional deceptions come easily.

5. Can I live with myself?

This question probably poses even more ethical problems than the others. If someone has, over the years, developed a business ethic that encourages sharp practice then, maybe, not only can the person live with himself or herself but he or she may actually celebrate the completion of a sharp deal. This question, however, may be of most relevance to senior managers because it is often they who profess all the ethical objectives of their organization and then apply such pressures to achieve other business objectives, such as sales targets, on the middle and junior managers that the latter cannot behave ethically.

6. Would I publicize my decision?

This is probably the best of tests of ethical behaviour. If, for example, cheaper products or substitutes are used, would a business advertise the fact? If the service charge is not distributed to the staff, would this be advertised to the world?

7. What if everyone did it?

The last question is really concerned with what would happen to commerce, maybe an industry or even a whole society, if everyone did the same. Some trades, usually because of the behaviour of a few, over the years have acquired reputations for dishonesty, making business life more difficult for everyone in those trades. This is the reason that the leading professions have developed codes of practice (see Appendix 5). It is through businesses aiming for and achieving a trustworthy level of service that consumers are made to have faith in an industry, trade or profession.

What are the ethical issues?

The questions above, just one writer's ideas on how to look at ethical issues, highlight the fact that questions of ethics range through fundamental policy issues such as 'Should we be in the business we are in?' through to straightforward operational issues such as ensuring that customers are not shortchanged. The range of ethical issues includes relationships with

- customers
- employees and managers
- supplies and suppliers
- sources of finance
- the community.

Customers

As indicated above, most ethical concerns appear to focus on relationships with customers. In many respects this is the easiest area to look at. Questions include the following:

- Are trade descriptions honest and complete or is only limited information given?
- Are customers told about controversial products, e.g. irradiated foods and genetically modified foods?
- Are prices misleading, with hidden extras?
- Are customers misled about past performance?
- Do staff bonus schemes put customers at risk?
- Is customers' ignorance of their rights exploited?
- Are significant facts hidden, e.g. hidden commissions in contract catering?
- Are risks taken with customers' health and safety, e.g. taking risks with food temperatures or fire exits?

Employees and managers

A major area of ethical concern is how employers treat their employees. One major fast food retailer attracted a lot of adverse publicity when it was found that some branches were offering 'zero hour' contracts, i.e. 'You will be present at the place of work but you will only be paid when you actually work.'

What about equal opportunities – are staff selected and promoted fairly, or are some candidates passed over because of their sex, race, disability or even age (see Figure 4.1)? Is discipline even-handed? There are questions also of job security, dignity and the like. Does an employer try to meet his/her employees' needs in these respects? From the treatment and fairness of young workers to the higher-order considerations of family-friendly policies in attempting to address the so-called work–life balance and any accusation of exploitation, HRM practitioners are faced with ethical as well as regulatory questions (see Legge, 1998: also Lucas, 2004). Woodall and Winstanley (2001) consider that contemporary HRM, with its emphasis on performance management and strategic alignment (see Chapters 2 and 7), is faced with a set of ethical issues, 'In particular, the preoccupation with flexibility, commitment, culture, quality and performance' (p. 41).

What should be of major concern to senior managers is the fact that, though they may profess ethical principles, they often put such pressure on their middle and junior managers that ethical behaviour becomes difficult and often impossible. Just one example will illustrate this – pizza home-delivery target times have caused serious road accidents and even death. Another factor within the hospitality sector may not lead to such a tragic outcome as this latter example but nevertheless is worthy of mention. Particularly with regard to front-line, customer contact roles, the hospitality sector requires its staff to show certain emotions as part of their job, the smiling welcome, the concerned listener to a customer's problems, the calm response to a vitriolic complaint from an angry, perhaps rude, guest. The need to display such behavioural responses, however contra to the employee's actual inner feelings, is known as emotional labour, and management need to consider just how much emotional stress and pressure its employees should be required to 'suffer' (see Mann, 1997).

Robbins (2005) reports that in the USA there is a significant increase in company training schemes which specifically deal with ethical issues. A survey conducted in the late 1990s found that around 75% of the workers in the 1000 largest US corporations received some level of ethics training. In the UK there has also been an increase in employee awareness of ethical issues and whistleblower protection supported in an attempt to encourage employees to alert external bodies of unethical or illegal practice.

Supplies and suppliers

The seven questions listed above could also be applied to a business's supplies and suppliers. These days, caterers and hoteliers are faced with a range of ethical problems concerning supplies. Should a caterer give a customer what the customer wants in spite of ethical considerations. Some animal products – frogs legs and sharks fins – for example, are obtained using very cruel methods. Some methods endanger whole species. Should a caterer offer these or even supply them if asked? Because it is legal to sell crate-reared calves' products, should caterers sell them or should they seek alternative, more humane supplies as did many restaurateurs during the veal export disturbances of 1995?

When stationery, furniture, etc., is bought, is the source of raw material checked out? Is it from a sustainable source or is it contributing, even in a very minor way, to ecological damage? Are cleaning materials, energy sources and other supplies environmentally friendly? How are the suppliers' employees treated? Are they treated ethically?

Sources of finance

Not many business people have a free choice of the sources of finance available. Most smaller- and medium-sized businesses will be obliged to use conventional banks. For various reasons they may be locked into one bank. However, where choices can be made about finance, the types of questions to be considered will be concerned with how the banks invest their money and from what sources the banks derive their funds and profits. One bank in particular makes a feature of its ethical investment policy.

In other cases a business may have surplus funds for periods of time, which they may invest. This could be in shares of a company, so it should be asked how the company makes its money? Does it conduct itself ethically?

Another source of finance is the taking of credit from suppliers. Are the periods taken as agreed originally or are 'unfair' periods of credit taken? Are smaller suppliers exploited because they cannot afford to lose the business even if credit periods are extended unilaterally?

The community

Finally, every business operates within a community and it has a responsibility to that community. How it meets these responsibilities varies considerably. Most hospitality businesses contribute to their community life in ways that bring many benefits. Others, however, can bring considerable problems such as late-night noise, litter and violence. At the time of writing, there is a hot topic concerning 'binge drinking' caused in part by cheap alcohol offers in pubs and the ensuing anti-social and often violent behaviour in town centres. The Government, police and licensed retailers will need to liaise effectively and with some degree of ethical consideration for the local community whose domesticity may be upset by such outcomes.

The community creates a whole range of laws and regulations covering taxation, planning, building, food safety, waste disposal, noise, pollution, fire precautions and licensing. Are these adhered to or are they ignored, putting people's comfort, health and maybe lives at risk?

Ethical and environmental issues are increasingly coming to the forefront of business generally and within the hospitality industry as well. The HCIMA, along with most other professional bodies, has a code of conduct (see Appendix 5). It has recently embarked on a major survey of environmental management practices in the hotel and catering industry and the Prince of Wales Trust has funded the International Hotels Environmental Initiative.

Many public companies now produce annual reports describing how they are meeting various environmental and social responsibilities. McDonald's, for example, participates in the National Spring Clean campaign and in 1989 they set up the Ronald McDonald Children's Charities. Among other things this charity funds 170 Ronald McDonald Houses which provide free accommodation to the families of children in hospital. Other companies such as BP Amoco, the Body Shop, P & O and companies in the hospitality industry report annually on their environmental and social initiatives. An interesting conflation of product policy and ethical behaviour is exemplified by the Pret a Manger coffee shop and takeaway group. Their strategic concern for quality baguettes and the like mean that the shelf life of a filled roll, e.g. tuna and sweetcorn baguette, is limited before it becomes somewhat less appetising, even soggy, and fails the quality test. Such products are removed from the shelves. As these products are still perfectly safe and healthy foods, Pret a Manger has purchased refrigerated vans which collect the unsold products from all their outlets and then distribute free of charge to centres for the homeless and other charitable institutions.

At the international level ethics and ethical issues become even more complex. As Mole (1990) writes, 'Values differ from country to country . . . conventions of behaviour can be misinterpreted . . . normal practice can engender mistrust. Faced with such diversity the best course is probably to reserve ethical judgement for one's own behaviour and suspend it when looking at others.'

Further Reading and References

Caterers Briefings (1994) Kingston-upon-Thames: Croner Publications.

Hall, S. (ed.) (1992) *Ethics in Hospitality Management*, New York: Educational Institute of the American Hotel and Motel Association.

Hoffman, W. M. and Frederick, R. E. (1995) *Business Ethics*, 3rd edn, New York: McGraw-Hill.

Legge, K. (1998) The morality of HRM, in Mabey, C., Salaman, G. and Storey, J. (eds) *Strategic Human Resource Management: A Reader*, London: Sage/Open University Press.

Lucas, R. (2004) *Employment Relations in the Hospitality and Tourism Industries*, London: Routledge.

Mann, S. (1997) Emotional labour in organizations, in *Leadership and Organization Development Journal*, Vol. 18, No. 1, 4–12.

Mole, J. (1990) *Mind Your Manners*, London: Industrial Society.

Robbins, S. (2005) *Organizational Behaviour*, 11th edn, New Jersey: Pearson Education Inc.

Trompenaars, F. (1998) *Riding the Waves of Culture*, 2nd edn, New York: McGraw-Hill.

Woodall, J. and Winstanley, D. (2001) The place of ethics in HRM, in Storey, J. (ed.) *Human Resource Management—A Critical Text*, London: Thomson Learning.

Questions

1 Describe a business's key stakeholders and the ethical considerations which can enter into the relationships between the business and the stakeholders.

2 Discuss using examples Steven Hall's test for ethical behaviour in business.

3 What are the key ethical considerations in the employment relationships? (You may find several of the following appendices of use in answering this question.)

4 Evaluate the ethical behaviour of an employer with which you are familiar using the key stakeholders as a basis.

5 To what extent do public companies' social responsibility statements accord with their actual behaviour?

The HCIMA code of conduct

HCIMA is an internationally recognised management organisation for managers and potential managers in the hospitality, leisure and tourism industries. It is a registered charity and has a worldwide membership which covers all sectors of the industry including hotels, restaurants, cost sector catering, pubs and clubs, as well as leisure outlets, theme parks and sports venues. Membership of the Association confers a respected acknowledgement of an individual's qualifications and specific industry experience through designatory letters; and enables members to progress professionally, network with industry contacts and enjoy a wide range of services and benefits.

The obligations of members

The Memorandum of the Association states that the main objectives of the HCIMA are:

 (i) The promotion of standards and management good practice
(ii) The advancement of education and training, in particular promoting research and the dissemination of the outcomes.

Members of the Association are committed to the achievement of these objectives and to the maintenance of the standards of professional conduct as established by the Code of Conduct. This defines the standards required by the Articles of the Association and is in two parts:

1 Rules of Conduct – These define the professional standards which members must maintain as a condition of membership. Adherence to these rules is obligatory. Failure to do so may lead to disciplinary action being taken against the member in accordance with the Bye-Laws.
2 Principles of Good Professional Practice – These principles expand upon the basic standards set down in the Rules of Conduct and indicate the standards which members should seek to achieve in the interests of good practice. Failure to achieve these standards alone would not lead to disciplinary action, but in the event of any complaint being considered under the disciplinary procedure, such failure would be admissible in evidence and taken into account in proceedings before the Disciplinary Committee.

The rules of conduct

In general, members of the Association are required to exercise their professional skill and judgement to the best of their ability and to carry out faithfully their professional responsibilities with integrity. In particular, members shall:

1 Comply with the laws and ethical customs and practices of any country in which they work.
2 Uphold and safeguard the reputation and standards of HCIMA.
3 Use their HCIMA designatory letters where possible:
   • for purposes, and in a style, which conform with the objectives and uphold the dignity of the Association and
   • in conjunction with their own name.
4 Declare to HCIMA any conflict of interest which might arise in the course of representing the Association.
5 Not misuse their authority for personal aggrandisement or gain.
6 Respect the confidentiality of information.
7 Maintain a proper balance between the interest of employer or proprietor and customers, clients and suppliers.

The principles of good professional practice

Members of HCIMA must accept the responsibilities and obligations implicit in their work. In respect of themselves and others with whom they interact in the course of their professional life, they should seek to maintain and promote the following standards:

(a) In respect of HCIMA and fellow members:
   • avoid injuring or damaging, directly or indirectly, the reputation, interests or prospects of fellow members
   • promote and recommend the Association and its standards
   • uphold the educational standards and policies of the Association and support the advancement and acquisition of education, training and qualifications
   • avoid bringing the Association into disrepute
   • when acting as a representative of HCIMA, the interests of the Association should be paramount to personal or employers' interests
   • not knowingly misrepresent the corporate views of the Association in public
   • avoid professional criticism, by maintaining a high standard of performance.
(b) Personally:
   • regulate their professional affairs to a high standard of integrity and uphold their statutory responsibilities in all respects
   • make proper use of resources available
   • when in pursuit of personal ambitions and interests take account of the interest of others
   • maintain their standards of professional competence, knowledge and skill; and
   • take advantage of opportunities for training and education offered to advance and improve personal professional standards.

(c) In respect of their employers:
- carry out duties and responsibilities conscientiously and with proper regard for the employer's interests
- apply the lawful policies of the employer obviating corrupt practice, particularly in relation to receiving gifts or benefits
- disclose immediately and fully to an employer any interest which conflicts with those of the employer
- consult with and advise the employer on the implementation or adoption of new developments in the profession or industry
- have full regard for the interest of the profession and the public interest in fulfilling obligations to the employer.

(d) In respect of colleagues and subordinates:
- help and encourage their professional development through the acquisition of skills, qualifications and training
- promote good relationships through effective communication and consultation
- establish their confidence in and respect for himself (the member) and his qualification
- protect at all times their health, safety and welfare.

(e) In respect of customers, clients and suppliers:
- promote the standing, impartiality and good name of the HCIMA
- establish good, but detached, relationships
- avoid endorsing any product through advertising in a way that impairs HCIMA's impartiality
- establish and develop with customers, clients and suppliers a relationship leading to mutual confidence
- protect at all times the health and safety of customers.

Note: Information adapted from the HCIMA Code of Conduct April 2005.

HCIMA management guide

Hospitality Assured

What is it?

Hospitality Assured is *The Standard for Service and Business Excellence* in hospitality, championed by the Hotel and Catering International Management Association (HCIMA) and supported by the British Hospitality Association (BHA).

The standard is fully endorsed by the British Quality Foundation and the Quality Scotland Foundation as meeting the criteria in the EFQM Excellence Model, which is owned by the European Foundation for Quality Management (EFQM). It is the only standard within the Hospitality Industry that focuses on the customer experience.

The process for achieving Hospitality Assured recognition is rigorous. It takes into account customer opinion and considers all the aspects of service from the customers' point of view. This is an accreditation which is not achieved easily. It is an ongoing process that provides a series of performance indicators against which an organisation can continually judge and measure itself.

Hospitality Assured gives customers the opportunity to choose an organisation where high quality service is guaranteed. The hallmark of Hospitality Assured accredited organisations is a powerful desire to exceed customer expectations, within a climate of continuous improvement and business excellence. Customers can therefore be confident that they will be satisfied by any organisation that is Hospitality Assured.

The Standard for Service and Business Excellence comprises 10 steps.

The ten steps comprise 49 key requirements or criteria. These are all measurable objectives. The standard, however, is not prescriptive. It does not lay down precisely how objectives will be met – they will vary organisation by organisation, according to that organisation's customer promise. For example a customer promise in a conference centre will be different to a cruise ship, a pub or a care home.

Why become Hospitality Assured?

Hospitality Assured was created for the industry, by the industry and is based on best international practice. Hospitality Assured is owned and managed by the HCIMA.

Hospitality Assured 'accredited' organisations enjoy a number of significant advantages. These include:

- Being seen as one of the very best organisations in the hospitality industry by customers, employees, stakeholders and competitors.
- Being able to use powerful business tools and objective external assessment to stimulate and measure performance improvement in service delivery and business excellence.
- Being able to Benchmark the accredited organisation against the best in class.
- Using the Hospitality Assured mark to promote the accredited organisation to existing and new customers.
- Demonstrating that the accredited organisation is a quality employer.
- The most appropriate standard for the particular area of business.
- For Local Authorities, it helps significantly with preparation for 'best value' reviews, by demonstrating 'best value'.

- It helps to protect existing business.
- It proves that a catering service is reputable.
- The methodology used in the Hospitality Assured process demonstrates the importance placed on customers.
- The standard's criteria stands up to the external scrutiny of stakeholders.
- Improved listening to customers.
- Faster reaction to customer needs.
- It encourages staff motivation and team-building at all levels.
- It can create a new mission statement and service promise.
- It finds the gaps in service delivery.
- It highlights good practice.
- It underpins ongoing improvement.
- It facilitates target-setting and performance monitoring.

Who can become Hospitality Assured?

Any organisation – small or large, single or multi-unit in hospitality, leisure and tourism, with a desire to improve its service to customers and improve its operational and business excellence – is eligible.

In the meetings and conference sector, Hospitality Assured has partnered The Meetings Industry Association (MIA). Members of the MIA can seek to achieve Hospitality Assured-Meetings (HA-M), which is promoted to meetings buyers as a mark of Service and Business Excellence in the meetings industry (for the updated list of accredited organisations, visit www.hospitalityassured.com).

Who has achieved Hospitality Assured?

There are currently over 130 corporate organisations (for the updated list of accredited organisations, visit www.hospitalityassured.com) – representing some 3500 trading outlets and involving more than 50,000 staff in the following sectors – which have been successful in achieving Hospitality Assured accreditation by meeting the minimum requirements of the standard.

Hospitality Assured sectors

- Bars, Pubs and Inns
- Clubs
- Colleges
- Conference Centres
- Foodservice and Facilities Management
- Healthcare
- Hotels
- Leisure
- Local Authority
- Meetings (MIA)
- Other
- Restaurants
- Transport
- Universities

Simple steps to achieving Hospitality Assured include:

1 Contacting Hospitality Assured.
2 Asking for a visit or attend an induction seminar.
3 Attending workshops – these are staged either at an organisation's premises or publicly, providing managers and supervisors with a sound working knowledge of 'The Standard for Service and Business Excellence', evidential requirements, and how to use the Hospitality Assured 'self-assessment' business improvement tool.
4 Carrying out 'Self-Assessment' – a fast and dynamic process to check an organisation's own strengths and weaknesses against the ten steps of the standard. This process should involve a cross-section of the operation's managers, supervisors and front-line staff.
5 Getting ready for 'Assessment' – a period (typically 6–12 months) of building on strengths and addressing areas for improvement, highlighted by the self-assessment process. Help is now available from consultants during this period.
6 Booking an 'External Assessment' – when confident, an organisation can request Hospitality Assured to organise an external visit from the scheme's assessment body, MQA. Assessment is mainly carried out by meeting and interviewing an organisation's management team and staff, in order to gather evidence of processes in action. The assessment will be planned with you in advance by the assessment team from MQA.
7 Achieving 'Accreditation' – this will be awarded if an organisation is judged to have scored at least 60% against the 'Standard for Service and Business Excellence', with a minimum score of 50% in each and every one of the standard's ten steps.
8 Planning for 'Re-Assessment' – to maintain accreditation, organisations must agree to be re-assessed annually and continue to meet the minimum requirement for accreditation. The focus in re-assessment is to measure positive change and continuous improvement.

Scheme Pack – Brilliant Business Improvement Tool

The Hospitality Assured Scheme Pack is the starter kit for Hospitality Assured. It contains the *standard; guidelines* as to the evidence required to meet the standard; and, importantly, a *self-assessment business improvement tool*. The cost is £100, or £75 to HCIMA members, available from hospitalityassured@hcima.co.uk or mia@meetings.org.

Quotes from Hospitality Assured accredited organisations
Hotels

One of the world's most famous hotels – the 133-bedroom The Ritz, London – became the first five-star hotel in the capital to achieve Hospitality Assured when it was initially assessed in 2001. Former Managing Director Luc Delafosse said: "The Ritz London has greatly benefited from participation in Hospitality Assured – it has been the right catalyst for the hotel. You cannot deliver good service unless you have happy employees. For our guests, it is the staff who make the difference, and this is where Hospitality Assured has had a major role to play in our success. I wanted an officially recognised organisation that could assess the service we offer, and take time to listen to the management and staff. Since the Hospitality Assured standard is industry specific, it fitted the bill perfectly. The process leading to accreditation has proved highly motivating for everyone concerned, and we have taken, and will continue to take, on board all the assessors' comments and recommendations."

Food and Service Management

Linda Halliday, Partner and HR Director in contract caterers Wilson Storey Halliday, says that the company was initially accredited with Hospitality Assured five years ago, and the key steps of the standard could be applied to all aspects of the business. "With an annual turnover of £55 million and 1,600 staff, our vision is to be the best independent food-service provider in the UK," she states. "The essential ingredients of our business are people, food and communication. People are the most important aspect in helping to cope with growth in the business, so recruiting the right staff is vitally important, as is a thorough induction to the business. It is crucial that employees feel they are part of the business – a factor that underpins the Hospitality Assured process. I am passionate about good customer care. I would recommend Hospitality Assured because it enables you to benchmark your performance; and discover your strengths and weaknesses, helping you to continuously develop the weaker areas of your business and further build upon the areas where you are doing well. You should not get too hung up over Hospitality Assured scores; instead concentrate on your people, be innovative and take risks!"

Healthcare

Anchor Trust is the largest not-for-profit provider of housing and support for older people in England. Bob Bird, Head of Lifestyle Services, Anchor Homes, says of Hospitality Assured: "Anchor Homes is delighted at being given Hospitality Assured accreditation. We were impressed at the professionalism and thoroughness of the assessing team who went into great detail to understand the ethos and culture of our organisation. The extremely constructive observations and recommendations made, will without doubt, enable us to further improve our service delivery to our customers in the next few months."

Leisure

West Ham United Hospitality Ltd scored a remarkable double by gaining both the HCIMA-led Hospitality Assured accreditation for its hospitality facilities and the MIA-led Hospitality Assured-Meetings (HA-M) accreditation for its conference and banqueting facilities. Director of West Ham United Hospitality, David Thorpe-Tracey MHCIMA, said: "We are delighted that all our efforts have been recognised with the HCIMA- and MIA-led Hospitality Assured awards. Our success will not go to our heads! My team and I have assured the Football Club that we will not be resting on our laurels and will be continuing to strive to achieve excellence."

Local Authorities

Irene Carroll, General Manager of City Catering at Southampton City Council, says she and her team are delighted at being awarded Hospitality Assured for school catering, civic hospitality, meals-on-wheels and a sixth-form college. "We are now building on the lessons learnt from achieving Hospitality Assured to formulate a strategy to ensure that continuous improvements are made to the whole service. Due to the accreditation, we have become far more focused on detailed business planning, strategic development and benchmarking. Embarking and working our way through the Hospitality Assured process was the best 'wake up' call City Catering could have had. We had every reason to be proud of what we had achieved in a very short space of time for a new organisation, but now we can achieve even more while working within the guidelines of Hospitality Assured. I would recommend it to any organisation!"

Lord Thurso, MP FHCIMA

Quality and profits have
always been inextricably linked.
Hospitality Assured is the
Simplest and the most cost
Effective method I have come across
for improving quality. It is
clearly a benchmark for our industry's future.

For further Information

To find out more about Hospitality Assured, contact: Tony Lainchbury MHCIMA, Hospitality Assured General Manager; or Steven Bulloch, Hospitality Assured Administrator, at: HCIMA, Trinity Court, 34 West Street, Sutton, Surrey SM1 1SH – on telephone: 020 8661 4918; fax: 020 8661 4901; email: hospitalityassured@hcima.co.uk or stevenb@hcima.co.uk. The website is www.hospitalityassured.com.

22 November 2004

Risk Management

Introduction

Risk Management is the process which aims to help organisations understand, evaluate and take action on all their risks with a view to increasing the probability of their success and reducing the likelihood of failure. (Institute of Risk Management, 2003)

Risk Management is a strategic management activity involving a systematic approach to the management of risk. By formalising the practice of risk management it is possible to reduce operational costs to a business by diminishing the risks incurring accidents or loss.

Service industries' profitability depends on people using facilities and services. Any perception that a business premise or its practices are unsafe can be damaging to the reputation of the business. Prioritising the application of risk management to every aspect of a business ensures that risk or damage to either the business or individuals is greatly reduced or removed.

What is Risk Management?

Risk Management is a strategic and systematic approach which:

- Carefully examines the diverse activities of a business
- Is continuous and developmental
- Identifies potential risks
- Assesses those risks for potential frequency and severity
- Removes those risks which can be eliminated
- Reduces the effect of those that cannot be eliminated
- Increases probability of successful actions taken to investigate risk
- Supports financially the consequences of the risks that remain.

Key aims of Risk Management

Risk Management is a quality management system which ensures that business is conducted to the highest possible standard with the best quality of customer care.

The result of this will also be a reduction in costs associated with risk taking. Key aims should be:

- Improved written policies and strategies for risk management
- Safer business practices
- Safer business premises
- Increased staff awareness of risk taking and risk management
- Better education and training for staff on risk management
- Reduction of potential financial loss.

Where do risks occur?

Risks may occur in any element of a business organisation. All of these elements have a critical influence on the manager's ability to control risk. Risk Management is concerned with compiling information about the risk elements of the business which are usually easily identified by the organisation or are within its level of expertise.

The Risk Management review brings together the knowledge and the expertise to provide an estimate of the probability of an incident happening and then puts in place solutions to prevent or mitigate that occurrence.

The key elements to review within this process may be both internal and external. They include:

Strategic	Competition/Customers/Industry/Management
Financial	Accountancy Systems/Credit/Interest/Exchange Rates
Operational	Absence Management/Recruitment/Staff Turnover/Buildings and Associated Operations/Supplies and Suppliers
Hazard	Environment/Equipment/Health and Safety/IT Systems

Risk Assessment

In the hospitality, leisure and tourism industries a systematic and regular Risk Assessment procedure is vital. Undertaking a Risk Assessment is time consuming but business failure is the possible alternative. Producing standardised documentation is helpful in formalising the process and in ensuring that all risks are clearly identified. There are also legal and insurance implications for ensuring that a successful Risk Assessment is completed on a regular basis.

A large organisation may have a dedicated Risk Manager who would ensure that all aspects of the assessment are undertaken or delegated to appointed staff. In smaller organisations a manager with significant training and knowledge of the business, including its Health and Safety Policy, business procedures and overall methods of operation, should be responsible for its completion. The Risk Manager should also compile lists of appropriate external emergency services so that all staff have access to points of contact in case of incident or emergency.

The elements of an assessment should be small enough to be manageable but big enough to identify the start and completion of the process. For example, running a food service area may be a significant element of a business operation but in assessment terms it may be split into a number of parts, which should be assessed separately.

It is very important that interviewing and listening to staff, as well as observation and measurement, forms part of the assessment. This should include preliminary discussions with those who work in the area to identify the scope of each assessment.

Legal requirement

The Management of Health and Safety at Work Regulations 1999 and their Approved Code of Practice require a Risk Assessment to be undertaken and, where more than five persons are employed, a record must be made of any 'significant' findings of the assessment and also of any specific group of employees identified by the assessment as particularly at risk.

Risk Identification

The Risk Assessor should approach Risk Identification in a systematic way. This should include all the elements identified previously: Strategic, Financial, Operational and Hazard.

Useful questions to ask are:

- What could go wrong?
- How could it happen?
- What would be the effect on the business and any individual?
- What should be done to remove, minimise and manage the risk?

Risk can arise from a single factor or a series of small factors, which can combine to cause loss or injury. Some risk is inherent in the operations of most businesses. The object of risk assessment and analysis is to determine how often the risk is likely to happen, what will be the financial effect on the organisation and how can the effect be minimised.

Legal requirement

Employers should be aware that an employee's act or default in violation of The Management of Health and Safety at Work Regulations 1999 *may not reduce the employers' liability nor does it provide a defence in any criminal proceedings that may result.*

Further Reading

Health & Safety Executive publications

Website: www.hsebooks.com/Books/
HSE Books, PO Box 1999, Sudbury, Suffolk CO10 2WA.
Tel: +44 (0)1787 881165
Fax: +44 (0)1787 313995

HSE publications website

Website: www.hse.gov.uk/pubns/index.htm
Information Line: +44 (0)8701 545500
Publications Line: +44 (0)1787 881165

Useful Risk Management publications

- A Guide to Risk Assessment Requirements – IND(G)218 – Free
- Risk Management – Frequently Asked Questions
- Five steps to Risk Assessment – IND(G)163 (rev1) – Free
- Five steps to Risk Assessment (Case Studies) ISBN 07 17615 804
- Good Practice and Pitfalls in Risk Assessment, Research Report 151, Health & Safety Laboratory, 2003
- Article 6(2)(a)-(i) of Council Directive 89/391/EEC (OJ No L 183, 29.6.89, p. 1)
- Fire Precautions (Workplace) Regulations 1997, Part II
- The Management of Health and Safety at Work Regulations 1999.

The Institute of Risk Management

Lloyd's Avenue House
6 Lloyd's Avenue
London EC3N 3AX
Tel: +44 (0)20 7709 9808
Website: www.theirm.org/index.html

Publications

A Risk Management Standard – **Free to download**

DISCLAIMER
This HCIMA Management Guide is intended as a brief summary to the topic. While the information it contains is believed to be correct, it is not a substitute for appropriate professional advice. The HCIMA can take no responsibility for action taken solely on the basis of this information.

HCIMA Trinity Court, 34 West Street, Sutton, Surrey SM1 1SH (UK)
Tel: +44 (0)20 8661 4900 Fax: +44 (0)20 8661 4901
E-mail: library@hcima.co.uk
Website: www.hcima.org.uk
Copyright HCIMA February 2005. Registered Charity No.326180

APPENDIX 4

Effective staff training

An abridged version of the publication *How to Get the Best from Your Staff: An Introduction to Staff Training Skills* by Michael J. Boella.

Author's note

This book sets out to cover the basics of staff training. It covers in a simple, step-by-step process, each of the main areas of knowledge and skills required by senior staff, supervisors and managers responsible for training. Because it is a partially programmed text it enables those who do not have the opportunity to attend a course to study and practise the basics. It also helps more senior managers to know just what is expected of their supervisors and staff trainers. Third, it can be used as a refresher for those who may have already attended a staff trainers' course. Finally, for those who themselves run staff training courses this makes a concise, easy-to-use guide and hand-out.

This book is not however to be seen as a substitute for attendance at a proper course.

Acknowledgements

My thanks are due to many people, known and unknown, who over the years have contributed the knowledge, experience and material which have made this short book possible. Regretfully, I cannot acknowledge everyone personally. However, I would like particularly to record my gratitude to the Tack Organization and the Industrial Society whose courses I attended and to the HCITB with whom I have collaborated on many occasions.

Introduction

The success of every business depends upon it staff and it has been found that people work most satisfactorily when they have confidence in their employer, in their surroundings and particularly in their own performance of their job.

Obviously no single factor contributes to creating this sense of confidence. But possibly more than anything else, effective induction, that is, the introduction of everything surrounding a person's job, and thorough training in the knowledge and skills necessary to do the job, are responsible for creating the confidence which can lead to a person doing his job in a competent and satisfactory manner. Unfortunately however there are those who feel that systematic training is unnecessary, is too costly, and is beyond their capabilities – or they feel that the ability to train others is something that one is born with. Yet most managers know that a person such as a secretary or a chef, who is skilled in his or her job, is more efficient than an unskilled person. This principle applies equally to the *skill of training* which is distinct from, and additional to, the *job skills* to be passed on. The skilled trainer trains more effectively than the unskilled trainer and, in contrast to the myth that there is not enough time to train, the skilled trainer makes training opportunities throughout the normal working day and will help to create a well-trained employee in a shorter time than an unskilled trainer.

Training others is a skill which can be learned by many normal staff and it makes sound business sense to train key staff, particularly the heads of departments, in this essential skill.

Benefits of training

Training, as with all other activities of an organization, should benefit the organization in the short or long term. These include:

1 Increased customer satisfaction
2 Increased customer demand
3 Better use of time
4 Safer working methods
5 Reduced waste
6 Reduced damage
7 Reduced staff turnover.

Hence – more efficiency.

However, because the staff are the people being trained they should also benefit in some way. These include:

1 Increased efficiency
2 Increased earnings
3 Improved job security
4 Improved job prospects.

Hence – increased job satisfaction and confidence in the job.

Planning training

If you are to train staff efficiently it will need to be properly planned and in order to do this four main elements have to be considered:

1 Who is to do the training?
2 What is to be taught?
3 How is it to be taught?
4 How is it to be judged?

Who is to do the training?

We all know that some people can do a job very efficiently themselves but when it comes to teaching others they are no good at all. This is because to teach others requires certain characteristics which are additional to being able to do the job well.

Anyone who is selected to teach others consequently will need to have certain characteristics. These include:

1 Wish to help others
2 Sympathetic and patient manner
3 Competence in the job
4 Understanding of trainees' needs and problems
5 Systematic approach to work
6 Knowledge and skill of teaching techniques
7 Ability to be self-critical.

From this description it is apparent that most trainers will be more mature people, generally employed at some supervisory level. However, this is not always the case as many craftsmen and even more junior staff make excellent trainers; they enjoy the responsibility and often they are in the best position to train their colleagues, and the task of training others can be a valuable step in developing such people for promotion.

As a principle, however, everyone who has to give some form of instruction or coaching during the normal working day should have or should develop some training skills. This applies particularly to every manager and supervisor. A trainer once trained is going to be able to:

1 Know what performance is expected of the staff
2 Recognize training opportunities and make use of them
3 Make training opportunities
4 Know which tasks and critical points need to be learned by trainees
5 Recognize shortcomings in performance
6 Analyse tasks
7 Plan training
8 Prepare and give instruction
9 Produce training aids
10 Keep records
11 Review training.

What is to be taught?

Training in a business context is concerned with bridging the gap between an individual's capabilities and the employer's requirements. This gap is a *training need*. Put this way it sounds simple but in practice it can be quite difficult. This is because what a person needs to bring to a job is a mixture of:

- General knowledge
- Technical knowledge
- Aptitudes
- Attitudes Skills.

Training needs, apart from consisting of knowledge, skills and attitudes, occur at different times in the working life of employees and organizations. For example when:

- A new employee starts
- Changes take place
- Things go wrong.

When a new employee starts

Of course a whole range of things need to be known. You should include items from each of the following:

- Relationships between staff and departments
- Hours and other conditions
- Safety and security practices
- Rules and regulations
- Methods of work.

When changes take place

A person needs training when the following occur:

- Changes in methods, products or standards of performance
- Changes in equipment
- Transfers and promotions.

When things go wrong (remedial training)

A person may need training when any of the following occur:

- Unsatisfactory trading results or standards
- Customer complaints
- Breakages, waste.

What can be taught?

Some things, such as knowledge and skill, can be transferred to most reasonable trainees quite easily given adequate training expertise on the part of the trainer.

Attitudes, on the other hand, are very difficult and in many respects it is better to aim to select people with the attitudes you want rather than to attempt to 'instil' attitudes into unwilling employees. If, for example, a person resents serving others, it is unlikely that you will have the time and psychological expertise to change his attitudes. Much better to avoid recruiting him in the first place. It is apparent therefore that most training should be concerned with transferring knowledge and skills. To do this the trainer will need to examine his own knowledge and skill and break it down so that he is completely aware of what he has to put over.

This process – job analysis – can be vital, because most skilled people take for granted large parts of their own knowledge and skill.

The managers' responsibility

These different activities have to be set in motion and monitored constantly by management. And as with most other management processes it is a cyclical one starting and finishing with the planning stage.

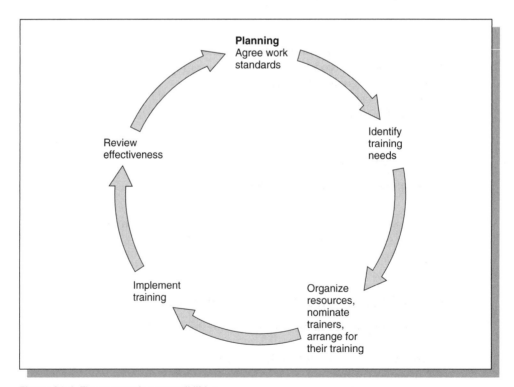

Figure A4.1 The manager's responsibilities

The manager responsible for training must:

1 Set training objectives. To do this, job descriptions may be needed and these will, so far as possible, set standards of performance. For example, if a person is expected to attend to twenty people in an hour, then the trainer should use this standard as his training objective and set progressively more difficult targets during the programme.
2 Select trainers and, where appropriate, he will arrange for them to be trained in training skills. Maybe he should be the first to attend such a course.
3 Delegate training responsibilities.
4 Provide training facilities such as rooms, equipment and training aids.
5 Inform staff of any changes and any training to be given to cope with changes.
6 Show that he really believes in training by participating in it himself.
7 Review the effectiveness of training by checking upon the work of people who have finished their training and occasionally by interviewing some or all of them or having informal chats with them to obtain their views on the training they received.

What is to be taught?

What has to be taught?

The types of factors staff may have to learn have been listed. One of the problems, however, of teaching others is that the experienced person automatically (even subconsciously) does many things which the trainee is going to have to learn step-by-step. A good example is the difference between a novice driver, who consciously thinks about each element of driving, and the expert who integrates each element unconsciously into the total driving process. Consequently, to be sure that all points are taught the trainer needs to use a systematic process for listing everything that is going to be taught.

If this is not done, many points, sometimes essential or even vital, may be overlooked in training. The omission will then only be highlighted when the trainee (or ex-trainee) does something wrong – possibly with expensive consequences for the employer. Unfortunately in these circumstances the trainee and not the inadequate training is usually blamed.

Here is a simple job broken down into duties.
A room-maid's duties:

1 Collection of guest departure list, and early morning tea and breakfast lists and keys from head housekeeper's office
2 Service of early morning tea and breakfasts in bedroom
3 Preparation of trolley for servicing rooms
4 Servicing of bedrooms
5 Servicing of bathrooms
6 Checking of all appliances
7 Checking of all literature
8 Final room check
9 Reporting back to housekeeper.

Task analysis

After this the duties may be broken down into tasks. Some tasks may be very simple to learn and they may not need to be broken down further. Such tasks usually draw upon a person's knowledge and skills which have been acquired in every day life (the life skills).

Servicing a bathroom • • •

1 Check quantity and take out dirty linen, leave outside bathroom on floor.
2 Check, empty and clean bin and ashtray, remove dirty soap.
3 Wash bath, tiles, clean all chrome fittings, mirrors and lights.
4 Wash toilet bowl, 'U' bend, seat and lid, wash tiles behind toilet and air vent.
5 Put toilet cleanser in bowl and leave.
6 Clean basin and top of vanitory unit then wash and dry drinking glasses after washing hands.
7 Replenish soap, towels, bathmat, disposal bags and toilet paper according to room quantities list.
8 Wash bathroom floor and door, wipe bath and wash basin pipes.
9 Replace bin also checking that shave socket is off.
10 Quickly check around and take out dirty linen to maid's trolley.

More difficult tasks, however, will need to be analysed into the various steps in order to identify exactly what a person has to learn and what he has to avoid. This is called 'task analysis'.

Task analysis – the main elements

Task analysis consists of:

1 *Listing WHAT is done*

This should be one word or a brief phrase describing each distinct step:
Greet guest
Take glass

2 *Describe HOW the action is performed*

This should be a brief description of how each step is carried out starting with:
by taking . . .,
by saying . . .,

3 *Describing CRITICAL points*

This should describe signs which inform the person carrying out the task that it is going well or otherwise. Such points should consist of sentences or phrases such as:
Check that totals cross-cast
See that the sauce has not curdled

4 *Adding any additional points that should be taken into account*, such as security, safety, sales promotion.

Note: This is omitted in some task analyses.

Lesson plans

Once the job has been broken down into the key words or phrases which list all the tasks, and once complicated tasks have been broken down into analysed tasks – the next step is to put all this knowledge and skill into a planned training session.

Not only does the trainer have to analyse and then organize what he is to transfer, but also he has to consider how he is going to:

1 Motivate his trainees to learn.
2 Present the knowledge and skill so that it is assimilated.
3 Give his trainees the opportunity to 'cement in' or consolidate the new knowledge and skills.
4 Ensure that what he has been attempting to transfer has been transferred permanently.
5 Motivate his trainees to use what they have learned.

These processes are incorporated into what is generally called a lesson plan. A lesson plan consists of:

- Introduction – motivate to learn
- Development – transfer knowledge
- Consolidation – make it permanent
- Close – motivate to use it

What	How	Critical point	Additional information
List each key step or stage, using short phrases starting with words such as:	Describe concisely the method to be used; start sentences with words such as:	Describe the critical signs which indicate that the operation is proceeding satisfactorily or otherwise. Use words which encourage a trainee to use his senses; look for, feel, taste. This column includes elements which involve using the senses in order to make judgements.	Add any additional information which may be necessary for the satisfactory performance of the task or to enhance a normal performance.
write, greet, cut, dispense	by writing by greeting by cutting by dispensing		This column is omitted in some task analyses.
For example, take a glass	For example, by taking a 6 oz Paris goblet by the stem	For example, check that the glass is clean and undamaged	—

Figure A4.2 Task analysis sheet

What is done?	How is it done?	Critical points (see/feel/smell/listen/taste)	Additional information
Select a grapefruit	By handling.	Feel for firmness—weight. Look for bruising.	
Cut off ends	By cutting downwards, on to a board with an 8 inch stainless steel knife across growing end, judging thickness of skin.	See the flesh is exposed. See and feel the fingers are bent away from knife.	Safety. Effect of acid on steel.
Cut off skin	By placing the fruit on end and cutting downwards, using all the blade of the knife, following the shape of the fruit. Turn after each cut.	See and feel the knife is cutting between the flesh and the pith.	Wastage.
Remove remaining pith	By lightly cutting downwards, using tip of knife.	See no pith remains on fruit. See any over-ripe patches are removed.	Bitter taste of pith.
Clear the waste	By scraping into bowl with hand.		Tidy work place. Safety
Segment grapefruit	By gently cutting between the membranes, with a stainless steel paring knife, using a 'V' cut for the first two large segments, then an in-out cut for the remainder and pulling the membrane out of the way with the thumb of the hand holding the fruit. Remove any pips while cutting to aid removal of unbroken segments.	Feel tough pith in centre. See all pips are removed.	
Remove excess juice	By hand squeezing what juice is left into bowl.	Feel 'skeleton' free from juice. See no pips fall into bowl.	

Figure A4.3 Task analysis work sheet preparing grapefruit segments

Source: Reproduced by permission of the HCITB.

The introduction

The introduction is concerned primarily with motivating the person to want to learn. It should be used to:

1 Establish a personal contact with trainees.
2 Reduce their nervousness.
3 Overcome any particular worries they may have, such as: when the training finishes, what it covers, what will be expected of them.

Unless the introduction is effective the trainee may not be receptive to what is to follow. To help in preparing the introductory phase a useful mnemonic or memory aid has been used by people for many years. It is:

I   interest
N   need
T   title
R   range
O   objective.

Interest

The first thing anyone communicating with others has to do is to attract their attention. This can be done in one of many ways, including:

• Making a personal connection between the trainee and the subject, for example, giving a taste or sample, and giving them useful information or news.
• Telling a funny story.
• Referring to something topical. Referring to (or inventing) something relevant from one's own personal experience.
• Stating something with an apparent contradiction, for example coffee is more important than caviar.
• Asking questions.
• Giving a demonstration or showing something relevant.

Whatever method is used, however, it should be relevant to the trainee and what is being taught.

Need

The need for the training session should be explained. This should be in two parts, from the employer's point of view and the employee's, but it is essential to emphasize why the trainee needs the training and what benefits he or she will receive.

Title

Obviously the trainee will need to know what is to be taught – usually this is incorporated early on and can be linked with one of the other elements of the INTRO.

Range

The trainee needs to know what is to be covered in the training session and sometimes it is equally important, in order to keep his attention or to reduce his anxiety, to tell him what is not to be covered. It is useful to link back to previous training sessions in order to check, to build confidence and to build on known material.

Objective

Finally the trainee needs to know what he will know or what he should be able to do as a result of the session.

While these five separate elements should be in an introduction, they may be combined skilfully into one or two sentences or, if the training is a long course, the introduction could take thirty minutes or more.

Development

The development stage is the main part of any training session and contains everything to be learned during the session. This should be organized so that:

1 Everything is in a logical sequence.
2 The trainer starts with a quick review of what the trainee knows so that the trainee starts from the known – and therefore feels confident – moving on to the new, the unfamiliar, material.
3 Essential material is picked out ensuring that it is covered, and desirable material is identified – to be covered if the time or opportunity presents itself.

The development stage is concerned with transferring the instructor's knowledge and skills to the trainee. It is, however, rather like serving a meal. The food has to be treated in certain ways to make it appetizing and digestible. In the same way any knowledge and skills to be transferred have to be presented so that they interest the trainee and are retained permanently by him.

There are a number of important rules which will help the trainer to prepare and present his material so that this happens, and these are covered in more depth on pages xxx–xxx.

Consolidation and close

Throughout a training session the trainer must use various means of assisting his or her trainee to learn. One major technique is the correct use of questions and this is covered on pages xxx–xxx. It is vital, however, that at the end of a session the trainer:

1 Tests that the training objectives have been achieved by questioning, testing or observing.
2 Reinforces the instruction by recapitulating and questioning so that key points will not be forgotten.

In addition to testing the effectiveness and reinforcing the instruction the instructor should also make quite clear what is now expected of the trainee in work terms and he will also arouse interest in the next session by explaining:

1 What it is about.
2 When it will be.
3 What the objective is.

A useful form for planning a lesson is as shown below.

Subject:	Aim:	Time:
Preparation and use of a room-maid's trolley	At the end of this session trainees will be able to: 1 Prepare their trolley for use 2 Recognize and know the use of all the contents of the trolley	30 minutes

Key point	Detail	Aids
Cleanliness of trolley	Emphasize that a clean trolley is necessary in order to ensure that clean linen is not made dirty	The actual items Questions
Linen	Show the different types of linen and how the number of each is arrived at, to include: towels sheets pillow cases	The actual items Questions
Cleaning	Show the different cleaning materials and explain what each is used for, to include: lavatory cleaner bath and basin cleaner floor polish	The actual items Questions

Figure A4.4 Lesson plan

The learning 'sandwich'

Every piece of instruction should be a sandwich consisting of a slice of motivation; motivating to want to learn; the filling; the main body of the instruction; a slice of motivation; motivating to want to use what has been learned.

How do we learn?

The ability of people to learn is dependent to a great extent upon their reasons for wanting to learn something. If someone is very keen to learn, he will apply himself. On the other hand, if he is not keen to learn, he will almost certainly bring little enthusiasm to the learning process.

Why do people learn?

Obviously there are many reasons for people wanting to learn and in a work setting these will be closely linked to why people work. If the trainer knows and understands why each individual wants to learn, he or she should be able to use this to motivate the person – and keep his or her interest. To attempt to treat all people in the same way is certainly not the way to being a successful trainer or supervisor. A key supervisory and training skill therefore is to discover what motivates each of his or her subordinates or trainees.

If a generalization is to be made, however, the main reasons are likely to be one or more of the following:

1 To obtain rewards such as pay, promotion, esteem.
2 To avoid punishment such as dismissal, reprimand, loss of esteem.
3 Interest.
4 Curiosity.

How do people learn?

Learning is the process of acquiring knowledge, skills and attitudes. It occurs when knowledge, skills and attitudes are transferred to the learner from other people or situations. The transfer is through five primary senses and is best when as many senses as possible are used – particularly in combination. For example, in teaching a person to cook it is possible merely to give him detailed recipes but the results are not likely to be edible! In addition to the recipes, however, the trainee would watch demonstrations and the results are likely to be an improvement. But to involve the trainee fully so that he sees, hears, smells, touches and tastes, is the best and only effective way of teaching cookery.

We learn: 1 per cent with our sense of TASTE
1.5 per cent with our sense of TOUCH
3.5 per cent with our sense of SMELL
11 per cent with our sense of HEARING
33 per cent with our sense of SIGHT.

(*Source*: Industrial Audiovisual Association, USA)

The transfer is made more effective by ensuring that:

1 The amount and type of material is suited to the person being trained. Frequent, short sessions are much more effective than infrequent long ones.
2 It is transferred in logical, progressive steps, building on the known.
3 The methods and choice of words used must suit the capabilities of the trainees.

How do we remember?

We remember: 10 per cent of what we READ
20 per cent of what we HEAR
50 per cent of what we SEE and HEAR
80 per cent of what we SAY
90 per cent of what we SAY and DO simultaneously

(*Source*: Industrial Audiovisual Association, USA)

In addition, trainers must recognize that there are many factors which inhibit a person's ability or desire to learn and consequently a trainee will have difficulty learning if he is:

1 Nervous, tired or frightened.
2 Worried about his or her job, money, family.
3 Distracted by noise, interruptions.
4 Uncomfortable, too cold, too hot.

So far as the training session itself is concerned people will not get the most out of it if they are bored by:

1 The trainer's style, tone and language
2 The length of the session
3 The content.

The rate at which people learn varies from person to person but most people learn in steps – sometimes making rapid progress and sometimes appearing to make very little progress at all. This is quite natural and a good trainer will recognize this and he will know when a trainee is stuck and needs sympathy and help rather than badgering. A trainer's main duty is to build up confidence and this will only be achieved by sympathy and understanding. Criticism and lack of patience reduce confidence and only slow down the learning process.

Question technique

A trainer can make use of questions in three main ways. These are, to test a person's level of attainment (test question), to stimulate a person to 'learn for himself or herself' (a teaching or extension question), and thirdly to generate understanding and exchange of information and attitudes between members of a group by tossing questions and answers back and forth (bonding questions).
Questions may be used principally for:

1 Testing the level of attainment before a 'training' session.
2 Testing the effectiveness of training.
3 Helping people to work out answers for themselves, thus teaching themselves.
4 Encouraging an exchange of knowledge and information, in a group.
5 Obtaining or focusing interest.
6 Maintaining interest.
7 Creating understanding between the group, and between the group and the instructor.

Question structure

Questions generally are more effective when they are 'open-ended'. This encourages a person to think for the answer. Where questions give simple alternatives or antici- pate yes or no, less thought is required by the trainee and the question consequently is less effective both in testing and in consolidating learning. Most questions should contain why, where, when, what, who or how.

Questions, particularly teaching questions, should be planned beforehand – and should relate particularly to the 'critical points' identified in the 'task analysis' stage.

Where questions are not answered satisfactorily by the trainee, the trainer must consider first if the question was properly framed and understood. If not the question should be rephrased and put again. If the question still remains unanswered the trainer must consider whether the training he has given is satisfactory or not.

Putting questions (the three Ps)

When questions are put to a group of people this should be done in a way which encourages everyone in the group to participate. This is achieved by:

1 Putting the question – without naming anyone to answer it.
2 Pausing so that everyone thinks about the question and answer.
3 Pointing out who is to answer the question.

Aids to training

Because people learn most easily by using a variety of their senses and their different faculties, trainers should always attempt to support their own instruction with training aids. These include visual aids such as blackboards and film slides and audio aids such as tape recorders. They should only be used to:

- Support but not substitute
- Simplify complex instruction
- Emphasize
- Interest
- Aid memory.

Training aids ideally should be the real thing, but in some cases the equipment or procedures may be too complex for a clear explanation, so a diagram may help. The preparation of training aids should be carefully planned to support the instruction given.

Training aids include:

- Actual equipment or equipment specially modified for training purposes
- Drawings and diagrarns
- Films, slides, recordings
- Graphs and charts.

Recently, for various reasons, the need for job descriptions and similar documents has grown considerably with the result that many employers – even small ones – now use such documents as an essential tool of effective management. Unfortunately these documents are rarely used for training purposes although with a little forethought they can be designed to serve the purpose of:

1 Job descriptions
2 Instructor's training programme and checklist
3 Trainee's training programme and checklist
4 Work manual.

Job aids

Many jobs can be made easier with descriptions of the methods or procedures to be employed. Such descriptions may be called job aids.

Job aids can be of value to the experienced worker as a reference, and to the trainee as a learning aid. As such, they can substitute for parts or all of certain training sessions because they enable trainees to teach themselves and they can relieve the trainees from having to attempt to memorize unnecessarily.

Job aids can be used:

1 Where supervision is minimal.
2 Where procedures are changed.
3 Where company standards need to be adhered to.
4 Where mistakes cannot be risked.
5 When memory needs assistance because of the complexity of a procedure, or the infrequency of its use.
6 Where staff may speak limited English but where a drawing or a design will describe what is required.

Job aids include:

1 Diagrams
2 Photographs
3 Price lists, menus
4 Procedural instructions, recipes.

Introducing staff to a new employer

How do people feel?

Most people approach a new job feeling nervous and worried. Sometimes this is quite apparent. In other cases, however, it is well-concealed. But whether it is obvious or not, until people have settled into an organization they will be nervous or worried and this will influence their ability to learn their job – to do it effectively and in particular to get on with their colleagues, supervisors and customers. They will not have the feeling of confidence which is essential to their being able to do a good job.

Success during the first few days in a new job is vital and while most managers admit this less than 10 per cent of managers in some industries actually carry out a formal induction of new employees.

What a job consists of

Induction is not something that takes place on the first morning of a new job, it can be a relatively long process, with some people taking many weeks to settle in. This is because every job has two parts to it. First, there is the work itself and secondly, there are all the peripherals to the job including conditions and social contacts.

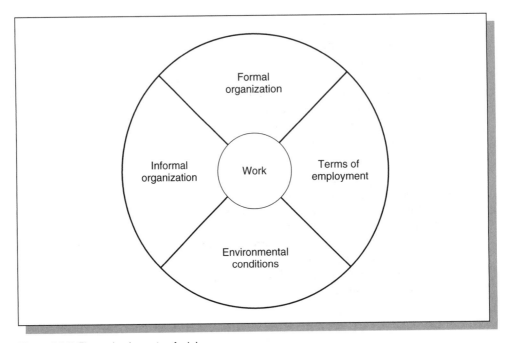

Figure A4.5 The main elements of a job

People will not be able to cope with the work part of their job unless they understand and are reasonably happy with the surrounding elements. These include:

1 Location and physical layout
2 Conditions of employment and contracts
3 Company and house rules
4 Customers
5 Management, supervision and formal relationship
6 Colleagues and informal relationships.

The induction process is concerned with introducing an employee to all these elements as quickly as possible so that he or she need not worry about them any more. This enables the trainee to concentrate on the work which is the main purpose of the job rather than having to learn and worry about all the elements surrounding the work.

Benefits of induction

The employer benefits from effective induction by:

1 Reducing staff turnover
2 Improving staff efficiency and work standards
3 Improving staff morale.

The employees benefit by:

1 Fitting in and feeling a part of the team.
2 Being accepted as part of the team.
3 Becoming competent and hence confident in the shortest possible time.

Every organization will need to induct its employees in its own particular conditions, rules and methods, so no example can cover all circumstances. However, the checklist below shows the type of subjects that need to be covered. This, however, shows only the formal aspects of induction, and managers and supervisors should ensure that newcomers are inducted into the informal aspects as well. By definition, however, this can rarely be done by managers or supervisors. Instead, what they need to do is to put a newcomer under the wing of a 'sponsor', that is someone who 'knows the ropes'. This person may well be the newcomer's trainer also.

Checklist for induction programmes:

1 *Documentation*
Are the following points covered?

Name   Address   Tel. no.
Next of kin   Name   Address
Tel. no.   National Insurance no.
P45   Bank address

2 *Information*
Are the following departments informed?

Wages/Pensions/Insurance/
Personnel/Training/etc.

3 *Terms of employment*
Are the following explained and understood?

Hours of duty/Meal breaks/Days off/
Method of calculating pay/Holiday
arrangements/Sick leave/Pension
scheme. Grievance procedures.
Rights regarding trade unions and Staff
Association
Additional benefits such as Group
Insurance rates or other discounts.

4 *History and organization*
Are the following explained and understood?

Origin and development of the
organization. Present situation/objectives.

5 *Establishment Organization*
Are the following explained and understood?

Layout of establishment including toilets,
showers, etc.
Names of relevant supervisors and colleagues,
introduction where necessary, to supervisor,
shop steward, etc.

6 *Rules and regulations*
Are the following explained and understood?

(a) Statutory; licensing laws and hours, food
hygiene, Innkeepers Liability Act, etc.
(b) Company rules; punctuality, drinking,
smoking, appearance, personal business,
use of employer's property, etc.

7 *The job*
Are the following explained and understood?

Purpose/methods/training needs

When things go wrong, who can help?

Frequently, when things go wrong, management and supervisors jump to quick conclusions regarding the cause. Quick conclusions are often wrong conclusions which lead to wrong solutions. Wrong solutions obviously do not solve the problem and frequently they do the reverse by aggravating people who recognize what is the real cause and just how ineffective is the solution.

Correcting errors depends upon the correct diagnosis of what causes things to go wrong. The correct procedure for putting things right consists of:

1 Identifying a fault as a variation or departure from a standard of performance which may be either specified verbally, in writing or by custom and practice.
2 Identifying the cause or causes.
3 Identifying the person or persons responsible. The person committing the error may not be at fault, but rather the person who issued the order or trained the person responsible.
4 Deciding what action to take, how to communicate this action and how to motivate the person who may take the new instructions as a criticism.
5 Deciding how to prevent a repetition.

Heads of departments and other senior staff are responsible for the prevention and correction of faults. They should, therefore, pay particular attention during training to 'critical points', that is, the points at which things could go wrong.

This book* is designed to assist managers and heads of departments to understand more clearly the knowledge and skills they need to bring to their responsibility in training their staff. The book, however, cannot substitute for thorough practical and theoretical training in the techniques of training because, as the book itself says, effective training makes use of various methods to transfer and consolidate knowledge and skill. Consequently the best way to become an effective trainer and supervisor, having attended a proper course on the subject, is to practice and to be critical always of one's own performance.

'There are no bad staff, only bad managers'

* *How to get the best from Your Staff.*

Index